enterprise
RISK ANALYTICS
for capital markets

enterprise
RISK ANALYTICS
for capital markets

Proactive and Real-Time Risk Management

Raghurami Reddy Etukuru

ENTERPRISE RISK ANALYTICS FOR CAPITAL MARKETS
PROACTIVE AND REAL-TIME RISK MANAGEMENT

iUniverse books may be ordered through booksellers or by contacting:

iUniverse
1663 Liberty Drive
Bloomington, IN 47403
www.iuniverse.com
1-800-Authors (1-800-288-4677)

ISBN: 978-1-4917-4491-8 (e)
ISBN: 978-1-4917-4492-5 (sc)

Library of Congress Control Number: 2014916842

Printed in the United States of America.

iUniverse rev. date: 10/9/2014

Contents

3 Fundamentals of Quantitative Finance 86

1 About the Book

Traditionally, risk management has been about looking for negative information after a decision has been made and reacting to negative events. Now risk management is maturing, and financial institutions are realizing that risk management must be integrated with business strategy. Traditional risk management relied heavily on quantitative models. While it is true that quantitative models are helpful for analyzing data quickly and detecting patterns, the effectiveness of the model depends on how and where it is used.

Quantitative models have been in use for several centuries. In physics, chemistry, engineering, and other fields, they have proven to be stable. When it comes to financial engineering, however, what drives the stability of the quantitative model is the needs of people. For example, a quantitative model developed to forecast the price of real estate in one place might not work in another place, as there are macroeconomic factors involved that are driven by human behavior.

The aftereffect of the wrong model is critical in the financial world. If the weather forecast says that there will be snowfall in the next two days and it doesn't snow, there will be no significant impact. If a forecast goes wrong in financial engineering, however, the impact will be heavy, causing other problems that can spiral out of control.

One of the main factors fueling such a crisis is the way data is maintained and analyzed. Though in the past it was possible to analyze data proactively and predict a crisis, it was not done. The quantitative models implemented by financial institutions have their own firewalls that restrict thinking to the broadest terms. Silo-based risk management failed to examine the connectedness among various investment strategies, departments, organizations, and countries. Quantitative financial models must be designed to use qualitative data and plug in the relationships among various instruments.

Risk management should become more proactive and real-time to influence investment decision making. Such changes require not only aggregated data but also faster processing. Managing risk, discovering prices, preventing fraud, following industry trends, processing derivatives, dealing with increased regulation, and providing granular reporting to regulators all demand new ways of storing and analyzing data.

Portfolios are sensitive to variations in interest rates, currencies, econometrics, catastrophic events, consumer confidence, and commodity prices, among other factors. Calculating the profit or loss of the portfolio for the past few days and making the assumption that we will probably see those levels in the coming few days is not enough anymore. It is necessary to simulate portfolio valuations across thousands of scenarios based on thousands of risk factors and to aggregate the results across all scenarios for each risk factor. This requires a huge volume of market data, qualitative data, and historical performance of various positions. This in turn requires an infrastructure that can read and process such data efficiently and generate the required analytics. The existing data warehouse infrastructures for external market data and internal data will have to go through several phases of change.

Market data, historical performance of positions, and contract terms and conditions belong to the category of structured data. This data is not enough to base decisions on. Much of the information about current market conditions, associated countries, counterparties, currencies, and opinions expressed in social media are only available in an unstructured format. Such information must be processed and structured into analytics engines to deliver pre-deal risk-reward metrics—such as CVA (Credit Valuation Adjustment), funding costs, and capital charges—that capture a variety of products, risk relationships, and scenarios.

The next big challenge after gathering this huge volume of data is processing that data quickly. Well-integrated hardware and software approaches are needed to meet end-user demands for analytics to deliver the required risk insights within the appropriate time frame of seconds, minutes, or hours. The level of demand for higher-quality information depends on the nature of the data. The trader may want to analyze the entire set of data and derive a conclusion before the trade is entered into the system, in which case the allowed time range expands from nanoseconds to microseconds.

Another example is rank-ordering trades with an individual counterparty by their standalone exposure or their CVA before placing a trade with a counterparty; the aggregated data for a regulatory report would need to be collected, processed, and stored in less than an hour, on a daily basis. Huge artifacts of data stored on disks and read/write hardware are the bottlenecks in this process, but that can be overcome to some extent by in-memory analytics.

Regulations like Basel III and Dodd-Frank require banks to track a trade's history and lineage and all events around it. This adds another dimension of governance risk and compliance in capital markets. Regulators are also becoming more stringent on what practices are acceptable, and reporting must prove that banks are following regulatory guidelines. For example, a big issue in capital markets is the shrinking liquidity of the CDS (credit default swap) market, which makes it more challenging to price credit risk into trades via measures like CVA. It is becoming more difficult to get regulators to accept hedges on the CVA capital charge, since the hedge must be 1:1 and cannot be from a proxy name.

Risk management practices must evolve from the current state to enterprise risk management. ERM does not mean simply pulling all the data into aggregated stores and generating various reports. It must be capable of analyzing the interconnectedness of various risk factors across asset classes and regions. Traditional risk management was capable of providing post-trading negative information that in turn could help avoiding the risk. However, risk management is not about *avoiding* risk. Avoiding risk will lead to loss of business opportunities. Risk management must be transformed into something that really *manages* risk instead of avoiding it.

ERM must be capable of redefining the value proposition of risk management by elevating its focus from the tactical to the strategic. It must be able to add value to the business strategy. ERM is about designing and implementing capabilities for managing the risks that matter. In my opinion, the following components are essential to ERM's effectiveness:

- risk knowledge
- risk quantification
- risk data management

- risk data aggregation
- risk architectures
- risk analytics and reporting
- risk regulation
- risk culture

This book is designed to bring these eight components (scattered across various chapters) to the attention of the professional who has just started in risk management or wants to enter the field.

2 Financial Products Explained

A financial instrument is an electronic or physical document that represents monetary value. It is the written legal obligation of one party to transfer something of value, usually money, to another party at some future date, under certain conditions. Financial instruments are designed to deliver value to both buyer and seller. They play a key role in the flow of capital among institutions and investors.

A customer buying a CD (certificate of deposit) from a bank, for example, receives a certificate. The certificate carries value to the buyer for its lifetime. The bank typically agrees to pay the money back to the customer after a predetermined time and also pay interest on the principal. Upon maturity, the customer receives the principal and interest. A CD is therefore classified as an instrument.

Other examples of financial instruments are stocks, bonds, and ETFs (exchange-traded funds). Financial instruments are intangible assets. For example, a gold coin is tangible, so it is not listed as a financial instrument, but the gold ETF *is* a financial instrument.

2.1 Bonds

Corporate structure is comprised of two things: equity and debt. Both the equity and the debt are sliced into smaller pieces to improve the liquidity of funding. Equity slices are called *stocks* and debt slices are called *bonds*. Bonds are issued for a few months to a few years. The issuer pays a specified rate of interest during the life of the bond and repays the face value of the bond at maturity. The buyer of the bond is nothing but a lender or investor.

For example, let's say that XYZ Inc. is planning to expand its business by raising $100 million in capital by issuing bonds. It plans to return the loaned capital in ten years. In this case, it issues one million bonds for $100 each. It pays interest of 5 percent (for example) annually. Every six months, it pays a coupon of $2.50, and at the end of the tenth year, it pays $102.50 ($100 principal plus the last coupon).

The issuing value of $100—called *face value* or *par value* or *principal*—is the amount of money the bondholder will get back at the end of the maturity period. The face value may differ from the amount the bond buyer pays to buy the bond. If the buyer is buying the bond from the issuer at the time of issuance, the purchase value may be the same as the face value. But the bond price may go up or down after issuance because of fluctuations in interest rates or the credit quality of the issuer.

Assume that the buyer purchased a bond at the time of issuance at face value and is receiving a 6 percent annual coupon. Let's assume the interest rates go down to 3 percent after a year. Newly issued bonds will typically pay around 3 percent, but an investor who purchases previously issued bonds, which are paying 6 percent, will continue to receive 6 percent interest even if market interest has fallen. However, the holder of a 6 percent bond will demand more than face value for the bond. For simplicity, assume that the investor pays $102. In this case, $102 is called the *bond price*. Similarly, if interest rates go up after issuance, the bond price goes down. Bond prices are inversely related to interest rates—if the credit quality of the issuer improves after the issuance, the bond price will go up, and vice versa.

Bonds can be customized based on certain features to fulfill the needs of investors and issuers. For example, an investor may think that interest rates will rise over time and so prefer to receive a coupon proportionate to market interest rates; or an issuer may want to withdraw the bond in the middle of the life of the bond. A variety of types are available in the bond market, and each has advantages and disadvantages to both the investors and issuers.

2.1.1   Zero-Coupon Bonds

A zero-coupon bond, also called a *discount bond* or *zero bond*, does not pay regular interest payments. Instead, the investor buys the bond at a steep discount price—that is, at a price lower than face value. At the time of maturity, bondholders will receive the face value of the bond. For example, a bond with a face value of $100 may be issued at $90 for the duration of two years. At the end of the two years, bondholders will get $100, implying an interest income of $10 per two years or $5 per year. The implied interest rate is (10/90)/2 = 5.5 percent.

Larger investors or dealers who have bought bonds may be receiving bulk coupons periodically. Such an investor may choose to separate coupons from the principal of the bond, which is known as the residue, so that he can sell them to different investors as zero-coupon bonds. Or a particular entity may need cash for the short term—say, six months—and therefore issue zero coupons.

2.1.2   Step-Up Bonds

Step-up bonds have coupon payments that increase (step up) over the life of the security according to a predetermined schedule. In the case of one-step bonds, the coupon will reset once during the life of the bond; with multistep bonds, the coupon will reset multiple times. The initial coupon paid on a step-up is usually lower than comparable market rates, and the step-up may eventually increase its future coupon payments and even yield higher than prevailing market rates. The step-up bondholder chooses to forgo some interest income in the near term in exchange for a potential higher yield over the life of the investment.

2.1.3   Step-Down Bonds

Step-down bonds have coupon payments that decrease (step down) over the life of the security according to a predetermined schedule. In the case of one-step bonds, the coupon will reset once during the life of the bond; with multistep bonds, the coupon will reset multiple times. The initial coupon paid on a step-down is usually higher than comparable market rates, and the step-down may eventually decrease its future coupon payments and yield less than prevailing market rates.

2.1.4   Callable Bonds

Bonds are usually issued with a specific maturity, but callable bonds have the provision that they can be redeemed by the issuer prior to maturity. A callable option gives the issuer the flexibility of withdrawing the bond prior to maturity, but it usually comes with a premium paid to the bond owner, either when the bond is called or in terms of interest rate.

Let's take the simple example of a home loan. When you take out a fixed-rate mortgage to buy a house, you usually have the option of prepaying the mortgage either by refinancing or paying down fully. You might refinance the mortgage because interest rates have gone down and you want a cheaper loan. All US mortgage loans come with embedded prepayment options, and no additional premium is required. Bond issuers, however, don't have such a provision by default. They must issue bonds with an embedded call option.

Investors who purchase callable bonds take a chance that an issuer may redeem them prior to the stated maturity date, typically when interest rates are low. If the bonds are called, investors may have to reinvest the proceeds at lower coupon rates. To compensate investors for the reinvestment risk and unknown final term, callable bonds generally offer higher yields than noncallable alternatives.

The three most common callable features are American, callable on any date, usually with thirty days notice; European, callable only at one specific future date; and Bermudan, callable only on interest-payment dates.

2.1.5   *Puttable Bonds*

Just as the issuer of a callable bond has the flexibility of withdrawing the bond from market when interest rates go down, the bondholder may also want to put the bond back to the issuer when interest rates go up or when the issuer's credit quality is trending down. Puttable bonds are considered investor-friendly. The same concept of premium applies to puttable bonds as to callable bonds, but in this case bondholders pay a premium, in lower coupon rates or at the point of putting it back.

2.1.6   *Step-Up Bonds with Call Option*

As discussed in 2.1.2, step-up bonds pay gradually increasing coupons. The risk to the issuer is that the coupon rate may rise above comparable rates over time. To mitigate such a risk, the issuer sometimes embeds a call option. The risk to the bondholder is that the bond is more likely to be called back by the issuer before the maturity date. As a result, the bondholder will not be able to enjoy the higher coupon payments.

Step-up securities are typically structured so that they are callable by the issuer at any interest payment date on or after the first step-up date. Some step-up securities have been issued so that they are continuously callable after the first step-up date, meaning they can be called at any time, not just on the payment dates.

2.1.7   Step-Down Bonds with Put Option

Since the bondholder has the risk of receiving lower interest rates in the future, buyers of step-down bonds prefer to have a put option so that they can put the bond back to the issuer if they start receiving coupons lower than prevailing market rates.

2.1.8   Convertible Bonds

Firms issue bonds to raise capital. But certain firms—such as early-stage companies, companies with a high potential for growth but poor credit, or established companies with weak financial health—may not be able to raise the capital in the bond market or will have to offer higher coupons to do so. At the same time, those companies may not want to issue additional stocks, as it would dilute the earnings of existing stakeholders. Such companies often issue convertible bonds, which give the investor the right to convert the bonds into common stock in the future. The right to convert the bond into common stock can be interpreted as the issuer implicitly selling the call option to the investor to purchase the issuer's stock. This option reduces the coupon payment on the convertible bond.

Convertible bonds have two components: a bond and an equity option. The option also acts as a long put on the bond, as the investor can put the bond back to the issuer with an exchange of stock. In this case, stock price acts as exercise price.

The convertible-bond market is considered to be high-risk, as firms with noninvestment credit ratings or emerging firms issue most of the convertible bonds. Since many institutional investors have constraints against investing in these issuers, the liquidity of the convertible bond market is not so attractive. As a result, convertible bonds are undervalued.

2.1.9   Treasuries

Treasury securities, or simply *Treasuries*, are backed by the "full faith and credit" of the US government, and thus by its ability to raise tax revenues and print currency. Treasuries are generally considered to be the safest of all investments. They are viewed in the market as having virtually no "credit risk," meaning it is highly probable that the interest and principal will be paid fully and on time. Treasures are divide into three types—bills, notes, and bonds—depending on term.

Bills

Treasury bills are short-term instruments with maturities of no more than one year. They can be used to hold investors' money so that they will be able to access it quickly as needed. The Treasury bill market is considered to be highly liquid, as investors can quickly convert bills to cash through a broker or bank.

Like zero-coupon bonds, Treasury bills do not pay periodic interest payments. Investors buy bills at a discount from the par or face value and then receive the full amount when the bill matures. The difference between the amount paid and amount received is the interest earned. Treasury bills play a key role in liquidity risk management that will be covered in forthcoming sections.

Notes

Treasury notes are intermediate- to long-term investments, typically issued in maturities of two, three, five, seven, and ten years. These are typically purchased for specific future expenses, such as college tuition, or used to generate cash flow during retirement. Interest is paid semiannually.

Bonds

Treasury bonds cover terms of longer than ten years and are currently being issued in maturities of thirty years. Interest is paid semiannually. Although Treasury bonds are considered to have very low credit risk, other types of risk—mainly interest-rate risk and inflation risk—do affect them.

Investors are effectively guaranteed to receive interest and principal payments as promised, but the underlying value of the bond itself may change depending on the direction of interest rates. As with all fixed-income securities, if interest rates in general increase after a US Treasury security is issued, the value of the security will fall, since bonds paying higher rates will come into the market.

Similarly, if interest rates fall, the value of the older, higher-paying bond will increase in comparison with new issues.

Newly or most recently issued bonds are called *on-the-run* and old ones are called *off-the-run*. Because on-the-run issues are traded most frequently, they provide the most liquidity and therefore typically trade at a slight premium. Some trading strategies successfully exploit this price differential through an arbitrage strategy that involves selling or shorting on-the-run Treasuries and buying off-the-run Treasuries.

2.1.10   Index-Linked Bonds

Inflation risk is a potential problem for many investors. If the inflation rate is higher than the coupon rate being received on a bond, it diminishes the purchasing power of the consumer. Inflation makes a dollar today worth more than a dollar tomorrow, even after ignoring the opportunity cost. Some investors—especially those who are managing inflation-related funds—or individuals who defer the purchase of certain products to the future prefer coupon or principal or both to be linked to the inflation index.

Inflation, however, is just one index. Bond payments can be linked to numerous indexes, including GDP (gross domestic product), consumer price index (CPI), earning measures, and foreign exchange rates. The need for index linkage depends on the type of business with which the investor is involved.

Treasury inflation-protected securities (TIPS) protect investors from inflation risk. The US Treasury created these inflation-indexed notes just for this purpose. The value of the principal is adjusted to reflect the effects of inflation with the CPI as a guide, in addition to a fixed rate of interest. At maturity, if inflation has increased the value of the principal, the investor receives the higher, adjusted value back. If deflation has decreased the value, the investor nevertheless receives the original face amount of the security.

2.1.11   Floating-Rate Notes

Bond investors purchase bonds to earn interest that matches the market interest rates. However, prevailing market interest rates can vary from time to time. Floating-rate notes (FRNs) protect investors from fluctuations in interest rates. The coupon is linked to a specific index, such as the London Interbank Offered

Rate (LIBOR). The interest is set for a certain period, typically three months, at the end of which it is reset.

Additional terms can also be added to the note, including when, where, and at what interest the rate can be reset. For example, a floor specifies the minimum level below which the coupon cannot fall; a cap specifies the maximum rate above which the rate cannot be reset; and dates specify possible redemption dates.

2.1.12   Inverse Floating-Rate Notes

Inverse floating-rate notes are just the opposite of FRNs. While FRNs are good when interest rates are trending upward, they are not favorable in declining periods. An inverse floater pays a coupon that increases as prevailing market rates decline. Inverse floaters can be linked to any reference index.

Let's say the borrower agreed to pay 15 percent minus (2 × LIBOR). Each time the LIBOR resets, the new coupon is calculated using the above formula. If the LIBOR is 3 percent at the inception, then the investor gets 9 percent per annum at the end of the first quarter of the life of the bond. If LIBOR is 2 percent at the end of the quarter, the investor gets 11 percent at the end of the second quarter.

Like FRNs, inverse floaters have additional features, such as caps and floors. For example, if the calculated coupon falls below 6 percent of the floor, the investor will continue receiving 6 percent.

2.1.13   Indexed Amortizing Notes

In regular bonds, the full principal is paid at the end of maturity, while the coupon can be either fixed or floating for a certain period. Indexed amortizing notes pay the specified coupon for a certain period called a *lockout period* and gradually pay down the principal from there on. For example, a $100 million bond on which it is agreed to pay a 5 percent coupon for three years will start paying down a certain portion of the principal every six months after the end of three-year lockout time. During the period of principal paying-down, the borrower pays the interest that is linked to a certain index, such as LIBOR.

These are called indexed amortizing notes because the principal pay-down is amortized based on a certain index. There are two flavors of maturities: one is a lockout period during which the principal is stable, and the other is actual maturity, before which the final schedule of principal is paid. For example, a $100, three-year lockout, twenty-five-year maturity bond pays a coupon on $100 for the first three years and $25 plus accrued interest for every six months after three years.

2.1.14   Interest-Differential Notes

IDNs are designed to pay the difference between interest rates in two countries or currencies. Investors use these bonds to take advantage of higher rates in other countries without actually investing in that country, thus avoiding the exchange-rate risk.

For example, let's assume interest rates in Country A and Country B are 4 percent and 5 percent respectively. That means a bond issued in Country B yields 25 percent higher than a bond issued in Country A. If an investor from Country A invests in Country B, he will have to convert the currency into Country B's currency and again convert back to home currency at the maturity. If at the end of one year—the time of repatriation—the currency of Country A depreciates by 25 percent of the original value, the investor will gain no net benefit.

In order to avoid currency risk, investors can buy IDNs, which will pay the difference in interest rates, such as 1 percent.

2.2   Derivatives

A derivative is a financial contract the value of which is derived from the performance of underlying market factors, such as interest rates, currency exchange rates, and commodity, credit, and equity prices. While most derivative transactions do not involve the exchange of underlying assets, certain derivative contracts dealing with currencies do involve such an exchange. Derivative transactions include options, forwards, futures, swaps, caps, floors, collars, and various combinations thereof.

Derivatives are meant for hedging and risk-transfer purposes. However, there are situation where investors can make a profit with little investment by applying derivatives or derivative strategies.

2.2.1   Options

An option is a derivative that represents a contract sold by one party to another party. The contract offers the buyer the right, but not the obligation, to buy or sell an asset at an agreed-upon price called the *strike price* during a certain period of time or on a specific date called an *exercise date*. Here the seller is called an *option writer* and the buyer is called an *option holder*.

Depending on whether the privilege is to buy or sell an asset, there can be options: a call option, which gives the holder the option to buy an asset at a certain price on or before a certain date, and a put option, which gives the holder the option to sell an asset at a certain price on or before a certain date.

The underlying asset in an option can be any allowed financial asset, such as a stock or interest rate. To buy an option, the buyer pays the premium. The buyer gets the benefit only if the contract value rises beyond the premium. If the value of the asset in the contract is reached, the strike price is called an *at-the-money option* to the buyer. If the value rises above the strike, then it is called an *in-the-money option*. If the value is below the strike price, it is called an *out-of-money option*.

2.2.2   Forwards

A forward contract is an agreement to buy or sell an asset on a specified date for a specified price. In a forward contract, the seller is obligated to sell the asset and the buyer is obligated to buy it as per the agreement, whereas in an option contract, the holder of the option has the option to buy or sell but is not obligated to do so. The following are the main features of the forward contract:

- There is an agreement to buy or sell the underlying asset.
- The transaction takes place on a predetermined future date.
- The price at which the transaction will take place is predetermined.

For example, suppose a food company is foreseeing that the demand for its products will be high in next six months. At the same time, it also foresees that the price of the raw material (wheat, for example) will also go up. The company thinks that it is not economical to buy and store the wheat because of the incurred storage costs. It will enter a forward agreement with farmers to buy X quantity of wheat at price Y on date Z. On that day, the farmer is obligated to sell

X quantity of wheat at price Y. At the same time, the food company is obligated to buy as per the terms.

Even if market rates are low, the buyer is obligated to buy at an agreed-upon price. Similarly, even if market rates are higher, the seller is obligated to sell at an agreed upon price. There are various contract terms, such as quality of material, delivery location, and delivery mode.

Let's consider another example. Suppose the farmer is expecting the crop in the next four months, and he foresees that the prices may go down by the time the crop is ready. He will enter a forward contract with the buyer to sell X amount of crop at Y price on Z date. On date Z, the farmer is obligated to sell as per the agreement, whereas the other party is obligated to buy the same.

2.2.3 Futures

Future contracts are similar to forward contracts. The difference is that forward contracts are bilateral, meaning buyer and seller can design the contract terms. Future contracts are executed on future exchanges, and both the buyer and seller need to obey the terms and conditions set by the exchange. Value to the buyer or seller is calculated on a daily basis, and the difference must be deposited with the exchange.

For example, let's say that a farmer enters a future contract to sell 1,000 pounds of wheat at $1 per pound on a certain date in future—say, in three months. On the next day, the price of wheat goes up to $1.10/pound. If for some reason the crop gets damaged and the farmer is unable to deliver the wheat, the buyer will end up buying the wheat in market at the higher price of $1.10/pound. In order to protect the future buyer, the exchange demands $1,000 \times 0.10 = 100 to be deposited in the buyer's account that is held with the exchange.

If wheat prices go down to $0.90/pound the next week, and if the buyer declines to buy the wheat as he thinks that he can get it in the market at a cheaper price, the farmer will lose the money. Therefore, the exchange will ask the buyer to deposit $1,000 \times ($1.10 - 0.90) = 200 in the seller's account. The revaluation and reimagining continues until the delivery date is reached.

Because of the requirement of margin deposits, future contracts are considered as not exposed to counterparty risk and are also much more liquid. However, the most recent regulations require the Futures to be given certain risk weight.

2.2.4   *Swaps*

Swaps involve returns on one type of product being exchanged with the returns on some other type of product. There may be a situation where investors are holding certain products and think those products are no longer suitable to their portfolios; selling those products and buying a different type of product may involve transaction costs and tax payments. Or it may be that certain parties are not qualified for the product they want but are qualified for similar products.

In such cases, the parties exchange the returns with the returns of the desired products, which are held by other parties. The whole mechanism of exchange of returns are created as products and called *assets*. There are several types of asset, depending on underlying assets. Interest rate swaps, equity swaps, and total return swaps are a few examples.

2.2.5   Combinations

Using multiple types of derivatives allows for customization of derivative products. For example, swaps provide the facility to exchange the returns of two products for their owners. However, a contract can be signed that gives an option to enter into such a swap agreement at a certain date in the future. If, on that date, the option holder thinks that the product he has is the right one for him, then he doesn't need to enter into a swap agreement. On the other hand, if he thinks that he would benefit from the swap agreement, he can enter into an agreement as per the terms set in the option contract. Such a product is called a swaption, as it combines *swap* and *option*. There are several such combo products.

2.3   Equity Derivatives

Equity derivatives are derivative contracts whose value is derived from the performance of the underlying stock. Equity-derivative transactions do not involve paying or receiving notional amounts. For example, buying an option on Apple stock does not require Apple stock to be bought or sold. Instead, options allow for transacting the fluctuations in stock price.

2.3.1   Equity Options

An option is a contract that allows the holder to buy or sell an underlying security at a given price, called the *strike price*. The two most common types of options contracts are *put* and *call*. A call option gives the holder the right to buy the underlying asset at the strike price if the price of the underlying asset crosses above the strike. Similarly, the put option allows the holder to sell the underlying asset at the strike price if the price of the underlying asset falls below the strike.

The three types of call or put options vary by exercise date. American options can be executed anytime on or before the date that is specified in the contract. European options can be executed only on an exercise date that is specified in the contract. Bermudan options can be executed only on certain dates (for example, every Friday) before the expiration date.

Say, for example, that a trader sees an announcement about the release of a product from Company ABC and thinks that the stock value will rise from its current price of $40 to $60. At the same time, he sees a risk of the price falling below $40 if the product fails. He would pay $40,000 for 1,000 stocks. If the stock went to $60, he would get a profit of $20,000. If the stock went down to $20, he would have a loss of $20,000. The investment of $40,000 might lead to a $20,000 profit or a $20,000 loss. Rather than purchasing the stock itself, he will purchase call options for a fraction of the price, with a strike price of $40 and an exercise date of the next three months.

Such an option will not come for free. The buyer will pay premium upfront. Valuation of option premiums is a very complex subject, and various quantitative models are used. For simplicity, assume that the option premium on this stock is $2. The buyer will pay $2,000 as a premium to get the right to purchase 1,000 stocks at $40. In next month, if the stock value rises to $60, the trader will buy 1,000 stocks at the price of $40 each and make a profit of $20,000 on his investment of $2,000. On the other hand, if the stock price falls to $20, the buyer will not exercise the option contract and forgo the $2,000 premium paid. He thereby reduces the loss to $2,000 from $20,000 (had he purchased stocks instead of options).

Payoff diagram for the call-option buyer

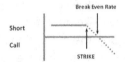

Payoff diagram for the call-option seller

Now let's consider a trader holding stocks of Company XYZ who thinks that the stock value may fall from its current price of $40 to $20. He may not want to sell the stock now because of tax considerations, or he may be seeing little chance of it rising too high. Rather than selling the stock itself, he will buy a put option at a strike price of $40 and an exercise date of the next three months. For simplicity, assume that the option premium on this stock is $2. He will pay $2,000 as premium to get the right to sell off 1,000 stocks at $40 each in the next three months. Next month, if the stock value falls to $20, the trader will exercise the option and sell the 1,000 stocks at the price of $40 each. On the other hand, if the stock price rises to $60, the trader will not exercise the option contract; he loses the $2,000 premium paid, but he can sell in the market at $60.

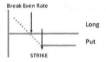

Payoff diagram for the put-option buyer

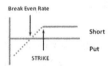

Payoff diagram for the put-option seller

2.3.2   Exotic Options

So far, we have discussed simple options. Complex products can be built using these simple options. The complexity gives investors more flexibility and can be used to customize hedging needs or to build arbitrage strategies. The customization lies in the exercise mechanism, strike price, and payoff amount, among other factors. While exotic options are complex in nature and can be priced using variants of the Black-Scholes model and other complex models, the scope of this book is limited to explaining the features of various exotic options.

Compound Options

A compound option is an option on an option—that is, the exercise payoff involves the value of another option. A compound option thus has two expiration dates and two strike prices. It is a two-dimensional, second-order derivative. There are typically four types:

1. *European style call on a call option.* On the first expiration date T1, the holder has the right to buy a new call using the strike price X1. The new call has expiration date T2 and strike price X2.
2. *European style call on a put option.* On the first expiration date T1, the holder has the right to buy a new put using the strike price X1. The new put has expiration date T2 and strike price X2.
3. *European style put on a put option.* On the first expiration date T1, the holder has the right to sell a new put using the strike price X1. The new put has expiration date T2 and strike price X2.
4. *European style put on a call option.* On the first expiration date T1, the holder has the right to sell a new call using the strike price X1. The new call has expiration date T2 and strike price X2.

Chooser Options

A chooser option gives the holder of the option the right to choose whether the option is a call or put at a specific time during the life of the option. Chooser options are similar to compound options except that the holder has an additional option of choosing the type of a second option. The value of the second option at the time of expiration determines whether the option is a call or a put. A chooser option is a two-dimensional, second-order derivative.

Barrier Options

Barrier options have payoffs that depend on the strike and the barrier. They work well in a market where the future is not clear—that is, it is not certain if the future is going to be bullish or bearish. A barrier above the current stock level is called an *up barrier*; if it is ever crossed, it will be from below. A *down barrier* is below the current stock level; if it is ever crossed, it will be from above. An *in-barrier* (knock-in) pays off only if the stock finishes in the money and if the barrier is crossed sometime before expiration. An *out-barrier* (knock-out) option pays off only if the stock finishes in the money and the barrier is never crossed before expiration.

There are four types of barrier options:

1. *Down-and-out call/put*, a call/put option that expires if the market price of the underlying asset drops below the barrier.
2. *Down-and-in call/put*, a call/put that becomes a standard call/put option if the market price of the underlying asset drops below the barrier.
3. *Up-and-out call/put*, a call/put option that expires if the market price of the underlying asset hits above the barrier.
4. *Up-and-in call/put*, a call/put that becomes a standard call/put option if the market price of the underlying asset hits above the barrier.

Out options are inversely related to volatility. Increased volatility increases the probability of the underlying asset price hitting the barrier, which in turn makes the options expire. Barrier options are two-dimensional, first-order derivatives.

Parisian Options

Parisian options are a special type of barrier option for which the barrier (in or out) feature is only triggered after the underlying asset price has spent a certain prescribed time beyond the barrier. Parisian options protect sellers and investors from market manipulation. Depending on the contract, the small fraction of the time outside the barrier can be reset or saved and added to future times. Parisian options are strongly path-dependent, three-dimensional (asset price, time, time spent outside the barrier), first-order derivatives.

Lookback Options

The payoffs of lookback options depend on the maximum or minimum underlying asset price attained during the option's life. Therefore, lookback options are strongly path-dependent. Lookbacks provide investors with the flexibility (if in the money) to buy at the ex-post low and sell at the ex-post high.

A *standard* or *floating-strike lookback call* gives the option holder the right to buy at the lowest price recorded during the option's life. Similarly, a *standard* or *floating-strike lookback put* gives the right to sell at the highest price. A *call on maximum* or *fixed-strike lookback call* pays off the difference between the realized maximum price and some predetermined strike or zero, whichever is greater. A *put on minimum* or *fixed-strike lookback put* pays off the difference between the predetermined strike and the realized minimum price or zero, whichever is greater.

Lookback options are three-dimensional—asset price, time, and maximum/minimum. They are first-order derivatives and quite common in the fixed-income sector, as interest rates fluctuate up and down during a specified time.

Ladder Options

Ladder options are special types of lookback options for which the highest asset price is set to the floor in the series for call options, and the lowest is set to the ceiling in the series for put options. For example, in the series of multiples 5, 10, 45, 50, and 55, the asset price 53 is reset to 50 for call options and to 55 for put options. This will reduce the payoff to the investor. Ladder options are cheaper than the regular lookback options.

Shout Options

In shout options, the special feature—the payoff upon shouting—is another derivative, with contractual specifications different from the original derivative. The embedded shout feature in a call option allows its holder to lock in the profit via shouting while retaining the right to benefit from any future upside move in the payoff. The holder should shout only when the underlying asset is above strike. The number of shouting rights throughout the life of the contract may be more than one, depending on the contract. The shouting instants may be limited to some predetermined times.

Binary Options

In regular European options, a *call option* pays off the difference between the asset price and strike if the asset price is above the strike. Similarly, a *put option* pays off the difference between the strike price and asset price if the asset price is below the strike. Binary options are similar to European options, but the payoff amount is based on a special clause. The payoff amount is either a constant amount or the value of the asset itself.

If the payoff amount is a fixed quantity, then the option is called *cash-or-nothing*. For example, in a binary cash-or-nothing call option, if the predetermined amount is q and the asset price closes above the strike at the time of expiration, then the call writer pays off q amount on the expiration day. In a binary cash-or-nothing put option, the writer pays off the amount q if the asset price closes below the strike at the time of expiration.

If the payoff amount is determined as the asset price, then the option is called *asset-or-nothing*. For example, in a binary asset-or-nothing call option, since the predetermined amount is the value of the asset at the time of expiration, if the asset price closes above the strike at the time of expiration, then the call writer pays off an amount equal to the asset price on the expiration day. In a binary asset-or-nothing put option, the writer pays off the amount equal to the asset price if the asset price closes below the strike at the time of expiration.

Asian Options

Asian options link the payoff to the average price of an asset over a period of time. Because of the averaging concept, Asian options exhibit lower volatility and are less prone to market manipulation. The average is determined by taking the complete set of prices en route to expiration. The complete set can be discrete or continuous. A discrete set includes only the closing prices of each day, while a continuous set includes prices of every transaction or the closing prices of very short intervals. Again, the average can be arithmetic or geometric.

Depending on how the average price is used in option payoff, there are two types of Asian options:

1. In the *average price option*, the average price is used in place of the asset closing price. Therefore, the average price Asian call option pays off $\max(0, S_{ave} - K)$, where K is a strike price. Similarly, the average price Asian put option pays off $\max(0, K - S_{ave})$.
2. In the *average strike option*, the average price is used in place of the strike price. That is, the strike price is variable and is not defined at the time of initiation. Therefore the average strike Asian call option pays off $\max(0, S_T - S_{ave})$, where S_T is a closing price of the asset. Similarly, the average strike Asian put option pays off $\max(0, S_{ave} - S_T)$.

Advantages of Asian options include the following:

- lower volatility
- less prone to market manipulation
- easy to manage hedge ratio because of stability observed in average
- less exposed to sudden jumps and crashes

Basket Options

In a basket option, the underlying asset is a basket of securities, currencies, or commodities, and the strike price is based on the weighted value of the basket's constituents. Basket options are a popular way to hedge portfolio risk. The cost of a basket option is significantly less than buying an option on the individual constituents of the portfolio. The buyer has the flexibility to choose the maturity of the option, the foreign currency amounts for the basket, and the aforementioned strike price. Basket options are also called *rainbow options*.

Forward Start Options

Forward start options are options whose strike price will be determined at some later date. A forward start option is paid for in the present, but the strike price is not fully defined until an intermediate date before expiration. An application of forward start options is employee stock options. An employee is typically promised that he will receive stock options at periodic dates in the future conditional upon his continued employment, and the strikes of these options will be set to be at-the-money on the periodical grant dates.

Bermudan Options

The Bermudan option can be exercised before maturity, but it can only be exercised at given times. Bermudan options are cheaper than American options but more expensive than European options. Investors prefer them when there is a lot of uncertainty about the dividends.

2.4 Option Strategies

In this section, we will discuss different options strategies that can be built out of option instruments and underlying assets.

2.4.1 Covered Call

Let's say we own stock, and we think that the price of stock will not increase beyond a certain value, X. However, there may be other parties who think that the stock price will go above X and want to purchase a call option on that stock. We can sell the call option on the stock that we hold, giving the other party the right to buy the stock at the price of X. In return, we receive the premium. If the stock price does not reach X within a specified time, the call buyer will not exercise it, and we are said to make a profit equivalent to the premium received. But if the stock price increases above X, we will have to forgo the increased price. Therefore, we will still be in a good position until the stock reaches X + premium but will have to forgo the market opportunity, as we have to sell the stock to the call buyer at the price of X.

Such a mechanism is called a *covered call*. In brief, the covered call involves selling a call option on a stock we own. Covered calls are good in downside markets, as we receive some premium, and not favorable in upside markets, as we have to forgo opportunities. In simple math, covered call = long stock + short call.

Consider a stock whose current value is $10. The holder of the stock does not believe that the value will rise above $15 in next two months but believes that there is a chance of it rising above $15 after two months. He wants to make some money out of this stock during these two months. He writes a call option at a strike price of $15, which expires in two months. In return, he receives $1, for example, as the premium. If the stock reaches $15, he is obligated to sell the stock at a price of $15, thus forgoing the profit opportunity beyond $15. If the stock does not reach $15, he keeps the premium received.

2.4.2   Protective Put

Let's say that we own stock and think that the value may go down in the next few days or weeks. But selling the stock may have some tax implications, or we may think that the stock value can rise again in the future and selling and buying will have some other implications.

In that case, we can buy a put option, which will give us the right to sell the stock at a certain price, X. If the stock price goes below X, we can sell the stock at the price X. The strategy is economical only if the stock price goes below X, as we already paid the premium to purchase a put option. The downside of this strategy is that we will be losing premium if the stock does not go below X. The protective put is an insurance-style strategy, meaning we buy insurance on the stock we own. In simple math, protective put = long stock + long put.

Consider a stock whose current value is $10. The investor believes that the stock price may go down in the future and does not want to sell it now because of the transaction costs and tax considerations. Therefore, he buys a put option at a strike price of $10 with an expiration date in two months. If the stock price goes below $10, he is protected, as he can exercise the put option and sell the stock to the put writer at $10. If the stock rises above $10 or remains the same, he will not sell the stock. The loss is limited to the premium he paid.

2.4.3   Simple Math on Option Combos

Based on the equation cover call = long stock + short call, different combinations of stock and options can be derived. Please note that negative of short is long, meaning shorting the short position creates the long position. This is similar to the negative of a negative being positive.

Long stock + short call = short put → Equation 1

Rewriting the above equation,

long stock – short put = –short call,

which is equivalent to

long stock + long put = long call → Equation 2.

Rewriting the above equation again,

long put = long call – long stock,

which is equivalent to

long put = long call + short stock → Equation 3.

Rewriting the above equation again,

–long call = –long put + short stock,

which is equivalent to

short call = short put + short stock. → Equation 4.

In summary,

long stock + short call= short put → Equation 1

long stock + long put = long call → Equation 2
long call + short stock = long put → Equation 3
short put + short stock = short call → Equation 4.

2.4.4   Straddles

In the above strategies, we used the underlying stock as one of the instruments. We can also create the strategies by using only options without the underlying stocks. The straddle is one such strategy.

Let's assume that we don't own any stock, and we want to make some profit from the movement of stock prices. If we buy a call option, we make some profit when the stock goes up, and if we buy a put option, we make some profit when the stock goes down. How can we make a profit on a put option if we don't own the stock? Since we have the right to sell the stock at a strike price of X, we can buy the stock in the market at a price below X and sell it to the option writer at the price of X. But we will be in the money only after the stock moves by the amount equivalent to the sum of the two premiums we paid. This strategy also assumes the expiration date is same for both the options.

The straddle strategy involves buying the same number of call and put options at the same strike price with the same expiration date. If both the call and put positions are long, then the straddle is called a *long straddle*; if both the positions are short, then the straddle is called a *short straddle*. In other words, selling a long straddle is nothing but a short straddle.

By employing a long straddle, the manager takes advantage of any sudden movement in the stock price regardless of the direction. However, there is a risk of losing both the premiums if the stock price does not move enough to cover the premium paid. The maximum risk in the position is equal to the net premium. Buying both a call and a put allows for upper and lower breakeven points.

While the profit is unlimited from upside movement, there is limited profit from downside movement bound to the zero price of the stock, but such limited profit can still be high. Some managers employ a straddle if the implied volatility is low, anticipating that the option prices will go up when the implied volatility returns to the normal level, regardless of stock-price movement. However, such a profit is very limited.

Managers expect profit from time decay of the option or a stable price of the underlying stock. The profit on a short straddle is limited to the premium received on both the call and the put, but the losses can be huge if the stock price moves in either direction. If the volatility falls for both or either option, the position could lose regardless of stock-price movement.

Example of a Long Straddle

Let's say the strategist buys one call option at the strike price of $15 and pays a premium of $1.50, and also buys one put option on the same stock at the strike price of $15 and pays a premium of $1.50. The total premium paid is $3. Scenarios for stock movement include the following:

- If the stock remains at $15 during the life of the contracts, the strategist would lose the $3 premium paid.
- If the stock touches $18, which is strike + premium, then he is at no loss no gain, as he can exercise the call option at a strike of $15 and receive $3, enough to cover the total premium paid.
- If the stock rises above $18, which is strike + premium, he would make some profit, as he can exercise the call option at a strike of $15.
- If the stock touches $12, which is strike – premium, he is at no loss no gain, as he can exercise the put option at a strike of $15 and receive $3, enough to cover the total premium paid.
- If the stock falls below $12, which is strike – premium, he would make a profit, as he can exercise the put option at a strike of $15.

Therefore, in order for the strategist to make a profit, the stock price should move up or down by an amount exceeding the sum of the two premiums paid. Any change in stock price beyond the breakeven level (strike +/– total premium) represents profit to the investor. Long straddles are good only if there is a chance of extreme movements in the stock price.

Consider the same example from the point of view of the strategy seller. The seller receives a $3 premium by selling one call and one put on the same stock at the strike price of $15. Consider the following scenarios for stock movement:

- If the stock remains at $15 during the life of the contracts, the strategist makes a profit of $3, which is the premium received.

- If the stock touches $18, which is strike + premium, he is at no loss no gain, as the buyer can exercise the call option at a strike of $15 and receives $3, enough to cover the total premium paid.
- If the stock rises above $18, which is strike + premium, the seller would lose money, as the buyer can exercise the call option at a strike of $15.
- If the stock value touches $12 which is strike − premium, he is at no loss no gain, as the buyer will exercise the put option at a strike of $15 and receive $3, enough to cover the total premium paid.
- If the stock value falls below $12, which is strike − premium, the seller loses money, as the buyer can exercise the put option at a strike of $15.

Investors who think that the stock price will fluctuate around the strike price and not show extreme movements sell the straddle to earn some premium.

2.4.5   *Strangles*

Strangles are a good strategy for long investors when there is movement in the stock price. Strangles are very similar to straddles, except that instead of having the same strike price for both call and put, the call will be at higher strike than the put position. By having a wider gap in strike price, the sum of the premium paid on the two positions can be reduced.

The seller of the strangle is in a good position until the stock moves beyond the two strike prices. Though he earns fewer premiums compared to the straddle, he is in safe mode for a wider gap in the stock movements.

A strangle strategy is employed by taking a long position in a call option and a put option on the same underlying asset, at the same maturity but different strike prices. These positions are cheaper to implement, as the options with strikes further from the current underlying price will have a lower theta (rate of change of option price with respect to time). Managers typically take a call position with a higher strike than that of the put position. The profit is not realized for slow movement of the stock. Large movements are required to lock in profits. However, the cost of strategy establishment is low because of lower premiums.

As with a short straddle, managers expect a profit from time decay of the option or stability or little movement in the price of the underlying stock. The profit on a short strangle is limited to the premium received on both the call and the put, but the losses can be huge if the stock price moves in either direction. If the volatility falls for both or either option, the position could lose regardless of stock-price movement. Within a certain band, the risk of a short strangle is less than that of a short straddle because of different strike prices.

Let's say the strategist buys one call option at the strike of $20 and pays the premium of $1.50. Additionally, he buys one put option on the same stock at the strike of $15 and pays the premium of $1.50. The total premium paid is $3. Consider the following possible stock movements:

- If the stock value remains between $15 and $20 during the life of the contracts, the strategist would lose the $3 premium paid, as he cannot exercise any of the call or put options.
- If the stock value touches $23, which is the strike + two premiums, he is at no loss no gain, as he can exercise the call option at a strike of $20 and receive $3, enough to cover the total premium paid.
- If the stock value rises above $23, which is strike + premiums, he would make some profit, as he can exercise the call option at a strike of $20.
- If the stock value touches $12, which is strike − premiums, he is at no loss no gain, as he can exercise the put option at a strike of $15 and receive $3, enough to cover the total premium paid.
- If the stock value falls below $12, which is the strike − premiums, then he would make a profit, as he can exercise the put option at a strike of $15.

In order for the strategist to make a profit, the stock price should move above the call strike by an amount equal to the sum of the two premiums paid or should fall below the put strike by an amount equal to the sum of the two premiums paid. Any change in stock price beyond the breakeven levels (call strike + total premium and put strike − total premium) is profit to the investor.

Let's say the strategist sells one call option at the strike price of $20 and receives the premium of $1.50. He also sells one put option on the same stock at the strike price of $15 and receive the premium of $1.50. The total premium received is $3. Consider the following scenarios of stock movement:

- If the stock value remains between $15 and $20 during the life of the contracts, the strategist would keep the $3 premium received, as the buyer cannot exercise any of the call or put options.

- If the stock value touches $23, which is strike + two premiums, then he is at no loss no gain, as the buyer can exercise the call option at a strike of $20 and receive $3, enough to cover the total premium paid.
- If the stock value rises above $23, which is strike + premiums, the seller would lose money, as the buyer can exercise the call option at a strike of $20.
- If the stock value touches $12, which is strike − premiums, then he is at no loss no gain, as the buyer can exercise the put option at a strike of $15 and receive $3, enough to cover the total premium paid.
- If the stock value falls below $12, which is strike − premiums, the seller would lose money, as the buyer can exercise the put option at a strike of $15.

In order for the strategist to make a profit, the stock price should not move above the call strike by an amount equal to the sum of the two premiums received and should not fall below the put strike by an amount equal to the sum of the two premiums received. Any change in stock price beyond the breakeven levels (call strike + total premium and put strike − total premium) is a loss to the seller.

2.4.6   Condors

Straddles and strangles involve only two positions—one from long and the other from put—and both of them should be either long or short. Condors are somewhat similar to strangles but involve four positions. A long condor involves four calls with different strike prices: the lowest and highest strikes as long calls and the two middle ones as short puts.

The short straddle and short strangle strategies are exposed to short volatility risk, which can lead to huge losses. In order to limit the losses from higher movements of prices, two additional positions can be added to the short strangle or straddle. The two positions stay at the edges. There will be a total of four positions:

1. One long put at the lowest strike in the range
2. One short put at the next lowest strike
3. One short call at the next highest strike
4. One long call at the highest strike in the range

A condor provides downside protection from short volatility risk. The rules of thumb are that condors should have four positions, and zero or an even number of puts or calls; also, extreme positions must be long. The following are various combinations of condors:

- Calls-only condor = long A + short B + short C + long D.
- Puts-only condor = long A + short B + short C + long D.
- Puts and calls condor = long call A + short call B + short put C + long put D.
- Puts and calls condor = long put A + short put B + short call C + long call D.

In all of the above examples, A < B < C < D.

2.4.7   Vertical Spreads

If we are very optimistic that the stock price of a particular company will only rise in next few days or weeks, we can buy a call option on that stock. At the same time, we must also be optimistic that the stock price will rise beyond a certain price. In order to offset the premium paid, we can sell the call option on the same stock at a higher strike price. If the stock price rises above the first strike price, we will take the profit but only until it reaches the higher strike price at which we sold the other call option.

Consider an example where an investor buys a call option with a strike price of $15 and pays a premium of $3. At the same time, he sells the call option on the same stock at the strike of $20 and receives a premium of $1. The net premium paid is $2. The expiration of the two options should match. If the stock is rising and crosses the $15 mark, the profit increases. The breakeven level is $17. If the stock touches $20, he should sell the stock to the other call buyer. Therefore, there is a ceiling of profit at $20, at which stage he is making a profit of $3 after covering the premium paid. This strategy, called a *vertical-call bull spread*, is good in a rising but not-so-optimistic market.

The vertical spread for the writer in the scenario above is called a *vertical-call bear spread*. The writer of the bear spread believes that the stock price will not go up, so he'll earn the premium, but on the safe side he buys a call option at the higher strike by paying a little premium just in case he has to sell the stock to the first buyer, thus minimizing the loss.

2.4.8   *Butterfly Spreads*

The butterfly spread is a combination of a bull spread and a bear spread. It involves four positions, two long and two short. The strike price for the middle positions is the same. In a bull spread, long call A and short call B are involved, and in a bear spread short call B and long call C, where A < B. Butterfly is a conservative strategy, meaning it has limited profit and limited risk.

2.4.9   *Equity Swaps*

Some investors have restrictions on owning certain stocks. For example, some countries restrict which stocks can be owned by foreigners. But foreign investors may see opportunities in the stock market of that country.

For example, let's say Party A, who is a foreign investor in Country B, wants to invest in the stocks of that country. Since he has restrictions on owning those stocks, he approaches Party B in Country B, who borrows the funds from elsewhere and buys the stocks on behalf of Party A. The interest on the borrowed funds is either fixed or variable. Let's say the interest is LIBOR. At the end of the reset period, typically three or six months, Party A pays the interest on the borrowed funds and Party B pays the returns on the stocks. If the stock price goes up, Party B pays the profit to Party A. If it goes down, Party A pays the loss amount to Party B.

In this case, Party B continuously earns some constant spread from the interest component. For example, if Party B borrows the funds at LIBOR and if Party A is paying the interest as LIBOR + 100bp, then 100bp is the commission for Party A.

Equity swaps are similar to interest-rate swaps and currency swaps, but the difference is that the swap payment is determined based on the stock returns.

2.5   *Interest-Rate Derivatives*

We've discussed equity derivatives, how and where are they used, the applications of equity options in risk management, and building arbitrage strategies using the options. For all those products, the underlying asset is a stock. While most option products do not directly involve the stock to be purchased, some are built by explicitly using the stock in the strategy.

Similarly, interest-rate derivatives are used to manage the risk in the fluctuations of interest rates and to build arbitrage strategies to fulfill the specific needs of investors and borrowers. The most common derivative types used for interest rates are options, forwards, futures, swaps, and a combination of these.

2.5.1   Interest-Rate Options

While some businesses deliberately engage in floating interest rates, some are restricted to borrowing the cash at floating rates only. This may be because their analysis suggests that interest rates will not go up, or the business may not be qualified for lower fixed-interest rates. But interest rates may move up against the borrower's favor or go down against the lender's favor. There are options contracts available to protect both parties from unfavorable movements of interest rates.

Interest-rate options protect against adverse-rate risk while allowing gains from favorable rate movements. There are three main types of interest-rate options: caps, floors, and collars. When buying any of these contracts, the buyer pays a premium, typically up front. The premium amount depends on the specified rate, market volatility, and time covered, which may range from a few days to many years. Interest-rate options are also used to protect complex products against rate risk. The interest-rate component is stripped out from such products and hedged using interest-rate options.

Caps

Caps are used to create a ceiling on floating-rate interest costs. When interest rates move above the cap rate, the seller pays the buyer the difference. Borrowers purchase caps. For example, let's say Company XYZ borrows funds on a floating-rate basis when three-month LIBOR is 6 percent. At the same time, the company purchases a 7 percent cap to protect against a rate increase above that level. If rates subsequently increase to 9 percent, the company receives a 2 percent cap payment to compensate for the increase in market rates. The cap ensures that the borrower's interest-rate costs will never exceed the cap rate.

Cap contracts can be customized in such a way that the protection is continued or discontinued after paying the first protection amount. The diagram below shows the payoff of the cap contract.

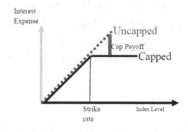

Floors

Floors are used to create a bottom on floating-rate interest costs. When interest rates move below the floor rate, the seller pays the buyer the difference. Floors are used by lenders as protection from downward movement of interest rates. For example, let's say Lender ABC lends it funds on a floating-rate basis when three-month LIBOR is 6 percent. At the same time, the company purchases a 5 percent floor to protect against a rate decrease below that level. If rates subsequently fall to 3 percent, the lender receives a 2 percent floor payment to compensate for the fall in market rates. The floor ensures that the lender's interest-rate receivables will never fall below the floor rate. Floor contracts can be customized in such a way that the protection can be continued or discontinued after paying the first protection amount. The diagram below shows the payoff of the floor contract.

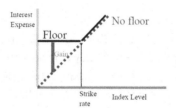

Collar

A collar is created by buying a cap and selling the floor or by purchasing a floor and selling the cap. The premium due for the cap/floor is partially offset by the premium received for the floor/cap, making the collar an effective way to hedge rate risk at a low cost.

For example, say Company ABC purchases an 8 percent cap and sells a 6 percent floor and is unaffected between 6 to 8 percent base rate on a floating-rate loan. The premium paid on call may have been offset by the premium received on the floor. If interest rates go above 8 percent, then Company ABC receives the protection. If interest rates go below 6 percent, Company ABC will be paying the difference to the other party.

2.5.2   Interest-Rate Swaps

Interest-rate swaps are used to exchange fixed interest rates with floating interest rates. A swap is an agreement to exchange interest payments in a single currency for a stated time. Only interest payments are exchanged, not principal.

Swap terms are customized to meet the users' specific risk management objectives. Terms include beginning and ending dates, settlement frequency, and the notional amount and reference rates on which swap payments are based. Reference rates may be published rates—such as LIBOR or benchmark Treasuries—or customized indexes crafted to meet the users' needs.

Why would the parties want to exchange rates instead of borrowing or lending the funds in the rate type they desire? Reasons include the following:

- Some lenders may not qualify for lower fixed rates because of credit quality.
- Some foreign entities in some countries are not qualified for fixed-rate loans.
- Certain companies' business strategy needs floating rates even though they're qualified for lower fixed rates.

The most basic swap is an exchange of floating-rate interest payments for fixed-rate payments. For example, a company that has cost-effective floating-rate bank debt can use its floating-rate borrowing power to create fixed-rate debt. To do so, the company enters into a swap to the target maturity (e.g. five years), agreeing to exchange floating-rate payments based on LIBOR for a five-year fixed rate. Through the swap, the company avoids the costs of issuing long-term debt, gains the protection of a fixed rate, and retains the cost advantage its bank debt enjoys.

2.5.3   Interest-Rate Swaptions

A swaption is nothing but a swap plus an option. Interest-rate swaptions give the holder the right, but not the obligation, to enter into or cancel a swap agreement at a future date. The buyer may purchase either the right to receive a fixed rate in the underlying swap or to pay a fixed rate.

A company's future financing needs may be uncertain or contingent upon other events. A swaption provides protection against rising rates without obligating the purchaser in the event the financing doesn't materialize. Swaptions can be used to translate the value of call options embedded in debt securities into cash.

2.5.4   Forward Rate Agreements

A forward rate agreement (FRA) is an agreement between two parties that one party will pay a certain interest rate on a certain principal amount at a specified future time. FRAs are traded over the counter and not on an exchange. Forward rate agreements are very flexible in nature and can be structured to mature on any date. They are off-balance-sheet instruments. They do not require a notional amount to be exchanged; instead, only the interest differentials are exchanged.

FRAs are not options; therefore, both parties are required to share losses and gains, depending on interest-rate movements. The efficiency of hedging depends on the manager's skill in forecasting the interest rates.

As an example of how an FRA works, let's say a manager is anticipating that interest rates will rise in two months and decides to hedge the interest-rate risk by buying a three-month FRA two months from now. It is called a 2 × 5 FRA. Assume that the broker quotes 7.50 percent. The broker may be dealing with counterparties on the other side, but the manager does not need to be aware of those details. The value date is two months from the spot date. The first fixing is two business days prior to the value date. Maturity will be three months from the value date.

Two months later, the interest rate rises to 8 percent, as the manager forecasted. Without the hedging, the manager would have paid 8 percent for the funding, but since he entered into a forward rate agreement, the broker would pay the differential of 0.5 percent on the agreed amount. Mathematically, the value the manager receives is equal to

$$P(R_y - R_{forward})(T2 - T1)\, e^{-R2 \times T2}$$

where

- P = principal;
- Ry = agreed annualized interest rate for the period T2 – T1;
- T1 and T2 = one year and two years, respectively;
- Rforward = forward interest rate between T1 and T2—for example, LIBOR rate—for the period T2 – T1; and
- R2 = discount rate used to calculate the present value of the payment on T2 date.

On the other hand, assume that the interest rate declined to 7.0 percent. In this case, the manager would need to pay the 0.5 percent differential to the broker. Mathematically,

$$P(R_{forward} - R_y)(T2 - T1)\, e^{-R2 \times T2}$$

is equal to the value the manager pays.

2.5.5   Interest-Rate Futures

Unlike the forward rate agreement, interest-rate futures trade on standard exchanges, such as CME (Chicago Mercantile Exchange) and CBOT (Chicago Board of Trade). In futures, bonds are exchanged rather than interest-rate differentials. If the manager anticipates that the interest rate will decline, then he will buy the futures. If interest rates decline as anticipated, then the manager will take delivery of the futures and sell them in the market at the higher prices. Similarly, if the manager is anticipating interest-rate hikes, then he will sell the futures. If interest rates move in an unfavorable direction in either case, then the manager would bear the loss.

In order to prevent market manipulation, the exchanges set a rule that any government bond with more than fifteen years to maturity on the first day of the delivery month is deliverable on that contract. Since the deliverable bonds have different market prices, the CBOT has created a conversion factor.

Cash paid by a long position = quoted future price × conversion factor + accrued interest

Cost to deliver the bond to buyer = quoted bond price + accrued interest

Profit/loss to future buyer = cost to deliver the bond to buyer – cash paid by long position

= Quoted bond price – quoted future price × conversion factor

Conversion factors are calculated as the present value of the bond minus accrued interest divided by face value. If interest rates decline as anticipated, the quoted bond price will go up, so the manager will profit from the deal. Otherwise, he will have to bear the loss.

Since the future seller has the option to deliver the bond from a wider list of bonds, the sellers choose the bond that minimizes the value of quoted bond price – quoted future price × conversion factor. Such a bond is called a cheapest-to-deliver (CTD) bond.

2.6   Foreign Exchange Derivatives

It is often necessary to hedge currency risk in foreign investment strategies. Depending on the strategy, some fund managers may want to retain the currency risk, expecting to earn a premium, while other managers want to hedge the currency risk away. Various currency-hedging techniques are discussed here.

2.6.1   Fx Forward

A foreign-exchange forward is a contract to buy or sell foreign currency at a fixed rate for delivery on a specified future date or time. If the date of the foreign-currency usage and the maturity date of the foreign-currency forward contract are matched up, the investor has in effect locked in the exchange-rate payment amount. Fx forward contracts are considered over-the-counter, as there is no centralized trading location and transactions are conducted directly between parties via telephone and online trading platforms at thousands of locations worldwide. Interestingly, unlike other forward contracts, currency forward contracts are more liquid than currency futures.

2.6.2   Fx Futures

Fx futures are similar to Fx forwards in that the underlying asset is a currency exchange rate, such as the US dollar to euro exchange rate. However, there is a major difference: currency futures are traded via exchanges, such as the CME, and are therefore well controlled.

2.6.3   Fx Options

Currency options are financial instruments that give the owner the right, but not the obligation, to buy or sell a specific foreign currency at a predetermined exchange rate. A call option gives the holder the right to buy the currency at an agreed-upon price, and a put option gives him the right to sell it at an agreed-upon price, irrespective of unfavorable market price for the same.

2.6.4   Cross Hedging with Forwards

In less-developed countries or frontier countries, capital markets are still in an infancy stage, and foreign exchange markets are heavily controlled. Therefore, currency forwards and futures are either unavailable or are just starting to develop at a rather slow pace. International firms that are exposed to currencies of these countries should look for alternative currency hedging; such an exchange-rate risk management technique is referred to as *cross hedging*. Cross hedging utilizes a triangular parity condition, which often exists among the home, foreign, and third currencies.

2.6.5   Cross-Currency Swaps

Cross-currency swaps are used to manage the currency risk in foreign-investment portfolios. A currency swap involves the exchange of payments denominated in one currency for payments denominated in another. Payments are based on a notional principal amount, the value of which is fixed in exchange-rate terms at the swap's inception.

Periodic swap payments are made in the appropriate currencies based on specified reference interest rates. When the swap matures, a final payment representing the change in the value of the swapped notional principal is made between the parties to the swap. Alternatively, the principal values can be reexchanged at maturity at the original exchange rate. Because currency swaps involve exchange risk on principal, the credit risk associated with these transactions is substantially greater than that of interest-rate swaps. Unlike interest-rate swaps, netting of notional amounts within a single swap is not allowed in currency swaps.

Fx Swaps

Fx swaps are different from cross-currency swaps. In Fx swaps, the notional amounts in two currencies are exchanged at spot price and reexchanged after a certain time at the forward exchange rate. These swaps are useful for parties who want the currency to be used in a foreign country for a particular period.

CIRCUS

CIRCUS stands for combined interest-rate and currency swap. Fixed-rate payments in one currency are swapped with floating-rate payments in another currency.

2.7 Credit Derivatives

Before actually getting into credit derivatives, let's briefly discuss credit ratings. As we discussed earlier, Treasuries are backed by the "full faith and credit" of the US government. Therefore, it is guaranteed that the principal and interest will be paid back on time. It is not necessary for every bond in the market to be issued or backed by the government. Corporate bond issuers are private issuers. If the bond issuers are financially strong, then it is anticipated that the principal and interest will be paid back.

For investors who do not have insights into the bond issuers, however, it is difficult to gauge the financial strength of the issuer. Private rating services were developed to fulfill the needs of bond/security investors. They provide evaluations of an issuer's financial strength and its ability to pay principal and interest in a timely fashion. There are several rating agencies, including Moody's, Standard & Poor's (S&P), and Fitch. Just as individuals have FICO scores, issuers and bonds have rating codes. The rating code represents the credit quality of the issuer and bonds.

The rating of a bond can stay stable, move downward, or move upward, depending on the creditworthiness of the issuer and market conditions. Investors who hold bonds seek protection from credit downgrades or defaults. Credit derivatives are designed to protect investors from credit-quality degradation and probable default of the issuer.

Let's examine a practical scenario. An investor bought AAA-rated bonds, but because of general economic conditions, he foresees that the rating may be downgraded or defaulted. Or the investor bought non-investment-grade or high-yield bonds, as they are paying higher coupons and may require him to buy protection from default. Or a bank has loans on the balance sheet and wants protection from customer defaults. In these cases, the bank will use credit derivatives to transfer the credit risk to a protection seller. Certain investment strategies—especially if they are using funds from pension plans and endowments—are required to purchase credit protection.

Credit derivatives are bilateral contact agreements. They are bought over the counter and do not involve exchanges, and therefore they are called OTC derivatives. Examples of credit derivatives include, but are not limited to, asset swaps, credit default swaps, total return swaps, and credit linked notes.

2.7.1   Asset Swaps

Asset swaps are used to swap two different types of assets that generate cash flow. With interest-rate swaps, we learn that fixed interest rates are exchanged for floating interest rates on a certain notional amount; the actual assets are not swapped. Let's consider an example where Investor A holds a bond that pays a fixed-interest coupon, and Investor B holds a floating-rate bond. Investor A sees an opportunity in rising interest rates, while Investor B foresees a risk of bond default because of rising rates. Neither wants to sell the existing bond and buy a different type, perhaps because of tax considerations. Investor B, the floating-rate investor, does not want to go to interest-rate swaps, as they do not protect from default.

In order to meet their needs, the investors exchange their bonds and cash flows for a certain period of time, with an agreement to swap back again on a certain date. During the swap period, Investor A will be holding the floating-rate bond and Investor B will be holding the fixed-interest bond. If the floating-rate bond defaults during the process, then Investor A is obligated to pay the face value to the original owner, Investor B. Therefore, Investor A is bearing the risk of bond default in order to receive higher interest rates. He is selling credit protection to Investor B. Similarly, Investor B is receiving fixed interest, which is less than the floating rate. He is willing to receive a lower rate in order to get protection on his original bond. Therefore, he is said to be buying protection or selling credit risk.

In this example, the transactions did not involve buying or selling the underlying bonds. Therefore, they are called *credit derivatives*. This is one example, but there are many other types of asset swaps.

2.7.2   Credit Default Swaps

In the case of asset swaps, the floating-rate investor avoided credit risk by exchanging the bond for another type of bond. What if there are no parties in the market to exchange bonds with? Can he still buy the protection? The answer is yes, using a credit default swap (CDS).

A default swap is a bilateral contract between two parties in which one party pays periodic premiums to buy protection against the risk of default or downgrade of an asset issued by a specified entity. In other words, he is buying the insurance to protect his assets. Upon a credit event, the buyer of protection receives a payment intended to compensate against loss on the investment.

For short-term assets, such as six-month bonds, the fee may be paid up front. For long-term bonds, the fee is paid over the life of the transaction at regular intervals. The contract is typically specified using the confirmation document and legal definitions produced by the International Swap and Derivatives Association (ISDA). Upon a credit event, the buyer of protection receives a payment in the form of a cash or physical settlement. Credit events may include the following:

- bankruptcy (not applicable to sovereigns)
- failure to pay
- obligation acceleration/default
- repudiation/moratorium
- restructuring

Single-name CDS contracts provide protection against a default event on the part of a single issuer.

2.7.3   Nth-to-Default Baskets

Nth-to-default swaps offer protection on a specified occurrence of default in a list of reference entities. For example, in a basket of ten reference entities, the basket-holder may want to purchase the protection only on the first default. He may do this because he wants to wind down the remaining positions after he sees the first default. Such protection is called a *first-to-default swap*.

First-to-default baskets are called *correlation products*. The investor in the first-to-default basket receives a periodic spread payment and agrees to bear the loss when any one of a specified group of credits defaults. Like equity tranches of collateralized debt obligations (CDOs), first-to-default baskets have a first-loss exposure to the reference portfolio and offer leveraged exposure to credit risk, and their value depends on the correlation. Unlike CDOs, first-to-default baskets typically involve small reference portfolios; five names are typical.

Alternatively, the basket-holder may want to purchase protection on the second occurrence of default in the basket. Such protection is called *second-to-default swap*. In this case, the basket investor does not receive any compensation for the first default. He will have to bear the risk.

The pricing of nth-to-default swaps depends on individual risks as well as on the way in which credit events on one name relate to credit events on another. In other words, the credit correlations among the individual names determine the price of the nth-to-default swap.

2.7.4   Contingent Credit Default Swaps

With a regular CDS, the payment-upon-credit event is determined based on an initially agreed-upon notional value. However, because of market fluctuations, the future exposure can be higher than the initial notional amount. For example, a bond issued with a principal of $100 may sometimes trade at $101. A contingent CDS is structured in such a way that payment is linked to exposure amount.

2.7.5   Total Return Swaps

A total return swap is a bilateral agreement between two parties that exchanges the total return from an asset between them. This is designed to transfer the credit risk from one party to the other. In addition, total return swaps are used as synthetic repo instruments for funding purposes. The total return swap (TRS) is sometimes called a *total rate of return swap* or *TR swap*. In a TRS, the total return of an asset or credit-sensitive security is exchanged for some other cash flow, usually tied to LIBOR or some other asset or credit-sensitive security. The maturity of the underlying asset does not need to match the contract maturity.

In a TRS, the total return from the underlying asset is paid over to the counterparty in return for a fixed or floating cash flow. This slightly distinguishes the TRS from a credit default swap, as the payments between counterparties to a TRS are connected to change in the market value of the underlying asset, as well as changes resulting from the occurrence of a credit event. So the TRS is used to transfer credit risk, interest-rate risk, or any other risks that influence the market value of the asset.

The buyer of a TRS receives the complete cash flow of the underlying asset without actually buying the asset, which makes it a synthetic bond product and therefore a credit derivative. An investor may wish to receive such cash flows synthetically for tax, accounting, regulatory-capital, external-audit, or legal reasons. This concept is especially useful for illiquid assets.

The total return on the underlying asset is made up of the interest payments and any change in the market value. A positive change in market value, which is called *capital appreciation*, makes the cash flow to the total return receiver, whereas a negative change in market value, which is called *depreciation*, makes the cash flow to the total return payer. The swap is usually paid on a quarterly or semiannual basis, with the underlying asset being revalued or marked-to-market on the resetting dates. The asset price is usually obtained from an independent third-party source, such as Bloomberg, or as the average of a range of dealer quotes.

If the obligor of the reference asset defaults, the TRS may be terminated immediately, with a net present-value payment changing hands according to what this value is. Alternatively, if a secondary market exists for the underlying assets, then the contract may be continued, with each party making appreciation or depreciation payments as appropriate. Upon termination of the swap, counterparties will be liable to each other for accrued interest plus any appreciation or depreciation of the asset.

In a TRS, one party purchases and retains rights to the underlying asset and transfers the total return of the asset to another party in return for a floating return, such as LIBOR plus spread. The spread is a function of the credit rating of the swap counterparty, the amount and value of the reference asset, the credit quality of the reference asset, the funding costs of the beneficiary bank, any required profit margin, and the capital charge associated with the TRS.

Suppose an investor wants to purchase a real-estate tower worth $10 million. However, his balance sheet does not allow any more assets to be bought, or he does not want to take care of day-to-day operations. Or he may not want to pay $10 million now, as he thinks that he could use those funds for some other purpose. What he wants to do is enter into a two-year agreement with the real-estate owner such that the owner agrees to pass on monthly profits (from leases or sales) from the tower to the investor. The tower is still owned by the real-estate owner.

In return for monthly profits, the investor pays a certain interest on $10 million, usually LIBOR + X. Let's say that at the end of the second year, the building is reappraised, and its value is $12 million. Had the investor owned it, he would have gained $2 million of appreciation. So the real-estate owner pays the difference of $2 million to the investor. The investor made some profit without having the tower on his balance sheet.

Assume that instead the value of the tower goes down to $8 million at the end of the second year. Had he owned the tower, the investor would have lost $2 million, so he will pay $2 million to the owner.

As the words "total return" indicate, the owner gives all the returns. Giving a negative amount (loss) is nothing but receiving an amount. By doing so, he has indirectly purchased loss protection.

In the above case, we used a real-estate tower as an example. The asset might also be a bond. If the bond value goes down because of downgraded credit quality of the issuer, the bondholder receives compensation for the lost value. In this case, it is said that the bondholder purchased credit protection.

2.7.6   Credit Linked Notes

A credit linked note (CLN) is a credit derivative under which the coupon or price of a note is linked to the creditworthiness or performance of a specific financial asset. It offers issuers a hedge on credit risk and gives investors a higher yield on a note for accepting exposure to a specified credit event. Credit linked notes are backed by collateral that is highly rated, such as Treasury securities. CLNs are created through special purpose vehicles (SPVs) or trusts that are collateralized with AAA-rated securities. Investors buy securities from the trust, which pays a fixed or floating coupon during the life of a note.

The holder of a CLN has credit exposure to the issuer of the note, as well as to the reference entity or entities as defined in the terms and conditions of the CLN. By purchasing a credit linked note, the investor is effectively selling credit protection in relation to the reference entity. In return, the investor receives a higher coupon representing the premium paid by the buyer of credit protection. While an investor bears the credit risk of the issuer of the debt instrument, he physically holds a credit linked note, which gives him synthetic exposure to the occurrence of predetermined credit events in relation to the underlying entity. If no credit event occurs during the term of the CLN, it is redeemed on its maturity date at its nominal amount. If the reference entity defaults or declares bankruptcy, the CLN buyer receives an amount equal to the recovery rate.

Credit linked notes have become increasingly popular since 1997, as banks try to reduce their exposure to the risk of default on loans to emerging markets. A credit linked note allows an investor to obtain credit exposure to a wide variety of underlying entities in order to enhance the return on the fixed-income investment portfolio. Since the features of a CLN resemble those of a regular corporate bond, institutional investors—who are typically restricted from investing in other credit derivatives like a CDS or TRS—are interested in them. In addition, because of the size of the minimum investment, they also attract retail investors. The presence of both institutional investors and retail investors increases the market for CLNs. In essence, there are more parties willing to write insurance against default.

An issuer may also issue a note that is linked to the credit of one or more reference entities. Such CLNs are called *basket CLNs* or *nth-to-default CLNs*.

A basket CLN is a note that references a basket of reference entities. Investors will receive a coupon until the earlier of the maturity date of the CLN or the date on which credit events have occurred in respect to every reference entity. If a credit event occurs, the nominal amount of the CLN will be reduced by the same proportion as the relevant reference entity bears to the basket, and the investor will be paid an amount equal to the recovery value of outstanding obligations issued by the relevant reference entity. Thereafter, as the nominal amount of the CLN has been reduced, coupon payments will be reduced proportionally and the coupon rate may be reset. As the basket CLN is not terminated following a credit event, the remaining nominal capital continues to be exposed to potential credit events throughout the remaining term.

An nth-to-default note is a note that also references a basket of reference entities. The difference between a basket CLN and an nth-to-default CLN is that upon occurrence of a predetermined number of credit events in relation to reference entities, the entire nth-to-default CLN terminates, whereas a basket CLN continues with a reduced nominal amount. An nth-to-default CLN would terminate after n reference entities suffered a credit event—that is, a first-to-default after one reference entity, a second-to-default after two reference entities suffered a credit event, and so forth.

A CLN is a structured note where the principal repayment is linked to the creditworthiness of the CLN issuer as well as to the reference entity. Here the reference entity is nothing but the issuer of the bond for which the CLN issuer is providing the protection. By purchasing the CLN, the investor is indirectly providing the protection on the bond issued by the reference entity.

An institution provides credit protection for a reference entity using a CDS and receives regular fixed payments from the protection (CDS) buyer. The institution then issues the CLN with the principal amount and maturity matching that of the CDS. The institution pays the investor regular interest until the maturity of the note. If there is a no credit event on the reference entity, the investor receives back the principal on the maturity of the note.

If the reference entity experiences a credit event, the CDS on which the institution sold protection is triggered. The institution pays to the CDS buyer the principal amount of the CDS in cash and receives the instrument/bond that was issued by the reference entity. Now the CLN is also triggered; as a result, the investor does not get his principal returned but instead receives the bond that is experiencing the credit event. The scale of the loss incurred to the CLN buyer will depend on the market value of the delivered bond.

Based on the above description, we know that the investor is exposed to the credit risk on the reference entity as well as the CLN issuer and therefore expects a higher return on the CLN than would have been achieved on a regular medium-term note. CLNs provide a way to gain exposure to credit market to investors who are restricted from using credit derivatives because of operational, legal, or regulatory constraints. CLNs are a relatively simple trade, as the investor does not need to enter into an ISDA master agreement. Unless the reference entity experiences a credit event during the life of the CLN, the principal will be repaid to the investor on maturity. During the life of the note, the investor will also have received regular interest payments in the form of coupons.

2.7.7   Credit Spread Options

A credit spread option is an option contract where the exercise is based on the credit spread of the reference credit relative to some strike spread. The strike spread can be Treasury spread or LIBOR spread. The delivery upon the exercising of the options involves an asset swap, a floating-rate note, or a default swap. Like equity options, the option contract can be put or call, and can be European-style, American-style, or Bermudan-style.

2.8   Repo-Style Transactions

2.8.1   Repos

Repo stands for "repurchase agreement." By using the word *repurchase*, we are explicitly saying that we are buying the one that was previously sold by us. It is essentially a secured loan. One party borrows cash from another and posts securities as collateral. In other words, the party sells the securities and receives the cash with an agreement that it will purchase the securities back. When the agreement expires, the borrower pays back the loan principal with interest and the lender returns the collateral—that is, the other party sells back the security. Agreements are typically overnight, but term agreements are struck for several months or longer. Collateral is typically US Treasuries, mortgage-backed securities, corporate bonds, municipal bonds, asset-backed securities, and equities.

In capital markets, financial institutions use repos as a form of overnight borrowing, with government securities (considered to have the highest credit grade) as collateral. The repo market plays many important roles in financial markets, as described in the following points:

- Broker-dealers want to participate in security markets by holding securities, but at the same time they do not want to lock in their capital by buying these securities outright. They use the repo market to borrow the money by posting these securities as collateral. When the repo expires, the borrower of cash must either sell the security to pay back the loan or renew the repo for another day or term.
- Leveraged investors and hedge funds buy securities and finance the purchases through the repo market.
- Non-leveraged investors—such as state and local governments, money market funds, other mutual funds, and foreign sovereign

entities—prefer the relative safety of lending money. Since repos virtually eliminate credit problems, they use the repo market to gain exposure to credit markets.

- The central banks use repo to add or remove liquidity from the financial system, particularly when such actions are expected to be unwound in relatively short order.

While repo transactions are relatively safer than other financial transactions, the repo market is not completely risk-free. If the borrower of cash defaults on a loan, the lender can sell the collateral and use the proceeds to cover the loan. But risk arises if the counterparty defaults on the loan at a time when the value of the collateral falls. Conversely, the risk to the borrower of money is that the lender defaults at the same time that the value of the collateral has risen. Haircuts are introduced to mitigate such risks. Haircuts are discussed at 5.1.14.

2.8.2   Reverse Repos

In a repo transaction, securities are sold by the borrower at a lower price to the dealer and repurchased at a higher price, with the difference attributed to the interest to be paid. A reverse repo does the opposite. Dealers buy at a lower price and then sell back the securities at a higher price at a later date, attributing the difference to the interest earned.

In other words, if an institution is borrowing the money, then it is a repo transaction for that institution. If the institution is lending the money, then it is a reverse repo for that institution.

2.8.3   Tri-Party Repos

Repo transactions involve several operations, such as trading settlement, selecting the right collateral, payment settlement, and custody during the life of the transaction. These activities bring certain operational risks to the repo market.

Tri-party agents or clearing banks are established to take care of these operations and to reduce the operational risks. There are two such clearing banks for the US repo market: JPMorgan Chase and Bank of New York Mellon. In brief, tri-party agents act as:

- *independent custody agents* to hold the collateral against loans so that this collateral is truly available to the lender of cash in the event of a default by the borrower;
- *pricing and margin collection agents* to price the collateral so that the agreed-upon amount of collateral, including margin, is held against the loans; and
- *settlement agents* to facilitate securities and cash movement to and from the accounts of borrowers and lenders as appropriate.

Daily operations of the repo market involving tri-parties are as follows:

- The borrower of cash first deposits securities into an account at the clearing bank, and the lender of cash deposits cash into the borrower's account.
- The clearing bank simultaneously moves the cash into the borrower's account and the securities into the lender's account.
- At the expiration of the repo contract, after the borrower deposits enough cash to repay the loan with interest, the clearing bank simultaneously passes the cash to the lender and returns the securities to the borrower.

About two thirds of US repo operations are outsourced to tri-party agents. Tri-party agents provide only operations. They do not act as guarantors; that is, they do not participate in the risk of transactions. If one of the parties defaults, the impact still falls entirely on the other party. This means that parties to the tri-party repo need to continue to sign bilateral written legal agreements.

2.8.4   Security Finance Transactions

Security finance transactions, also called security lending transactions, are pretty much like repo-style transactions. They involve an exchange of securities and collateral. In either case, the legal titles are exchanged for the period of the contract. The main difference comes from voting rights and corporate actions. In security lending transactions, the security lender or collateral receiver has the right to recall the security if is needed for voting-rights purposes. Since the security borrower holds the legal title during the contract, the contract terms specify the option of calling back the security when the lender needs it for voting. This is not possible in the case of repos.

It should be noted that the bondholder does not have voting rights; only stockholders have the voting rights. Therefore, repos are mainly limited to lending the bonds, whereas security finance transactions are used to lend the stocks. In either case, the collateral can be cash or other security.

2.9 Commodities

Commodities are broadly categorized as grains, such as corn, wheat, oats, and rice; soft commodities, such as coffee, cocoa, sugar, potatoes, orange juice, and cotton; precious metals, such as gold, silver, platinum, and palladium; industrial metals, such as aluminum and copper; and energy commodities, such as crude oil, heating oil, natural gas, gasoline, and electricity.

Commodities are different from traditional financial instruments in that they cannot be priced using the capital asset pricing model (CAPM) and net present values. Moreover, they typically perform well during the last stage of the business cycle, where both stocks and bonds start declining. Therefore, the commodity asset class is said to be countercyclical in nature. Supply, demand, inventory levels, and storage costs drive commodities prices and leasing rates. Commodity future returns are positively correlated with the inflation rate, and the positive correlation increases as the time horizon increases. Positive correlation with inflation is good for investors in the sense that bonds and stocks are negatively correlated with inflation and so the negative correlation between commodities and bonds/stocks helps the portfolio manager achieve greater diversification.

Historically, commodities were used as a hedge against inflation. Now they have become a special class of assets and are widely used by hedge funds to enhance portfolio returns in addition to diversification. For example, oil prices are negatively correlated with both the S&P 500 and the FTSE 100. The negative correlation becomes even more negative as the time horizon increases. The addition of commodities to a portfolio of bonds and stocks will shift the efficient frontier upward and left, enhancing the return and reducing the overall risk.

Within the commodity class, the returns of any commodity have low or even negative correlation with the returns of other commodities. This suggests that holding a diversified commodity portfolio can have significant benefits over holding a single commodity investment. Commodities provide a better inflation hedge than real estate. But the emerging-markets bonds and stocks are positively correlated with commodities as the emerging markets are said to be net producers of commodities while the developed markets are said to be net consumers.

There are several ways of gaining exposure to commodity markets, including the following:

- *Spot markets* provide direct access to commodities and may deal with the producer directly or through an intermediary. However, the investor or fund manager has to deal with storage costs—and for some commodities, such as gas and electricity, the storage will be challenging. Spot markets are good for precious metals, which do not require much space to store. One other disadvantage of the spot market is that it requires full initial payment. If all the overheads can be managed properly, spot markets provide a better hedge against unfavorable movements of prices.
- *Pure play* is a concept of buying stocks of desired commodity-producer companies. For example, an investor who wishes to gain exposure to the copper market will purchase stocks of Freeport-McMoRan Copper & Gold Inc.'s stock, which moves in the direction of copper performance. However, the pure play is subject to operational risk of the company and depends on the effectiveness of company management.
- *Commodity futures* are another way of gaining exposure to commodities through the futures written on those commodities. Futures contracts are standardized agreements and are backed by the faith of exchanges and clearinghouses. They can be purchased through licensed futures-commission merchants. In contrast to the spot market, futures purchases require little initial upfront margin. Futures contracts may result in margin calls depending on the direction of spot prices. Investors can roll the futures contracts to future expirations if delivery is not required.
- *Commodity swaps* are used by producers and consumers to hedge against commodity price variations. The commodity swap can be settled in either cash or by physical delivery. Consumers whose businesses prefer fixed-rate payments for commodities hold the floating leg to receive the variance while the producers who agree to pay a floating rate hold the fixed leg. There are two main types of commodity swaps: fixed-floating commodity swaps, where both the legs are commodity based, and commodity for interest swaps, where a total return on the commodity is exchanged for some money market rate plus or minus a spread.

- *Commodity indices* provide access to commodities or to a particular sector of commodities. Commodity-linked notes are also available, where prices are linked to total returns of commodities.

2.9.1   Structure of the Commodity Market

The basic structure of the commodity market primarily involves four parties: exchange corporations, clearinghouses, futures commission merchants (FCMs), and FCM customers. The exchange corporation has members in terms of clearing members and non-clearing members.

Exchange Corporations

Exchange corporations provide an organized marketplace with uniform rules and standardized contracts. Exchanges operate markets for spot commodities, options, futures contracts, and other financial securities. Membership fees and transaction fees paid on contracts back exchanges.

There were more than 1,600 exchanges in the United States during the second half of the nineteenth century in the vicinity of harbors or railroad crossings. Today, they are limited to six. Among them are the Chicago Board of Trade (CBOT), which was originally dedicated to agricultural commodities, trades futures, and options on corn, soybean, soy meal, wheat, rice, and precious metals like gold and silver; the New York Mercantile Exchange (NYME), trading crude oil, gas, copper, aluminum, and precious metals; and the New York Board of Trade, trading contracts on coffee, sugar, cocoa, cotton, and orange juice.

Clearing members of the exchange are entitled to clear their own transactions and those of affiliated companies without a clearing license, as well as their clients' transactions. Non-clearing members of the exchange are not able to clear transactions on their own and pay clearing members to clear their trades.

Clearinghouses

The clearinghouse provides the facility to close out positions without having the buyer and seller interact with each other. The clearinghouse supervises the delivery of commodities and guarantees each futures contract that it clears.

Futures Commission Merchants

FCMs are the brokerage firms that execute, clear, and carry advisor-directed trades on the various exchanges. Some FCMs also act as commodity-pool operators and trading managers, providing administrative reports on investment performance.

FCM Customers

FCM customers are end-users who open and close the future positions.

2.9.2   *Pricing of Commodity Futures*

Since commodities do not yield any cash flows, they cannot be priced using the theory of net present value of cash flow. Instead, they are priced based on expected future price, lease rates, convenience yield, and storage costs. Expected future value depends on factors like supply and demand. Agricultural commodity prices depend on weather conditions and production capacity, while energy commodities depend on season. Electricity commodity prices change even during the day, as storing of electricity poses some challenges.

In a simple pricing technique, under a no-arbitrage assumption, the total cost of the commodity forward contract is equal to the present value of the expected future price. Mathematically:

$$Ft = S0 \times e^{rt}.$$

The above equation illustrates that the commodity price at time 0 is equivalent to the present value of a unit of a commodity received at time t. The risk-free rate r represents the discount rate or opportunity cost. The above technique is simple and assumes that there are no storage costs or lease rates, which will be discussed later in this topic.

If the above equation does not hold, then arbitrage opportunities exist. There are two types of arbitrage opportunities: *cash-and-carry arbitrage* and *reverse cash-and-carry arbitrage.*

If Ft is greater than $S0 \times e^{rt}$, then a cash-and-carry arbitrage opportunity exists, in which case the present value of the expected future spot price is greater than the current spot price. Under this scenario, investors buy the commodity in the spot market and store and simultaneously sell the futures contract on the same. At contract expiration, they deliver the commodity and receive the future contract price. Investors may use funds borrowed at risk-free rate r to buy the commodities in the spot market, which will be repaid at the time of contract expiration by receiving the future contract price.

If Ft is less than S0 × e^{rt}, then a reverse cash-and-carry arbitrage opportunity exists, in which case the present value of the expected future spot price is less than the current spot price. Under this scenario, investors short the commodity in the spot market and simultaneously buy the futures contract on the same. At contract expiration, they receive the commodity and cover the short position. Investors receive funds by shorting the commodities in the spot market and lending at the risk-free rate until the time of contract expiration, at which time they pay the futures contract price.

From the above opportunities, it can be observed that investors buy whichever (either spot commodity or futures contract) is low and sell high, which can be generalized as "buy low and sell high." There are three characteristics that influence arbitrage opportunities: lease rates, storage costs, and convenience yield.

Lease Rates

In the simple pricing technique, it was assumed that the opportunity cost is equal to the risk-free rate, which actually represents the return that the investor can receive without any risk by investing in Treasuries or similar securities. However, if the commodity can yield some rental/lease income, then the investor must forgo that return by not holding the commodity. In other words, holding the commodity may help the investor by fetching some lease income. Therefore, the opportunity cost is reduced by the amount of the lease rate. Assuming a continuous lease rate of δ, the effective opportunity cost will become r − δ.

Mathematically, the commodity forward price for time t with an active lease rate of δ is

$$F0, t = S0 \times e^{(r-\delta)t}$$

where

$$S0 = \text{commodity current spot price}$$

$$r - \delta = \text{effective opportunity cost.}$$

Storage Costs

In contrast to lease rates, the holder of the commodity will have to pay a fee for storing the commodity until the delivery of the contract. This will increase the opportunity cost by an amount equivalent to the storage cost.

Assuming that continuous storage cost is equal to γ, the effective opportunity cost will become $r + \gamma$ Therefore, the commodity forward price for time t with an active storage cost of γ is

$$F0, t = S0 \times e^{(r + \gamma)t}$$

where

$$S0 = \text{commodity current spot price}$$
$$r + Y = \text{effective opportunity cost.}$$

Convenience Yield

Convenience yield represents the benefit that the holder of a commodity receives. The benefit can be in a form other than a lease. For example, a manufacturer may need raw materials on a continuous basis. If the manufacturer runs out of stock of the materials, the production process may slow down or even shut down temporarily. As a result, the manufacturer may lose part of his business income. Having the material purchased ahead of need and keeping it ready for manufacturing purposes increases the benefit, called the *convenience yield*.

Convenience yield has the same effect as lease rate and represents the benefit the holder of a futures contract loses or the benefit the holder of a commodity receives. Assuming a continuous convenience yield of α, the effective opportunity cost will become $r - \alpha$.

Therefore, the commodity forward price for time t with an active convenience yield of α is

$$F0, t = S0 \times e^{(r - \alpha)t}$$

where

$$S0 = \text{commodity current spot price}$$
$$r - a = \text{effective opportunity cost.}$$

Impact of Lease Rate, Storage Cost, and Convenience Yield on Arbitrage Opportunity

Often there are situations where a combination of lease rate, storage cost, and convenience yield are applicable when determining futures prices. For example, manufacturing units may be paying a storage cost while enjoying the benefit of convenience yield, or a jewel manufacturer may lease old jewels while receiving the benefit of convenience yield before remanufacturing them. Taking all three into consideration,

$$F0, t = S0 \times e^{(r - \delta + \gamma - a)t}$$

It is necessary to set any non-applicable terms to zero. Therefore, investors should consider the above equation while assessing the arbitrage opportunities.

2.9.3 Market Conditions

Normal Backwardation Market

A market in which the futures price is below the expected future spot price is called a *normal backwardation market*. In the agriculture market, for example, farmers want to protect themselves from the fluctuations that may be caused by weather. For this purpose, they sell the futures ahead of the harvest. Speculators, on the other hand, bear the risk and expect a risk premium. The risk aversion of farmers puts downward pressure on futures prices, which fall below the current spot prices. This phenomenon is referred to as *normal backwardation*. Normal backwardation occurs if hedgers are net short in futures and speculators are net long in futures.

Contango Market

A market in which the futures price is above the expected future spot price is called *normal contango*. When hedgers are net long in futures, the futures price will be higher than the expected spot price to compensate speculators for the risk of selling short. For example, Kellogg's, a cereal company, wants to protect itself from pricing fluctuations of grain and buys long futures in grains. Speculators, on the other hand, bear the risk of pricing fluctuations and expect a risk premium. To compensate the speculators for bearing the risk, Kellogg's will pay more than the spot price for future deliveries. This will put upward pressure on prices. Speculators expect that the spot price at the time of delivery will be less than the price they receive for futures and cash in the profit. Normal contango occurs if hedgers are net long in futures and speculators are net short in futures.

There is a difference between normal contango and contango. As discussed above, normal contango refers to the price pattern where the futures price is above the expected future spot price while contango refers to a situation where the futures price is greater than the spot price. There are many factors that make the market contango. One such factor is the storage cost. Holding a commodity requires storage costs, which may make the opportunity cost higher than the risk-free rate. So the parties may pay a higher premium for futures, which will result in a price higher than the spot price. Similarly, backwardation refers to the price pattern where futures prices are below spot prices. For example, a stock that pays the dividend falls in price by an amount equivalent to the dividend when the dividend is announced. So the futures buyer prefers to pay a lesser amount than the spot price. In the case of commodities, the lease rate replaces the role of dividend.

In other words, if $r - \delta + \gamma - \alpha > r$, then the market is said to be contango, and if $r - \delta + \gamma - \alpha < r$, then the market is said to be backwardation.

2.10 Securitized Products

Capital markets have been going through lots of innovative changes over the past few decades. Securitization is one of those innovations. Most banks issue loans. Every bank has limits on balance sheets either set by internal management or regulators. When the bank reaches the limit, it is in a position where it cannot offer new loans to customers. At the same time, it may be in a position where it cannot sell the existing loans to other institutions because of perceived illiquidity.

In such cases, banks make the loans into slices-and-dices called securities and sell them in the secondary market. This way, the bank can reduce the balance sheet—creating room for additional lending—and can also earn some profit in the secondary market. The buyers of securities in turn gain the exposure to underlying assets. Since these are different from straight bonds, which are considered to be organic securities, they are called *securitized securities*. Depending on the underlying assets and the structure of the securitization, the structured products are called *asset-backed securities, residential-mortgage-backed securities, commercial-mortgage-backed securities, collateralized mortgage obligations*, or *collateralized debt obligations*. Before discussing each of these products, let's see how the securitization process works.

2.10.1   Securitization Process

Originators originally lend the loans. A special purpose vehicle (SPV) then acquires the pool of loans. Some SPVs provide credit enhancements. The loans are then divided into multiple securities and sold in the secondary market. Let's examine each of these participants more closely.

Originators

Originators are the parties who lend the money to borrowers. While some originators sell the loans to other institutions, others create SPVs and transfer the loans. The motivation for selling the loans to other institutions is willingness to serve existing customers even after reaching lending capacity, reducing the risk assets, and arbitrage purposes. In some cases, the originators still continue as servicers even after selling the loans. Servicers monitor the loans and collect the payments. The assets from the originators are pooled and transferred to the SPV.

Asset Pools

Assets from the originators are pooled according to their maturity and other characteristics. An asset pool is managed by a special purpose vehicle.

Special Purpose Vehicle

An SPV is a legal entity created by the sponsors or originators by transferring assets to the SPV. They are intended to carry out some specific activity or a series of such activities. The special purpose can be registered as a limited partnership, limited liability company, trust, or corporation. An SPV is a kind of virtual entity that has no employees, makes no substantive economic decisions, and has no physical location. SPVs cannot go bankrupt. Trustees perform the administrative functions, such as collection and distribution of cash.

Credit Enhancements

Credit enhancements provide protection to investors in the form of financial support to cover losses on securitized assets in adverse conditions. They are a kind of escrow that enables bankers to convert pools of low-quality loans into high-quality securities. Depending on how the protection is offered, there are many types of credit enhancements:

- *Excess spread* is net interest left over after all expenses are covered that is deposited into a separate account. SPVs usually collect extra money on the spread so they can make up for potential missed payments in the future.
- *Surety bonds* are a type of external credit enhancement and mimic insurance policies. These bonds guarantee to pay if the securitized security does not meet its obligations. Banks and other financial institutions generally issue these bonds.
- *Wrapped securities* are another type of insurance-style credit enhancement where a third-party insurance company insures the security against any losses. However, the insurance company has the option to pay back a certain amount of pending interest or principal on a loan or to buy back some of the loans in the portfolio of the investor.
- *Cash collateral accounts* are another type of credit enhancement in which the SPV uses a certain amount of cash inflow to purchase low-risk commercial paper instruments. If there is any problem with the loan payments, the SPV can get the cash out of the commercial paper and use it in place of defaulted loan.
- *Overcollateralization* is an internal credit enhancement to ensure that cash inflow is always greater than outflow. This is done by using a loan to value ratio.

2.10.2   *Mortgage-Backed Securities*

Mortgage-backed securities (MBS) are securitized assets backed by a pool of residential or commercial mortgages. Three government-sponsored entities (GSE)—Fannie Mae, Freddie Mac, and Ginnie Mae—or private equities purchase loans from banks, mortgage companies, and other originators and then assemble them into pools. The entity then issues securities that represent claims on the principal and interest payments made by borrowers on the loans in the pool.

The securities are primarily assumed to be protected because homeowners have equity in the house or have mortgage insurance, and also GSEs act as credit enhancers in the case of GSE securities. Depending on the cash flow and risk distribution to investors, mortgage-backed securities exhibit three types of structures: pass-through securities, collateralized mortgage obligations (CMOs), and stripped MBS.

Pass-Through Securities

Pass-through securities pass through pro rata cash flows generated from mortgage payments made by the underlying mortgage holders in the pool. Cash flows from borrowers come in three forms: interest, principal installment, and principal prepayment. One of the key drivers that determines the level of payment to the investor is prepayment rate, which increases the possibility of principal repayment in advance at any time with no penalty. Therefore, pass-through securities are exposed to prepayment risk and reinvestment risk.

Assume, for example, that investors in MBS purchase the securities when market interest rates are high. Also consider the pools, which are backed by floating-rate mortgages. Investors can easily think that they will get steady coupons throughout the life of the security and final payment at maturity. If market interest rates go down, homeowners will have an incentive to refinance the loan, so there will be a prepayment to the pool. However, the refinanced (new) loan will not come to the same pool. If many loans in the pool are refinanced, there will be a sudden increase in the principal payment. Therefore, the SPV will pay the security principal to the earlier-than-stated maturity date. Now the investor has to find other securities in which to invest. Since market interest rates are lower, the investor will end up investing in them at lower returns. Had the investor originally invested in securities that were not exposed to prepayment, he would have been continued receiving higher coupons or returns.

Such a risk is called *prepayment risk*. Various quantitative models are used to calculate the prepayment risk and price the securities accordingly.

Collateralized Mortgage Obligations

Not all investors have the same level of interest to prepayment risk embedded in pass-through securities, even if the security price is adjusted to reflect such risk. Some investors prefer more exposure to prepayment risk and then expect higher risk premium, and some investors prefer little exposure to prepayment risk.

Collateralized mortgage obligations (CMOs) repackage the cash flow generated by the mortgage pool into different tranches, each tranche having a different mixture of prepayment risk/reward. A CMO is fundamentally similar to a CDO in that the risk of a portfolio of bonds has been redistributed such that some investors are exposed to more risk and some are exposed to less, but the principal difference is that the CMO is designed to redistribute prepayment risk, whereas the CDO is designed to redistribute default risk. We will be discussing CDOs shortly.

The most common type of CMO is a *planned amortization class (PAC)*, which is amortized based on the sinking fund schedule that is established within a range of prepayment speeds—meaning that, within a certain range of prepayment rates, the payments to the PAC remain stable. PAC security is structured with a companion tranche called the *support tranche*, which provides prepayment protection for the PAC security.

If the prepayment rate is higher than the upper prepayment rate, then the support tranche absorbs the excess payment, while the PAC receives payments as originally scheduled. If the prepayment rate is less than the lower prepayment rate, then payments to the support tranche are deferred and paid to the PAC. Therefore, the stability of the PAC security cash flows comes at the expense of increased risk to the support tranche. If the excess continues until the support tranche is paid off, then the PAC tranche will start receiving the excess payments. Similarly, if the payments are less than supported by the support tranche, then the PAC will receive lesser payments. At this stage, the PAC is said to be broken or busted.

Stripped MBS

In contrast to pass-through MBS, stripped MBS do not distribute cash flows on a pro rata basis. Stripped MBS receive either the principal or interest component of cash flow generated from the underlying pool. The strips that pay only the principal component are called *principal-only strips* or *PO strips*, and the strips that pay only the interest component are called *interest-only strips* or *IO strips*.

PO securities are purchased at a considerable discount to par. The PO cash flow starts out small and substantially increases with the passage of time. Basically, the faster the prepayments occur, the faster PO securities receive their principal back and the higher the yield on the investment. PO tranches benefit from lower interest rates, where prepayments are much faster. This is because anyone who borrowed at a higher interest rate will want to take advantage of current low interest rates and so will prepay the loans through refinancing. That means the yield on PO price is inversely related to interest rates and exhibits negative convexity at lower rates of interest.

IO securities' cash flow starts out big and gets smaller as time passes. In contrast to POs, IO prices move in the same direction as interest rates. That is the reason why certain hedge-fund managers prefer IOs during times of rising interest. If interest rates are falling, then the underlying pool will be paid off faster than expected, and IO investors will be left with no-interest cash flows.

MBS prices are more volatile because of the prepayment option embedded in mortgage loans. In the United States, mortgage borrowers can prepay the home loan at any time without penalty—that is, the borrowers can avail themselves of the prepayment option at no explicit cost. Mortgage loans include this option price implicitly. Since mortgage loans can be paid at any time, pricing MBS is a complex process, and therefore investors require a large premium for bearing prepayment risk. MBS arbitrage hedge-fund managers develop various mathematical models and utilize Monte Carlo simulations to calculate option-adjusted spreads. MBS arbitrage hedge-fund managers take long positions in MBS with higher AOS values and short positions in Treasury bonds to fund the long positions. Therefore, MBS arbitrage-fund managers are said to be long prepayment risk.

2.10.3   Asset-Backed Securities

After seeing the success of MBS markets, financial institutions started exploring other forms of non-mortgage assets to be used in securitization pools. They discovered lots of self-liquidating financial assets. For example, a financial institution with a pool of less-liquid auto loans can transfer them to the SPV to create publicly traded, highly rated liquid securities. These securities are called asset-backed securities. While the mortgage loans used in MBS are also financial assets, the term *asset-backed securities* (ABS) became more familiar for non-mortgage financial assets.

2.10.4   Collateralized Debt Obligations

CDOs are similar to ABS or MBS in that an SPV assembles all of these categories. However, with CDOs, an entire pool is structured based on credit risk exposures—with segments that divide exposure into different tranches with unique risk, return, and maturity profiles—and then issues CDO securities transferring the risk to investors.

The reference pool can be assembled with physical cash-flow assets, such as bonds, loans, MBS, or ABS, or with synthetic credit risk exposures. A CDO structure can have any number of tranches depending on attachment points. However, a typical CDO structure comprises three tranches—senior, mezzanine, and equity.

The *equity tranche*, or *first-loss tranche*, absorbs the losses up to a predefined percentage of the sum of the notional amount on a portfolio of reference names. Once the equity tranche is exhausted, the *mezzanine tranche* starts to absorb the additional losses. The *senior tranche* is considered to be the least risky and typically gets an AAA rating. The senior tranche performs well until both the equity and mezzanine tranches are exhausted, and then it too will experience losses.

CDOs provide investors with a way to gain exposure to various classes of risky credit assets. Investors have the option of choosing different levels of risk–risk combinations. CDOs give banks a way to unload risky assets from balance sheets, thus reducing regulatory capital. Depending on the type of cash inflows and outflows, CDOs are divided into balance-sheet, arbitrage, and synthetic types.

Balance-Sheet CDOs

In balance-sheet CDOs, the assets in the pool are typically loans. The originators of these loans are mostly banks. Banks use balance-sheet CDOs to reduce risky assets. The incentives for the bank for creating balance-sheet CDOs are numerous. They can get rid of illiquid loans and replace them with liquid loans. Long-term loans can be replaced with short-term loans. They can raise more capital as the size of the balance sheet comes down below the limit. They can reduce the regulatory capital.

In order to insure investors from deterioration of quality of the underlying loans, the structuring entity provides credit enhancements, such as a cash collateral account. A CCA is a kind of an escrow account where the portion of payments is retained to fund potential shortfalls in expected cash inflows.

Balance sheet CDOs are typically static in that the assets are purchased, placed in a pool, and distributed based on the cash flows of underlying assets. There is no active management of underlying assets.

Arbitrage CDOs

Arbitrage CDOs are funded by securities that are actively traded. In other words, arbitrage managers acquire the assets, typically bonds, in the open market, actively managing the pool by constantly selling and buying the securities. The structuring of tranches is similar to balance-sheet CDOs.

Arbitrage CDOs use quantitative engineering to determine when to sell the assets and what to buy, hedge the cash flows, and keep the spread at a desired level. Their main purpose is to provide innovative products to investors, utilizing market inefficiencies to make some profit. Arbitrage CDOs are of two types: *cash-flow CDOs* and *market-value CDOs*. Payments to cash-flow CDO investors depend on principal and interest received by the pool, whereas with market-value CDOs, the distribution depends on sale of underlying assets.

While balance-sheet CDOs are considered static, arbitrage CDOs are considered to be managed, as they require active management to buy, sell, and hedge the underlying assets.

Synthetic CDOs

A synthetic CDO is a transaction that transfers the credit risk on a reference portfolio of assets made up of credit default swaps. Thus, a synthetic CDO is classified as a credit derivative.

The risk of loss on a reference portfolio is divided into tranches of increasing seniority. Losses will first affect the *equity* or *first-loss tranche*, next the *mezzanine tranche(s)*, and finally the *senior* and *super-senior tranches*. CDO investors take on exposure to a particular tranche, effectively selling credit protection to the CDO issuer. The issuer, in turn, hedges its risk by selling credit protection on the reference portfolio in the form of single-name credit default swaps. Parties on the other side of these hedging transactions are the ultimate sellers of credit risk to the CDO investor, with the CDO issuer acting as an intermediary.

Synthetic CDO tranches can also be either funded or unfunded. If a tranche is funded, the CDO investor pays the notional amount of the tranche at the beginning of the deal, and any defaults cause a write-down of principal. Throughout the deal, the investor receives LIBOR plus a spread that reflects the riskiness of the tranche. The investor's funds are put into a collateral account and invested in low-risk securities (government or AAA-rated debt).

Unfunded tranches are similar to swaps. No money changes hands at the beginning of the deal. The investor receives a spread and pays when defaults in the reference portfolio affect the investor's tranche (after any subordinate tranches have been eaten away by previous defaults). Because unfunded tranches rely on the investor's future ability and willingness to pay into CDO, they create counterparty credit risk that must be managed.

Synthetic CDOs in the market can be customized so that the payment structure of a tranche doesn't depend on the payment structures of other tranches. Such CDOs are thus sometimes called *single-tranche CDOs*. The most popular single-tranche CDOs are exchange-traded standardized tranches. The reference credit pools of such CDOs are CDS indices, such as CDX and ITRAXX series. Other (non-standard) single-tranche CDOs are often called *bespoke tranches*.

2.10.5   Asset-Backed Commercial Paper

The term *asset-backed commercial paper (ABCP)* refers to short-term debt notes. These are either offered on a discount basis or are coupon-based. ABCP conduits issue the debt notes and receive the principal. The principal is then used to obtain stakes in various assets, such as trade receivables, consumer debt receivables, and auto and equipment loans and leases. The acquired assets are either undivided assets or individual securities, such as ABS and MBS, corporate and government bonds, or commercial paper (CP) issued by other entities. Repayment to maturing ABCP depends on the collections received from the asset interests. Alternatively, the conduits can issue new CP or draw on liquidity facilities to repay maturing CP, provided the performance of the assets financed through the original issuance of the maturing CP is satisfactory.

Financial institutions or large corporations usually sponsor ABCP programs. They are established to finance the assets of the sponsor or the sponsor's clients. ABCPs are also used to unload assets off of a sponsor's balance sheet. Let's explore the life cycle of ABCP, the various parties involved in the process, and key terminology used.

Sponsor

A program sponsor initiates the creation of an ABCP program but typically does not provide the equity for the conduit. Unaffiliated third-party equity providers usually own the conduits. The sponsor of ABCP programs often refers assets and borrowers to the programs. Typically, transactions referred to the program must meet minimum credit-quality standards based on the sponsor's standard credit-approval process.

Though the sponsor does not own the conduit, it can retain a financial stake in the program by providing credit enhancement, liquidity support, or both. Depending on the sponsor's role in referring the assets to be financed, ABCP programs have four different structures:

1. In a *single-seller program*, the sponsor is the sole originator of the financed assets and uses the conduit as an alternative source of funding for its own business activities. Sponsors usually provide credit enhancement in the form of over-collateralization.
2. In a *multi-seller program*, the sponsor is generally a financial institution seeking to provide financing alternatives to its clients. Sponsors usually provide credit enhancement in the form of a letter of credit, subordinated interest, or purchase commitment.
3. In a *securities-backed program*, the sponsor is a financial institution seeking arbitrage opportunities or capital relief associated with unloading assets off balance sheets. Sponsors usually provide credit enhancement in the form of a letter of credit, subordinated interest, or purchase commitment.
4. In a *mix of securities-backed and multi-seller strategies,* the sponsor has the flexibility to serve its own needs, as well as those of its clients. Sponsors usually provide credit enhancement in the form of a letter of credit, subordinated interest, or purchase commitment.

Conduits

The issuing vehicles of an ABCP program are called *conduits.* They are usually nominally capitalized SPVs structured as bankruptcy remotes and are owned by management companies independent from the sponsor. Due the bankruptcy remoteness, they have a limited scope of business activities and restricted liabilities. ABCP conduits use various servicing agents—such as the administrative agent, the issuing and paying agent, the collateral agent, the referral agent, and the manager—to perform the administration and operation of the program.

Liquidity Support

Because of asset servicers or cash-flow timing mismatches between the underlying asset portfolio and CP repayment obligations, there is potential for repayment shortfalls and missing payments. These problems are not generally associated with credit risks. To overcome these problems, the ABCP programs are structured with liquidity facilities to assist in the timely repayment of CP. They also serve as alternative-funding sources in the event a conduit is unable to issue new CP to repay a maturing CP or to acquire additional asset interests under a committed transaction. Liquidity support can be either internal or external sources of funds available to ABCP conduits to repay maturing CP on a timely basis. Since internal sources of liquidity are insufficient to repay maturing CP, most ABCP programs are structured with at least 100 percent external liquidity support.

Credit Enhancements

Credit enhancements protect the program against losses on the underlying asset portfolios. They are either internal or external supports provided either at transaction level or program-wide, or a combination of both. Individual transaction-level credit enhancement cannot be used to cover losses stemming from other transactions in the conduit's asset portfolio. On the other hand, program-wide credit enhancement can cover losses stemming from any asset in the portfolio.

In a mixed credit-enhancement mode, where both transaction-specific and program-wide enhancements are implemented, transaction-specific enhancements usually serve as a first layer of loss protection, while the program-wide facility serves as a second layer of loss protection, absorbing losses in excess of applicable transaction-specific enhancement.

Administrative Agents

Administrative agents perform the day-to-day operations of the program and credit-advisory services. The administrative agent can be the sponsor itself or a subsidiary of the program sponsor, or even an independent third-party entity. As part of the day-to-day operations of the program, the administrative agent may:

- arrange for the execution and safekeeping of the program documents;
- maintain operating accounts;
- invest excess funds in permitted investments;
- maintain general accounting records;
- prepare financial statements and arrange audits;
- preserve books and records;
- give notice to other key parties; and
- prepare monthly portfolio reports.

In connection with the issuance and repayment of CP, the agent may:

- instruct the issuing and paying agent and the depositary;
- purchase and sell assets;
- extend loans to borrowers; and
- determine when draws on liquidity and credit-enhancement facilities are necessary.

The administrative agent's role can also include credit-advisory services, in connection with which the agent may:

- identify and refer new sellers to the conduit;
- conduct due diligence reviews of prospective sellers;
- structure the acquisition of asset interests and any necessary hedging arrangements; and
- monitor the ongoing performance of each transaction.

Issuing and Paying Agent and Depositary

The issuing and paying agent is responsible for the settlement and record-keeping pertaining to the issuance and repayment of CP, whereas the depositary is responsible for maintaining a special-purpose trust account into which the proceeds from the issuance of CP are deposited and from which funds to repay maturing CP are withdrawn. Often, the roles of issuing and paying agent and depositary are assumed by the same third-party entity acting under a single agreement.

CP Placement Agent

CP placement agents coordinate the actual sale of CP. They usually work closely with the administrative agent to determine the face or principal amount, maturity, interest or discount rate, and denominations of CP to be issued.

Collateral Agent

For programs in which the ABCP is a secured obligation, a collateral agent may be appointed to maintain a first-priority security interest in the conduit's assets, property, rights, and interests for the benefit of the secured parties, which include CP investors. In addition, collateral agents may reserve the right to assume control of the program's operating accounts to ensure that collections are applied in accordance with the program's payment-priority schedule. Furthermore, upon the occurrence of certain program's termination events, collateral agent may be required to enforce a conduit's rights under purchase and lending agreements, which may include seizing and liquidating asset interests.

ABS versus ABCP

ABCP differs from term securities in the following ways:

- The invested assets can be revolving and fluctuate in size.
- They typically create diversified portfolios.
- They can fund long-term assets by issuing short-term debt.
- They rely on liquidity support for potential repayment shortfalls caused by asset and liability timing mismatches.
- There is no scheduled amortization of assets and liabilities.
- Additional issuance of CP may be used to maintain the conduit's investment in assets.

2.11 Other Derivatives

2.11.1   Property Derivatives

Unlike the stock and bond market, derivatives offer no liquid market or facile means of hedging the attendant real-estate risk. Case, Shiller & Weiss introduced the concept of real-estate futures in 1992. The introduction of futures and options based on the S&P/Case-Shiller Home Price Indices at

CME represents the fulfillment of that vision, forging the creation of a novel derivatives asset class. CME housing futures and options are designed to provide a facile way for institutional and individual investors to gain exposure to real-estate risk and effectively diversity their portfolios. Commercial and private asset holders are afforded an efficient hedging mechanism. In the process, this novel market may have the effect of reducing transaction costs for trading real estate.

Cash settlement is based on the reported value of S&P/Case-Shiller Home Price Indices of home prices for the cities of Boston, Chicago, Denver, Las Vegas, Los Angeles, Miami, New York, San Diego, San Francisco, and Washington DC, and an index that represents a composite of the ten cities. Commercial real-estate property derivatives based on indices published by the National Council of Real Estate Fiduciaries (NCREIF) became available for trading in March 2007.

Property derivatives have some advantages over direct property investment, such as ease of execution, customization, and no property management. Property derivatives are associated with certain risks as well. Investment risks and returns may not be aligned with direct property investment. Derivatives have as drawbacks counterparty risk and lack of control over the referenced assets, and among other things there are index shortcomings.

2.11.2   Operational Risk Derivatives

As operational risk is mainly related to the way of doing business operations and external events, it is certainly difficult to find the specific source of operational risk. Moreover, operational risk measurement is a highly subjective process requiring certain judgments. Even if various operational risks are identified, aggregated risk may not be reliable, as the correlations among risks are merely assumptions.

For these reasons, it is difficult to price the operational risk and hedge it away. Nonetheless, there are certain products available in the market that can be used to hedge operational risk depending on its nature. Some of the operational risk-hedging instruments are insurance; catastrophe options like underwriting derivatives and weather derivatives; and catastrophe bonds like indemnified notes, indexed notes, and parametric notes. Firms willing to hedge operational risk may have to depend on multiple products, as there is no single product that can protect or insure against firm-level operational risk.

Insurance companies write policies to cover different types of operational risks. One of the operational-risk insurance companies is Fidelity Insurance, which protects firms from employees committing fraudulent acts. Directors' and officers' insurance companies cover legal expenses resulting from litigation concerning the fulfillment of directors' and officers' fiduciary duties. The Chicago Board of Trade (CBOT) trades catastrophe options, which have payoff linked to an index of underwriting losses written on a large pool of insurance policies. These options have deductibles and maximum limits and closely resemble collar or cover below and above certain limits.

2.11.3   Weather Derivatives

Weather derivatives are linked to an index that is based on weather conditions, such as average temperature, precipitation, and wind speed. Indemnified bonds offer relief to the debt issuer based on internal events, such as a large underwriting loss. Indexed note payoffs are based on established insurance loss indices. The most commonly used index is the one produced by Property Claims Services. Parametric notes are linked to the magnitude of an external risk event, such as a hurricane.

2.12 Financial Markets and Data Explained

In this section, we'll discuss various participants in the capital markets and how the data is organized.

Investment Banks

Investment banks provide services related to the sale of IPOs (initial public offerings). They advise corporations to raise the capital by various means, including bonds, stocks, and structuring of debt. They, as underwriters, provide guarantees on a price on the securities they offer. They do this either individually or by forming a syndicate of investment banks.

Brokers

Brokers facilitate trades by locating buyers for sellers and sellers for buyers to complete the desired transaction. The broker neither maintains an inventory of traded assets nor takes positions in these assets. Brokers make profits from commissions.

Dealers

Dealers match buyers and sellers to facilitate trades, but instead of doing it on a commission basis, they buy the assets at relatively low prices and resell them at relatively high prices. The bid–ask spread represents the dealer's profit margin.

Broker-Dealer

The firm that acts as both broker and dealer is called a *broker-dealer*.

Intermediaries

Intermediaries do the business of broker-dealer in a different manner. They buy one kind of asset from customers and a sell different kind of assets to other customers. That way, they add liquidity to the market. For example, in an interest-rate swap, they match the clients by paying floating leg to one party and fixed leg to another party. Unlike broker-dealers, instead of creating an inventory of assets for resale, they create portfolios.

Exchanges

Exchange corporations provide an organized marketplace with uniform rules and standardized contracts. Exchanges operate markets for spot commodities, options, futures contracts, and other financial securities. Exchanges are backed by membership fees and transaction fees paid on contracts.

Clearinghouses

Clearinghouse make it easy to close out positions without having the buyer and seller interact with each other. The clearinghouse supervises the delivery of commodities and guarantees each futures contract that it clears.

Hedge Funds

Hedge funds are private partnerships that seek to optimize profits. Though hedge funds were originally established to hedge portfolios against downside risk by using short selling, they have become opportunistic and seek to profit by using complex and advanced strategies. Hedge funds are only available for accredited investors who have a net worth of $1 million or a history of income greater than $250K.

Since hedge funds are offered only to sophisticated investors, they are typically unregulated. If a fund has less than one hundred accredited investors, then the fund does come under the regulatory oversight of the Securities and Exchange Commission (SEC). However, since institutional investors like pension funds and endowments started investing in hedge funds, and since they are restricted from investing in unregulated funds, most hedge funds are seeking to register with the SEC even if they have less than a hundred investors. In contrast to mutual funds, hedge funds are restricted from advertising and soliciting and must concentrate marketing efforts on wealthy individuals and institutions.

Buy-Side Firms

Buy-side firms make investments that align with investors' expectations. They establish sophisticated research teams and build proprietary strategies. Based on their research and strategy, they buy large quantities of securities. Examples of buy-side firms include hedge funds, asset managers, mutual funds, pension funds, and insurance firms. Buy-side firms are restricted from brokerage activities.

Sell-Side Firms

Sell-side firms sell securities and assets to money-management firms like buy-side firms and to corporate clients. They are registered members of a stock exchange. They are also considered to be intermediaries and are very similar to prime brokers, depending on how they are structured. Sell-side firms establish sophisticated research firms. They also purchase securities off the market directly.

Custodians

Hedge-fund assets, including cash and funds, are typically held with a custodian who essentially deals with dividend collection and margin payments. However, it is not mandatory for the hedge fund to hold assets with a custodian. In the event that the custodian becomes insolvent, the hedge-fund assets will be at risk. Therefore, the investor needs to find out the exact role of the custodian related to the hedge fund in which the investor wants to invest.

Prime Brokers

Prime brokers provide various standard and premium services to hedge funds. Standard services include executing trades on behalf of the hedge funds, lending securities for short sale, and leverage or margin financing. Some larger-dealer banks that act as prime brokers provide premium services, such as custody of securities, clearing, cash management, and reporting. Other premium services include leasing space to start-up hedge funds, start-up services, capital introduction, compliance, and risk management.

Since prime brokers provide margin, the hedge funds will pledge the securities in their brokerage account to serve as collateral. The prime broker, in turn, uses this as collateral against their loans through a process called *rehypothecation*. In the event of the prime broker's bankruptcy, the protection of hedge funds/ investors against rehypothecation depends on the country of the prime brokers. In the United States, there is a legal process to segregate, identify, and return the assets, whereas in the United Kingdom the assets remain frozen until the broker works through the bankruptcy process. That is the main reason why investors under the US division of Lehman Brothers had an advantage over the investors in the UK division during the collapse of Lehman Brothers in 2008.

When hedge funds are concerned about the solvency of the prime broker, they typically demand margin loans, but the prime broker may not be able to use those same securities as collateral against his loans with other lenders, since the other lenders may also have concerns about the prime broker's solvency. When clients or hedge funds start leaving a prime broker, the prime broker will start facing a liquidity crisis, causing systemic risk. Therefore, hedge funds may need to consider diversifying against multiple prime brokers.

2.12.1   Trade Life Cycle

To better understand the nature of trading data, I would like to provide a brief overview of the trading cycle. There are several sequential steps involved in trading, from inception to settlement and maturity.

1. *Pre-trading*: While certain trades are simple, there are some with structured deals comprising many parts. These will require a provisional trade to be created and due diligence to be performed before the agreed upon time. During this phase, the provisional trade will go through legal departments for scrutiny, and risk management departments to assess the risks (such as market risk and credit risk) and prepare any other trades required to hedge any inherent risk. At this stage, the trade lies in a non-trading portfolio but will be ready to convert into a real trade.

2. *Order*: When the trader is instructed to perform a trade, the instruction is called an order.

3. *Execution*: The trade is executed when both the parties agree to a trade. The execution can occur over the telephone, over e-mail, over an electronic system, or in person.

4. *Booking:* The trade is entered in the books of both counterparties.

5. *Matching*: When the trade is entered, the parties must match their records to ensure they match. If the records are not matched, then it may be a case that the trade was not received and executed by a counterparty, or it was executed with different a counterparty, or the counterparty details are incorrect in the book. Mistakes should be corrected to ensure that the records are identical in the books of both parties.

6. *Confirmation*: Upon ensuring that the trade is matched at both the counterparties, the trade will be confirmed. Before the confirmation, the back office may sometimes make changes to the records if there is any missing information other than the pricing information—for example, if the currency symbol is missing, then the inclusion has to be agreed upon by the trader.

7. *Post-booking scrutiny*: When the trades are entered in the trading system, they are scrutinized by the middle office to ensure that they fit into other processes. At this stage, additional details—such as counterparty, settlement, or custodian information—is attached to the records. At this stage, the calculation of cash flows related to the trade may be performed.

8. *Settlement*: This is the stage at which the counterparties to a trade fulfill their obligations to exchange. What is exchanged depends on what is traded. Certain derivatives involved an exchange of cash from both sides. Certain trades involve paying or receiving the net cash flow. For example, currency trade involves exchanging one currency for another; interest-rate swaps involve calculating the net cash flow and either paying or receiving; and credit default swaps involve one party paying periodical premiums and receiving nothing unless there is a credit event.

9. *Oversight*: This is the stage at which the trades are aggregated to assess how individual trades and the whole portfolio stand up to market price changes, to assess the overall effect of a group of trades on an entire book or department. The next-level aggregation starts with enterprise-wide risk data aggregation.

2.12.2   Financial and Risk Data

Pre-Trade Data

Pre-trade data is the category of data based on which firms valuate the products to be traded. This category includes the following:

- fundamentals
- estimates
- macroeconomic data
- ratings
- indices
- derived data
- time-series data
- output of quantitative models

This data can be broadly subcategorized into several types. A major subcategory is public information. Public companies file their financial statements into databases like EDGAR. In certain jurisdictions, private companies must also file some information. In addition, corporations like Thomson Reuters provide financial news, such as macroeconomic data, financial results, patents, and key hiring. There is a lot of unstructured data from social media to mine for insights about capital markets and products. Public indices, though they are not called on as research data, provide direction of market, products, and geography.

The following are other subcategories of pre-trade data:

- *accounting data*
- *business-specific data*
- *proprietary information*, including internal research, quantitative analytics, fundamental research, portfolio structures, settlement instructions, trading strategies, idea generation, and price discovery
- *vendor-supplied data* that is commercially sourced, including terms and conditions, pricing data, ratings, real-time data, corporate actions, and sponsored research
- *in-house time-series data* used to back-test a trading strategy and infer patterns to construct new trading strategies, including real-time streaming data referring to direct quotes and prices from brokers; snapshots for OTC markets, in which OTC products are revalued

at certain cut-off points, since there is no official closing price; and historical data, including both official close prices and snapshot data, preserved for risk management purposes and in keeping with regulations requiring histories of internal credit ratings and operational losses

- *operational limits*, including position limit, counterparty limit, exposure limits, level of interest rate risk and credit risk, and list of approved instruments

Trading Data

Trading data can be logically grouped into pricing data, time dimensions, aggregated data, and market rules. Pricing data contains trade facts, trade value, date time, frequency, and price type. The trade facts include open price, high price, low price, bid price, ask price, list price, close price, and volume. The trade value represents the actual observed value for the trade fact. Data and time represents the data and time of the trade value was produced. The frequency represents the periodicity on which the trade values are collected. The examples include tick-by-tick, daily, weekly, monthly, quarterly, and yearly.

Product-Specific Data

This data is made up of instrument details, features, asset classes, asset subclasses, and security identifiers, among other things. Asset classes include the following:

- debt (or fixed income)
- equity
- money market
- derivatives
- security finance transactions
- indices
- commodities
- currencies

Asset subclasses includes the following:

- common stock
- preferred stock
- rights
- warrants

- corporate bonds
- government bonds
- agency bonds
- munis
- structured products
- RMBS
- CMBS
- ABS
- CDO
- CMO
- CLO
- commercial papers
- interbank rates
- deposits
- options
- futures

- forwards
- swaps
- repos
- reverse repos
- security lending
- security borrowing
- exchange indices
- agency indices
- bond indices
- geographic indices
- spots
- forwards
- futures
- spots
- forwards
- currency swaps.

Asset-Class Matrix

Asset Class	Assets
Equities	common shares, preferred shares, private equities, American depository receipts, private placements, initial public offerings, block trades
Fixed Income	corporate bonds, municipal bonds, mortgage-backed securities, asset-backed securities, Treasury bonds, Treasury notes, zero bonds, euro dollar bonds
Money Market	Treasury bills, certificates of deposit, commercial papers, repos, banker's acceptance
Fx	Fx spot, Fx forwards, Fx futures, Fx swaps, Fx options, Fx windows
Commodities	grains, such as corn, wheat, oats, rice; soft commodities, such as coffee, cocoa, sugar, potatoes, orange juice, cotton; precious metals, such as gold, silver, platinum, palladium; industrial metals, such as aluminum, copper; energy commodities, such as crude oil, heating oil, natural gas, gasoline, electricity

Derivative Type

Asset Class	Derivative Type	Derivative Subtypes
Equity	Options	American options, European options, Bermudan options, compound options, chooser options, barrier options, Parisian options, lookback options, ladder options, shout options, binary options, Asian options, basket options, forward start options
	Swaps	equity swaps
Interest Rates	Options	caps, floors, collars
	Forwards	forwards, FRAs
	Futures	
	Swaps	interest-rate swaps, currency swaps
	Combinations	swaptions, forward swaps
Credits	Options	
	Forwards	
	Futures	
	Swaps	credit default swaps (CDS), total return swaps, asset swaps, contingent CDS, single-name CDS, nth to default swaps
	Combinations	
FX	Options	
	Forwards	
	Futures	
	Swaps	
	Combinations	
Commodities	Options	
	Forwards	
	Futures	
	Swaps	

Exchange-Traded Funds (ETFs)

ETFs are essentially index funds that track the performance of a specific stock or bond market index or other benchmark. There are quite a few different real-estate funds available on the market. Investors can get exposure to global real estate, country-specific real estate, or REITs. Inverse ETFs are also available. There are even ETFs related to real estate, such as home-builder ETFs and mortgage-backed funds. They are highly liquid and tax efficient. Investors can take long or short positions. Below is partial list of available real-estate ETFs:

- Direxion Daily Real Estate Bull 3X Shares ETF (DRN)
- Direxion Daily Real Estate Bear 3X Shares (DRV)
- WisdomTree International Real Estate ETF (DRW)
- First Trust FTSE EPRA/NAREIT Global Real Estate ETF (FFR)
- iShares FTSE NAREIT Industrial/Office Cap Index ETF (FIO)
- First Trust S&P REIT ETF (FRI)
- Focus Morningstar Real Estate Index ETF (FRL)
- iShares FTSE NAREIT Real Estate 50 ETF (FTY)
- Cohen & Steers Global Realty Majors ETF (GRI)
- iShares Cohen & Steers Realty Majors ETF (ICF)
- iShares FTSE EPRA/NAREIT Developed Asia Index ETF (IFAS)
- iShares FTSE EPRA/NAREIT Developed Europe Index ETF (IFEU)
- iShares FTSE EPRA/NAREIT Developed Real Estate ex-US Index ETF (IFGL)
- iShares FTSE EPRA/NAREIT North America Index ETF (IFNA)
- iShares Dow Jones US Real Estate ETF (IYR)
- PowerShares KBW Premium Yield Equity REIT Portfolio (KBWY)
- PowerShares Active US Real Estate ETF (PSR)
- ProShares Short Real Estate ETF (REK)
- iShares FTSE NAREIT Mortgage Plus Capped Index ETF (REM)
- iShares FTSE NAREIT Residential Plus Capped Index ETF (REZ)
- iShares FTSE NAREIT Retail Capped Index ETF (RTL)
- SPDR Dow Jones Global Real Estate ETF (RWO)
- SPDR Dow Jones REIT ETF (RWR)
- SPDR Dow Jones International Real Estate ETF (RWX)
- Schwab US REIT ETF (SCHH)
- UltraShort Real Estate ProShares ETF (SRS)
- Claymore/AlphaShares China Real Estate ETF (TAO)
- Ultra Real Estate ProShares ETF (URE)
- Vanguard REIT ETF (VNQ)
- Vanguard Global ex-US Real Estate Index Fund (VNQI)
- Wilshire US REIT ETF (WREI)

Derived Data

Risk Type	Parameters
Market Risk	delta, beta, DV01, gamma, vega, theta, rho, duration, convexity, yield, yield-to-maturity, risk-free rate, VaR, mark-to-market value, volatility
Counterparty Credit Risk	PFE, PE, EE, EPE, EEPE, CS01, cross gamma
Liquidity Risk	

Reference Data

Reference data exists in every database across the bank. It is a set of predefined domain values. Reference tables link via foreign keys in other tables. Examples of reference tables are country codes storing country name and ISO code, and lists of allowable transaction statuses with definitions. Reference data changes slowly; therefore, it is called *slowly changing data*.

Master data is data about the business entities on which the bank performs transactions. Examples of master data include counterparties, vendors, products, and financial structures. Master data is business-critical data that provides context for transactions.

For example, say that a trading group is involved in trading a certain type of bonds. It needs to know about the issuer of the bond, issue date, maturity date, type of bond, issuer rating, and lots more. All such information is maintained in a specific set of tables, which are referenced by trading application. When the trading data is flowed into an enterprise data system, a similar reference needs to be made to obtain such details. If there are several trading systems and several sets of master data, it becomes challenging for the enterprise data system to contact each master set for the details. If there were a source where all the master data was available in one place, it would become easy for enterprise systems to obtain the details. Managing such data is called master-data management.

Master-data management provides a linked view of all the references for a given financial product or otherwise to provide the understanding of the total relationship and facilitate the analysis of the data. Effective reference-data management is an imperative for financial institutions because of increased globalization and data-driven businesses.

Reference data elements include the following:

- exchange codes
- ISIN (International Securities Identification Number)
- CUSIP number (Committee on Uniform Securities Identification Procedures)
- SEDOL code (Stock Exchange Daily Official List)
- valoren number
- currency
- industry classification
- issuer name
- issuer type
- country of headquarters
- instrument name
- instrument type
- issue data
- issue status
- primary market
- legal entity identifier
- market type
- client type

Legal Entity Identifiers

The best way to start describing an LEI is to revisit the problems faced during the financial crisis in the form of special purpose vehicles. SPVs are legal entities used to isolate a corporation's risk. SPVs involve complex transitions in acquiring loans from the entity that created the SPV and securitizing them for sale in a secondary market. The investors failed to understand the relationship between the SPV issuing the securities and the party responsible for repayment. The lack of clarity and transparency in the market was further complicated by increasing globalization, which intensified the degree of systemic risk.

Regulators from across the globe identified the need for a global system that that would uniquely identify the legal entity, enabling the parties to a transaction to fully assess the true nature of the risk. An LEI is a unique ID assigned to a corporate entity. In the US, the Dodd-Frank Act mandated initiatives to create LEIs, and the effort is being driven by the Office of Financial Research (OFR) and Commodity Futures Trading Commission (CFTC) to issue guidelines around derivatives.

The LEI system is an alphanumeric code and associated set of six reference-data items to uniquely identify a legally distinct entity that engages in financial-market activities. This global standard is endorsed by the G-20 and is consistent with the specifications put forward by the International Organization for Standardization (ISO 17442:2012) in May 2012: a 20-digit code and associated "business card" information.

Successful operation of a global LEI system will require support from the global regulatory community, private sector firms, and industry associations. The endorsed recommendations define clear roles for the public and private sectors through a "federated" model. Regulators oversee through a regulatory oversight committee (ROC); private industry participates and consults on the development and operations of a central operating unit (COU); and local implementation is conducted through local operating units (LOU), which will benefit from local knowledge of infrastructure, corporate organizational frameworks, and business practices. The COU will ensure that all parties that implement the LEI adhere to governing principles and standards—including reliability, quality, and uniqueness—that will result in "one golden standard" for the LEI.

To support the use of the global LEI, the recommendations of the Financial Stability Board (FSB) allow for jurisdictions to serve as early adopters of a global LEI. In the United States, the CFTC issued a rule requiring swap counterparties to be identified by a legal entity identifier. Because the global LEI system would not yet be functioning at that time, the CFTC provided for a CFTC Interim Compliant Identifier (CICI) that conformed to the endorsed global LEI standard and made an explicit commitment for the CICI to transition to the global LEI. The US Securities and Exchange Commission has also issued a proposed rule that would require the use of an LEI, if available, for derivatives reporting and a final rule for private-fund use of an LEI in meeting reporting requirements.

As the global LEI becomes more widely used, many industry participants expect the LEI to decrease costs and improve risk management at the firm level and across the system. These savings would come primarily from operational efficiencies, such as reducing the volume of transaction failures; lowering data reconciliation, cleaning, and aggregation costs; and reducing regulatory reporting costs. In addition, a global LEI would provide long-term benefits by enhancing the ability to perform business functions like "know your customer" and improving enterprise risk management.

By providing a universal, unique, authoritative identifier for each entity in a financial transaction, a global LEI will provide a valuable risk management tool for aggregating data on exposures. However, while the LEI is critical on its own, it is not sufficient to provide a complete view on the aggregate exposures of any one entity to another. As noted in the FSB report, information on ownership and corporate hierarchies is also essential for aggregating risks on a broader level (such as the parent-entity level), which is a key objective for the global LEI system.

3 Fundamentals of Quantitative Finance

We've discussed various financial products that are used to fulfill the needs of borrowers and investors, thus facilitating cash flows among markets. We also learned that the investor does not have to be a direct lender but instead can gain the exposure to credit or debt markets by participating in secondary markets and derivatives. The derivative-style products are also used to hedge against market volatilities or counterparty credit quality deterioration.

Before choosing a particular product, combination of products, or market sector, it is essential for both investors and issuers to evaluate such factors as credit quality, market economics, product type, historical performance of products, and risk characteristics. Manually evaluating all such factors is time-consuming, and a significant delay in decision making can lead to losing investment opportunities. Mathematical algorithms have evolved slowly to aid investors in picking the right product according to their risk-return preference.

One situation is that the investor wants to know how much a stock value will increase if the Dow Jones index goes up by 1 percent and how that fits in the existing portfolio. Another situation is that using a complex algorithm to predict the chances of increase in interest rates, what products are good in rising markets, and what kind of losses can be incurred if the interest rates dip again. As investors started adding more and more factors to algorithms, they became complex models leading to the evolution of quantitative finance. Mathematicians and investment firms have put a lot of effort into developing models in order to improve their trading and risk management. There are several models that became the industry standard and, later, base models for several variations.

In this chapter, we will be discussing the various statistical measures, how they are calculated and interpreted, how bonds are priced, how to monitor bond prices with respect to changes in market factors, how interest rates are predicted, and how the default is estimated. We will get deep here into developing the models, discussing them qualitatively and quantitatively.

3.1   Statistical Measures

Statistical models have been widely used since the seventeenth century in the fields of physics and engineering, with high degrees of precision in predicting outcomes that are repeatable and consistent. The same models and measures applied to finance provide performance and risk overview to an organization's board and its external stakeholders, with a sense of the likelihood that a loss greater than a certain amount would be realized over a given time frame. Statistical measures quantify the risk into a single number with some supplemental information on the extent of "tail risk." There are several performance and risk measures that have evolved over time, and we'll look at some of them here.

3.1.1   Mean, Median, and Mode

Mean, median, and mode are three variants of averages of a data set. The *mean* represents the average and is calculated by adding up all the numbers and then dividing by the total count. The mean is also called *expected value*. The *median* is the middle value in the list of numbers after listing in numerical order. The *mode* is the value that occurs most often. If no number is repeated, then there is no mode for the list.

3.1.2   Standard Deviation

Standard deviation measures the degree of variation of returns around the mean return and is often used as a measure of investment risk. The higher the fluctuations in the returns, the higher the standard deviation will be. The square of standard deviation is called the *variance*.

Standard deviation, also known as *volatility*, is a widely used measure in the financial industry, as it provides a precise measurement of how varied an investment's returns have been over a particular time frame both on the upside and the downside. With this information, investors can judge the range of returns the investment is likely to generate in the future. It allows an investment's performance swings to be captured into a single number.

Standard deviation is calculated as follows:

1. Calculate the mean or average from the daily returns of the fund.
2. Prepare a new set of values from the set by subtracting the mean from each value. In other words, get the difference between the values and mean for each sample in the set.
3. Take the squares of the above values.
4. Take the average of the above values.
5. Take the square root of the above value.

The calculated mean and the standard deviation are used to make certain assumptions about the future performance of an investment. For example, say an investment fund has a standard deviation of 4 and an average return of 10 percent per year. These two measures indicate that the investor can expect the investment fund's future returns to range between 6 percent and 14 percent, or its 10 percent average plus or minus its standard deviation of 4.

It is a standard assumption that investments with smaller standard deviations tend to lose less money over short time frames than those with high standard deviations. For example, the one-year average standard deviation among ultra-short-term bond funds is typically around .6 percent.

The drawback with the standard deviation is that it is not intuitive enough. It does not care if there is a greater number of positive returns than negative returns or vice versa over a period. To overcome this problem to some extent, there are two variations of standard deviations:

- *Upside standard deviation* uses the average return of only gains and then measures the variation of only the gain periods around this gain mean. This statistic measures the volatility of upside performance.
- *Downside standard deviation* uses the average return of only losses and then measures the variation of only the loss periods around this loss mean. This statistic measures the volatility of downside performance.

Standard deviations or volatility is widely used in option pricing models, such as the Black-Scholes model, determining haircuts for collaterals. The volatility that is calculated (by reverse engineering) from option-pricing models by using the market prices of options and risk-free interest rates is called *implied volatility*. The implied volatility is widely used as a standard measure, as it is assumed that the market prices are already adjusted because of volatility.

The volatility measure is also known as the *fear factor*. Chicago Board Options Exchange (CBOE) has developed a market volatility index, called VIX, that measures the implied volatility of S&P 500 index options over next thirty days. It gives an idea of stock-market expectations.

3.1.3   Skewness

Skew is a very important statistical measure in the analysis of return distribution, as it tells us how the returns deviate from the normal distribution. The normal distribution is symmetrical, with equal frequency of loss and gains.

If we take daily profits and losses and place them on a graph, we will see different heights. In a perfect market, the returns (profit or loss) exhibit a normal distribution, indicating an equal number of values on both sides of the mean. But in reality, it is not always expected for any investment to show the normal distribution, as there will be either more number of profits or more number of losses. Such a graph is prolonged on either the positive side (for more number of profits) or the negative side (for more number of losses). Such distribution is called *skewed distribution*.

Skewness refers to the extent to which the distribution is not symmetrical. By looking at the graph, we can easily identify the nature of the investment fund. For example, for investments that employ complex option-like strategies, the return distribution is not always symmetrical, but may be positively or negatively skewed. In negatively skewed distribution, a greater number of outliers lie in the left tail, indicating potential for heavy losses; in positively skewed distribution, a larger amount of outliers lies in the right tail, indicating the potential for higher returns. For a normal distribution, the skewness is zero.

The following three diagrams depict normal distribution, distribution with positive skew, and distribution with negative skew:

Normal distribution

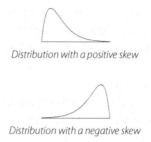

Distribution with a positive skew

Distribution with a negative skew

Since it is not feasible to draw a graph for every investment and variety thereof, there is a mathematical calculation to determine skewness, which is equal to the average of the cubed deviations from the mean divided by the sample standard deviation cubed.

$$\text{Skewness} = \frac{E[(x - \mu)^3]}{\sigma^3}$$

where μ is the mean and σ is the standard deviation.

3.1.4 Kurtosis

Kurtosis, which accompanies skewness, is another significant statistical measure. Just as there is a possibility for extreme outliers on either side, there is a possibility for either higher values or lower values around the center. Such behavior is called *peakedness*.

Kurtosis measures the peakedness of the distribution. Distribution that is more peaked than a normal distribution is referred to as *leptokurtic*, whereas distribution that is less peaked than a normal distribution is referred to as *platykurtic*. Kurtosis for the normal distribution is 3. The difference between non-normal kurtosis and 3 is called *excess kurtosis*.

Excess kurtosis is negative for platykurtic distribution and positive for leptokurtic distribution. Leptokurtic distribution will have more returns either around the mean or far from the mean, whereas platykurtic distribution will have fewer returns around and far from the mean.

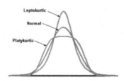

Efficient risk management puts more emphasis on skewness and kurtosis, as the risk estimated by traditional models either overestimates or underestimates the real risk of investments. Investments that exhibit negative skew and excess kurtosis are indicated by the fat and prolonged left tail. But there is a mathematical measure to calculate the kurtosis:

$$\text{Kurtosis} = \frac{E[(x - \mu)^4]}{\sigma^4}$$

3.1.5   Covariance

Covariance is a statistical measure that explains the degree to which returns on two assets move in tandem. A positive covariance indicates that the asset returns move in the same direction. A negative covariance indicates that the returns move inversely. Covariance is used to calculate the correlation coefficient.

The covariance for two random variables X and Y, each with sample size N, is calculated as follows:

$$cov(X, Y) = \sum_{i=1}^{N} \frac{(x_i - \bar{x})(y_i - \bar{y})}{N}.$$

where X bar and Y bar are the means of samples X and Y.

3.1.6   Correlation Coefficient

The correlation coefficient is derived from the covariance by scaling it per unit of each standard deviation.

$$cor(X, Y) = \frac{cov(X, Y)}{\sigma_X \, \sigma_Y}$$

Correlation coefficients are widely used in investment strategies to find out the relative direction of investments. They plays a key role in achieving portfolio diversification and also in hedging. A correlation coefficient of 1 indicates that both returns move in the same direction at the same pace. A correlation coefficient of −1 indicates the returns of two investments move in the opposite direction.

For example, low volatility funds and commodities exhibit low correlations to traditional asset classes like stocks and bonds, and adding such investments to a portfolio can reduce volatility without sacrificing part of the return. Some asset classes, such as commodities and real-estate investments, provide a good inflation hedge. Commodities and real estate are negatively correlated with interest rates and, therefore, are positively correlated with inflation and negatively correlated with stock and bond markets.

The correlation coefficient is used also in Basel capital calculations, portfolio diversification, securitization, and wrong-way risk monitoring, among other situations.

3.1.7   Beta

Beta is somewhat related to the correlation coefficient but is derived in a slightly differ manner. Beta gives a measure that shows how a particular investment varies with respect to another investment, usually a major index like Dow Jones or S&P 500. Therefore, it is used as a measure of systemic risk.

Beta is calculated as the ratio of the covariance of two investments and the variance of a reference investment. For example, if we are calculating the beta of ABC Corp with respect to the S&P 500, then beta is the ratio of the covariance between ABC Corp and S&P 500 and the variance of S&P 500. If the market is expected to return 6 percent, a stock with a beta of 2 should return 12 percent. In other words, it is expected to yield either profit or loss that is double for the market.

Beta is a good way to measure the risk of any stock. Stocks with a beta of near 1 may be considered a safe investment, but returns are lower. Young technology stocks typically carries high betas, whereas standard utility companies carry betas below 1.

Beta is used in the capital-asset pricing model (CAPM), which gives portfolio based on market returns. According to CAPM, a portfolio returns:

$$E[r_p] = r_f + \beta(E[r_m] - r_f)$$

where Rf is the risk-free interest rate, Rp is expected portfolio return, and Rm is expected market return.

3.1.8   Alpha

Alpha measures the excess return over the return predicted by the CAPM. According to CAPM, portfolio return = $E[r_p] = r_f + \beta[E[r_m] - r_f]$.

Since the beta does not capture all the risk exposure, a portfolio's actual return may be higher than that predicted by the above formula. The higher returns are attributed to the manager's skill in exploiting market inefficiencies. Therefore, the CAPM should be adjusted as follows:

$$E[r_p] = r_f + \beta[E[r_m] - r_f] + \alpha$$

The excess returns in the above formula are called the *alpha*. Alpha is a key measure used in hedge funds.

3.1.9   Treynor Ratio

The Treynor ratio measures return adjusted for systemic risk. It gives portfolio excess returns over the risk-free rate per unit of systemic risk. The Treynor ratio is also called the *reward-to-volatility ratio* or *Treynor measure*. The higher the Treynor ratio, the better the performance of the portfolio.

$$Treynor\,Ratio = \frac{r_p - r_f}{\beta}$$

It may be possible that one portfolio will return more profits than another, but at the same time that portfolio may be taking higher risk, creating a potential for higher losses in the future. Therefore, it is useful to scale the returns for systemic risk. Investors may actually prefer the portfolio that is giving lower returns as it involves less risk. The higher the Treynor ratio, the better the portfolio.

3.1.10   Sharpe Ratio

The Sharpe ratio is one of the most important measures in the investment space, determining the risk-adjusted returns of a portfolio. It is similar to the Treynor ratio, but it gives excess returns over the risk-free rate per unit of portfolio risk instead of per unit of systemic risk. If the Sharpe ratio needs to be calculated per security, portfolio return and volatility are replaced with those of the security.

$$Sharpe\,Ratio = \frac{r_p - r_f}{\sigma_p}$$

The Sharpe ratio can be used as a hurdle rate to determine whether or not to add a fund to a portfolio. A Sharpe ratio comparison tells whether a fund can be added to a portfolio or not. The higher the Sharpe ratio, the better the performance of the fund. When comparing the Sharpe ratio of portfolios, the fund's Sharpe ratio must be higher than the portfolio's Sharpe ratio.

$$\frac{r_m - r_f}{\sigma_m} > \rho \frac{r_p - r_f}{\sigma_m}$$

where

$$\frac{r_p - r_f}{\sigma_m} = \text{manager's Sharpe ratio}$$

$$\frac{r_p - r_f}{\sigma_p} = \text{portfolio's Sharpe ratio}$$

ρ = correlation between manager's return and portfolio's return
σ_m = standard deviation of manager's return
σ_p = standard deviation of portfolio's return

Similarly, when comparing two funds, a fund with a higher Sharpe ratio is a better candidate for the portfolio.

3.1.11   Sortino Ratio

Standard deviation is not a good measure of risk, especially when there are more observations above the mean or below the mean. That means standard deviation is not good for non-normal distributions, which are quite common in alternative investments.

The Sharpe ratio, which adjusts the performance to the standard deviation, can often be misleading because the standard deviation penalizes portfolios for positive upside returns as much as the undesirable downside returns. An alternative to the Sharpe ratio is the measure that uses an alternative to the standard deviation. The downside semi-variance or downside semi-standard deviation is a better alternative to standard deviation or total risk.

The Sortino ratio takes only the downside size and frequency of returns into account and measures the reward to the negative volatility trade-off. The Sortino ratio can be expressed mathematically as follows:

$$SortinoRatio = \frac{r_p - r_f}{\sigma_{down}}$$

where σ_{down} = downside substandard deviation

3.1.12   D-Statistic

The D-statistic is another measure of downside risk. It gives the percentage of negative returns with respect to the absolute returns of all months.

$$D - Statistic = \frac{\sum |NegativeReturns|}{\sum |AllReturns|}$$

The lower the value of the D-statistic, better the performance of the fund or portfolio.

3.1.13   Omega

While the D-statistic takes zero as a demarcation, the omega can be calculated by using any value as a threshold. It is the ratio of the sum of absolute returns above the reference point and the sum of absolute returns below the reference point. The threshold point is similar to the required rate of return and is positive.

$$Mathematically, omega = \frac{Sum\,of\,absolute\,returns\,above\,the\,threshold\,point}{Sum\,of\,absolute\,returns\,below\,the\,threshold\,point}$$

$$Omega(L) = \frac{\sum Returns+}{\sum |Returns-|}$$

where

$$L = \text{threshold point}$$
$$Returns+ = \text{returns above the threshold}$$
$$Returns- = \text{returns below the threshold.}$$

The higher the value of the omega, the better the performance of the fund or portfolio. The omega can be used to monitor the style and performance of the fund manager. While standard deviation, skewness, and kurtosis take relative values above or below the mean, omega takes the actual value of returns. Therefore, omega represents the actual distribution and provides the combined effects of standard deviation, skewness, and kurtosis. Omega is the most often preferred measure for investors.

3.1.14   Limitations of Statistical Measures

Though statistical measures can be useful, they do have limitations. Keep the following in mind when relying on the statistics mentioned in this section:

- Statistical measures are backward-looking—they use analysis of historical data as a basis for predicting the future with a particular degree of confidence. They don't capture actual reasons behind the quantified value and also don't make any adjustments for the repetitious nature of such events.
- Statistical measures will underestimate the risk, as the historical data do not capture the potential for severe shocks.
- Similarly, the statistical measures will overestimate the risk, as the historical data can contain highly stressed periods of performance.
- The statistical models typically ignore, or insufficiently address, liquidity and funding risks.
- Statistical models tend to be built with a heavy focus on the statistical and analytical aspects of the process, often with less attention given to accuracy of static data and accuracy of historical market data.
- When the measures look strange, it is extremely difficult to track down the source of the error or discrepancy.

3.2   Probability Distributions

Probability distributions provide insight into how the returns are distributed over a period of time. They are helpful for quantifying the nature of the behavior based on certain known characteristics. There are several probability distributions in the mathematics; some of them are provided in this chapter.

3.2.1   Normal Distribution

Normal distribution, also known as the *normal curve* or *Gaussian distribution*, is a continuous distribution function. The normal distribution is a two-tailed distribution with a bell shape. Its skew value is 0, kurtosis is 3, and mean = mode = median.

Normal distribution

The value of z is used to measure the area of the curve, which is the equivalent probability of an observation or confidence level.

The z value based on confidence level or probability is calculated from exponential mathematical formulas but is readily available to anyone using a scientific calculator. Similarly, confidence level is calculated for a given z value using scientific calculators.

A z value of –1.645 gives a probability of 95 percent; in other words, 95 percent of the mass is distributed in the right side of –1.645. Since the normal distribution is symmetric, the same is true for the positive value of 1.654—that is, 95 percent of the mass is distributed to the left of 1.645. Hence, 90 percent of the mass is distributed between –1.645 and 1.645.

The z value is sometimes expressed as one-tail or two-tail. For example, 90 percent two-tail means each tail has 5 percent, and in such a case, it is necessary to find z value for 95 percent confidence level.

The value of z is calculated using the following formula, standard deviation, and mean:

$$z = \frac{(x - \mu)}{\sigma}$$

where x is a normal random variable with mean μ and standard deviation σ. The confidence level is then calculated using the exponential formula or a scientific calculator. Therefore, the z value is also called the *deviation of variable from mean per unit of standard deviation*.

For standard normal distribution, mean is 0 and standard deviation is 1. In terms of standard deviations:

- 68 percent of samples lie within 1 standard deviation, which indicates a 68 percent confidence interval.
- 90 percent of samples lie within 1.645 standard deviations, which indicates a 90 percent confidence interval.
- 95 percent of samples lie within 1.96 standard deviations, which indicates a 95 percent confidence interval.
- 99 percent of samples lie within 2.58 standard deviations, which indicates a 99 percent confidence interval.

Risk-averse investors prefer that returns of financial assets be normally distributed. In reality, very few asset classes exhibit normally distributed returns.

Most financial-asset classes exhibit skewed and fat-tailed distribution. In a skewed distribution, less probable but large deviations appear in either tail, and in a fat-tailed distribution, mass is distributed in the tail and around the mean. Distributions with high excess kurtosis exhibit fat tails.

A series of returns within smaller units of time may sometimes exhibit the normal distribution, whereas the total series can be non-normal. In other words, a non-normal distribution can be a series of normal distributions. Such behavior is called *regime switching*.

Let's consider a simple example. Suppose x is a normal random variable with mean 150 and standard deviation 38. What is the probability that x will take a value greater than 215?

$$z = \frac{(x - \mu)}{\sigma} = \frac{x - 150}{38}$$

where x is 215, as the question is to find the randomness. Therefore, z is 1.71.

3.2.2   *Lognormal Distribution*

The model is a variant of the normal distribution. If the returns are normally distributed, then the underlying asset prices themselves are lognormally distributed. This can be derived as follows: If one day return is r, then price on the day t = P0(1 + r × t), where P0 = initial price and t is the time period.

This can be simplified as

$$P1 = P0 \times e^{\wedge}rt$$

$$R_t = ln(\frac{P_1}{P_0})$$

Therefore, if the returns are normally distributed, then the prices are lognormally distributed. The lognormal distribution is used, as the prices can never be less than zero.

A lognormal distribution has a longer right tail compared with normal, or bell-shaped, distribution. In lognormal distribution, the values are spread between 0 and infinity, and therefore no negative prices are observed and there is an upward bias. This distribution is useful when the variable representing the fact—for example, stock price—can only drop to zero but can rise by more than 100 percent.

In practice, underlying asset price distributions often depart significantly from the lognormal. For example, historical distributions of underlying asset returns often have fatter left and right tails than a normal distribution, indicating that dramatic market moves occur with greater frequency than would be predicted by a normal distribution of returns— more very high returns and more very low returns

If a data set is known to follow a normal distribution, transforming the data by taking the logarithm of variables yields a data set that is lognormally distributed. Since the normal distribution allows variables to have negative values, and negative values are not observed in asset prices, the lognormal distribution is used instead, in which the observed values take zero and above.

Let x be the continuously compounded asset return. Then the asset price at the end of the return period is calculated as $pe^x e^x$. When x is normally distributed, the log value of e^x is said to be lognormally distributed.

As the standard deviation increases, the probability of an observation falling in the tail increases and shows skewness. Standard deviation σ determines the shape of the distribution.

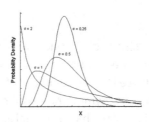

Lognormal distribution is left-skewed with heavy tails. This can be observed from the above figure. Such a distribution is mostly observed in high-yield bonds.

In the financial sector, the survival of certain investments is uncertain until a certain period has passed, and if the investment survives for that certain period, the probability of failure decreases dramatically. In other words, assets with a lognormal distribution have a higher chance of failing as they age for a particular period, but after survival to a specific age, the probability of failure decreases as time increases.

3.2.3   Poisson Distribution

The Poisson distribution is a discrete-probability distribution. It views distribution as a function of the expected number of successes and is derived from the binomial distribution. The Poisson distribution is called *the law of small numbers*. When applying the Poisson distribution to analysis, the following conditions must be met:

1. The events must be countable whole numbers.
2. Each occurrence is independent of the other.
3. The average frequency of occurrence for the period must be known.
4. The number of counts must be measurable.

The Poisson distribution is very useful in operational risk measurement to estimate loss frequency distribution.

3.2.4   Student's T-Distribution

The z-statistic of a normal distribution is good for analyzing various financial data series. However, one drawback with the normal distribution is that it requires a very large number of observations, which is sometimes impractical. Instead of the z-statistic, the alternative t-statistic is used, which is derived from a small number of available samples. The t-statistic is very similar to the z-statistic, except that the standard deviation is replaced with the sample standard deviation.

This distribution is called student's t-distribution, with n – 1 degrees of freedom. The t-statistic varies based on the number of degrees of freedom. Therefore, it is a function of both confidence level and number of degrees of freedom. The t-distribution is centered at 0 and symmetric—that is, the area to the left of 0 is half, and the area to the right of 0 is half. The total area under the curve gives the cumulative probability, which is 1. The area in the tails of the t-distribution is larger than the area in the tails of the normal distribution. As sample size n increases, the distribution becomes approximately normal.

3.2.5   Chi-Square Distribution

The chi-square distribution is used to test the variance of a normally distributed population. The chi-square distribution has the following properties:

- The mean of the distribution is equal to the number of degrees of freedom.
- The variance is equal to twice the number of degrees of freedom.
- As the degrees of freedom increase, the chi-square curve distribution approaches a normal distribution.

3.3 Equity Option Quantitative Models

3.3.1   Black-Scholes Model

Fischer Black, Myron Scholes, and Robert Merton developed a model in the 1970s that became very popular and is widely used to price stock options. Called the Black-Scholes model or the Black-Scholes-Merton model, it became the foundation for many models to come. This book is not aimed at showing the derivation of the Black-Scholes model; rather, it uses the model equation and discusses how the model is being used.

Fisher Black was initially working to create a valuation model for stock. Myron Scholes later joined Black, and the result of their work was a pricing model to evaluate options. The model assumes that the price of heavily traded assets follows a geometric Brownian motion—a stochastic process—with constant drift and volatility. When applied to stock options, the model incorporates the constant price variation of the stock, the time value of money, the option's strike price, and the time to the option's expiration.

The stochastic process, also called the *random process*, is a theory that explains that the process may take many unknown directions before evolving into some system over time. In a deterministic system, the process can only evolve in one way, whereas in a stochastic process, there is some indeterminacy—even if the initial condition or starting point is known, as there are several directions in which the process may evolve.

For example, if we drop a heavy metal ball in a jar of liquid, it reaches the base more or less in a straight path. By applying chemical physics, we will be able to find out the time taken to reach the bottom. Provided the conditions are same, the time taken to reach the bottom will be same for each instance.

On the other hand, if we drop very lightweight particles—for example, broken wheat—on the surface of the liquid, they move slowly to reach the bottom. Moreover, they travel random paths. Each particle makes its own way. Even if we drop just one particle at a time repeatedly, the path it takes each time is going to be different as it travels in random paths. This is a stochastic process.

Now if we put the prices of the stock in a probability distribution, they will exhibit lognormal distribution, whereas the returns of the underlying asset are normally distributed. A lognormal distribution has a longer right tail compared with normal, or bell-shaped, distribution. The lognormal distribution allows for a stock price distribution of between 0 and infinity and has an upward bias representing the fact that the stock price can only drop 100 percent but can increase by more than 100 percent.

In practice, the asset return distribution often departs significantly from the normal distribution. For example, historical distributions of underlying asset returns often have fatter left and right tails than a normal distribution, indicating that dramatic market movements occur with greater frequency than would be predicted by a normal distribution of returns—that is, more very high returns and more very low returns. But the Black-Scholes model assumes the normal distribution of returns. Let's discuss various limitations of Black-Scholes model before getting into the applications of the model.

$$\text{Call Price } C = S * N(d_1) - X * e^{-rt} * N(d_2)$$

$$\text{Put Price } P = X * e^{-rt} * N(-d_2) - S * N(-d_1)$$

where

$$d_1 = \frac{ln(\frac{S}{X}) + (r + \frac{\sigma^2}{2})t}{\sigma\sqrt{t}}$$

$$d_2 = d_1 - \sigma\sqrt{t}$$

r = expected return on stock per year,
equal to continuously compounded risk-free rate

σ = volatility of the stock price per year

S = price of the stock at the time of valuation of the option

K = Exercise price

T = Period until expiration in years,
normally measured as the number of trading days until expiration
divided by the number of trading days in one year—that is, 250.

The function N(x) is the cumulative probability distribution function for a standardized normal distribution.

European options on dividend-paying stocks are valued by adjusting the stock price such that the present value of dividends will be deducted from the stock price. However, only dividends with ex-dividend dates during the life of the option should be included. The dividend should be the expected reduction in the stock price expected. According to the Black-Scholes formula, a non-dividend-paying European call-and-put option is priced as follows:

$$\text{Call Price } C = S * e^{-qt} * N(d_1) - X * e^{-rt} * N(d_2)$$

$$\text{Put Price } P = X * e^{-rt} * N(-d_2) - S * e^{-qt} * N(-d_1)$$

$$d_1 = \frac{ln(\frac{S}{X}) + (r - q + \frac{\sigma^2}{2})t}{\sigma\sqrt{t}}$$

$$d_2 = d_1 - \sigma\sqrt{t}$$

where q = continued dividend rate.

The assumptions and limitations of the Black-Scholes model are as follows:

- The model assumes that there are no transaction costs. In fact, buying and selling of options or hedging and re-hedging of assets often are exposed to bid–ask spreads. This is even more pronounced for over-the-counter options.
- The model assumes that volatility is known and constant. In fact, the volatility is a function of both time and the underlying asset, and time series show that volatility is highly unstable.
- The model assumes that the risk-free rate is known and constant. In fact, risk-free rates change often, as short-term interest rates are uncertain.
- The model assumes that dividends are known and constant. This is not true in fact.
- The model assumes that the underlying asset path is continuous. In fact, market prices are discontinuous, and from time to time they jump

downward and upward. The sudden and large movements of prices are not contained in the lognormal distribution, and the assumption that returns are normally distributed does not hold true.

- The model assumes that price changes are exogenous. In fact, the buying and selling of large quantities of underlying assets move the prices either in a fairly predictable fashion or an unpredictable fashion.
- The model assumes that there is no autocorrelation in returns. In fact, in most cases, the returns are random and independent from what happened in the previous day or anytime in the past.
- The model is applicable to only European options. That is, it assumes that options are exercised only at the time of expiration. In fact, most stock options are American options and can be exercised at any time.
- The model assumes that delta hedging eliminates the risk completely. In fact, there is always some residual risk.

European options on dividend-paying stocks are valued by adjusting the stock price such that the present value of dividends will be deducted. However, only dividends with ex-dividend dates during the life of the option should be included. The dividend should be the expected reduction in the stock price expected.

3.3.2   Greeks Explained

From the Black-Scholes model, we learn that the price of call or put option depends on the following five parameters:

- r = expected return on stock per year, equal to continuously compounded risk-free rate
- σ = volatility of the stock price per year
- S = price of the stock at the time of valuation of the option
- K = exercise price
- T = time period until expiration in years,

If any of these parameters changes, then the option price will change even if the underlying asset is same. The Black-Scholes model can be used to derive the rate of change of the option price with respect to any one of these parameters (except with strike price, as strike price is fixed throughout the life of the option contract) while assuming the others are constant. Such a rate of change is represented by Greek letters and so is called *Greek*. Since the strike price does not change during the life of the contract, the Greek is not applicable to the strike price. Instead, there is an additional Greek called gamma, which is related to delta. Let's discuss a few of these Greeks and their relationships.

The rate of change with respect to a variable is a derivative function. For example, velocity gives the rate of change of distance with respect to time. So it is a first-order derivative. Velocity also changes with respect to time and is called *acceleration*. Greeks are also called *sensitivities*. They play a very important role in sensitivity analysis.

Delta

Say we purchased a call option on a stock with a strike price of $15. Also assume that the current stock price is $20. So if we exercise the option today, we will realize a profit of $5. But the option may be trading at $6 as the expiration date is not near, and there may be an expectation that the stock price will increase. Now, if the stock price increases by $1 to reach $21, then one may think that the option price is increased by $1 to $7. While this seems logically correct, this is not how it works in reality. So how much will the option price move if the stock increases or decreases by $1? That's where delta comes in.

Delta is the amount an option price is expected to move based on a $1 change in the underlying stock. In other words, delta gives the rate of change of the option price with respect to the price of the underlying asset. For example, if delta is 0.4 for a call option, a $1 increase in stock price will result in a $0.40 increase in the call option price.

Delta is a first-order derivative and is a very useful measure in designing hedging strategies. It is expressed mathematically as follows:

$$\Delta = \frac{\partial V}{\partial S}$$

where V = call option price and S = stock price.

The Black-Scholes formula is mathematically expressed as:

$$V = S * N(d_1) - X * e^{-rt} * N(d_2)$$

where

$$d_1 = \frac{ln(\frac{S}{K}) + (r + \frac{\sigma^2}{2})t}{\sigma\sqrt{t}}$$

$$d_2 = d_1 - \sigma\sqrt{t}$$

Taking the derivative of V with respect to S by keeping all other parameters constant,

$$\Delta = N(d1).$$

Therefore, we will need to calculate the new value of d1 with new value of S and find the corresponding value in normal distribution, as explained in probability distribution function.

Based on the historical data, the following patterns are observed, though they don't have to be true always. For a call option on a non-dividend-paying stock, delta is approximately 0.5 for the at-the-money option, 1 for a deep-in-the-money option, and zero for a deep-out-of-the-money option.

In other words, for the options for which the underlying price is at the strike price, $1 change in underlying asset price will result in $0.50 change in the call option price. If the underlying stock price is much higher than the strike price, the $1 change in stock price will result in a $1 change in the call option price. If the underlying stock price goes much lower than the strike price, the change in stock price will not have any impact on the option price.

From the put-call parity, the delta of a put option can be derived as follows:

$$Call + Ke^{-rt} = Put + Stock$$

$$C + Ke^{-rt} - P = S.$$

Taking the derivative with respect to S,

$$\Delta(call) - \Delta(put) = 1$$

$$\Delta(put) = \Delta(call) - 1$$

$$= N(d1) - 1$$

Therefore, for a put option on a non-dividend-paying stock, we find that delta is approximately −0.5 for the at-the-money option, −1 for a deep-in-the-money option, and 0 for a deep-out-of-the-money option.

Gamma

The rate of change of the option price with respect to stock price is not the same throughout the path of the stock price. Therefore, delta also changes with respect to the underlying stock price. Gamma gives the rate of change of delta with respect to stock price. Therefore, it is a second-order derivative of an option with respect to underlying asset price. It is the rate that the delta will change based on a $1 change in the stock price. So if delta is similar to speed (change of distance with respect to time), then gamma is similar to acceleration (change of speed with respect to time). The option with the highest gamma is the most responsive to changes in the price of the underlying stock.

$$\Gamma = \frac{\partial \Delta}{\partial S} = \frac{\partial^2 V}{\partial S^2}$$

Gamma provides the convexity of the option–price relationship. Gamma is more sensitive for at-the-money options and less sensitive for in-the-money and out-of-the money options. Gamma is also a function of time-to-maturity. For at-the-money options, gamma decreases as the time-to-maturity increases. For out-of-the-money options, near-to-expiration and far-from-expiration options will have lower gamma and medium-term options will have higher gamma. Gamma of in-the-money options also behaves like that of out-of-the-money options but is high at not-so-near but near expiration. Gamma is very useful in convertible arbitrage strategies and option strategies.

Theta

Theta provides the rate of change of the option price with respect to time-to-maturity. Theta is always negative, regardless of asset price and type of option. In other words, out-of-the-money, at-the-money, and in-the-money call-and-put options will all have negative theta. Therefore, option value increases with increased length of time—that is, far-from-maturity options will have a higher option price than those near to expiration. At-the-money options will have a higher absolute theta.

Theta, a time-decay function, is an enemy for the option buyer, as the time to expiration decreases the value of option decreases. On the other hand, it's actually the best friend for the option seller. Theta is the amount the price of calls and puts will decrease for a one-day change in the time to expiration.

Theta is more pronounced for at-the-money options and will result in more significant dollar losses over time than in- or out-of-the-money options with the same underlying stock and expiration date. That's because the higher premium is already priced in at-the-money options. For out-of-the-money options, theta will be lower than it is for at-the-money options as the dollar amount of the time value is smaller. However, the out-of-the-money options experience greater losses because of the smaller time value.

The formula for theta is derived from the Black-Scholes model by taking the first derivative with respect to time, assuming all other variables are constant.

Vega

Vega provides the rate of change of the option value with respect to the volatility of the underlying asset. Vega is always positive and is higher for at-the-money options. As market volatility increases, the value of options will increase because an increase in implied volatility suggests an increased range of potential movement for the stock.

The formula for Vega is derived from BSM by taking the first derivative with respect to volatility, assuming all other variables constant.

Rho

Rho gives the rate of change of the value of an option with respect to the interest rate. The option is more sensitive to rho at lower strike prices; as the stock value goes down, the probability of the company value falling below the debt value increases, and the bond value in turn is more sensitive to the interest rate.

In the Black-Scholes formula, the term $N(d_2)$ gives the probability of a call option being exercised or the probability of debt being survived. The probability of a call-option exercise involves the stock being above the strike, which can also be interpreted as the company value being higher than the debt value.

The Black-Scholes formula provides the following equation for rho:

$$Rho\ (call) = Kte^{-rt}N(d_2)$$

As we know from put-call parity,

$$C + Ke^{-rt} = P + S$$

$$Rho\ (put) = Kte^{-rt}N(d2) - Kte^{-rt}$$

$$= -Kte^{-rt}[1 - N(d_2)]$$

$$= -Kte^{-rt}N(-d_2)$$

3.4   Quantitative Concepts of Bonds

From the analysis of Black-Scholes formula and Greeks, we have learned how equity options are priced. Now we'll discuss the same for bonds. Like any other assets, bonds are valued based on the principle that a dollar today has more value than dollar tomorrow. For the purposes of discussion and simplicity, consider that a dollar today has more value than a dollar next year, because we can invest the dollar today and earn some profit. In addition, because of positive inflation, we will get fewer things next year than today for the same dollar amount.

Let's assume that we need to receive some amount from someone. We are told that we have the following options:

- Get $98 today or $100 next year. We prefer $98, because if we buy a CD for $98 it may become $102 by the end of the year.
- Get $95 today or $100 next year. We may prefer $95 because we think that we cannot earn more than $5 without taking risk. For example, if we buy a CD then we may get $4 for $95 in one year.

The profit we earn without taking risk is called the risk-free rate. This is the core parameter used in bond valuations. Let's call the risk-free rate r. Then the amount we invest today plus the interest (at the risk-free rate) we earn should be equal to the amount we are supposed to receive at the end of the year. Therefore,

$$95 + 95r = 100$$

$$95(1+r) = 100.$$

To put it in proper terms,

$$95 = \frac{100}{(1+r)}$$

Calculating the r, we get 5.2 percent.

In general, the present value PV = 100/(1+r). Bonds are priced on the concept of present value. The amount we can demand today rather than taking $100 next year depends on our earning potential. Such an earning potential is called *opportunity cost*. In a riskless business, the opportunity cost is same as the risk-free rate. If we think that we can earn more than the risk-free rate by taking some risk, we may prefer to take less than $95 and invest in that business. Let's assume that we can earn 7 percent on our own. Then what is the amount we can accept today instead of $100 next year?

$$P = \frac{100}{(1+0.07)} = 93.45$$

So for a person who thinks that he can earn 7 percent per year, $93.45 today is same as $100 next year. If there is a bond that is paying a coupon rate of 7 percent, then that is the preferred one for the investors whose opportunity cost is 7 percent. Here the P is also called a present value of expected payment of $100.

Bond Yield

Two parameters that determine how a bond is creating value to the investor are *coupon rate* and *yield*. Bonds that are issued with a face value of $100 may be traded above or below $100. Let's say the bond is being traded at $97. If we buy a bond for $97 today, at the end of one year we will get $100 + coupon (say 5 percent). Therefore,

$$PVof97 = \frac{105}{(1+y)}$$

$$y = 8.24\%$$

where y is the yield.

Though the coupon rate (also called interest the issuer is paying) is 5 percent, the bond is actually paying 8.24 percent, since we have purchased it at discount for $97. Since 8.24 percent is greater than the investor's opportunity cost (7 percent in our example in the discussion), the investor prefers this bond, which is trading at $97.

Bond investors prefer bonds with higher yield. It is sometimes called an *internal rate of return* or *opportunity cost*. If we invest $100 today and then reinvest it at the end of the year, the value at the end of the second year is 100(1 + y)(1 + y), as $100 will become 100(1 + y) at the end of the first year and then reinvesting the received amount will fetch 100 (1+ y)(1+ y).

Rewriting the same,

$$100 = \frac{P}{(1+y)(1+y)}$$

and so the present value of the amount that we can expect to receive at the end of t year is

$$P(1+y)^t$$

This is a concept we use in assessing the bonds.

Bonds Paying Multiple Coupons

Most bonds pay coupons semi-annually. The coupon rates are discounted to present value using half of the opportunity cost or yield. Let's assume that there is bond trading at $97 and paying semi-annual coupons of 5 percent per year for two years. At the end of six months, we receive the coupon of $2.50 and so on. At the end of maturity, we will receive the principal and last coupon.

$$97 = 2.5/(1+y/2) + 2.5/[1+y/2^2 + 2.5/(1+y/2)]^3 + 102.5/(1+y/2)^4$$

If we are evaluating the bonds on the assumption that the opportunity cost is equal to the risk-free rate, then we replace y with risk-free rate r.

3.4.1   Duration

From the previous formula, we learned that the bond value decreases with increasing interest rate. In other words, bond prices vary inversely with interest rates. If y increases by one basis point (1 percent of 1 percent or 0.01 percent), we will have to reevaluate the bond price by using the new value of y. The change in bond price for a change in interest rate or yield can be calculated by revaluing the present values of coupons and par value using the new interest rate as the discount rate.

However, this process is time-consuming. Therefore, the duration, which is a simple and less-intensive measure that gives the percentage change in a bond's price for a 1 percent change in its yield to maturity (YTM), is used to calculate the new value of the bond.

By applying mathematics to the previous formula, we can get the rate of change of bond price with respect to yield. In other words, by taking the derivative of the bond price with respect to y, we can get the rate of change of the bond price with respect to the interest rate. This is similar to velocity, which gives us the rate of change of distance with respect to time. In the bonds world, it is called *duration*. Rising interest rates mean falling bond prices, and declining interest rates mean rising bond prices.

For investors, this indicator is a standard data point provided in the presentation of comprehensive bond information. The duration is measured in years, and it is more useful to interpret duration as a means of comparing the interest-rate risks of different securities. Securities with the same duration have the same interest-rate risk exposure. The longer the duration, the longer the average maturity, and therefore the higher the sensitivity to interest-rate changes.

In fact, duration is nothing but the weighted average of the present value of the bond's payments and can be viewed as the average, or effective, maturity of the bond. For small changes in interest rates, the implied duration can be calculated using a simple formula, as follows:

$$\text{Duration} = \frac{P_- - P_+}{2P_0 \Delta_y}$$

where

$$P_0 = \text{bond price}$$
$$P_- = \text{bond price when interest rate is incremented}$$
$$P_+ = \text{bond price when interest rate is decremented}$$
$$\Delta_y = \text{change in interest rate in decimal form.}$$

The duration for a bond portfolio is equal to the weighted average of the duration for each type of bond in the portfolio.

$$\text{Portfolio Duration} = w_1 D_1 + w_2 D_2 + \ldots + w_i D_i$$

where

$$w_i = \text{market value of bond i / market value of portfolio}$$
$$D_i = \text{duration of bond i}$$
$$K = \text{number of bonds in portfolio}$$

Macaulay Duration

Frederick Macaulay developed the concept of duration, equating it to the average time to maturity or the time required to receive half of the present value of a bond's cash flow. The relationship between modified duration and Macaulay duration can be expressed as follows:

$$D_m = \frac{D_{Mac}}{1 + \frac{y}{k}}$$

where D_m = modified duration and D_{Mac} = Macaulay duration.

As the number of payments per year increases, y/k will become smaller, and the value of modified duration will approach Macaulay duration. In other words, for continuous interest rates, k is equal to infinity and y/k will be 0, in which case modified duration and Macaulay duration will become equal.

Price Value of a Basis Point

PVBP or dollar value of 01 (DV01) provides the change in value of the bond for one basis point change in interest rate. Since duration gives the percentage change in bond value for a 1 percent change in interest rate, the change in value for one basis point (100th of 1 percent) is calculated as follows:

$$PVBP = \frac{Duration}{100}$$

Impact of Coupon Rate, Yield, and Maturity on Duration

Duration also depends on the coupon rate of the bond. For a given yield, the lower the coupon, the higher the duration. For example, US Treasuries usually have lower coupon rates and current yields than corporate bonds of similar maturities. Therefore, US Treasuries should have higher durations than corporate bonds.

Limitations of Duration

The first of the limitations is that duration, just like the delta of an option, is not constant throughout the path of interest rates. This issue can be addressed by using convexity, which will be discussed shortly.

The second limitation is the reinvestment risk. Since the duration is equal to the weighted average of the present value of the bond's payments, it assumes that the coupon payments are reinvested at the same yield. However, the yield may change from time to time, and the investor may sometimes end up reinvesting the coupon payments at lower rates. Reinvestment risk applies not only to coupon cash flows but also to principal repayment.

A third limitation is that all the interest rates change in parallel and duration assume that the yield curve is shifted in parallel. However, in reality, only a certain part of the yield curve may change while the other part stays the same. For example, in an interest curve over five years, the interest rates between second year and third year may change, and the rate before the second year and after the third year may stay the same. This issue can be addressed using the key-rate-shift and bucket-shift methods, as discussed below.

Key-Rate-Shift Approach

In contrast to the duration, which assumes that all the rates change in parallel, the key-rate-shift approach allows analysts to calculate price sensitivities by changing the rate at a particular area of the yield curve. This method is useful to hedge the instruments against certain areas of yield curves. The key-rate-shift techniques assume that a change in interest rate of a particular term affects that term and terms on each side of it. The five-year interest rate affects five-year bonds and also three-year and seven-year bonds proportionately.

In order to implement efficient hedging strategies, risk managers typically choose a higher number of key rates. However, additional key rates will also need higher transaction costs and more monitoring time.

Bucket-Shift Approach

In contrast to the key-rate-shift approach, the bucket-shift approach incorporates much potential change within the region of the yield curve. This approach stands in between the key-rate change and the duration method; that is, the bucket shift assumes the parallel shift only within the range. For example, when a manager anticipates that interest rates of terms three to five years will change, then the price sensitivity is calculated by assuming a parallel shift between three and five years while keeping all other interest rates constant.

3.4.2   Convexity

Duration works well only for small changes in yield. As shown in the figure below, the rate of change of bond price with respect to yield also changes as the yield moves further away. Thus, the duration underestimates the resulting bond prices. Convexity measures the rate of change of duration with respect to yield, and so it is the second derivative. The negative slope indicates the inverse relationship between interest rate and bond price.

The duration is very similar to the delta of options, and convexity is very similar to the gamma of options.

Convexity can also be calculated using the following approximate formula:

$$Convexity = \frac{P_+ + P_- - 2P_0}{2P_0(\Delta_y)^2}$$

where

$$P_0 = \text{bond price}$$
$$P_- = \text{bond price when interest rate is incremented}$$
$$P_+ = \text{bond price when interest rate is decremented}$$
$$\Delta_y = \text{change in interest rate in decimal form}$$

The change in bond prices with respect to interest rates can be calculated as follows:

$$Change in bond price \frac{\Delta_p}{p} = Duration + Convexity Adjustment$$

$$\frac{\Delta_p}{p} = -D_m \Delta_y + \frac{(\Delta_y)^2}{2} Convexity$$

where

$$\Delta_y = \text{yield change}$$
$$\Delta_p = \text{bond price change}$$

Convexity is usually a positive term, regardless of whether the interest rate is rising or falling; hence, it is positive convexity. From the above, it can be seen that the convexity increases the change in price when interest rates decline—that is, when Δ_y is negative, the convexity acts as an add-on. Similarly, when interest increases, that is, when Δ_y is positive, the convexity reduces the price decline. In either case, convexity helps the investor.

However, some securities with embedded options or interest-only mortgage securities exhibit negative convexity. In this case, bond prices will increase with falling interest rates but will reach a ceiling at a particular point of yield.

Callable bonds exhibit negative convexity. Similarly, the embedded prepayment option in mortgage loans makes the mortgage securities exhibit negative convexity. The other instrument that exhibits negative convexity is IO mortgage securities or asset-backed securities. The falling interest rates make the borrowers prepay the loans, thus depleting the outstanding balance on which the interest is calculated to pay the IO investors. Puttable bonds also exhibit negative convexity.

For callable bonds, the price-yield curve follows the same positive convexity below the call price as an option-free bond, but as the yield falls and the bond price rises to near the call price, the positive convexity becomes negative convexity, where the bond price is limited at the top by the call price.

For a given yield, bonds with lower coupons will have higher convexity. For a given yield and duration, lower-coupon bonds will have lower convexity.

Duration is linearly related to maturity; that is, long-term bonds will have a higher maturity. The convexity increases with the square of maturity.

A Special Behavior of Convexity

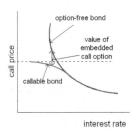

From the graph above for option-free bonds, we can see that the bond price is rising with falling interest rates. However, there are certain exceptions. Let's take mortgage-backed securities (MBS) as a second example. Interest and principal received from loans are used to create the securities. If interest rates go down, the homeowners think they can refinance at lower rates, so the loans are returned to the pool earlier than maturity time. Therefore, MBS holders are paid their principal early, and they will end up investing at lower market rates. This is called *prepayment risk*. Because of prepayment risk, investors try to stay away from MBS when interest rates fall. These bond prices do not increase as much as option-free bonds.

Let's take puttable bonds as a third example. A puttable bond gives the investor the option of putting back the bond to the issuer before it matures. If interest rates are going up, the investor can sell the bond back to the issuer and get the face value and then invest in newly issued bonds that are paying higher rates. Because of this option, investors prefer to buy puttable bonds, as they think they can put it back at any time. So the decrease in the puttable-bond price is not as much as that of option-free bonds.

For option bonds like callable bonds, puttable bonds, and MBS, the rate of change of bond price decreases as interest rates fall. This is called *negative convexity*.

3.5   *Interest Rate Models*

One of the key parameters used to evaluate financial products is the interest rate. We know the current interest rate at any one time, but it is necessary to know the future interest rates to forecast the prices. There are several mechanisms to forecast the interest rates, including rate curves, binomial model, stochastic models, one-factor model, and two-factor model. Let's discuss some of these mechanisms briefly.

3.5.1   Rate Curves

Yield Curve

Bond yields vary based on maturity. Long-term bonds typically pay more interest than short-term bonds. If we take yields of bonds of various maturities and draw a graph with rate on the Y-axis and maturity on the X-axis, we get a curve that rises from left to right. This tells us that long-term rates are higher than short-term rates and investors or lenders expect better rates for bearing the risk. The longer the period, the longer the risk of repayment. The shape of the curve changes based on economic conditions and rate policies. Four popular forms are as follows:

- *Steep curve* indicates that long-term rates are growing faster than short-term rates.
- *Flat curve* indicates that short-term rates are growing faster than long-term rates.
- *Inverted curve* indicates that short-term rates are higher than long-term rates. This is possible if the central bank is expected to cut the rates down the line.
- *Humped-shape curve* indicates that medium-term rates are higher than short-term and long-term rates.

In addition to these, a roller-coaster shape is also seen sometimes.

Spot Curve

The spot curve, also called the *zero-coupon yield curve*, is graphed using zero-coupon bonds and their yields. Let's take a simple six-month zero-coupon bond with a market price of $99.15. Upon maturity, the bond pays $100, meaning $99.15 pays an interest of $0.85 for six months. Therefore,

$$99.15 \, (1 + r) = 100$$

$$1 + r = \frac{100}{99.15}$$

$$r = \frac{0.85}{99.15} = 0.8573$$

The equivalent annual interest rate is 1.7146 percent.

Similarly, we can calculate interest rates of one year, one and a half year, up to three years. By drawing a graph, we will get a curve with interest rates of different maturities. If we want seven-month interest or sixteen-month interest, we can easily plot it from the graph.

Forward Rate Curve

In the spot curve, we assumed that zero-coupon bonds pay one-time interest at the end of the maturity. If that is the case, then a one-year zero-coupon bond can be decomposed as follows:

$$Discount\ Bond\ Price \ast \left(\frac{1+r1}{2}\right)\left(\frac{1+r2}{2}\right) = 100$$

where r1 is the six-month interest rate and r2 is the six-month interest rate six months from now. We can calculate r1 using six-month zero bonds and then r2 from the above formula.

Similarly, r3, the six-month rate after one year, can be calculated from a one-and-a-half-year zero bond by using r1 and r2.

By drawing the graph with forward rates on the y-axis and the maturity on the x-axis, we get the forward rate curve. Using the interpolation method, we can the forward rates for odd periods like seven months, thirteen months.

Interpolation

Interpolation is a mathematical method used to determine the value of an unknown data point based on the values of known surrounding data points. Linear interpolation assumes that the data points follow a straight line. This method relies on the fact that the slope is same throughout a straight line.

Financial market often uses linear interpolation to determine the value of missing interest rates on the yield curve. For example, assume that a bank wants to calculate the present value of the bond that matures seven months from today; the calculation will need an interest rate of seven months. Since there are no seven-month rates but only six-month and twelve-month rates, it will be necessary to interpolate the required rate.

Please note that interest rates vary based on the maturity time. It is not a true assumption that if the six-month rate is 3 percent, then the nine-month rate will be 4.5 percent. The nine-month rate may be different, as length of maturity determines the rate.

For example, assume that there are three data points—a, b, and c—on the y-axis, with corresponding x-axis values of x, y, and z. If we know any of these five values, we can calculate the sixth data point. Since the slope = distance y-axis/distance x-axis,

$$\frac{c-a}{z-x} = \frac{c-b}{z-y}$$

Imagine that a is the six-month interest rate which is a known value; b is the seven-month interest rate, which is an unknown value; and c is the twelve-month interest rate, which is a known value. Using the above interpolation formula, we can calculate b, the seven-month interest rate.

3.5.2   Vasicek Model

The Vasicek model is one of the earliest no-arbitrage and stochastic interest-rate models based on the evolution of an unspecified short-term interest rate. The Vasicek model provides an explicit formula for the zero-coupon yield curve. It also provides an explicit formula for derivatives, such as bond options. Additionally, it can be used to create an interest-rate tree. The model is based on mean-reversion theory and assumes that the short rate follows the stochastic process, which is expressed as follows:

$$\text{Drift } dr = a(b - r)dt + \sigma \times dz$$

where

- dz is a standard Wiener process;
- r is the current level of the interest rate;
- b is the long-run normal interest rate;
- a is a coefficient that adjusts the speed of the interest rate toward its long-run normal level; and
- σ is a volatility of interest rate and is assumed to be constant.

The mean-reversion theory states that the factor approaches its long-run mean from its current level. From the above model, it can be observed that if the interest rate is above the long-run mean—that is, r > b—then the drift (dr) becomes negative and the rate will be pulled down in the direction of r. Similarly, if the rate is less than the long-run mean—that is, r < b—then the drift becomes positive and the rate will be pulled up in the direction of r.

This feature is particularly attractive because without it, interest rates could drift permanently upward or downward, which is not possible practically speaking. Mean reversion is reasonable for interest rates because it is economically unreasonable to think that interest rates can become infinite or arbitrarily large.

In the Vasicek model, the mean reversion of interest makes the interest rate become normally distributed. Based on the normal distribution, the Vasicek model gives an explicit formula for the zero-coupon yield curve, as follows:

$$\text{Expected rate } E[R] = r \times e^{-a(T-t)} + b \times (1 - e^{-a(T-t)}).$$

One drawback with the normal distribution is that the variable can become negative. However, if the chosen value of the coefficient is greater than zero, the expected value will converge to b, which indicates mean reversion.

Weaknesses of the Vasicek Model

- While the model is based on no-arbitrage theory, real prices exhibit some arbitrage. In other words, the Vasicek model generates prices that are inconsistent with the current term structure, and this could permit other dealers and counterparties to arbitrage against them.
- The Vasicek model is a one-factor model and cannot capture the most complex term structural shifts that occur.
- The Vasicek model assumes that all rates have the same volatility.
- Unless the coefficient is chosen properly, interest rates can go negative, which is not possible in any economy.

3.5.3   Cox-Ingersoll-Ross Model

While the Vasicek model assumes that all rates have the same volatility, empirical evidence suggests that interest-rate changes are more volatile when the level of interest rates is high. The Cox-Ingersoll-Ross (CIR) model has been developed to address such a limitation and is based on conditional volatility. The model also shows that interest rates will remain positive.

Thus, the CIR model has the same drift term as the Vasicek model, but with a modified volatility term:

$$Drift\,dr = a(b-r)dt + \sigma * \sqrt{rt} * dz$$

When the short rate *rt* is high, the volatility of interest rate changes is high, and vice versa. The parameter σ no longer represents the volatility of interest-rate changes. It is just a parameter. The model provides solutions for bond prices and complete characterization of the term structure that incorporates risk premiums and expectations for future interest rates. The CIR model process has the non-central chi-square distribution. The chi-square distribution always makes the interest rate positive.

3.5.4   Heath-Jarrow-Morton Model

All the models discussed so far use short-term interest rates to predict the expected future interest rate. Heath, Jarrow, and Morton modeled the whole forward rate curve, and this model is a breakthrough in the pricing of fixed-income products.

The process for the short rate r in the Heath-Jarrow-Morton (HJM) model is a non-Markov process. In a Markov process, only the present state of a variable determines the possible future state. The general HJM model makes the motion of the spot-rate non-Markov—that is, it utilizes the vector of past and present values of interest rates and bond prices at time t that are relevant for determining bond-price volatilities at that time.

The non-Markov process is the real challenge of the implementation of the HJM model. It is required to generate a Monte Carlo simulation of the different paths. Using a Monte Carlo simulation can be a slow process and requires powerful computers.

The one-factor HJM model's extreme popularity is due to its simplicity and mathematical tractability. The one-factor model essentially assumes that the term structure is affected by a single source of uncertainty. However, such a model can occasionally be insufficient in describing the full evolution of term-structure movements. Multifactor models can provide a more realistic description of the transition behavior of the term structure of interest rates. Multifactor HJM models are outside of the scope of this book.

The drawbacks of the HJM model are that the expressed instantaneous forward rates are not directly observed in the market. It is also difficult to calibrate the model to prices of actively traded instruments. These drawbacks are addressed by the Brace-Gatarek-Musiela model.

3.5.5   *Brace-Gatarek-Musiela Model*

The Brace-Gatarek-Musiela (BGM) model, a discrete version of the HJM model, is also called the *LIBOR market model* (LMM). It models the actively traded, observable quantities in the fixed-income sector. Many traders favor this model, as it can price any contract whose cash flows can be decomposed into functions of the observed forward rates. The model uses the discrete-compounding definition of "interest rate" rather than continuous compounding. The model uses the most convenient approach of valuing interest-rate derivatives by working in a world that is always forward-risk neutral with respect to a bond maturing at the next reset date. This phenomenon is referred to as *rolling-forward risk-neutral world*. The LMM can be extended to incorporate many independent factors.

The LMM can be used to value nonstandard caps, such as ratchet caps, sticky caps, and flex caps. In a ratchet cap, the cap rate equals the previous reset date plus a spread. In a sticky cap, it equals the previously capped rate plus a spread. In a flex cap, there is a limit on the total number of caplets that can be exercised. Either the HJM or LIBOR market model can be used to simulate the behavior of interest rates month by month throughout the life of the MBS.

3.5.6   *Markov Process*

Transition matrices can be used to observe different non-Markovian behaviors. According to Markov properties, the next time's distribution is only dependent on the present state and not on any developments in the past. The Markov assumption, while convenient, may be unrealistic. A Markov process has no memory: to compute future state, only knowledge of the current state is required, not the path of how the firm arrived at that state. The basic belief is that, for example, issuers who have experienced previous downgrading are prone to further downgrading, while issuers who have been upgraded before are less frequently downgraded. In other words, state transitions depend on the path, which contrasts with the Markov property.

Industry heterogeneity and time variation, due in particular to the business cycle, are some of the causes for non-Markovian performance in rating transitions. To determine whether the rating transition depends on the previous state, path dependency analysis can be performed on rating-transition matrices. Path dependency analysis shows whether any one year's rating action has an impact on the following year's rating movement. It shows whether the frequency of upgrades in any year is conditional on previous upgrades, and likewise, whether the frequency of downgrades in any given year is conditional on prior downgrades.

3.6   Hedging Principles

We have discussed that such sensitivities as DV01, delta, gamma, and beta are used to measure the movements of prices with respect to underlying factors. There are many situations where assets are purchased to receive the expected cash flows and investors want to ensure that their market prices are unchanged. For example, say an investor purchases a bond that is paying a coupon of 7 percent per year. As his goal is to receive the coupon, he will need to ensure that the bond price will not change. For example, if interest rates are increasing, the price goes down for certain bonds. Selling the bond may not be economical for the investor because of tax terms or the transaction costs involved. There may be other bonds where the prices are inversely related to the interest rates. Alternatively, there can be indices that behave inversely with the bond.

Sometimes the investor may want to short other bonds or indices to mimic the inverse performance. Such a mechanism is called *hedging*. For this purpose, it is necessary to find the DV01 of both the bond and the hedging instrument so that the proportionate shorting units are determined. As we discussed earlier, DV01 represents a change in bond price for one basis point change in yield.

Consider a thirty-year semiannual-coupon bond with a DV01 of 0.19. The portfolio manager wants to hedge it using a fifteen-year semiannual coupon bond that has DV01 of 0.12. The hedging ratio is calculated as the sensitivity of the original instrument and the sensitivity of the instrument being used for hedging. Therefore, the hedging ratio is

$$\frac{0.19}{0.12} = 1.583$$

This implies that the portfolio manager will need to short $1.583 of notional for every $1 notional of the original bond.

The DV01 sometimes doesn't yield a perfect hedge. While the bond price increases with respect to yield decreases, the decrease in bond price with respect to decrease in yield may be slower or vice versa. This is because of the convexity effect. Positive convexity makes the bond price increase as yields decrease when compared with higher yields.

Hedging mechanisms need to be rebalanced to incorporate the convexity effect. In the case of callable bonds and MBS, the convexity is negative and the increase in bond price at lower interest rates is slower and may reach a stable value. Similarly, if the portfolio contains options, and if the manager determines that the options need to be hedged for a short period to be protected from market volatilities, delta and gamma are used to create the hedging.

In summary, the asset is protected from volatility in the underlying factor by using its corresponding first-order derivative—such as duration/DV01, delta, beta, and credit delta—and then adjust it using second-order derivatives, such as convexity and gamma. The portfolio will need to be rebalanced periodically based on the alignment of the hedging.

3.7 Quantitative Strategies

So far, we have discussed financial instruments, derivatives, and basic quantitative concepts. Now we'll see how investment strategies are built. Hedge-fund strategies are discussed here for better understanding of capital markets and investment strategies. However, the concepts of hedging are the same whether applied by banks or at hedge-fund firms.

3.7.1 Long/Short Equity

Long/short equity strategies are designed by employing both long and short positions. The returns are not intended to correlate with market performance; instead, they are constructed by buying the undervalued stocks and selling the overvalued stocks. The portfolio benefits from increased value of long positions and decreased value of short positions.

The portion of absolute value of exposure is allocated to long assets, while a certain portion is allocated to short assets. For example, if a portfolio is constructed with $100 million in long stocks and $50 million in short stocks, then the absolute exposure is $150 million and the net exposure is $50 million. In other words, $150 million of exposure is created using the funds of $50 million. These types of portfolios are called *100:50 portfolios*. The first number stands for the long portion while the second number stands for the short portion. Typically, for long/short portfolios, the net exposure is 100 percent.

For example, traditional investment funds, such as mutual funds, typically have a constraint of 130:30 ratio of long and short, and therefore they are called *130/30 funds*. A 130/30 fund has a gross exposure of 160 percent but a net exposure of 100 percent, meaning they are effectively equivalent to 100 percent long.

On the other hand, nonconventional funds like hedge funds do not have any constraints on net exposure, and so the long/short ratio can be anything, but typically they end up with a net long exposure. The advantage of the long/short equity strategy is that it provides greater gross exposure with a lesser exposure to systemic risk. Since the beta of the long/short equity portfolio is the weighted average of the individual betas, and since short positions have negative beta, the net beta will be less.

Short positions generate profit as well as providing downside protection to the portfolio. Short positions also provide greater leverage. For example, if the portfolio is constructed with $80,000 of long and $40,000 of short, then, since the net exposure is $40,000, the portfolio manager is able to establish $120,000 (gross) worth of positions using $40,000. In this example, for simplicity, it has been assumed that the prime broker does not require any margin to be posted for a short position. In reality, fund managers may be required to deposit a portion of the funds received for the short position with the prime broker.

Long/short equity strategies may also use derivatives for both long and short positions and are typically concentrated. The payoff of the long/short strategy resembles a call option. The return profile of the long/short equity strategy is shown in the diagram below. The long position usually outperforms in a bull market, and short positions generally outperform in bear markets, thus providing downside protection to the overall portfolio.

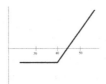

Typical payoff diagram of a long/short strategy

Since long/short equity funds tend to have a long bias, they are exposed to market risk, also called *systemic risk*. Therefore, returns are partially attributed to market risk premium, also called *beta return*. Historical performance of long/short equity funds demonstrates significant excess returns, called *alpha returns*. Major sources of alpha are market inefficiencies, idiosyncratic risk (firm-specific risk), short selling, and use of leverage and derivatives.

The capital-asset pricing model (CAPM) assumes that markets are efficient and states that idiosyncratic risk is not rewarded by excess returns. In reality, market inefficiencies do exist. Long/short equity managers exploit market inefficiency with manager skills like stock selection and trading talents. Various stock-selection approaches engaged in by long/short equity managers are described in the following section. Long/short managers earn excess returns from risk factors not covered by CAPM—such as firm-specific risk, small-cap risk, liquidity risk, and event risk—in addition to merger announcements, possible bankruptcy protection filing, and so on. The other factors that commonly influence returns are long positions in high book-to-market stocks and short positions in low book-to-market stocks; long positions in small-cap stocks and short positions in large-cap stocks; and long positions in past outperforming stocks and short positions in past underperforming stocks.

Many institutional investors are not qualified for short selling because of internal or external compliance restrictions, and therefore they are not able to utilize the profit opportunities that arise from short selling. Since hedge-fund managers do not have such constraints, they earn excess returns from short selling stocks that are not performing well, are overvalued, or have the potential for bankruptcy.

Long/short equity fund managers follow a variety of approaches to find stocks suitable for building a portfolio. Some of the most common approaches are bottom-up, top-down, value, growth, large cap/small cap, sector concentration, trend and countertrend, activist, black-box trading, and equity market timing. Long/short equity fund managers may also combine two or more of these approaches in portfolio construction.

Bottom-Up Approach

This is the most common approach employed by many long/short equity fund managers. They engage their researchers to perform ground-level research on companies that have limited analyst coverage to analyze company-specific information that is not yet known to the public. Company-specific information includes product offerings, intellectual rights, competitive advantage, regulatory compliance, slots in major retail stores, traffic to retails, and so on. They do not concentrate on macroeconomic trends and relative performance. They focus on strengths, weaknesses, opportunities, and threats, which is called the *SWOT framework*. Long/short equity fund managers following this approach typically build concentrated portfolios.

Top-Down Approach

In contrast to the bottom-up approach, the top-down approach focuses on macroeconomic metrics, such as the business cycle, monetary and fiscal policy, purchasing power, consumer confidence, and inflation forecast. Fund managers have a clear understanding of the interdependencies of macroeconomic factors and their impact on sector returns. They pay little attention to firm-specific analysis. Long/short equity fund managers following this approach may also invest in sector ETFs (exchange-traded funds) and build diversified portfolios.

Value Approach

In the value approach, hedge-fund managers use both fundamental and technical analysis. They conduct fundamental analysis of book-to-market, P/E (price/earnings) ratios, dividend yield, and earnings growth by often sitting with the firm's management and comparing with competitors to look for undervalued firms. Managers usually pick firms that are temporarily unfavorable and use technical analysis, such as volatility of stock, to determine when to open a position.

Growth Approach

In the growth approach, managers look at past and current behavior of the stock and analyses to see if there is a potential for growth. To forecast potential growth, managers often look for the most recent sales and forecasted sales. Managers prefer small-cap companies, as they usually offer higher potential for growth than matured companies.

Large Cap/Small Cap

Small-cap companies typically have less analyst coverage and are less liquid in nature. However, they will have higher growth potential. The fund managers gather private information. Large-cap companies typically have higher trading volume and analyst coverage, and so much of the company-specific information is known to the public. Long/short equity fund managers using this approach usually go long in small cap and go short in long cap.

Sector Concentration

Long/short equity fund managers following this approach utilize domain experts or research analysts who have been following sectors like oil, biotech, health care, alternative energies, real estate, and so on. Portfolios are constructed by going long in strong performers and going short in weak performers.

Trend and Countertrend

Managers who follow the trend-and-countertrend approach typically wait for market momentum to be established and invest in individual stocks or sectors when the trend is detected and reverse the position before the trend reverses. Managers following this approach believe in mean reversion, thus thinking that excess market value will be eventually wiped out, establishing the countertrend.

Activist Approach

Managers following the activist approach find companies with poor management and deal directly or indirectly with the board of directors to engage in corporate governance. They involve themselves with company activities and make recommendations to improve operating performance and dividend payout, thus increasing the shareholders' wealth.

Black-Box Trading

The black-box approach, also known as the *quantitative approach*, uses computer-automated tools to find undervalued and overvalued stocks. Managers typically use screeners to filter out certain groups of stocks based on predefined criteria and establish a weighting scheme to shortlist the stocks. Managers may also use stratification in order to gain diversification.

Equity Market Timing

Managers using equity market timing look for various buy-and-sell signals in the market to enter or exit the positions. Common signals employed by equity market timing funds include the following:

- A buy signal is generated when the price is above the moving average.
- A buy signal is generated when a short-term moving average crosses above a long-term average.
- A buy signal is generated when a group of moving averages are all increasing.
- A sell signal is generated when the price is below the moving average.
- A sell signal is generated when a short-term moving average crosses below a long-term average.
- A sell signal is generated when a group of moving averages are all decreasing.
- A buy signal is generated when RSI crosses below 30.
- A sell signal is generated when RSI crosses above 70.
- When the price difference between two securities (price of A – price of B) crosses below 30, then buy security A and sell security B.
- When the price difference between two securities (price of A – price of B) crosses above 70, then sell security A and buy security B.
- A channel-breakout strategy generates a buy (sell) signal when the price crosses above (below) the previous high (low) in a specific look-back period.

Some managers employ this strategy across different time zones of the globe. If managers expect that the price will go up the next day, they may buy the stock in their counterpart funds in Japan and then sell at market open in the United States. Risks involved in this strategy include trend reversals, wrong signals, and failure of trade execution in time.

3.7.2   *Relative-Value Arbitrage*

Relative-value arbitrage strategies involve purchasing undervalued securities and simultaneously short selling overvalued securities. Relative-value arbitrage fund managers maintain zero market exposure as they build a portfolio in such a way that market risk of long positions is cancelled out by that of short positions. Therefore, the relative value strategy is said to be nondirectional.

Relative-value arbitrage managers take advantage of price disparities caused by market inefficiencies that occur because of either a lack of public coverage for the securities or market segmentation. Relative-value arbitrage managers also employ dedicated arbitrage strategies, such as merger arbitrage, fixed-income arbitrage, convertible arbitrage, and volatility arbitrage. Relative-value arbitrage strategies are broad in scope in that they can involve a combination of any two securities—including but not limited to stocks, bonds, options, forwards, futures, and swaps—and may contain a combination of strategies, such as merger arbitrage, fixed-income arbitrage, convertible arbitrage, and volatility arbitrage. That is why the relative-value arbitrage strategies are often called an *arbitrage smorgasbord*. A special type of relative-value strategy is a stub-trading strategy that involves the piece of an equity security left over from a merger or recapitalization, which is called a *stub*.

3.7.3   Convertible Arbitrage

Companies with great potential for growth but poor credit ratings or established companies with weak financial health often issue convertible bonds in order to avoid immediate stock dilution and to lower the coupon rate. Convertible bonds give the investor the right to convert the bonds into common stock. The right can be interpreted as the issuer implicitly selling the call option to the investor to purchase the issuer's stock. This call option reduces the coupon payment on the convertible bond.

Convertible bonds comprise two components: a bond and an equity option. The option also acts as a long put on the bond, as the investor can put the bond back to the issuer with an exchange of stock. In this case, the stock price acts as the exercise price. Since the options are embedded and cannot be traded separately, pricing disparities occur, especially in volatile markets. Convertible arbitrage fund managers apply various quantitative techniques to price the bond and option and profit from arbitrage trading.

The convertible-bond market is considered to be kind of risky, as firms with non-investment credit ratings or emerging firms typically issue most of the convertible bonds. Many institutional investors have constraints against investing in these issuers, making the liquidity of the convertible-bond market not so attractive. As a result, convertible bonds are undervalued. Convertible arbitrage fund managers take advantage of this undervaluation.

The most common arbitrage strategy is buying convertible bonds and selling the underlying stock, thus gaining profit from the convertible bond coupon, stock depreciation, and short rebate. If prices move up—that is, in an unfavorable direction—the loss from the short sale will be offset by the gain from the bond price.

Depending on the volatility of the stock, the manager builds various forms of convertible arbitrage strategies, such as static trading and dynamic trading. The latter are also referred to as *volatility trading strategies* and take various forms, such as the delta-neutral strategy, gamma trading, and skewed trading. Depending on the credit quality of the issuer, the manager builds various credit arbitrage strategies.

Static Trading

This is the basic form of convertible arbitrage strategy. A hedge-fund manager buys a convertible bond or convertible preferred stock and short sells the underlying stock. The fund receives a coupon payment from the convertible bond or a dividend from the preferred stock. The fund invests the amount received from the short sale but pays the dividend back to the stock lender. Interest earned minus the dividend is called a *short rebate*. So the fund manager is compensated by a static return represented by the coupon payment and a short rebate, even if gains from bond-price appreciation are cancelled by loss on a short sale. Any transaction costs and leverage costs need to be subtracted from this static return.

Delta-Neutral Strategy

In contrast to static trading, volatility trading is dynamic. In volatility trading, the fund manager re-hedges the convertible bond positions according to stock-price movements in order to maintain delta neutral. The delta measures the sensitivity of an option price to the changes in the price of the underlying stock. Therefore, the delta of the convertible bond measures the convertible price sensitivity to the underlying stock price changes. The delta is used to calculate the hedge ratio, which gives the number of stocks to be shorted to achieve a delta-neutral portfolio of convertible bonds and short stocks.

$$Hedge\ Ratio = \Delta * \frac{convertible\ price}{conversion\ price}$$

where conversion price = underlying stock price + conversion premium if any.

As the delta changes from time to time, the hedge ratio also changes, so the fund manager needs to adjust the stock position periodically in order to remain delta neutral. This is called *delta hedging*. Delta is approximately 1 for deep-in-the-money options, 0.5 for at-the-money options, and 0 for out-of-money options. As the stock value increases, the delta increases; it decreases when the stock value decreases. The fund manager needs to sell more stocks as the delta increases and cover part of the short position when the delta decreases in order to maintain delta neutral. If the gain (loss) from the convertible bond price is offset by loss (gain) from the stock price increase (decrease) because of portfolio rebalancing, then how will changes in the convertible bond price help the manager to gain profit? The profit comes from the convexity of the bond.

Because of the convexity effect, the convertible-bond price will increase more rapidly than the stock price. So the gain from the bond is higher than the loss from the short position. Similarly, because of the convexity effect, the convertible bond price falls more slowly than the stock price decreases. So the loss from the convertible-bond price is smaller than the gain from the short position. In other words, the fund manager gains from movements of the stock in either direction. This explains why the delta-neutral strategy can also be called a *long volatility strategy*.

Gamma Trading

Like the delta-neutral strategy, gamma trading is also dynamic in nature and is long volatility. In fact, gamma trading is an extension of the delta-neutral strategy and is built on top of it. This strategy requires more dynamic trading than delta trading. Gamma measures the rate of change of delta with respect to changes in the underlying stock. Gamma is more sensitive for at-the-money options. The rate of change of delta or gamma increases as the stock value increases. As the gamma increases rapidly, fund managers of the delta-neutral strategy need to short more stocks. This will increase the short-position value by the change in delta times the change in the underlying stock.

Since the convertible-bond market is relatively small, heavy short selling will force the stock prices down. When stock prices revert back to their previous position, for example, the fund manager needs to cover part of the short position because of decrease in delta. Since the fund manager can buy back the stocks at a lower price, he will lock in a profit of the change in delta times the change in the underlying stock. The higher the gamma, the higher the profit for the manager. Since gamma trading requires more frequent trading, the transaction costs will also be higher. Gamma traders prefer to buy at-the-money convertibles near to expiration, as gamma is more pronounced for at-the-money and near-expiration options.

Credit Arbitrage

Because of the embedded option, a convertible bond can fall into four sections of prices, known as deep-out-of-the-money, out-of-the-money, at-the-money, and in-the-money. As described earlier, delta and gamma are higher for at-the-money and in-the-money, which helps the convertible-fund manager profit from volatility trading strategies. For deep-out-of-the-money and out-of-the-money, the convertible bond hits the bond floor, acts more like a straight bond, and may not be useful for volatility arbitrage.

Fund managers employ the credit arbitrage strategy when the convertible bond goes to one of two stages. Convertible bonds deep-out-of-the-money are called *distressed convertibles*, and convertible bonds out-of-the-money are called *busted convertibles*. The issuer is said to be in financial distress in either case, and investors have concerns about payment of scheduled coupons and par value at maturity. At this stage, the bonds are exposed to both credit risk and interest-rate risk. Convertible arbitrage fund managers profit by building credit arbitrage strategies using distressed and busted convertibles.

Distressed and busted convertibles come with a cheap equity option but are exposed to credit risk. Credit-arbitrage managers strip out the fixed-income portion of the convertible and sell it to credit buyers at a discount price, typically entering into an asset-swap agreement. Credit buyers provide the credit arbitrage with the option to repurchase the convertible at a slightly higher price. The difference between the repurchase price and the sale price is the premium that the credit arbitrage manager pays to the credit buyer or protection seller. An asset swap also provides protection against interest-rate risk, as the credit arbitrager no longer needs to worry about interest-rate fluctuations that will impact the bond price.

At a later time, if the credit quality of the issuer improves, then the distressed or busted convertibles will be at-the-money or in-the-money. At this juncture, the credit arbitrage manager buys the convertible back from the credit buyer at a predefined price and either sells it at a premium or converts it into common stock, gaining profit from the strategy.

3.7.4   Bond Strategies

Various arbitrage and non-arbitrage strategies are built with fixed-income securities by using term-structure theories, exploiting market inefficiencies, using forecasting models, and best utilizing the manager's skill level. There are three main term-structure theories:

1. The *pure expectation theory* states that the yield received in long investments is equivalent to the effective yield received by periodically reinvesting using short-term bonds. According to this theory, the rising term structure reflects that the market expects the short-term rates to rise in the future; the declining term structure reflects that the market expects the short-term rates to decrease in the future; and the flat-term structure reflects that the market expects the short-term rates to remain unchanged in the future. For example, if a one-year bond returns yield higher than that of a six-month bond, then investors anticipate that the yield six months from now should be higher than the six-month rate available now.

2. The *liquidity preference theory* states that long-term investments pose a higher interest-rate risk than short-term investments, and therefore long-term bonds are less marketable and less liquid in nature. So investors either prefer short-term bonds or expect sufficient compensation for bearing interest-rate risk and liquidity risk in long-term bonds. As a result, yield premium increases with maturity.

3. The *market segmentation theory* states that the bond market is segmented by maturities, and thus supply and demand are determined by bond maturities. Market inefficiencies also exist, as certain market participants are restricted from investing in noninvestment-grade securities.

Fixed-income strategies can use any of the following securities:

- US Treasury bonds
- corporate bonds
- municipal bonds
- sovereign bonds
- asset-backed securities
- mortgage-backed securities
- fixed-income futures
- fixed-income swaps

- fixed-income options
- credit protection products

Using these theories and securities, fund managers build various arbitrage and non-arbitrage strategies. Arbitrage strategies involve two opposite positions profiting from pricing disparities. Non-arbitrage strategies involve investing using the mean-reversion theory and forecasting models, especially in structured products. Various possible arbitrage and non-arbitrage strategies are described below. While each strategy has its own characteristics, fund managers often employ more than one compatible strategy in a portfolio.

Yield Curve Arbitrage

Yield curve arbitrage strategies employ the analysis of the level, slope, and curvature of yield curve and trading bonds with different maturities and duration. Managers can use the yield curve of the same country or can use two yield curves across two countries.

Butterfly Strategy

This strategy also takes advantage of information that exists in the yield curve. It involves taking one short position and two long positions, one on each side of the short position, or one long position and two short positions, one on each side of the long position.

TED Spread

TED stands for Treasuries over Eurodollars. Yield anomalies often appear between government bonds and the LIBOR rate with the same maturity. Funds profit from the disparity by taking two opposite positions.

On-the-Run versus Off-the-Run

On-the-run bonds are bonds that were recently issued and off-the-run bonds are bonds that were issued in the past. On-the-run issues are more liquid than off-the-run issues, so off-the-run issues require the liquidity premium and therefore are cheaper than on-the-run issues with the same remaining expiration time. Both prices converge to their par value at maturity. Hedge-fund managers take a long position in the off-the run and simultaneously take a short position in on-the-run with the same remaining expiration time as that of off-the-run. At the time of maturity, the hedge-fund manager will have captured profit that is equivalent to the difference between the basis points of the two positions. So the on-the-run versus the off-the-run strategy profits from the noise level in the yield curve rather than from its curvature.

Basis Trade

In Treasury-bond futures contracts, the counterparty has the provision to choose the securities to be delivered from any government bond with more than fifteen years to maturity. This provision reduces the likelihood of market manipulation and produces a large supply of potential bonds that are deliverable on the contract. Fixed-income arbitrage managers profit from this embedded deliverable option on a future contract; technically speaking, the fund managers hold the long position in the delivery option.

Cash received by the short position = QFP × CF + accrued interest

where

QFP = quoted future price
CF = conversion factor set by CBOT for the bond delivered
Cost to purchase the bond = quoted bond price + accrued interest.

Arbitrage managers develop mathematical models that minimize the value of quoted bond price − QFP × CF to determine the cheapest-to-deliver bond. Strategies include

- *structured-products arbitrage*, employed by fund managers when they take a long position in equity tranches of a CDO and a short position in mezzanine or equity tranches or selling a CDS. These strategies' failure during crises is due to the highly correlated nature of the underlying securities.
- *barbell strategy*, a non-arbitrage strategy built on the concept of a core-satellite approach. Fund managers implementing this strategy take a long position in ultra-safe, high-liquid, short-term government bonds as part of their core position and a long position in high-yield, high-risk, long-term bonds. Short-term bonds have lesser duration, and long-term bonds have a higher duration. This strategy does not invest in

intermediate bonds. It employs the principle that extreme shocks do not exist for a long time and things will revert to the normal condition. If the fund can survive the extreme event, the temporary losses in long-term bonds can be recovered by holding the position until recovery happens. Since short-term bonds are safe bonds, it is expected that they won't be affected by extreme events, and after expiration they can be rolled over to take advantage of market conditions that exist at that time.

• *bullet strategy*, a non-arbitrage strategy that, in contrast to the barbell strategy, invests in concentrated intermediate-term bonds by employing forecasting models. Since the duration is proportional to the square of maturity, the effective duration of the bullet strategy is less than that of the barbell strategy.

3.7.5   *Volatility Arbitrage Strategy*

The volatility arbitrage strategy is an actively managed, derivative-based strategy that aims to generate absolute returns. Some volatility arbitrage strategies involve either short-lived positions, which typically range from a few hours to two days, or long-term capital growth, minimizing short-term volatility. The strategies exploit arbitrage opportunities both within equity derivatives and between derivative and equity markets.

Volatility arbitrage strategies are capable of generating returns that are negatively correlated with equity markets in a bear market while producing returns that are positively correlated during a bull market. The special advantage of volatility arbitrage is that, though it can generate returns that are negatively correlated with equity markets, it can also generate returns that are positively correlated with equities during a bull market. As a result, allocation to volatility arbitrage can significantly improve fund performance during periods of high volatility without impacting performance in normal or bull-market conditions. Various sub-strategies involving volatility arbitrage include gamma trading, volatility surface trading, and skewed trading.

Volatility Surface Strategy

Price volatility in option futures can be estimated using either backward- or forward-looking methods. Backward-looking methods forecast future volatility based on statistical measures, such as using time-series models ranging from moving averages to GARCH (generalized autoregressive conditional heteroskedasticity) models. Forward-looking methods estimate future volatility as the implied volatility obtained from observed option premiums by reverse-engineering a theoretical option-pricing model, such as the Black-Scholes model. Forward-looking methods typically yield better predictions of future volatility than backward-looking methods, as it is believed that market prices quickly get adjusted to current market conditions.

The Black-Scholes option-pricing model for European-style options assumes that volatility of the underlying asset, expressed as the standard deviation of its returns, remains constant over the life of the option. However, empirical research shows that the volatility of an asset's returns varies over time. Therefore, implied volatility may be different from real volatility.

A term structure of implied volatility can be plotted, as different implied volatilities are extracted from options with different maturities. Similarly, *volatility smiles* present as different implied volatilities are extracted from options with different strikes. The combination of volatility term structure and volatility smiles, a three-dimensional plot, is called *volatility surface*.

When a volatility smile is detected, the manager buys the cheaper option in the volatility surface that is nearer the money and sells the more expensive option in the volatility surface that is further out of the money on the same underlying asset and the same expiry. This type of spread trade can be constructed using either put or call options. If the manager has a negative view on the underlying market, bear spread would be used—that is, long the put with a high strike and short the put with a low strike. Alternatively, writing a call option with a low strike and buying the long with a higher strike can also execute a bear spread. If the manager is positive on the market, bull spread would be implemented using call options, longing the call with a low strike and shorting the call with a higher strike, or selling the put option with a high strike and buying a put with a low strike.

Another form of surface trading uses term structure according to which options further from expiry are cheaper than those nearer to expiry. In order to profit from this opportunity, the trader can sell near-to-expiry options in volatility terms and buy further-from-expiry options. This is called a *calendar spread*, and the trader aims to profit through time decay.

The third type of surface trading is using both the term structure and the volatility smile. Such a strategy involves taking a long position in an option far from expiry, with a high strike price, and a short position in an option near expiry, with a low strike price.

The above strategies can be implemented to be delta neutral by buying and selling differing amounts of options, because the options for different expiries will have differing deltas on the same futures contract.

4 Market Risk Analytics

Earlier we discussed the way bond prices go down when interest rates go up and vice versa. If we think in a fundamental manner, we can interpret it as investors' ability to buy newly issued bonds that are paying coupons at current interest rates instead of purchasing the bonds issued last year that are paying low coupon. The investors expect to pay lower value to the bond. The percentage of returns on lowered value will be comparable to market interest rates. In terms of financial mathematics, yields are increasing. That means investors expect more returns on bonds because of increased market rates and so prefer to pay less for the bond.

Yields increase strongly if the timing or pace of policy changes surprises investors. A swift rise in bond yields would result in capital losses for investors and other assets. Parties that benefit from increased rates are holders of floating-rate bonds and balance sheets with variable interest-rate loans.

Now we know that the bond price is linked to the market-factor interest rate. We also learned that there is a possibility of loss to the bond portfolio because of fluctuations in market factors. Similarly, other financial instruments or products—such as stocks, foreign exchanges, commodities, and derivatives of these products—react to the market movements.

Therefore, *market risk* can be defined as the risk of financial loss to the portfolio resulting from movements in market prices that in turn are affected by changes in interest rates, foreign exchange rates, commodity prices, equity prices, earning announcements, unemployment rates, gross domestic product, consumer good prices, inflation, and so on. Other forms of financial risk, such as credit and liquidity risks, may also propagate market risk. For example, a downgrading of the credit rating of an issuer could lead to a drop in the market value of securities from that issuer. Likewise, a major sale of a relatively illiquid security by another holder of the same security could depress the price of the security.

On the other hand, perceived market risk can impact liquidity and credit risk. Depending on the asset or security, exposure to other factors may also arise. The firm that is intended to manage market risk should capture all risk factors that it is exposed to, and it must manage these risks soundly.

The goal of market risk analysis is to determine or predict possible deviations from the expected value. If that is the case, why can't we only use standard deviation? Standard deviation does not provide the confidence level. That means there is no guarantee that the standard deviation is an accurate measure. Then what is the alternative? The answer is value-at-risk that can be used to quantify the market risk. Value-at-risk or simply VaR gives the potential loss that can occur in the future at certain confidence level.

Let's say we have a portfolio with several instruments. Each instrument price either increases or decreases at the end of the day. Even if we do not sell that instrument, we can get the price from market data. Based on individual prices, we can calculate the portfolio returns on a daily basis.

Assume we have daily returns for the past thirty days. After arranging them in descending order, we will have both positive and negative values. If there are no negative values at all, that means the portfolio value is rising continually, and there is no loss. If there are negative values, the sum of the bottom 5 percent of the values gives the loss that occurs 5 percent significance level or 95 percent confidence level. Call such a loss amount X. Assuming that the performance of the portfolio will stay at the current pace, we can say that the maximum loss that can occur to the portfolio in next days with a confidence level of 95 percent is X. Here, the X is value-at-risk.

For example, a risk manager tells the portfolio manager that thirty-day VaR for the portfolio is $100 million, with a confidence level of 95 percent. That means the maximum loss does not exceed $100 million in the next thirty days but only with a confidence level of 95 percent. There is a 5 percent chance that the loss can exceed $100 million in the next thirty days. However, the VaR cannot determine the loss that can occur beyond 95 percent confidence level or 5 percent significant level.Low-probability (5 percent of probability in our example) catastrophic occurrence can create a loss that exceeds $100 million.

So what do we need to know about VaR or value-at-risk?

- It denotes the loss that can occur to a portfolio.
- There is a percentage-of-confidence level above which the VaR is not reliable.
- There is a period above which the VaR is not applicable.
- It is appropriate to only that portfolio on which it is calculated.
- It does not indicate the loss that can occur beyond the confidence level.

Is the VaR a final answer? No. It has several shortcomings, and there are alternatives. The purpose of this chapter is to discuss how VaR is measured, what are its variations and alternatives, what are the advanced market risk analysis mechanisms, and how market risk management can be improved.

4.1   VaR Measurement Methodologies

There are three basic methods that are used to compute value-at-risk, though there are numerous variations within each approach. The measure can be computed analytically using parametric methods by making an appropriate assumption about return distributions—that is, if the returns follow normal distribution or lognormal distribution. It can also be estimated by running hypothetical portfolios through historical simulation or from Monte-Carlo simulations.

4.1.1   Parametric Approaches

Under the topic of probability distributions, we learned that the returns under normal circumstances take the bell shape called *normal distribution*. The normal distribution is a two-tailed distribution with a bell shape. Its skew value is 0, kurtosis is 3, and mean = mode = median.

The value of z is used to measure the area of the curve, which is the equivalent probability of an observation or confidence level. A z value of −1.645 gives the probability of 95 percent; in other words, 95 percent of the mass is distributed in the right side of −1.645. Since the normal distribution is symmetric, the same is true for the positive value of 1.654—that is, 95 percent of the mass is distributed to the left of 1.645. Hence, 90 percent of the mass is distributed between –1.645 and 1.645.

Since the standard normal distribution has a mean of 0 and a standard deviation of 1, z is equal to the number of standard deviations below (or above) the mean. In other words, 90 percent of samples lie within 1.645 standard deviations, which indicates a 90-percent confidence interval.

Similarly, we can determine the following:

- 68 percent of samples lie within 1 standard deviation, which indicates a 68 percent confidence interval.
- 95 percent of samples lie within 1.96 standard deviations, which indicates a 95 percent confidence interval.
- 99 percent of samples lie within 2.58 standard deviations, which indicates a 99 percent confidence interval.

The percentage of samples that lie on the left of –1.645 is not enough to calculate the loss amount. We must calculate the area that lies left of –1.645. The area left of –1.645 provides the loss that can occur in the 5 percent probability band and similarly, the area right of 1.645 gives the profit that can occur in the 5 percent probability band. The same concept is applicable to other percentages. The area to the left side of confidence levels indicates the VaR at that confidence level. The z value for any confidence level can be obtained from standard financial calculators.

In reality, the normal distribution may not necessarily be standard normal distribution. The mean can be non-0, and standard deviation can be other than 1. A value from any normal distribution can be transformed into its corresponding value on a standard normal distribution using the following formula:

$$z = \frac{(x - \mu)}{\sigma}$$

where

z = the value on the standard normal distribution
x = the value on the original distribution
μ = the mean of the original distribution
σ = the standard deviation of the original distribution.

The purpose of using the parametric approach is to calculate the area in the loss tails. To calculate the area, we use risk factors like beta, delta, and duration, depending on the underlying assets in the portfolio. For the asset classes that exhibit a normal distribution, the returns are said to be linear with respect to risk factor. For example, duration—which is a risk factor—gives the rate of change of bond price with respect to interest rate. Similarly, beta gives the rate of change of stock price with respect to market index, and delta provides the rate of change of the option price with respect to underlying stock price.

In simple words, if we know that the percent increase in interest can change the bond price by x amount (in case of duration), then we can estimate the change in bond price as a loss or profit to the portfolio manager. This way we can calculate value-at-risk using the risk factors, such as duration, beta, and delta.

The parametric approach is also known as a *linear approach*. The approach is parametric in that it assumes that the probability distribution is normal and then requires calculation of the variance-covariance parameters. The approach is linear in that changes in instrument values are assumed to be linear with respect to changes in risk factors. For example, for bonds, the sensitivity is described by duration, and for options it is described by the Greeks. The assumption that the asset returns are normally distributed provides a straightforward formula to calculate the value-at-risk.

These approaches are called *parametric approaches* because they require parameters, such as mean, standard deviation, and correlation. Historical data is used to measure mean, standard deviations, correlations, and risk factors like beta, delta, duration, and so on. Measuring VaR with normal distribution uses one tail (only the loss part of the tail), so the significance level used in the formula is one-tailed. From the earlier formula we know that

$$z = \frac{(x - \mu)}{\sigma}$$

$$x = z \times \sigma + \mu.$$

In a simplistic form, VaR with normal distribution, or normal VaR, is calculated as follows:

$$VaR_\alpha = (\sigma \times z_\alpha + \mu) \times \text{asset value}$$

where

- σ = standard deviation of asset per holding period in percentage;
- μ = Mean returns for the holding period in percentage;
- α = one-tailed significance, or 1 – α = confidence level; and
- z is a negative value, as the VaR is interested only in the left tail.

If the population mean and standard deviation are not available, the researchers use the sample mean and standard deviation.

VaR with lognormal distribution, or lognormal VaR, is calculated as follows:

$$VaR_\alpha = (1 - e^{\sigma z - \mu}) \times \text{asset value}$$

When the asset exhibits a linear relationship with the risk factor, the VaR is adjusted to the risk factor. The delta-normal method is used to calculate VaR for the options that exhibit a linear relationship. The delta-normal approach requires one additional parameter, which is the delta (Δ). Delta is defined as the rate of change of the option price with respect to the underlying asset price.

$$VaR_\alpha = \Delta \times \sigma \times z_\alpha \times \text{asset value}$$

For instruments that exhibit risk factors like beta and duration, the Δ should be replaced accordingly with that risk factor. The above formula ignores the mean because of its smaller value. If the μ value is significant, then we can use the term $z \times \sigma + \mu$ instead of $z \times \sigma$.

The delta-normal method described above is appropriate when there is only one asset type in a portfolio or the assets are not correlated. That means the simple delta-normal method ignores the diversification benefit. The variance-covariance method, on the other hand, utilizes both the variance and covariance, considering the correlation between assets. Some researchers call the variance-covariance method the *delta-normal method*. Whatever name we give it, the difference between the two approaches (diversified and undiversified) should be noted.

Measuring VaR using the variance-covariance method involves the following steps:

1. Obtain the risk factors.
2. Get the transpose of the risk-factor matrix.

3. Obtain the variance-covariance matrix.
4. Multiply the transpose of the risk-factor matrix with the variance-covariance matrix.
5. Multiply the resultant matrix of the above with the risk-factor matrix.
6. Take the square root of the above value.
7. Multiply the above square root with the z-value of corresponding significance.

Using Δ as an example risk factor, the above steps can be expressed mathematically as follows:

$$VaR_\alpha = Z_\alpha * \sqrt{(\Delta T \Omega \Delta)} * portfolio\, value$$

where

Δ = Risk factor matrix
Ω = Variance-covariance matrix.

Advantages of Parametric Approaches

- It is typically many times faster to calculate parametric VaR compared with Monte Carlo or historical simulation.
- They are simple to implement.

Disadvantages of Parametric Approaches

- They gives a poor description of nonlinear risks.
- If conditional returns are not normally distributed, the computed VaR will understate the true VaR. In other words, if there are far more outliers in the actual return distribution than would be expected given the normality assumption, the actual VaR will be much higher than the computed VaR. In reality, the risk-factor distributions have high kurtosis, with more extreme events than would be predicted by a normal distribution.
- Even if the standardized return distribution assumption holds up, the VaR can still be wrong if the variances and covariances that are used to estimate it are incorrect. To the extent that these numbers are estimated using historical data, there is a standard error associated with each of the estimates. In other words, the variance-covariance

matrix that is input to the VaR measure is a collection of estimates, some of which have very large error terms.

- A related problem occurs when the variances and covariances across assets change over time. This non-stationary behavior in values is not uncommon because the fundamentals driving these numbers do change over time. For example, the correlation between the US dollar and the Japanese yen may change if oil prices increase by 15 percent. This, in turn, can lead to a breakdown in the computed VaR.

4.1.2   *Historical Simulation Approaches*

Historical simulation approaches are called *nonparametric approaches*. The parametric approaches assume that the returns are distributed normally or lognormally. In reality, most assets do not follow the normal distribution. Historical simulation makes an assumption that near-future returns will likely follow the pattern of most-recent returns.

The historical simulation methodology uses past performance. *Performance* means both profit and loss. It makes the assumption that the past is a good indicator of the near future. In other words, the recent past will reproduce itself in the near future. It gets the profit/loss for longer historical time if available.

Using historical simulations to find VaR requires a long history of returns in order to get a meaningful result. Computing VaR on a portfolio with only a year of return history will not provide a good VaR estimate. Assume, for example, that we have historical returns for the past two years for various asset types. We get about 504 records for two years (trading years will have about 252 trading days) for each asset type. However, the assets in the portfolio change every day. We will need to simulate the existing portfolio value by applying the collected historical-asset returns to each of the assets in the portfolio, assuming that the portfolio exists for the past two years.

Now we get a new set of returns for our portfolio. We rank the historical data in the order of returns and then separate the bottom x percent of samples. The variable x is the significance level at which VaR is being calculated. For example, if there are a hundred samples in the data, then the bottom five values are separated from the list after being ranked in descending order, and the top value in the separated list—the cutoff point—is used to calculate the VaR.

One basic assumption that traditional historical simulation makes is that the future returns pattern will likely follow the historical return pattern, and therefore equal weight is placed on all returns. However, the past influential things that contributed to the profit and loss don't hold true today. Therefore, it is necessary to give less weight to older returns and give more weight to more recent returns.

There are several methods that adjust the series of historical returns. Three such methods are described below.

Age-Weighted Historical Simulation

The age-weighted simulation weighs the recent observations more and distant observations less. Let us assume w1 is the weight given to a one-day-old observation. All subsequent past observation is decayed using the parameter λ..

So the weight of a two-days-old observation is λw1, the weight of a three-days-observation isλ^2w1, and so on. Since λ is a fraction, the square of λ is smaller than λ and so on. The weight of an i-days-old observation is λ^{i-1}w1.

Since all the weights must sum to 1,

$$\lambda w1 + \lambda^2 w1 + \ldots + \lambda^{i-1} w1 = 1$$

$$w1(\lambda + \lambda^2 + \ldots + \lambda^{i-1}) = 1$$

$$w1 = \frac{1-\lambda}{1-\lambda^n}$$

$$w(i) = \lambda^{i-1}\frac{1-\lambda}{1-\lambda^n}$$

The main goal of the decay parameter is to reduce the impact of ghost effects that may not reoccur.

Volatility-Weighted Historical Simulation

The volatility-weighted historical simulation approach weighs the observation by volatility rather than the age. Let us assume R_{ti} is the actual return for asset i on day t, σ_{ti} is the volatility forecast for asset i on day t, and σ_{Ti} is the current forecast of volatility for asset i. The volatility-adjusted return is given by

$$R_{ti}^* = \frac{\sigma_{Ti}}{\sigma_{ti}} R_{ti}$$

Thus, the volatility-adjusted return, R^*_{ti}, is replaced by a larger value if the current forecasted volatility exceeds the previous forecasted volatility, and similarly by a smaller value if the current forecasted volatility is below the previous forecasted volatility. The volatility-weighted historical simulation approach allows the current forecasted VaR to be more sensitive to current market conditions.

Filtered Historical Simulation

Empirical evidence suggests that negative shocks increase market volatility more than positive shocks of the same magnitude, a phenomenon that has been called *asymmetric volatility*. Therefore, the traditional historical simulation method may not be efficient during asymmetric volatility periods. The filtered historical simulation method refines the basic historical simulation by using standardized residuals from a time-varying volatility model. Because the standardized residuals are likely to be independent and identically distributed, they are ideally suited for bootstrapping. Second, filtered historical simulation uses Hull and White's volatility updating so that increases in volatility during the risk-measurement period affect the risk measures themselves. Thus, the method contains both the advantages of the basic historical simulation method and sophisticated volatility models like GARCH.

Advantages of Historical Simulation Approaches

- They are intuitive and often computationally simple.
- Since they do not depend on the assumption of distribution, they can accommodate fat tails, skewness, and any other non-normal features that can underestimate the actual VaR.
- They avoid complex variance-covariance matrices.
- They use data that is often readily available either in-house or from vendors.
- Historical simulation approaches can be modified to allow a weighting scheme either by age or volatility.
- There is no need to calculate the correlations.
- There is no need to assume they are joint-normal with stable correlation.
- Empirical evidence suggests that the historical simulation works quite well.

Disadvantages of Historical Simulation Approaches

- Quiet periods may underestimate VaR and expected shortfall.
- Volatile periods may overestimate VaR and expected shortfall.

- It is difficult to detect structural/regime shifts in the data.
- They ignore plausible extreme events if they do not occur in the past.
- New financial instruments and markets may not have enough data.

4.1.3   Monte Carlo Simulation

The VaR measurement methodologies described thus far possess several disadvantages. The delta-normal method does not work well for complex instruments, such as exotic options. Historical simulation methods do not work well if there is not enough data available. To overcome these issues, researchers use the Monte Carlo simulation approach. This process is both parametric and a full valuation model, and it is tailor-made for this purpose.

This process involves five basic steps:

1. Specify the stochastic process and parameters—for example, Brownian motion.
2. Simulate a large number of outcomes based on assumptions.
3. Calculate the value of the asset for each outcome.
4. Run several iterations of steps 2 and 3. The more the iterations, the higher the accuracy. The number of iterations ranges from five thousand to a few hundred thousand.
5. Rank the asset values. The VaR at alpha percent of significance level corresponds to the cutoff value at alpha percent of the calculated values.

Monte Carlo simulation techniques are the most flexible and powerful, since they are able to take into account all nonlinearity of the portfolio value with respect to its underlying risk factor and to incorporate all desirable distributional properties, such as fat tails and time-varying volatilities. Also, Monte Carlo simulations can be extended to apply over longer holding periods. However, these techniques are also by far the most expensive computationally.

Advantages of Monte Carlo Simulation

- descriptive for both linear and nonlinear risks
- can include time-decay factor
- flexible and extensible to other risk factors
- produces perfect distribution using an unlimited number of scenarios

Disadvantages of Monte-Carlo Simulation

- slow process
- intellectual and technical expertise is required
- subject to model risk of the stochastic process chosen
- subject to sampling error at lower number of simulations

4.2   *Application of VaR Models to Various Portfolios*

VaR will change each time the positions are changed in a portfolio. Portfolio managers would like to know which position should be altered in order to achieve the desired level of VaR or what will be a change in VaR if a particular position is added or subtracted. There are three tools available to address these issues: marginal VaR, incremental VaR, and component VaR.

4.2.1   *Marginal VaR*

Marginal VaR provides the per-unit change in a portfolio VaR with respect to additional investment in a portfolio. That is, the marginal VaR is the partial derivative of the portfolio VaR with respect to the position. The marginal VaR of asset i in a portfolio P is given by the following equation:

$$MVaR_i = \frac{VaR_p}{P}\beta_i$$

where β_i is the risk factor of asset i and VaR_p is the value-at-risk of the portfolio

If the portfolio manager wants to reduce the portfolio value by x amount, then the manager should rank all marginal VaRs and pick the asset with the highest marginal VaR. Similarly, if the portfolio manager wants to increase the portfolio value by x amount but not add new instruments, the manager should choose the asset with the lowest marginal VaR.

4.2.2   *Incremental VaR*

While marginal VaR gives the impact of changing an existing position on the portfolio VaR, incremental VaR gives the change in VaR from the addition or deletion of an entire position in a portfolio. Thus, the incremental VaR is the difference between the portfolio VaR after adding/deleting the position and the VaR before adding/deleting the position. For accurate measurement of the incremental VaR, it is necessary to reevaluate the portfolio fully. Since the full revaluation of VaR is a complex process and time-consuming, for small changes to a portfolio, the incremental VaR may be calculated approximately by using the variance-covariance matrix.

The portfolio manager will need to consider the tradeoff between accuracy and faster computation. Since most arbitrage opportunities exist for a very short time, and since the number of calculations in full revaluation increases with the square of the risk factors, the shortcut method provides a good approximation of a large portfolio, where a proposed trade is likely to be small relative to the entire portfolio.

4.2.3   Component VaR

The component VaR of an asset i is the amount of risk that the asset contributes to the portfolio of assets N. Because of the diversification effect, it is generally less than the individual VaR of that asset.

Mathematically, component VaR is the marginal VaR multiplied by the dollar weight in position i:

$$\text{Component VaR} = \text{MVaR} \times wi \times P$$

From the equation of the marginal VaR, it is known that $\text{MVaR} \times P$ is equivalent to the portfolio VaR × beta of the asset. Therefore,

$$\text{Component VaR} = \text{portfolio VaR} \times \beta i \times wi.$$

Component VaR can be used to break down the risk contributions of the portfolio by a desired criterion, such as by type of currency, class of asset, geography of an asset, or even business unit.

4.2.4   Annualizing the VaR

Normal value-at-risk at an α of significance is defined as

$$\text{VaR}_\alpha = (\sigma \times z_\alpha + \mu) \times \text{asset value}.$$

If the VaR is calculated on a daily basis and returns are assumed to be normally distributed, then the mean will be assumed to be zero. Therefore,

$$\text{VaR}_\alpha = \tau \times z_\alpha \times \text{asset value}.$$

In this case, the annual VaR can be calculated as

$$Daily\ VaR * \sqrt{250}$$

where the number 250 represents the number of trading days in a year. However, the above approximation does not hold true in the following cases:

- When the returns are auto-correlated
- When the mean is not zero

When the mean is not zero, the annual mean is calculated by multiplying the daily VaR by 250, whereas the standard deviation is calculated by multiplying with the square root of 250. Therefore, the VaR approximation using the square root of the time-period rule will be biased and overestimate the actual value-at-risk. This is because the higher positive mean and negative z value should reduce the actual VaR by a higher value. The actual value-at-risk is

$$VaR_a = (\sigma \times z_a + \mu) \times asset\ value.$$

Though a one-year (or 250-day) horizon was used above as an example, the same error is applicable for any time horizon. Therefore, it would be more accurate to calculate the direct annual VaR instead of using the square root of time rule.

However, for some securities that are newly issued, the data may not be available for longer periods. In that case, risk managers should make subjective decisions when using short-term VaR to measure long-term VaR. The significance error increases with the time horizon chosen. The square root of time rule may be approximate for three months but will over-penalize the fund for long time periods.

4.3   Advantages and Shortcomings of Value-at-Risk

4.3.1   Coherent Risk Measures

In order to measure and understand the risk involved in any event, it is necessary to find out if the risk-quantification method is meeting coherent risk measures. The following are coherent risk measures:

1. *Translation invariance.* The risk of a portfolio is dependent on individual assets. If a deterministic quantity of I is added to a portfolio with a quantified loss of rho (R), then the resulting loss will be rho (R) – I. Similarly, if the same quantity is subtracted, the resulting loss will be rho (R) + I.
2. *Subadditivity.* Subadditivity reflects the idea that the total risk of a portfolio can be reduced by diversification and makes decentralization of risk management possible. Thus, the total risk of a portfolio is at most equal to the sum of the risks of the individual assets. Rho (R1+R2) <= rho (R1) + rho (R2).
3. *Positive homogeneity.* The risk of a portfolio will increase with its size. For a constant value of X, the risk of a portfolio with XR events, rho (XR) = X × rho (R).
4. *Monotonicity.* A portfolio with higher potential returns will likely have less risk. For R1 >= R2, rho (R1) <= rho (R2).

4.3.2   Disadvantages and Alternatives

VaR does not meet all of the coherent measures. It meets at most only three of the coherent risk measures—that is, VaR is translation invariant, positive homogeneous, and monotone. VaR is not generally subadditive. VaR is subadditive only if the portfolio returns are linear and the risk-return distribution follows a normal or elliptical distribution. Most portfolios in alternative investments contain options or events that cause the distribution to be skewed. Therefore, VaR is not subadditive in this case.

Alternative: Expected shortfall or expected tail loss or conditional tail can be used, all of which meet the subadditive measure.

VaR assumes a normal distribution of returns. Calculation of the confidence level assumes a normal distribution. But most alternative investment returns are not normal and contain fat tails. Some extreme events, such as the short volatility risk of short options, can lead to fat tails.

Alternative: The extreme value theory is used to measure VaR for non-normal distributions.

The VaR measure gives a maximum loss level at a given confidence level. It does not tell what the loss will be beyond the given confidence level.

Alternative: Expected shortfall.

VaR assumes the portfolio position is constant over time. However, trading positions change frequently, and the VaR will need to be revalued. Revaluing VaR is complex and time-consuming.

Alternatives: As an alternative to revaluation of VaR, marginal VaR, incremental VaR, and component VaR can be used in order to determine the possible change of VaR due to a change in positions.

VaR methodologies assume the database with historical information is large enough. Because of the nature of products and continuous evolution of new ones, there may not be enough historical information.

Alternative: If historical information on a particular financial instrument is not available, then the instruments are mapped to known instruments. This process is called the *mapping method.*

VaR models do not work efficiently in contagion markets, where correlations are broken. And VaR models are also not good if strategic risks are significant.

4.4   *Alternatives to Value-at-Risk Models*

As described earlier, the VaR process has some disadvantages, such as the assumption of a normal distribution, market conditions that are not always normal, and VaR that does not meet the subadditive property. VaR does not give the losses that can exceed the confidence level. Moreover, VaR should never be used as the sole measure of risk. Instead, it must be used in conjunction with other risk measures, such as conditional VaR, tail analysis, stress tests, and measures of exposure to risk factors and to issuers.

While VaR provides useful risk information under normal market conditions, in stressed markets its usefulness relative to these other risk measures should be expected to reduce. However, this is not to suggest discarding VaR models in such times; rather, risk management practices should continue to consider VaR, but with due adjustment for current conditions. Let's discuss few alternatives or supplements to VaR models.

4.4.1   *Conditional VaR (ETL and ES)*

Expected tail loss (ETL) and expected shortfall (ES), known as conditional VaRs, address some of the VaR drawbacks. The assumption of a normal distribution underestimates extreme losses and fails to capture skewness and kurtosis. For example, a portfolio manager who writes options receives the option premium. If asset prices move as expected and options expire worthlessly, then the manager will keep the premium, profiting from the strategy. However, in unfavorable price movements, the losses will be extreme. This is called *short volatility risk,* and it is one of the sources of fat tails in the return distribution.

Since the traditional VaR measurement does not consider kurtosis and skewness, the actual VaR is underestimated. ETL is simply the average of losses larger than VaR. This VaR acts as a benchmark for ETL. ETL is not a substitute for VaR; it only supplements VaR.

The following are attractive properties of ETL:

- It reveals the loss hidden in tails.
- It gives the losses beyond the VaR.
- It is subadditive.
- It is risk averse.
- It is very useful for scenario-based portfolio optimization.

Although it has numerous advantages, ETL is not yet a popular risk measure for the financial industry, whereas it is widely used in the insurance industry. Because of the nature of certain illiquid assets, it is very much required to adopt the expected tail loss in measuring risk.

If the value-at-risk used in ETL is measured relative to the benchmark, it is called the *expected shortfall.* ES is the same as ETS except that it measures the average of relative VaRs beyond the confidence level.

4.4.2   Extreme Value Theory

ETL and ES overcome some of the disadvantages of traditional VaR, but they are still based on a central-limit theorem with certain assumptions about the changes to the shape of the normal distribution by considering skewness and kurtosis. In reality, extreme events may cause a complete deviation of normal distribution. Extreme values of the distribution are important for proper risk management, as they are associated with extreme events, such as large market declines, market crashes, the failure of major financial institutions, the outbreak of political crises, and natural disasters. The challenge of analyzing and modeling extreme events is that only a few extreme events occurred in the past and there is a range of extreme events that have yet to occur.

One solution to this problem is to use stress tests and scenario analysis. These can simulate the changes in the value of the portfolio under hypothesized extreme market conditions. While these are certainly very useful, they are inevitably limited, as it is not possible to explore all possible scenarios. Extreme value theory (EVT), a special branch of statistics, attempts to make the best possible use of a limited amount of information about the extremes of the distribution and draw meaningful conclusions. EVT applies only to the tails and is inaccurate for the center of the distribution. The two parameters that play important roles in EVT are scale (beta) and shape (epsilon).

According to the Fisher-Tippett theorem, as the sample size gets larger, the distribution of tail converges to the generalized extreme value (GEV) distribution. The shape parameters determine the speed at which the tail disappears. Depending on the shape of epsilon, the GEV takes three forms of distribution:

1. *Frechet distribution,* a shape parameter of greater than 0 that indicates heavy tails
2. *Gumbel distribution*, a shape parameter of 0 that indicates light tails
3. *Weibull distribution,* a shape parameter of less than 0 that indicates very thin tails.

The peaks over threshold (POT) approach, a special application of EVT, is used to analyze the tail distribution over a high threshold. Instead of analyzing the entire data in tails, the POT limits the analysis to maximum and minimum ranges by setting a threshold.

VaR calculated from EVT will be higher than historical-simulation VaR and normal VaR, especially at high confidence levels, proving the assumption of normality or lack of sufficient past events can lead to underestimation of risks.

EVT has several advantages over traditional parametric and nonparametric VaR approaches. In the parametric approach, because of the assumption of normality, most observations lie close to the center of distribution, whereas tail observations are more important for VaR calculation. Nonparametric or historical simulation approaches estimate VaR by using a histogram of returns. However, the histogram may not contain events that have yet to occur.

4.4.3　VaR with Cornish-Fisher Formula

Return distributions of certain asset classes exhibit close to normal distribution. Such a distribution is not completely away from normal but deviates slightly with skewness. The Cornish-Fisher expansion is a formula for approximating the VaR for such a distribution. It provides an adjusted z-score based on the value of skewness:

$$\text{Adjusted } z = z + \tfrac{1}{6} \times (z^2 - 1) \times \text{skewness}$$

Since the VaR is only interested in the left tail, the z-score is negative. Therefore, it is necessary to use the negative value of the z-score in the above formula.

The negative sign of the z-score and skewness magnifies the adjusted z-score, which in turn increases the VaR. Thus, the normal VaR, which is underestimated for skewed tail distribution, can be adjusted using the Cornish-Fisher formula:

$$\text{Adjusted VaR} = \text{adjusted z-score} \times \text{standard deviation.}$$

4.4.4　VaR for Leptokurtic Distribution

Depending on the level of confidence, the VaR will be either underestimated or overestimated for leptokurtic distribution, as there is a higher probability of mass distribution in fat tails. For a lower confidence level (such as 95 percent), the normal assumption can overestimate VaR if the actual distribution is leptokurtic. On the other hand, for a higher confidence level (say 99.5 percent), the normal assumption underestimates the actual VaR if the distribution is leptokurtic. The underestimation or overestimation depends on the value of excess kurtosis or fatness of the tails.

One approximate distribution for fat-tail distribution is student's t-distribution.

$$\text{Let V} = \text{the degrees of freedom.}$$

$$Student'st - distribution = \mu + t_a * \sqrt{\frac{-v - 2}{v}} * \sigma$$

As the number of samples increases, the VaR with student's t-distribution approaches that of the normal distribution.

4.5   Scenario Analysis and Stress Testing

As we discussed earlier, VaR does not tell the worst-case loss beyond a certain confidence level. It can only predict the maximum loss over a specified horizon at a given confidence level. A stress test can help to gauge the worst-case loss. However, a stress test cannot be viewed as a substitute for VaR; instead, it is used as a supplement. A scenario analysis involves estimating the loss from extreme movements. A combination of stress testing and scenario analysis provides intuitive feedback regarding the extreme loss that can occur to the portfolio. In other words, stress testing is useful to explain how VaR can change in various sorts of scenarios, such as extreme market moves, abnormal events, and distress conditions.

In abnormal circumstances, unrelated markets can become linked quickly, and correlation breakdown occurs. Hedging mechanisms will not work, and orderly execution will become difficult. Markets will experience sudden drops in liquidity. The need for funds may result in selling liquid assets, leaving concentrated illiquid portfolios.

Over the last century, markets have seen several abnormalities. The following are various extreme market movements in the recent past:

- 1987—Stock-market crash. Dow Jones Industrial Average (DJIA) fell 23 percent in a single day and caused contagion effects.
- 1990—Nikkei crash. Nikkei fell 48 percent over the year.
- 1992—European currency crisis. The European Rate Mechanism (ERM) prescribed set of currency bands broke down.
- 1994—US federal funds' short-term target rate was raised.
- 1997—Asian crisis. The Thai baht fell 16 percent on July 2, 1997, leading to contagion risk.
- 1998—Russian crisis. Russia defaulted on its internal government debt, and as a result, the Russian ruble fell 41 percent from August 25, 1998, to August 27, 1998, with a one-day fall of 29 percent on August 27, 1998.
- 1998—Failure of Long-Term Capital Management
- 1999—Brazil crisis
- 2001—Internet bubble was burst.
- 2007–2008—Global financial crisis

A stress test involves both qualitative and quantitative analysis, and firms perform stress testing based on the characteristics of the investments. Regardless of the nature of the investment, the following are the most common scenarios for stress testing:

- *Historical event analysis.* This involves simulating past events, such as the 1987 Dow Jones crash, and calculating the worst loss that could happen to the present portfolio.
- *Tuning historical events.* The above is repeated, but updating the events for current conditions.
- *Portfolio-specific analysis.* Identify scenarios based on the portfolio and identify vulnerabilities and worst-case loss events specific to the portfolio.
- *Extreme standard-deviation analysis.* Measure the portfolio value for the extreme moves of standard deviation, such as –2, –3, –4, and –5.
- *Parallel shifts in the yield curve.* Calculate the interest-rate risk and portfolio result of a 1 percent shift in the yield curve.
- *Yield curve twists.* Identify the impact of changes in the shape of the curve.
- *Price jumps.* Evaluate the impact of price jumps in equities, commodities, and other asset classes, such as real estate, and their impact on the portfolio.
- *Currency devaluations.* Estimate the impact to the portfolio of currency devaluations and the effect on related markets and currencies.
- *Liquidity.* Test what happens when market liquidity dries up so that hedging techniques no longer work.
- *Contagion.* Evaluate the portfolio impact of all positions and markets moving in the wrong direction.
- *Modifying covariance matrix.* As the correlation changes dramatically during abnormal markets, it is helpful to modify the correlations in the covariance matrix and recalculate the portfolio risk. In this approach, first change the correlations of assets for which the underlying returns on any two factors change relative to each other and then find out how the correlations of other assets change with respect to the change. The correlation modification method involves both quantitative and qualitative judgments.
- *Sensitivity analysis.* Find the uncertainty in the output of the model and different sources of uncertainty in the model input.
- *Factor-push method.* This method involves pushing each risk factor in a direction that results in a loss for the portfolio.
- *Prospective scenarios.* Based on subjective analysis and experience, hypothetical and reasonable events that have not yet occurred should be predicted and applied to portfolio risk analysis.

• *Extreme value theory.* The theory applies to extreme observations in the sample.

4.6 Regime-Switching Analysis

Many quantitative models, such as the Black-Scholes model and the Markowitz mean-variance portfolio optimization model, assume that returns follow a normal distribution. Events like financial crises typically lead to dramatic breaks in time-series data. Many economic variables behave quite differently during economic downturns than their long-run tendency. As a result, the returns appear non-normal. Although the time-series data of longer periods appear non-normal, they may sometimes exhibit local normal distributions, meaning portions of time-series data appear normal. The time-variation in a normal distribution is often referred to as *regime switching*.

The concept of regime switching is not necessarily restricted to normal data appearing non-normal. It is applicable to any time-series data that behaves abnormal based on what it used to be. For example, a right-skewed distribution may suddenly exhibit normal distribution, which is not a favor for the investors. Certain types of investments exhibit right-skewed normal distribution, meaning they fetch unexpected positive returns from time to time. But because of a breakdown in relationships, among other economic factors, they may suddenly start showing normal distribution or left-skewed normal distribution behaving in a way that investor did not expect.

The concept of regime switching is not necessarily restricted to returns. It can be applicable to interest rates or currencies as well.

Because of regime switching, quantitative models start behaving differently. While several researchers developed models to detect regime switching, there are not any models to predict it. The difference between detection and prediction is that detection involves utilization of historical time-series data to find out irregular relationships; prediction involves forecasting the possibility of breakdown in relationships—among other factors used in the model—while continuously detecting the regime switching.

4.6.1 Regime-Switching Models

Regime-switching models are time-series models in which parameters are allowed to take on different values in each of some fixed number of regimes.

A stochastic process assumed to have generated the regime shifts is included as part of the model, which allows for model-based forecasts that incorporate the possibility of future regime shifts. In certain special situations, the regime in operation at any point in time is directly observable. More generally, the regime is unobserved, and the researcher must conduct inference about which regime the process was in at past point in time.

Regime-switching models have become an enormously popular modeling tool for applied work. Of particular note are regime-switching models of measures of economic output, such as real gross domestic product, which have been used to model and identify the phases of the business cycle. A sampling of other applications includes modeling regime shifts in inflation and interest rates, high and low volatility regimes in equity returns, shifts in policy rules, and time variation in the response of economic output to monitor policy actions.

There is substantial interest in modeling the dynamic behavior of macroeconomics and financial quantities observed over time. A challenge for this analysis is that these time series likely undergo changes in their behavior over reasonably long sample periods. This change may occur in the form of a structural break in which there is a shift in the behavior of the time series due to some permanent change in the economy's structure. Alternatively, the change in behaviors might be temporary, as in the case of wars or pathological macroeconomic episodes like economic depressions, hyperinflations, or financial crises. Finally, such shifts might be both temporary and recurrent, in that the behavior of the time series might cycle between regimes.

4.7 Valuation Models

Probability, calculus, and stochastic calculus have been used widely in evaluating securities and quantifying risk. Based on the output, the buyers or sellers determine the fair value of the security. While quantitative finance is useful for pricing and risk management, it cannot be the only factor used. Let's look at an example in which quantitative techniques are used and see why they fail or failed.

Probability is widely used in collateralized debt obligations. CDOs collect the payments from a pool of loans. Payments include both principal and interest. The payments are divided into three sections. Each section is divided into multiple securities with a face value of $100 or so. Such a mechanism is called *tranchization*.

The buyers of securities receive periodic coupons, and in the end they receive principal. For whatever reason, if the payments received by the pool are not enough to cover, then the bottom tranche of CDOs are first affected. The payments are first distributed to top tranche and then to middle or mezzanine and then to the bottom tranche. Therefore, regardless of the qualities of the underlying loans, the top tranche is considered as high-graded securities.

Because of the risk of receiving lower or no payments, the securities in the bottom tranche are available at a discount. The bottom tranches are called *risky* or *high-yield tranches.*

Here the complexity lies in valuating these securities. Since there is a chance of losing money because of the default in underlying loans, there is chance in losing the money in securities. The buyers of the securities do not know the characteristics of the underlying loans. Therefore, they won't be able to calculate the probability of default of such loans.

The probability of default of a security (not the underlying loan) is calculated as follows:

1. Collect the history of all CDO securities for the available period.
2. Find out how each of those is rated.
3. Segment the securities based on rating and year of rating.
4. Find out how many of the securities in each rating category defaulted or downgraded in the next year.
5. Based on the survival rate and the downgraded rate, calculate the percent of default of each rating category.
6. Calculate the probability of default of each security.

This is a complex mechanism. The fundamental flaw is that the model assumes the conditions applicable to past years will stay the same, and therefore applies the same probability of default to the future. The model ignores the information of the underlying loans. If the characteristics of all the loans are the same and there is a chance of a borrower defaulting, then the same reason is applicable to all the loans. And there is high probability that all the loans will default. Regardless of the seniority of the tranche, whether it is senior or mezzanine or equity tranche, all the securities can default. If there is no problem, the owners of all tranches of securities receive payments. If there is a problem, all the owners lose the money. The concept of seniority does not work.

The most complex quantitative models treat CDO equity and senior tranches as corporate equity and debt structure and calculate the default probability based on the approach as equity level to debt level. What is ignored here are the details of the loans. For example, if the loan was issued when the interest rates were high, borrowers tend to refinance when interest declines. Such loans do not come back to the same pool. The owners of the securities are paid their principal early, and they will end up investing at lower interest rates. The model does not consider the econometrics.

From the above analysis, we can say that there was enough information about the underlying loans that was not maintained and used. There is no mechanism for using such information even if it was collected. Instead, easily computerized though complex models were used.

4.8 Correlation Risk

Several hedge funds, which are classified as pair trading funds, rely on a correlation coefficient to manage risk and achieve consistent returns. The correlation coefficient is calculated based on historical data and used to observe the relationship between the historical performance of instruments or products. The observed relationship is assumed to continue into the future and applied in structuring investment strategies. However, the quantitative measure does not explain why those instruments are related. The correlation coefficient ignores the underlying fundamentals of the investments. Since it does not know why they are related, it won't be able to guarantee that the relationship will continue into the future.

There are situations where the expected correlation was broken in the past, leading to failure of investment strategies. *Correlation risk* refers to the risk of a loss when correlations in the market change. It plays a central role in risk management and the pricing of a single, paired, or portfolio of assets. Under stressed market conditions, correlation breakdown and divergence occur. Two uncorrelated asset classes may become correlated, and two oppositely correlated asset classes may tend to move in the same direction. This is partly because investors become risk averse during stressed markets and may even prefer to forgo profit opportunities.

For example, historically, commodities are negatively correlated with stocks and bonds or positively correlated with inflation. This was true even during the first half of 2008: when bonds were falling off, commodities were rising.

However, with the collapse of Lehman Brothers, more investors—including commodity investors—moved to risk-free assets, such as Treasuries. Since the market was facing a lack of investor base, commodity prices started falling off in correlation with bonds and stocks. This was mainly due to the fact that the same class of investors started investing in multiple and heterogeneous asset classes. For example, institutional investors now invest in both capital markets and commodity markets. When the investor faces losses in capital markets, he may be forced to sell even profitable and uncorrelated asset classes, such as commodities, in order to meet margin calls on capital markets. This will result in the breakdown of traditional relationships, and negative correlation will become positive correlation.

The important component of fluctuations in correlations is linked to liquidity risk. Market liquidity risk, funding liquidity risk, and correlation risk are all interrelated in a nonlinear fashion, with the same underlying asset return uncertainty. These relationships between different dimensions of liquidity risk and the seemingly unrelated correlation and asset return risks have important implications on hedging strategies.

Correlations work as expected, at least to some extent, in a normal market. This is because more lenders are ready to lend money and more investors are ready to borrow and participate in the market. In stressed markets, fewer lenders will be ready to lend money. Moreover, lenders try to withdraw loans. As a result, investors sell both performing and nonperforming assets. This results in reduced market participation and increases the correlation among asset prices. Therefore, the correlation risk is directly proportional to liquidity and is procyclical.

Correlation was one of the biggest risks that CDO investments faced during the financial crisis. One of the determinant factors of credit quality of the tranches is the estimation of correlation of defaults in the asset pool. Lower default correlations will result in higher quality for senior tranches. At the beginning of and during the financial crisis of 2008, the default correlations increased dramatically above what was estimated. Some of the reasons for increased default correlations were common vintage year and credit-quality characteristics of the underlying assets in the pool. The increased correlations resulted in large losses even to the senior tranches.

4.8.1   Correlation Breakdown in Commodities

Historically, commodity prices were negatively correlated to the prices of stocks and bonds. This was because when corporations start seeing significant returns, stock prices go up. Increased corporate returns result in increased employment opportunities, which in turn result in increased household income and inflation.

While the increased prices of raw materials and inflation cause corporate profits to pull down, commodities remain on the rise because of a lag between the unemployment rate and the fall of the stock market. To hedge against inflation, investors used to look for commodity investments. But that trend is changing. Because of the increased complexity of the economic system and increased participation, historical relations start breaking down.

If we observe the relationship between oil and the stock market in 2008, it is apparent that both commodities and the stock market trended downward simultaneously. This was against the historical economic theory that the stock market and commodities are negatively correlated. Let's examine the behavior of the oil market and causes for this unexpected change in correlation.

United States Oil Fund LP (USO), an exchange-traded fund (ETF), doubled between September 14, 2007, and July 11, 2008—from $60 to $120. While the increased demand came from the growth of emerging markets, two events were particularly influential:

- On May 12, 2008, a 7.9-magnitude earthquake hit Sichuan, a province in the western region of China, causing massive power outages. Firms had to use diesel-based generators to continue their business or manufacturing operations. This led to a rapid spike in diesel fuel, which in turn increased the prices of other oil products worldwide.
- China had built massive infrastructure to host the 2008 Olympics, boosting an already existing construction boom. In order to meet the demand, China had to import large quantities of construction materials. This increased the shipping traffic. China also stockpiled oil products as a precautionary measure.

These two factors increased demand for oil products, which was already following a rising curve because of the growth of other emerging markets.

Since many commodities transact over-the-counter, there was not enough transparency to ascertain the influence of the oil positions held by China. After the Olympics, Chinese companies started liquidating the piled positions and thus became a net exporter of oil products. This triggered a downward movement of oil prices. The crash of Fannie Mae and Freddie Mac in August

2008 and Lehman's bankruptcy filing in September 2008 further intensified the downward pressure on oil prices.

Traditionally, the buyers of commodities were regular consumers, such as industries and retail distributors. But recently, the investment style of commodities changed. Because of the increased availability of derivatives and ETFs, investment firms also started investing in commodities. So the parties that invest in stocks and bonds also started investing in commodities. When the crash of stock and bond market in September 2008 required investors to meet margin demands, they liquidated commodity positions to meet the margin demands of traditional investments.

So both traditional instruments (such as stocks and bonds) and commodities started falling together. At this point, it was said to be a phenomenon of correlation breakdown, as historical negative correlation between stocks and commodities did not repeat.

4.9   Sources of Market Risk: Macroeconomic Factors

Measuring and quantifying market risk is not enough to protect you from market fluctuations. Continuous monitoring of underlying sources that cause market fluctuations is required. While there are several factors that affect the overall market, the major sources are macroeconometrics, commodity-price risk, interest-rate risk, foreign-exchange risk, and equity price risk. Not surprisingly, all these sources are interconnected.

Macroeconometrics refers to the aggregation of micro or individual-level economic parameters and modeling the relationships and interactions among them.For example, *household savings* refers to the process that an individual uses to decide how much to save out of current income, whereas per capita savings, which is a macro-level parameter, depends on several other individual economic agents, such as employment rates, export and import level, local infrastructure, and rain conditions. At a microeconomic level, individuals are different from one another in terms of their needs and opportunities, where the macro level considers how these individual behaviors are related and impact each other.

Understanding economic aggregation is very much essential for understanding economic policy. In the economy, there are several types of aggregated or macroeconomic agents across goods, across households, across regions, and so on. The above-mentioned individual agents are just examples. There are several micro-level agents that constitute macro-level metrics, and there are several macro-level metrics that are interrelated. Analyzing the relationship among individual parameters and their relationship with macro-level metrics is a complex subject, and therefore requires not only a well-advanced model but also a gathering of volume of data and managing the data in the order.

For example, as in our scenario of household savings and per capita savings, suppose that there is an increase in aggregate savings, together with an increase in aggregate income and interest rates. Now the question is whether the savings are increasing primarily because of wealthy people or from those with moderate incomes. Is there a difference in savings for the elderly than for the young? Is the income level sustainable? These types of questions help financial institutions learn how and where to use the aggregated metric. Though there can be a readily available macro metric in the market, analyzing the individual or micro-level data helps institutions in the process of utilizing the macro data and making decisions based on that data. The mortgage-backed securities (MBS) models developed before the financial crisis ignored the underlying micro level data.

Now let's examine how global macro fund strategies build investment strategies. The global macro investments rely on price movements of assets across the globe. There is a potential for price movements driven by supply-and-demand effects, or by investor behavior of moving prices away from rational efficient market equilibrium, or by the instantaneous shift or drift in an equilibrium measure itself. Global macro managers monitor changes in global economic activity to identify these movements regardless of the asset type on which the price movements are observed. These are then mapped into price forecasts for the major asset classes, such as real assets or commodities.

Gather a reasonable number of drivers and build a reasonably efficient portfolio, and one would have the beginnings of a global macro strategy. From the risk management point of view, there should be a thorough analysis of micro-level agents and their relationship to the macro-level agent. However, for some global macro-strategies, forecasting the cause of price movement does not capture the reasons for inflation. It's also necessary to keep forecasting government policy decisions, as such announcements can impact the market's price behavior immediately after the policy decisions are announced.

A large number of macroeconomic risk factors must be used, as these factors can describe different macroeconomic sources of risk to a portfolio in a specific economy and the same source of risk in different economies. There is no limitation on the types of macroeconomic factors that can be modeled and included as component risk factors. The following are some of the types of risk factors that can be modeled:

- consumer price index (CPI) for a specific country
- gross domestic product (GDP) index for a specific country
- purchasing power index (PPI) for a specific country
- personal consumption index for a specific country
- unemployment rate for a specific country or geographical subdivision
- industrial production index for a specific country
- balance of trade for a specific country
- housing starts index for a specific country or geographical subdivision

4.10 Contagion Risk and Interconnectedness

Contagion risk is defined as the risk that financial difficulties at one or more banks will spill over to a large number of other banks or the financial system as a whole. Contagion risk is also called *systemic risk*. Prior to the Asian and Mexican crises, structural adjustment problems in one country remained within those borders. The Asian crisis of 1997 originally started with devaluation of Thai currency and spread to other countries at a surprising speed, causing contagion. After the Asian crisis episode, the literature on systemic risk and contagion grew at a rapid pace as researchers and analysts scrambled to explain the nature of the events that led to the massive system breakdown. There are two main issues that intensify contagion: interconnectedness and runs on banks.

Interconnectedness between banks speeds up the transmission of losses from affected banks to many other banks. Suppose Bank A loaned funds to Bank B and is now facing a problem with a downgraded credit rating. In order to meet the required capital reserves, Bank A either has to sell its assets, probably at discount, or force the other bank to repay the borrowed funds. In the latter case, Bank B may need to sell assets, which may result in losses. Though Bank B is not facing a credit problem, it is forced to sell assets and see losses. These losses may result in a downgrade of credit rating. The interconnectedness among more banks intensifies the problem even more.

The illiquidity of investments provides the rationale for the existence of banks and for their vulnerability to runs. Excessive withdrawals of deposits would force a bank into costly liquidation. Hence, if a depositor expects that others will withdraw, he will also withdraw to avoid losses from such liquidation. This is called a *run on the bank*. Contagion can be either pure or noisy. Pure contagion occurs when negative information—such as fraud or losses on specific risky investments—about one bank adversely affects all other banks, including those that have nothing in common with the first bank. Noisy or firm-specific contagion arises when the failure of one bank reveals a bad signal regarding other banks with common characteristics. If one bank fails, other banks with a similar asset and liability structure may also face a run. In a world with imperfect information, runs on other banks can be triggered by perceived, not actual, similarities with the failing bank.

There are numerous potential channels for contagion from one country to another. Notably, external linkages could stem from direct and indirect equity exposure of local banks in overseas banks or, conversely, shareholdings of local banks by foreign banks; direct exposures through loan books; deposit and funding sources from overseas or from foreign banks; payments and settlement systems; and holdings of credit risk transfer instruments written on assets held by local or overseas institutions.

Contagion risk is more pronounced in the banking and investment sector than any other. However, contagion risk resulting from the banking and investment sector may have an impact on other sectors because of their systemic exposure. Contagion risk can better be analyzed using the extreme value theory (EVT) framework. The EVT approach to contagion better captures the information that large, extreme shocks are transmitted across financial systems differently than small shocks. Multivariate EVT techniques are used to quantify the joint behavior of external realizations of financial prices or returns across different markets.

The interconnectedness of the global economy has become a wider subject these days. There were scenarios in the past where one interconnected event helped one hedge fund make billions, whereas the other event caused a prestigious hedge fund to collapse. While interconnectedness is not limited to just the currency, it is a coincidence that both scenarios discussed here are related to currency.

The key factors that led to serious currency crashes are high inflation, a large current account deficit, insufficient internal growth, and rising unemployment. Often, these three are interconnected. High inflation or expansionary macroeconomic policies can stimulate demand for imports and thus reduce the current account balance. Also, a decline in external demand for a country's exports can create a current account deficit and rising unemployment.

Currency risk is driven by domestic pressures and then proceeds to other countries. It even flows to unrelated countries, leading to contagion risk. Domestic currency risk originates from declining growth, which prompts devaluation of currency to promote the growth. The top five components of GDP are consumption, investment, growth, exports, and imports. In a country where consumption, investment, and growth become stagnant, the last resort to increase the GDP is boosting exports through currency devaluation.

Globalization increases the reachability of advanced products. An advanced product cannot be built solely based on domestic raw materials. It could be because of a lack of domestic availability of natural resources or human resources. For example, an end product that reaches a client in Indonesia may include technology from US, manufacturing from China, components from Taiwan, and programming from India. A country whose growth is exclusively dominated by exports may improve its growth temporarily but will hurt the local economy in the long run because of deep complexities of the economic system. If political leadership is weak and does not have control over economic policies, local manufacturers will not be protected.

Because of the nature of products, there may be lag between exports and imports. While the devaluation helps the exports temporarily, it will cause the imports to get expensive. In a country where imports are balanced out with exports, this may not be an issue. However, no single product can be built solely based on domestic products. The repercussions of this can be seen in the two main currency crashes of recent years, the 1992 European crash and the 1997 Asian crash.

4.10.1   1992 European Currency Crash

In 1979, the European Monetary System (EMS) was established in order to stabilize exchange rates, reduce inflation, and prepare for monetary integration. The system was originally started with France, Germany, Italy, Netherlands, Belgium, Denmark, Ireland, and Luxembourg, with the United Kingdom joining later. One of the main components of the EMS was the exchange rate mechanism (ERM). The ERM gave each participating currency a central exchange rate against a basket of currencies, the European currency unit (ECU). Each country was required to maintain its exchange rates within a 2.25 percent fluctuation band above or below each bilateral central rate. Some large countries, such as Italy and the United Kingdom, were given a band of 6.0 percent.

The ERM appeared to be a success, and the disciplinary effect reduced inflation throughout Europe under the leadership of the German Bundesbank. Starting in mid-1992, international investors worried that the exchange-rate values of several currencies within the ERM were inappropriate. After German reunification in 1989, the nation's government spending surged, forcing the Bundesbank to print more money. This led to higher inflation and forced the central bank to increase interest rates, which in turn put upward pressure on the German mark. This forced the central banks of other participatory countries to increase their interest rates as well so as to maintain the pegged currency exchange rates.

In 1992, the United Kingdom was in recession, with an unemployment rate above 10 percent. Because of the progressive removal of capital controls during the EMS years, international investors at the time had more freedom than ever to take advantage of perceived disequilibrium. At first, the Bank of England tried to defend the pegged rates by buying 15 billion pounds with its large reserve assets, but its sterilized interventions were limited in their effectiveness. The pound was trading dangerously close to the lower levels of its fixed band.

On September 16, 1992, a day that would later be known as Black Wednesday, the bank announced a 2 percent rise in interest rates in an effort to strengthen the pound's appeal. A few hours later, it promised to raise rates again, to 15 percent. Traders kept selling pounds in large volumes, and the Bank of England kept buying them. However, these efforts were inadequate, and eventually the United Kingdom was forced to leave the ERM, resulting in rapid depreciation in the pound's effective value.

4.10.2   1997 Asian Currency Crisis

In the early 1990s, the US economy began to experience growth, and so inflation. The US Federal Reserve had started increasing its interest rate to address possible inflation and to reduce overall spending and price hikes. Since money always looks for a higher interest rate or return from financial and real investment, there had been a capital inflow to US assets that caused the US dollar to appreciate.

Since many Asian currencies maintained a fixed or close alignment to the US dollar, their currencies were also appreciated with the appreciation of the US dollar. As a result, these Asian economies were losing export competitiveness and, hence, continued to face current account-balance deficits. Rising interest rates in the United States attracted fund managers' hot money to gain higher returns compared to East Asian assets. This caused a plunge in the demand for Asian currencies in the security market.

The Asian financial crisis began on July 2, 1997, when the Thai Central Bank withdrew its support of its currency, the Thai baht, which resulted in the 20 percent depreciation of Thai currency within a month. Currency depreciation in Thailand brought a similar depreciation in all the neighboring Asian currencies and, hence, intensified the financial crisis. The first round of currency depreciation happened in the Thai baht, Malaysian ringgit, Philippine peso, and Indonesian rupiah. The second round began with the Taiwan dollar, South Korean won, Singapore dollar, and Hong Kong dollar. To counter the weakness in currencies, governments started selling foreign exchange reserves and raised interest rates, which slowed economic growth. This made the interest-bearing securities more attractive than equities.

The contagion risk spread to Russia. In August 1998, Russia unexpectedly defaulted on its debt, crushing the value of the ruble. The overall effect caused the yields on emerging countries' debt to increase and resulted in a flight to quality government bonds in developed nations. Yields on both high- and low-grade corporate bonds were increased. The increased credit spreads caused immense losses to Long-Term Capital Management (LTCM), which was employing strategies based on relative value and credit spreads. You can read more about LTCM in Chapter 6.3.1.

4.11 Model Risk Management

Any model is only as good as the input. A model does not generate all the required input on its own. For example, the Black-Scholes options valuation model asks a user for an estimate of future volatility and then translates that estimate into a fair option value. If the estimated volatility is not correct, the estimated option value may not be fair in reality. In other words, a model may be correct, but data like rates, volatilities, correlations, and spreads may be badly estimated. Potential problems include the following:

- An insufficient number of factors make the model imperfect. For example, a one-factor model of interest rates may be reasonable for valuing Treasury bonds, but much less reasonable for valuing options on the slope of the yield curve.

- A model that was developed for one type of variable will not work for other variables. For example, assumption of a normal distribution of prices automatically makes the implicit assumption of returns to be lognormally distributed. A model developed on the assumption that bond prices are normally distributed for the sake of analytic simplicity will not work for yield analysis, as the bond yields are more likely to be lognormal. Transforming the variable using exponents of yields may not work perfectly all the time. They may be approximate for the short term, but will be erroneous if used for long-term bonds.

- A missing correlation factor, ignoring the correlation between corporate credit spreads and corporate stock prices in valuing convertible bonds, leads to incorrect pricing.

- The model developed may be inappropriate under current market conditions, or some of its assumptions may have become invalid. For example, interest-rate volatility is relatively unimportant in currency option pricing at low interest-rate volatilities but may become critical during exchange-rate crises.

- Unexpected trading costs can make the model imperfect. Market panic or sentiment can make the theoretically correct model imperfect, at least for a short time during the life of the model.

- Programming mistakes can lead to widespread and hard-to-detect errors. These include, but are not limited to, logic, rounding, and miscounting the days between dates or the coupons to maturity. In addition, there are occasional hardware flaws, such as the widely publicized Pentium floating-point error.

4.11.1   Controlling Model Risk

Model risk cannot be hedged. There is no single factor to which model risk can be mapped. There is no magic strategy for avoiding model risk. Developing sound risk management principles across the board and following general guidelines based on experience can *reduce* model risk, however.

A closer working relationship among model users, modelers, and model developers will reduce some of the potential errors. Model users are traders, salespeople, or capital-markets personnel who may be physically and organizationally separated from the model creators. Furthermore, the model implementers are programmers, who are often similarly separated from the model theorists. To avoid risk, it's important to have modelers, programmers, and users who all work closely together, understand each other's domains well enough to know what constitutes a warning symptom, and have a good strategy for testing a model and its limits.

Highly complex models tend to model the noise rather than the information. They may sometimes mistakenly identify patterns. However, the simpler models tend to discard important information. Therefore, the model should be optimal to discard noise while detecting as much information as possible.

Test the model against simple and known solutions. Small disagreements often serve as warnings of potentially large disagreements and errors under other scenarios. Therefore, small discrepancies noticed by users or programmers cannot be ignored. Reevaluate models frequently to ensure the fitness of the model to current market conditions. Ensure the quality of data from third-party vendors.

4.12 Market Risk Measurement Under Basel III

Under Basel III, market risk is measured as the sum of the following:

- VaR-based capital requirement
- stressed VaR-based measure
- specific risk
- incremental risk
- comprehensive risk
- capital requirement for *de minimis* exposures

For standardized measure, the institution may not use the supervisory formula approach (SFA); and to use the advanced approaches, the institution must have completed the parallel-run process and received notifications from the federal supervisor. Let's discuss each of these components in more detail.

4.12.1   VaR-Based Capital Requirement

The VaR-based capital requirement equals the greater of the following:

- previous day's VaR-based measure
- the average of the daily VaRs measured for each of the preceding sixty business days multiplied by three, with back-testing exceptions included if present

The daily VaR must be measured using one or more internal models reflecting the general market risk of all covered positions. It may reflect the specific risk for one or more portfolios of debt and equity positions, if the internal models meet the requirements of modeled specific risk. It must also reflect the specific risk for any portfolio of correlation trading positions that is modeled under comprehensive risk. Repo-style transactions may also be included, provided they are included consistently over time.

Basic Requirements for VaR-Based Measure

- The internal models must use all of the applicable five categories: interest-rate risk, credit spread risk, equity price risk, foreign-exchange risk, and commodity price risk.
- For material positions in the major currencies and markets, the models must incorporate segments of the yield curve—in no case less than six—to capture differences in volatility and less-than-perfect correlation of rates along the yield curve.
- If available, correlations across risk factors must be used; otherwise, the aggregated VaR can be measured by adding the VaRs of individual risk factors.
- The risks arising from the nonlinear price characteristics of options positions or positions with embedded optionality and the sensitivity of the fair value of the positions to changes in the volatility of the underlying rates, prices, or other material risk factors must also be included.
- The volatility of options positions or positions with embedded optionality by different maturities and/or strike prices, where material, must be included.
- Any omitted risk factors must be explained.
- Any proxies used to capture the risks of the actual positions must be demonstrated.

Quantitative Requirements for VaR-Based Measure

VaR must be calculated on a daily basis using a one-tail, 99.0 percent confidence level and a holding period equivalent to a ten-business-day movement in underlying risk factors. Such measure can be directly from ten business days or converted to the equivalent of a ten-business-day holding period if there is satisfactory explanation of converted value.

The data should include at least one year of historical observations relevant to actual exposures, with sufficient quality to support the calculation of risk-based capital requirements. The data sets must be updated at least monthly or more frequently, as changes in market conditions or portfolio composition warrant.

In order to use a weighting scheme or other method for the historical observation period, the institution must do one of the following:

- Use an effective observation period of at least one year in which the average time lag of the observations is at least six months.
- Demonstrate to the supervisors that its weighting scheme is more effective than a weighting scheme with an average time lag of at least six months representing the volatility of the institution's trading portfolio over a full business cycle. The institution using this option must update its data more frequently than monthly and in a manner appropriate for the type of weighting scheme.

Other Requirements

For back testing at sub-portfolio level, the portfolio must be divided into a number of significant sub-portfolios approved by the supervisors. These sub-portfolios must be sufficient to allow the institution and the supervisors to assess the adequacy of the VaR model at the risk-factor level. The supervisors will evaluate the appropriateness of these sub-portfolios relative to the value and composition of the institution's covered positions.

The institution must retain and make available to federal supervisors the following information for each sub-portfolio for each business day over the previous two years (five hundred business days), with no more than a sixty-day lag:

- a daily VaR-based measure for the sub-portfolio calibrated to a one-tail, 99.0 percent confidence level
- the daily profit or loss for the sub-portfolio
- the p-value of the profit or loss on each day (that is, the probability of observing a profit that is less than, or a loss that is greater than, the amount reported for item 2 above, based on the model used to calculate the VaR-based measure described in item 1)

4.12.2   Stressed VaR-Based Measure

The institution, at least weekly, must calculate a stressed VaR-based measure using the same internal model(s) used to calculate its VaR-based measure.

Quantitative Requirements for Stressed VaR-Based Measure

- Though the same internal models used to calculate VaR-based measure could be used to calculate the stressed VaR subject to the same confidence level and holding period, it must use the inputs calibrated to historical data from a continuous twelve-month period that reflects a period of significant financial stress appropriate to the institution's current portfolio.
- Must have in place policies and procedures describing how the period of significant financial stress is determined.
- Must be able to provide empirical support for the period used.
- Must obtain prior approval of the federal supervisors for, and notify them of, any material changes the institution makes to these policies and procedures.
- The policies and procedures must address the following:
  o How the institution links the period of significant financial stress used to calculate the stressed VaR-based measure to the composition and directional bias of its current portfolio.
  o The institution's process for selecting, reviewing, and updating the period of significant financial stress used to calculate the stressed VaR-based measure and for monitoring the appropriateness of the period to the institution's current portfolio.
- Nothing in this section prevents the federal supervisor from requiring an institution to use a different period of significant financial stress in the calculation of the stressed-VaR-based measure.

4.12.3   Specific Risk

There are two ways to measure specific risk for each of its debt, equity, and securitization positions: modeled specific risk and non-modeled specific risk.

Modeled Specific Risk

While the institution may choose to use models to measure the specific risk of covered positions, it must use the models to measure the specific risk of correlation trading positions. General requirements for calculating the modeled specific risk are:

- Explain the historical price variation in the portfolio.
- Be responsive to changes in market conditions.
- Be robust to an adverse environment, including signaling rising risk.
- Capture all material components of specific risk for the debt and equity positions in the portfolio. Specifically, the internal models must capture event risk and idiosyncratic risk and must capture and demonstrate sensitivity to material differences between positions that are similar but not identical and to changes in portfolio composition and concentrations.
- If the institution calculates an incremental risk measure for a portfolio of debt or equity positions, the institution is not required to capture default and credit-migration risks in its internal models used to measure the specific risk of those portfolios.

Non-Modeled Specific Risk

If the institution's VaR-based measure does not capture all material aspects of specific risk for a portfolio of debt, equity, or correlation trading positions, the institution must calculate a specific risk add-on for the portfolio under the standardized measurement method. The institution must calculate a specific risk add-on for all of its securitization positions that are not modeled under comprehensive risk.

4.12.4   *Incremental Risk*

The *incremental risk measure* is the measure of potential losses due to incremental risk over a one-year time horizon at a one-tail, 99.9 percent confidence level, either under the assumption of a constant level of risk of constant positions. Such risk must be measured at least on a weekly basis. If equity positions are included in the model, for modeling purposes default is considered to have occurred upon the default of any debt of the issuer of the equity position. The correlation trading positions or securitization positions may not be included in incremental risk measure.

Requirements for Incremental Risk Modeling

- A constant level of risk assumption means that the institution rebalances, or rolls over, its trading positions at the beginning of each liquidity horizon over the one-year horizon in a manner that maintains the institution's initial risk level.

- The institution must determine the frequency of rebalancing in a manner consistent with the liquidity horizons of the positions in the portfolio.
- The liquidity horizon of a position or set of positions is the time required for the institution to reduce its exposure to, or hedge all of its material risks of, the position(s) in a stressed market.
- The liquidity horizon for a position or set of positions may not be less than the shorter of three months or the contractual maturity of the position.
- A constant position assumption means that the institution maintains the same set of positions throughout the one-year horizon. If an institution uses this assumption, it must do so consistently across all portfolios.
- The institution's selection of a constant position or a constant risk assumption must be consistent between the incremental risk model and its comprehensive risk model, if applicable.
- The treatment of liquidity horizons must be consistent between the incremental risk model and its comprehensive risk model, if applicable.
- The model must recognize the impact of correlations between default and migration events among obligors.
- It must reflect the effect of issuer and market concentrations, as well as concentrations that can arise within and across product classes during stressed conditions.
- It must reflect netting only of long and short positions that reference the same financial instrument.
- It must reflect any material mismatch between a position and its hedge.
- The model must recognize the effect that liquidity horizons have on dynamic hedging strategies. In such cases, the institution must do the following:
  - choose to model the rebalancing of the hedge consistently over the relevant set of trading positions
  - demonstrate that the inclusion of rebalancing results in a more appropriate risk measurement
  - demonstrate that the market for the hedge is sufficiently liquid to permit rebalancing during periods of stress
  - capture in the incremental risk model any residual risks arising from such hedging strategies.

- The model must reflect the nonlinear impact of options and other positions with material nonlinear behavior with respect to default and migration changes.
- It must maintain consistency with the institution's internal risk management methodologies for identifying, measuring, and managing risk.
- The incremental risk-capital requirement is the greater of the average of the incremental risk measures over the previous twelve weeks or the most recent incremental risk measure.

4.12.5   Comprehensive Risk

Comprehensive risk captures all price risk. The institution that uses internal models to measure the price risk of correlated positions in the portfolio must calculate comprehensive risk measure at least weekly. The comprehensive risk measure can be either of the following:

- the sum of the modeled measure of all price risk and a surcharge for the institution's modeled correlation trading positions, which is equal to the total specific risk add-on for such positions multiplied by 8.0 percent
- the greater of the modeled measure of all price risk or the total specific risk add-on that would apply to the bank's modeled correlation trading positions multiplied by 8.0 percent (with approval of the FDIC and provided the institution has met the requirements of this section for a period of at least one year and can demonstrate the effectiveness of the model through the results of ongoing model validation efforts including robust benchmarking)

Requirements for Modeling All Price Risk

- The internal model must measure comprehensive risk over a one-year time horizon at a one-tail, 99.9 percent confidence level, either under the assumption of a constant level of risk, or under the assumption of constant positions.
- The model must capture all material price risk, including but not limited to the following:
    - o   the risks associated with the contractual structure of cash flows of the position, its issuer, and its underlying exposures
    - o   credit spread risk, including nonlinear price risks

- o the volatility of implied correlations, including nonlinear price risks like the cross-effect between spreads and correlations
- o basis risk
- o recovery-rate volatility as it relates to the propensity for recovery rates to affect tranche prices
- o the static nature of the hedge over the liquidity horizon, to the extent the comprehensive risk measure incorporates the benefits of dynamic hedging; in such cases, the institution must do the following:
  - choose to model the rebalancing of the hedge consistently over the relevant set of trading positions
  - demonstrate that the inclusion of rebalancing results in a more appropriate risk measurement
  - demonstrate that the market for the hedge is sufficiently liquid to permit rebalancing during periods of stress
  - capture in the comprehensive risk model any residual risks arising from such hedging strategies
- The market data used must be relevant in representing the risk profile of the institution's correlation trading positions in order to ensure that the institution fully captures the material risks of the correlation trading positions in its comprehensive risk measure.
- The institution must be able to demonstrate that its model is an appropriate representation of comprehensive risk in light of the historical price variation of its correlation trading positions.

Requirements for Stress Testing

The institution must, at least weekly, apply specific, supervisory stress scenarios to its portfolio of correlation trading positions that capture changes in the following:

- default rates
- recovery rates
- credit spreads
- correlations of underlying exposures
- correlations of a correlation trading position and its hedge

The comprehensive risk capital requirement is the greater of the average of the comprehensive risk measures over the previous twelve weeks or the most recent comprehensive risk measure.

4.12.6   *Standardized Measurement Method for Specific Risk*

The institution must calculate a total specific risk add-on for each portfolio of debt and equity positions for which VaR-based measure does not capture all material aspects of specific risk and for all securitization positions that are not modeled under comprehensive risk. The specific risk add-on for an individual debt or securitization position that represents sold credit protection is capped at the notional amount of the credit-derivative contract.

The specific risk add-on for an individual debt or securitization position that represents purchased credit protection is capped at the current fair value of the transaction plus the absolute value of the present value of all remaining payments to the protection seller under the transaction. This sum is equal to the value of the protection leg of the transaction.

For debt, equity, or securitization positions that are derivatives with linear payoffs, an institution must assign a specific risk weighting-factor to the fair value of the effective notional amount of the underlying instrument or index portfolio, except for a securitization position for which the institution directly calculates a specific risk add-on using the SFA.

A swap must be included as an effective notional position in the underlying instrument or portfolio, with the receiving side treated as a long position and the paying side treated as a short position. For debt, equity, or securitization positions that are derivatives with nonlinear payoffs, an institution must risk weighing the fair value of the effective notional amount of the underlying instrument or portfolio multiplied by the derivative's delta.

For debt, equity, or securitization positions, the institution may net long and short positions (including derivatives) in identical issues or identical indices. A set of transactions consisting of either a debt position and its credit derivative hedge or a securitization position and its credit derivative hedge has a specific risk add-on of zero if the following are true:

- The debt or securitization position is fully hedged by a total return swap or similar instrument where there is a matching of swap payments and changes in fair value of the debt or securitization position.
- There is an exact match between the reference obligation of the swap and the debt or securitization position.

- There is an exact match between the currency of the swap and the debt or securitization position.
- There is either an exact match between the maturity date of the swap and the maturity date of the debt or securitization position; or, in cases where a total return swap references a portfolio of positions with different maturity dates, the total return swap maturity date must match the maturity date of the underlying asset in that portfolio that has the latest maturity date.

The specific risk add-on for a set of transactions consisting of either a debt position and its credit derivative hedge or a securitization position and its credit derivative hedge that does not meet the above criteria is equal to 20 percent of the capital requirement for the side of the transaction with the higher specific risk add-on when the following are true:

- The credit risk of the position is fully hedged by a credit default swap or similar instrument.
- There is an exact match between the reference obligation of the credit derivative hedge and the debt or securitization position.
- There is an exact match between the currency of the credit derivative hedge and the debt or securitization position.
- There is either an exact match between the maturity date of the credit derivative hedge and the maturity date of the debt or securitization position, or, in the case where the credit derivative hedge has a standard maturity date, one of the following is true:
  - The maturity date of the credit derivative hedge is within thirty business days of the maturity date of the debt or securitization position
  - For purchased credit protection, the maturity date of the credit derivative hedge is later than the maturity date of the debt or securitization position, but is no later than the standard maturity date for that instrument that immediately follows the maturity date of the debt or securitization position. The maturity date of the credit derivative hedge may not exceed the maturity date of the debt or securitization position by more than ninety calendar days.

The specific risk add-on for a set of transactions consisting of either a debt position and its credit derivative hedge or a securitization position and its credit derivative hedge that does not meet the criteria of any of the above two sets but in which all or substantially all of the price risk has been hedged is equal to the specific risk add-on for the side of the transaction with the higher specific risk add-on.

The specific risk add-on for individual debt or securitization positions is the multiplication of the absolute value of the current fair value of each net long or net short debt or securitization position in the portfolio and the appropriate specific risk weighting factor.

Specific Risk-Weighting Factors for Sovereign Debt Positions

The specific risk-weighting factor for a sovereign debt position is based on the country risk classification (CRC) applicable to the sovereign and, as applicable, the remaining contractual maturity of the position; or if there is no CRC applicable to the sovereign, based on whether the sovereign entity is a member of the Organization for Economic Cooperation and Development (OECD). Sovereign debt positions backed by the full faith and credit of the United States are treated as having a CRC of 0.

The institution may assign a specific risk-weighting factor that is lower than the applicable specific risk-weighting factor if the following are true:

- The position is denominated in the sovereign entity's currency.
- The institution has at least an equivalent amount of liabilities in that currency.
- The sovereign entity allows banks under its jurisdiction to assign the lower specific risk-weighting factor to the same exposures to the sovereign entity.

The institution must assign a 12 percent specific risk-weighting factor to a sovereign debt position immediately upon determination a default has occurred, or if a default has occurred within the previous five years. They must assign a 0 percent specific risk-weighting factor to a sovereign debt position if the sovereign entity is a member of the OECD and does not have a CRC assigned to it.

The institution must assign an 8 percent specific risk-weighting factor to a sovereign debt position if the sovereign is not a member of the OECD and does not have a CRC assigned to it.

The specific risk-weighting factor is 0 for certain supranational entities and multilateral development bank debt positions, such as Bank for International

Settlements, the European Central Bank, the European Commission, the International Monetary Fund, or a multilateral development bank (MDB).

The specific risk-weighting factor is 1.6 percent to a debt position that is an exposure to a government-sponsored entity (GSE). Notwithstanding the foregoing, it is 8 percent specific risk-weighting-factor to preferred stock issued by a GSE.

With certain exceptions, the specific risk-weighting factor to a debt position that is an exposure to a depository institution, a foreign bank, or a credit union, in accordance with table below, is based on the CRC that corresponds to that entity's home country or the OECD membership status of that entity's home country if there is no CRC applicable to the entity's home country, and, as applicable, the remaining contractual maturity of the position.

Exceptions

The specific risk-weighting factor is 8 percent for a debt position that is an exposure to a depository institution or a foreign bank that is includable in the depository institution's or foreign bank's regulatory capital and not subject to deduction as a reciprocal holding.

The institution must assign a specific risk-weighting factor of 12 percent to a debt position that is an exposure to a foreign bank immediately upon determination that a default by the foreign bank's home country has occurred or if a default by the foreign bank's home country has occurred within the previous five years.

With certain exceptions, the institution must assign a specific risk-weighting factor to a debt position that is an exposure to a public-sector entity (PSE) depending on the position's categorization as a general obligation or revenue obligation based on the CRC that corresponds to the PSE's home country or the OECD membership status of the PSE's home country if there is no CRC applicable to the PSE's home country, and, as applicable, the remaining contractual maturity of the position.

The institution may assign a lower specific risk-weighting factor to a debt position that is an exposure to a foreign PSE if the following are true:

- The PSE's home country allows banks under its jurisdiction to assign a lower specific risk-weighting factor to such position.

- The specific risk-weighting factor is not lower than the risk weight that corresponds to the PSE's home country.

The institution must assign a 12 percent specific risk-weighting factor to a PSE debt position immediately upon determination that a default by the PSE's home country has occurred, or if a default by the PSE's home country has occurred within the previous five years.

Specific Risk-Weighting Factors for Corporate Debt Positions

With certain limitations, the institution must assign a specific risk-weighting factor to a corporate debt position in accordance with investment-grade methodology. That is, for corporate debt positions that are exposures to entities that have issued and outstanding publicly traded instruments, the specific risk-weighting factor is based on the category and remaining contractual maturity of the position. For this purpose, the FDIC-supervised institution must determine whether or not the position is in the investment grade category.

The specific risk-weighting factor is 8 percent for corporate debt positions that are exposures to entities that do not have publicly traded instruments outstanding. Limitations include the following:

- The specific risk-weighting factor is at least 8 percent to an interest-only mortgage-backed security that is not a securitization position.
- The institution shall not assign a specific risk-weighting factor that is lower than the specific risk-weighting factor that corresponds to the CRC of the issuer's home country, if applicable.

Specific Risk-Weighting Factors for Securitization Positions

The institution that is not an advanced-approaches institution must assign a specific risk-weighting factor to a securitization position using either the simplified supervisory formula approach (SSFA) or assigning a specific risk-weighting factor of 100 percent to the position.

Advanced-approaches institutions must calculate a specific risk add-on for a securitization position if the institution and the securitization position each qualifies to use the supervisory formula approach (SFA). If the securitization position does not qualify, the SFA may assign a specific risk-weighting factor using the SSFA or assign a specific risk-weighting factor of 100 percent to the position. A short securitization position must be treated as if it is a long securitization position for calculation purposes when using the SFA.

To calculate the specific risk add-on for a securitization position using the SFA, an advanced-approaches FDIC-supervised institution must set the specific risk add-on for the position equal to the risk-based capital requirement as calculated.

Specific Risk-Weighting Factors for Nth-to-Default Credit Derivatives

Regardless of whether the institution is a net protection buyer or seller, it must determine a specific risk add-on using the SFA or assign a specific risk-weighting factor using the SSFA to an nth-to-default credit derivative. It must also determine its position in the nth-to-default credit derivative as the largest notional amount of all underlying exposures. For purposes of the SFA or SSFA, the institution must calculate the attachment point and detachment point of its position as follows:

- The attachment point (parameter A) is the ratio of the sum of the notional amounts of all underlying exposures that are subordinated to the position to the total notional amount of all underlying exposures. For purposes of the SSFA, parameter A is expressed as a decimal value between 0 and 1.For purposes of using the SFA, parameter A must be set equal to the credit enhancement level (L) input to the SFA formula. In the case of a first-to-default credit derivative, there are no underlying exposures that are subordinated to the position. In the case of a second-or-subsequent-to-default credit derivative, the smallest (n- 1) notional amounts of the underlying exposure(s) are subordinated to the position.
- The detachment point (parameter D) equals the sum of parameter A plus the ratio of the notional amount of the position in the nth-to-default credit derivative to the total notional amount of all underlying exposures. For purposes of the SSFA, parameter A is expressed as a decimal value between 0 and 1. For purposes of using the SFA, parameter D must be set to equal the L input plus the thickness of tranche (T) input to the SFA formula.

The institution that does not use the SFA must assign a specific risk-weighting factor of 100 percent to the position.

Specific Risk-Weighting Factors for Modeled Correlation Trading Positions

The comprehensive risk measure for modeled correlation trading positions require a total specific risk add-on which is the greater of the following:

- sum of the specific risk add-ons for each net long correlation trading position
- sum of the specific risk add-ons for each net short correlation trading position

Specific Risk-Weighting Factors for Non-Modeled Securitization Positions

For securitization positions that are not correlation-trading positions and for securitizations that are correlation-trading positions not modeled, the total specific risk add-on is the greater of the following:

- sum of the specific risk add-ons for each net long securitization position
- sum of the specific risk add-ons for each net short securitization position

Specific Risk-Weighting Factors for Equity Positions

The total specific risk add-on for a portfolio of equity positions is the sum of the specific risk add-ons of the individual equity positions. The specific risk add-on of individual equity positions is the multiplication of the absolute value of the current fair value of each net long or net short equity position and the appropriate specific risk-weighting factor. The risk-weighting factors are determined as follows:

- For each net long or net short equity position, the factor is 8 percent
- For equity positions that are index contracts comprising a well-diversified portfolio of equity instruments, the factor is 2 percent.
- For equity positions arising from the following futures-related arbitrage strategies, the factor is a 2 percent specific risk-weighting factor to one side (long or short) of each position with the opposite side exempt from an additional capital requirement:
  - long and short positions in exactly the same index at different dates or in different market centers; and
  - long and short positions in index contracts at the same date in different, but similar indices.

- For futures contracts on main indices that are matched by offsetting positions in a basket of stocks comprising the index, there is a 2 percent specific risk-weighting factor to the futures and stock-basket positions (long and short), provided that such trades are deliberately entered into and separately controlled, and that the basket of stocks is comprised of stocks representing at least 90 percent of the capitalization of the index.

5 Counterparty Credit Risk Analytics

Counterparty credit risk represents the combination of market risk and credit risk (default risk). The core of the counterparty risk relies on using two factors: exposure for market risk and credit quality for credit risk.

Counterparty credit risk is the risk that the opposite party of the contract will not meet its contractual obligations plus the expected credit loss because of credit-quality deterioration. Depending on transaction type, counterparty risk can be one-directional or bidirectional.

The total counterparty credit risk is calculated to cover default, migration, potential future exposures, and spread risks.

Total CCR risk = CCR default risk + CVA risk.

CVA stands for credit valuation adjustment. It helps to detect the changes in expected credit losses in derivative trading. The CVA is not calculated by an individual instrument; it is calculated at counterparty level and allocated to individual trades.

The CCR excludes the credit risk that arises from the bonds in the trading book. For example, a bank lends money to corporate by purchasing bonds from the issuer anticipating periodical coupons and final payback of principal at maturity. If the issuer defaults before the bond matures, then the issuers lose part or all of the principal. However, such risk is calculated under issuer risk instead of counterparty credit risk. Therefore, the definition of counterparty risk does not include direct lending and bond issuance.

Over-the-counter (OTC) derivatives, which are contracts privately negotiated between counterparties, are subject to counterparty credit risk. Contracts that are traded on an exchange are not affected by counterparty credit risk, because the exchange guarantees the cash flows promised by the derivative to the counterparty. So the exchange collects the margin with daily valuation of contracts. However, the Basel III require certain risk weightage given to exchange traded derivatives as well.

Counterparty credit risk is applicable to derivatives and repo-style transactions, including the following.

- repurchase agreements
- reverse repurchase agreements
- foreign exchange
- dollar rolls
- interest rate derivatives (swaps, caps, floors)
- futures (according to Basel III)
- forwards
- bond insurance (CDs)
- secondary mortgage trading
- mortgage insurance
- letters of credit
- credit insurance

Let's consider an example to demonstrate the CCR. In an interest-rate swap, one party pays fixed rate and the other pays floating rates. The net payment is exchanged on a quarterly basis. Since the floating rates changes periodically and depending on whether the floating rate is above or below the fixed rate, the direction of payment changes—if floating rates are higher than the fixed, say, then the fixed leg is on the recipient side and is exposed to counterparty risk. It is deterministic to calculate the net exposure at any given date based on the interest rates of that day. The direction of payment and the amount of payment varies from time to time.

Therefore, it is essential to consider the credit exposure at future times. This is known as *potential exposure*. Only the current exposure is known with certainty, while the future exposure is uncertain. Therefore, the parameters that impact the counterparty credit risk are the credit quality (probability of default) of the opposite party, future exposure, and the recovery rate (the portion of the amount that can be recovered if the party defaults).

5.1   Basic Metrics of Counterparty Credit Risk

5.1.1   Mark-to-Market Value

If a bank issues loans, then the value of the loan at any time is its remaining balance plus any unpaid or accrued interest. This is the amount the bank loses if the borrower defaults, assuming that there is no recovery. The derivatives and repos do not have any fair value of balance. The value of the contract is calculated based on market value of the underlying instruments. Certain mathematical models are used that involve volatility, interest rates, and other factors.

An alternative to using the model is getting market quotes as if the asset or contract were being announced for sale. If there is no trading activity in the market for such a product, then a very similar product is used. The value obtained from the market is called *mark-to-market (MTM) value*. Simply, the MTM price refers to the price at which the asset, or a similar asset, is trading at in the market.

MTM value is also called *replacement cost*. However, there are two flavors of replacement cost, one that includes accrued interest or dividends and the other that excludes accrued interest or dividend. If the accrued interest is extracted from the MTM, it is called *clean replacement cost*; otherwise, it is called *dirty replacement* or simply *replacement cost*.

5.1.2   Exposure at Default

Let's assume that an investor bought a call option from Party A. The call option is to purchase the stock at strike price X on or before a certain date. Assume that stock price Y is now above the strike. If the investor exercises the option today, it will have a profit of Y − X. However, the investor may want to wait for more time, as he thinks the stock will still rise from the current level. If the party defaults today, the investor will lose the profit of Y − X. Here, the amount Y − X is called *exposure at default* or EAD. If the stock value is below the strike price and if the counterparty defaults today, then there is no loss to the investor. EAD can be expressed as the maximum of 0 and Y − X. EAD is also called *current exposure* or simply *exposure*. Therefore, exposure at default is defined as the maximum loss if the counterparty defaults today.

5.1.3   Potential Future Exposure

In the case of the same call option, the value of stock may be different at a given point in the future before the expiration date. Calculating future value today is a bit complex and involves various evaluation procedures. Future exposure is the maximum value of 0 or the difference between estimated value Y and the strike price. However, the future value of the stock is just an estimate. There is no 100 percent confidence that the stock price on certain date will be Y. Therefore, the word *potential* is included and is conditional based on confidence level.

Potential future exposure (PFE) is an estimated market value of a particular transaction or set of transactions at some point in the future, and there is no mention of probability of default. In other words, it provides estimated value of maximum loss assuming that the counterparty defaults. Therefore, PFE is defined as the loss that can occur with certain confidence level if the counterparty defaults at some point in the future. In this way, PFE is compared to VaR (value-at-risk).

There are three main approaches used to measure PFE: add-on, semi-analytical, and Monte Carlo:

- *The add-on approach* is the simplest of the three. A value representing the volatility of the class and maturity is added to the current positive exposure. The Basel current exposure method (CEM) provides a matrix of add-ons for each asset class and time horizon. While this method is very simple and faster to compute, it is not very effective, as it ignores several underlying factors.
- *The semi-analytical method*, a bit sophisticated yet not very effective, makes some simple assumption regarding the underlying risk factors of the exposure and draws the distribution of the exposure based on the risk factors. This approach ignores the path-dependent nature of the contracts and the impact of collateral and netting.
- *The Monte Carlo simulation* is very sophisticated and complex, and involves a time-consuming process. Since it is not preferable to apply add-on or semi-analytical methods to certain derivatives, the Monte Carlo simulation is most preferred for derivatives.

Monte Carlo Simulation Approach for PFE for a Simple FX Contract

Let's take a simple example in which the bank enters into an FX (foreign exchange) forward contract with Counterparty A. The bank agrees to take delivery of a certain amount of US dollars in one year in exchange for foreign currency. At the inception of the contract, the value of the contract is usually set to 0.

The value of the contract at the time of maturity as seen as of today is

notional amount × (forward rate − strike rate).

The current MTM value is

price value of [notional amount × (forward rate − strike rate)].

For simplicity and illustration purposes, assume that interest rates are constant. Since the notional and strike rate are also constant, the forward exchange rate is the main risk factor, and this is therefore the driver that will need to be simulated in order to generate the PFE profile.

The spot exchange rates are assumed to follow a geometric Brownian motion (GBM), meaning that the forward exchange rate curve will retain the same shape over time but with parallel shifts up and down driven by changes in the spot rates. For simplicity, the mathematical equation of Brownian process is not included here.

The next step is to divide the duration of the contract into a certain number of steps—twelve, for example. Simulate the value of the exchange rate for twelve time steps over the life of the contract. The GBM process uses the volatility and drift that are estimated using a one-year history of spot exchange rates. For each simulation, we will get twelve values of forward rates (as we divided the contract period into twelve equal parts) and twelve MTM values.

The procedure is repeated 10,000 times, and there will be 10,000 MTMs for each of the twelve time steps. Upon drawing the graph with MTM on Y-axis and time step (twelve steps total) on X-axis, we will get a distribution of MTMs of the contract. The final step is to take the 95th percentile of the 10,000 values of the each of the time step. We have used 95th percentile as an example, and it indicates the confidence level. We can choose the percentile (confidence level) depending on internal requirement.

Now we finally have twelve values of MTM, each representing the potential value of MTM at the end of each month until the maturity of the contract.

Monte Carlo Simulation Approach for PFE for Interest-Rate Swap

Now let's consider a special derivative contract where there is an amortization effect. The PFE of an interest-rate (IR) swap will increase initially but then decrease as a result of the resetting effect. The risk on an interest-rate swap tends toward 0 as time tends toward maturity because of the realized quarterly payments. Let's discuss the detailed process for estimating PFE of a fixed-for-floating rate swap.

The MTM value of the interest-rate swap is determined by the difference in present value of the fixed leg and present value of the floating leg. Since the fixed-leg value is a known value, the MTM of an IR swap fully depends on the value of the floating leg that in turn depends on the floating interest rate. Therefore, the main risk factor of IR swap is floating interest rate.

Assume that the maturity of the IR swap is five years. Since there are quarterly resets and quarterly payments, we can divide the contract period into twenty time steps.

Next, we choose the quantitative model. There are many scholastic models to choose from for the interest rates. For the purpose of our simulation, assume that we have selected the Cox-Ingersoll-Ross (CIR) model. The CIR model is a good approximation for short-term interest rates. It assumes that the zero curve follows the same shape but with parallel shifts up or down, similar to our FX forward contract example. The CIR model does not capture the changes in the shape of the yield curve, and there are more advanced models available for such scenarios. For discussion purposes, assume the curve follows the same shape with parallel shifts.

The CIR model involves a mathematical formula that is not repeated here. Just as we used one-year historical volatilities for the FX forward GBM process, here we can use the zero curve obtained at bond prices. In other words, by observing the prices of bonds and similar instruments with various maturities, we can derive the current market prices by changing the market prices.

Using the model, it is possible to simulate the required paths of the short interest rate and MTM values at various points in time over the life of the swap. The next step is to calculate the 95th percentile at each time point using the calculated MTM values of each time point. Each 95th percentile value corresponds to PFE at that point in time.

The Monte Carlo simulation process is very time-consuming and requires sophisticated architecture and infrastructure. Let's assume that the bank has 100 counterparties, 100 trades with each counterparty, and 20 time steps (for example, a 5-year swap has 20 quarters). To run 10,000 simulations, there will be $100 \times 100 \times 20 \times 10,000$ revaluations. That means the total number of instrument revaluations will be 2,000,000,000 or 2 billion revaluations.

There are several statistical measures that can be obtained from simulated PFEs, including the following:

- maximum PFE
- expected exposure
- effective expected exposure
- expected positive exposure
- effective expected positive exposure.

5.1.4   Maximum PFE

Maximum PFE refers to the maximum peak exposure that occurs at a given date or any prior date. In our FX contract example, we have obtained a set of ten thousand values for each time step. Therefore, there will be twelve maximum values, one from each of the twelve sets, and therefore twelve maximum PFEs. The maximum PFE is always greater than PFE.

5.1.5   Expected Exposure

As we know, the expected value is typically an average of set of values.Therefore, the expected exposure is the average of the distribution of exposures at a particular future date. Only positive values of the distribution are considered to calculate EE. In our FX contract example, we have obtained twelve values of 95th percentile from each step. Instead of taking 95th percentile value, if we take an average of positive values, that will become EE at a given time step. EE is always less than maximum PFE.

5.1.6   Effective Expected Exposure

In the same example of our FX contact, we have twelve expected exposures, each corresponding to one time step. If we draw a graph with the expected exposures on Y-axis and time on X- axis, there will be one maximum on or before each period. The maximum EE on or before a particular date is called an effective expected exposure of that date. For example, effective expected exposure of an FX contract at six months is the maximum value of EE on or before the sixth time step.

This information is useful if we want to continue this exposure measure to the rest of the maturity period. For example, if we decide to use EEE of the sixth month for the maturity period after the sixth month, the maximum EE on or before the sixth month will be carried over to rest of the months. Simply, effective EE says that the EE will never decrease from its maximum value.

5.1.7   Expected Positive Exposure

The definition of EE included the term *particular future date*. However, expected exposure can vary from time to time. A weighted average of the expected exposure across time horizons is called *expected positive exposure (EPE)*.

In our FX contract example, we have twelve EEs. If we multiply each EE by a corresponding time horizon, add all the multiplications, and then divide the total by twelve, we will get EPE. Please note that the negative EE must be converted to zero. In other words, we will consider only positive EEs to calculate EPE. In summary, the EPE is defined as the weighted average over time of expected exposures.

5.1.8   Effective Expected Positive Exposure

The calculation procedure for EEPE is same as that of EPE, except we will use the effective expected exposure of each time step to calculate EEPE. This is very helpful if the portfolio has short dated transactions. The calculation of EPE does not take maturity date into consideration. For example, assume that the basket has twenty transactions, ten of which are short-dated transactions. Those short-dated transactions may be rolled over into new transactions, which are not considered by the EPE calculation.

If we assume that the short dated transactions are replaced with new transactions after maturing, the recalculated EPE will be higher than it would have been without replacement. Therefore, the EEPE is calculated by replacing a short-dated transaction within transaction after maturity date. It is defined as the weighted average over time of effectively expected exposures.

5.1.9   Effective Maturity

For an instrument subject to a predetermined, minimum amortization schedule, the weighted maturity of the remaining minimum contractual principal payments is defined as the weighted average of the minimum amount of principal contractually payable in each month in the future. Effective maturity is measured as Macaulay (M) duration under the assumption that interest rates are zero.

For simple fixed wholesale exposures, M is the weighted average remaining maturity (in years) of the expected contractual cash flows from the exposure, using the undiscounted amounts of the cash flows as weights. The bank also has the choice of using the nominal remaining maturity of the exposure as effective maturity. For transactions subject to a qualifying master netting agreement—such as repo-style transactions, eligible margin loans, and OTC derivative contracts—the effective maturity is calculated as the weighted average remaining maturity of the individual transactions, with the weight of each transaction equal to the notional amount of the transactions.

For most exposures, the Basel Accord caps the effective maturity to five years and floors to one year. If the original maturity of the exposure is less than one year and is not a part of the bank's ongoing financing of the obligor, the effective maturity is subject to a floor equal to the largest minimum holding period of the transactions in the netting set. If we calculate effective maturity using the known values of EPE, then it is equivalent to the ratio of the present value of EPE over the life of the portfolio and the EPE over one year.

5.1.10   Probability of Default

In all of the above scenarios and definitions of various exposures, we have assumed that the counterparty defaults. However, there is no 100 percent guarantee that the counterparty always defaults. Depending on the credit quality of the counterparty, there is certain the possibility of default, and then the exposure is adjusted based on default probability.

Let's say the exposure at default is calculated as $100 million. So the probability of default is calculated as 30 percent. Then the adjusted exposure is

$$\$100,000,000 \times 30\% = \$30,000,000.$$

The calculation of probability of default (PD) is a cumbersome process. It involves various data points, factors, and mathematics. PD calculated using the historical data is called *real-world PD*, and PD that is calculated from current market prices is called *risk-neutral PD* or *market-implied PD*. Current bond prices and credit-default-swap premiums can be used to calculate risk-neutral PDs. It is assumed that current prices are automatically adjusted to reflect the credit qualities of the issuer.

Risk-neutral PDs are said to be *market-implied*. PDs can also be obtained from rating agencies. For short-term trades, risk-neutral PDs are suitable, and for long-term trades, the real-word PD is useful.

5.1.11   Recovery Rate or Loss Given Default

In the above calculations, we assumed that we would not get anything from the counterparty as part of recovery. However, there is a possibility that a certain portion of the amount can be recovered. Such a recovery portion is called the *recovery rate* or simply RR. As with the calculation of PD, the calculation of recovery rate is a cumbersome process.

The remaining portion after the recovery of exposure is called *loss given default* (LGD). Mathematically, LGD is expressed as 1 – RR. PDs and RRs are used to calculate the expected loss (EL):

$$EL = EAD \times PD \times LGD.$$

5.1.12   Collateral

Collateral is something that is provided as a guarantee for the debt. If the borrower is not able to repay the debt, the lender has the right to sell the collateral in the market and use the proceedings toward the debt. For example, if a mortgage loan is taken and not paid, the bank has the right to sell the house and use the proceedings toward the loan payment.

Similarly, a counterparty provides certain assets, such as securities or gold, as collateral. The collateral reduces the exposure by an equivalent amount. For example, if cash of $1 million is borrowed from an investor, the borrower becomes counterparty to the investor. Securities worth $1 million are provided as collateral to the investor. In this case, the exposure is 0.

Let us say the recalculated value of securities is $900,000. So the loan amount after adding the accrued interest is $1,100,000. The net exposure is $200,000. If the borrower does not pay $1,000,000, then the investor sells the securities in the market. Assuming zero recovery, the net loss is $200,000. Therefore, the use of collateral reduces the potential loss the investor.

5.1.13   Rehypothecation

In repo markets, one asset is pledged as collateral in exchange for another asset, such as cash or securities. A party—for example, a prime broker—who receives the collateral can use the same as collateral to some other party to borrow funds or initiate another repo transaction. The repledging or recollateralization of collated assets is called *rehypothecation*. Rehypothecation is different from the concept of selling the collateral in the market in case the borrower does not repay. Rehypothecation is related to reusing the collateral prior to maturity of the original repo transaction.

The borrower will need to grant the right of rehypothecation to the brokerage firm. Otherwise, rehypothecation is not allowed. With the rehypothecation, the ownership is transferred to the third party to whom the collateral has been rehypothecated. In return, the original collateral-giver receives the contractual right to the return of collateral.

Here the problem comes when the brokerage defaults or the counterparty in rehypothecation defaults. This is what happened in the case of the Lehman Brothers collapse. There are certain regulations around the rephypothecation, and these regulation rules vary from country to country. In the United States, Regulation T and SEC Rule 15c3-3 limit the amount of a client's assets that the prime broker may rehypothecate to a certain percent of liabilities. In other markets, there are no such limits. Such differences may encourage regulatory arbitrage.

5.1.14   Haircut

In a repo-style or security finance transaction, the collateral is offered to the lender to provide protection against default. If the borrower defaults, the lender has the right to sell the collateral in the market. But what if the lender doesn't get enough from the market to cover the receivables? Market conditions may have changed, and collateral may have decreased in value from the date it was collated. By considering these situations, lenders usually lend the amount less than the market value of collateral.

This is similar to getting 80 percent of home financing. The remaining 20 percent down payment is to compensate the lender from home-value fluctuations just in case he needs to sell it in the market. Please note that the transaction does not need to involve lending the cash only. It can be any security or cash.

This concept is called the *haircut*. Collateral is intended to protect the lender from default risk. Haircut is intended to hedge the risk on that collateral from market fluctuations.

The repo market defines the haircut as "adjustment to the quoted market value of a collateral security to take account of the unexpected loss that the repo buyer in a repo may face because of the difficulty of selling a collateral security in response to a default by the repo seller." The fair amount that can be lent against the collateral is calculated as

$$I (1- \text{haircut}) \times \text{market value of collateral}.$$

5.2   Advanced Concepts of Counterparty Credit Risk

5.2.1   Wrong-Way Risk

Counterparties that are protection sellers or derivative sellers are obligated to pay the in-the-money portion to the buyers upon claim or exercise. Under normal circumstances, the buyers receive full claim. There may be circumstances where the credit quality of the counterparty deteriorates over time. If the buyers do not have any exposure to the counterparty at the time of default, they will replace the contracts with the new counterparty. Depending on the new economics of the underlying assets and markets, the new contract may be more expensive or cheaper.

Consider an example in which a farmer sold forward contracts on wheat to a food company. By entering the contract, the buyer agreed to buy a certain amount of wheat at a certain price on a certain date. For some reason, if the price of wheat goes down, the farmer still receives the price that is agreed upon. If the price goes up in the market, the farmer is still obligated to sell at the agreed-upon price.

Think about what happens if the price goes up and the food company defaults. There is no impact on the farmer, as the prevailing market rates are higher. This is called *right-way risk*. Therefore, the right-way risk is the risk counterparty defaults when the party is not exposed to the counterparty.

The problem arises when buyers are exposed to the counterparty by a large amount at a time when the counterparty is in trouble—for example, if the counterparty has sold call options to the buyer and they are in the money.

If a counterparty is unable to pay the claimed amount, such risk is called *wrong-way risk*. Wrong-way risk can be defined as a risk that occurs when exposure to a counterparty is adversely correlated with the credit quality of that counterparty.

Specific wrong-way risk, also called *idiosyncratic wrong-way risk*, arises when the exposure to a particular counterparty is positively correlated with the probability of default of the counterparty because of the nature of the individual trades with the counterparty. For example, a company writing heavy put options on its own stock creates wrong-way exposures for the buyer that are specific to the counterparty.

In a credit default swap (CDS), where one buys protection on Bank A from Bank A's competitor Bank B, if the credit quality of Bank A deteriorates, the CDS will be in the money, and the exposure to Bank B will increase. Since they both have similar profiles, it is highly likely that the credit quality of Bank B will also be deteriorating, therefore increasing the possibility of default.

While banks are required to develop procedures to identify, monitor, and control trades from inception through their entire life cycle, Basel III requires that trades with specific WWR carry an "explicit Pillar I capital charge" with higher EAD. This is the place where financial institutions must take advantage of high-performance hardware, software, data management, and big data. Basel III requires them to identify the legal connection between the counterparty and the issuer or underlying company in case of equity derivatives, and jump-to-default of the underlying security while identifying specific wrong-way risk. Continuously monitoring exposure connection between the issuer/underlying party and counterparty by measuring the exposures and detecting jump-to-defaults requires sophisticated infrastructure.

General wrong-way risk or systemic wrong-way risk arises when the probability of default of counterparties is positively correlated with general market risk factors. The wrong-way risk has a material impact on the exposures of a portfolio, particularly on the "cross gamma" effect. Portfolio profit and loss are very sensitive to simultaneous movements of market factor and counterparty spread. For example, consider a cross-currency swap with a large emerging market bank. It is very probable that if the bank defaults, local currency will significantly devalue. Thus, if we receive dollars and pay local currency, around the time of counterparty default the exposure is likely to become larger.

Measuring and managing this cross-gamma exposure is critical for effective exposure management. This mechanism requires banks to identify exposures that give rise to a greater degree of general wrong-way risk and to conduct stress testing and scenario analyses designed to identify risk factors that are positively correlated with counterparty credit worthiness. These stress and scenario analyses need to include the possibility of severe shocks occurring when relationships between risk factors change.

Wrong-way risk arises from two scenarios. The first is specific to the counterparty itself. For example, the buyer purchases contracts that are collateralized by the counterparty's own or related party shares. Alternatively, a company simply sells put options on its own shares, and the buyer won't exercise them as the company stocks are trending downward; at the same time, the company may not be able to honor the put option claims as it is in trouble. This type of wrong-way risk is called *specific* or *idiosyncratic* wrong-way risk.

The second scenario is that the seller is affected by general macroeconomic conditions not specific to the seller's internal problems. An example of general wrong-way risk is that fluctuations in the interest rate cause changes in the value of the derivative transactions but could also impact the creditworthiness of the counterparty. Another example is a cross-currency swap with a large emerging market bank, where one party pays in dollars and receives local currency. When economic conditions deteriorate in that country, the local currency significantly depreciates. Because of the devaluation of local currency, the receiver gets more money, but because of the country problems the bank may go into trouble. So the counterparty is in trouble at the time it needs to receive payment. This type of wrong-way risk is called *general* or *systemic* wrong-way risk.

The most dangerous wrong-way risk arises from monoline counterparties— parties that focus on operating in one specific financial area. During the financial crisis of 2008, dealers suffered billions of dollars of losses from wrong-way counterparty credit exposures with monoline insurers.

Prior to the financial crisis, monoline insurers guaranteed a series of structured credit products, such as collateralized debt obligations (CDOs) of residential mortgage-backed securities (RMBSs). Arrangers bought protection against the default of senior CDOs of RMBS tranches from monoline counterparties, often in the form of a CDS. Delinquencies in mortgage loans increased suddenly, and so the delinquencies in the collateral pools of many CDOs of RMBSs also exploded, causing the mark-to-market values on these CDS hedges to increase strongly.

However, the monoline insurers did not anticipate mass defaults and therefore were undercapitalized. The undercapitalization of the insurers resulted in the loss of their AAA ratings, which in turn triggered a widening of the credit spreads of monoline insurers. The deterioration of credit quality of the monoline insurers increased the credit risk to the dealers holding the CDOs. The monoline counterparties were not required to post collateral or make margin payments. The most dangerous thing was that the deterioration occurred at the very time the underlying CDS contracts had become most valuable. In other words, the insurers became helpless at the time the need arose.

Measuring wrong-way risk is challenging, as this type of risk occurs once in a while but with higher magnitude. Wrong-way risk is measured by means of monitoring and needs a lot of subjective analysis and high-performance analytics. A banking organization should have a process to systematically identify, quantify, and control both specific and general wrong-way risk across its OTC derivatives and securities financing transaction (SFT) portfolios. To prudently manage wrong-way risk, banking organizations should do the following:

- Maintain policies that formally articulate tolerance limits for both specific and general wrong-way risk, an ongoing wrong-way-risk identification process, and the requirements for escalation of wrong-way risk analysis to senior management.
- Maintain policies for identifying, approving, and otherwise managing situations when there is a legal connection between the counterparty and the underlying exposure or the associated collateral. Banking organizations should generally avoid such transactions because of their increased risk.
- Perform wrong-way risk analysis for OTC derivatives, at least at the industry and regional levels.
- Conduct wrong-way risk analysis for SFTs on broad asset classes of securities (for example, government bonds and corporate bonds).

5.2.2   Credit Value Adjustment

Prior to the crisis, simple mechanisms, such as collateral and haircuts were used to hedge the risk involved in counterparty transactions. Most counterparties were assumed to have high-grade credit quality. Moreover, the concept of collateral and haircut were used only in repo-style transactions. So valuation of counterparty credit risk is ignored for derivative exposures because of relatively smaller size and the given rating of AAA or AA to the counterparties.

As the size of derivative exposure increases and the credit quality of the counterparty deteriorates, the valuation of counterparty credit risk can no longer be ignored and must be appropriately priced and charged for. Credit valuation adjustment (CVA) is the process through which counterparty credit is valued, priced, and hedged.

CVA is defined as the expected value of credit losses over the lifetime of the trade. In other words, it is a statistical estimate of the expected future losses from counterparty risk and is intended to hedge in order to absorb future potential credit risk losses.

$$CVA = (PV \text{ of } EE) \times LGD \times PD$$

EE is the expected exposure as described earlier in this chapter. PV of EE is the present value of expected exposure. It is calculated by dividing the EE by the discount factor. LGD or loss given default is either calculated or assumed as 50 percent. Probability of default (PD) is derived through market CDS spreads.

From the above formula, we can see that there are two components involved: market risk in terms of exposure and credit risk in terms of LGD and PD. In very simple terms, the CVA is the value investors expect to deduct from the risk-free value. For example, if a CDS contract was priced at $100 in normal markets and if the credit quality of the issuer deteriorates, then the investors are not willing to pay the price of $100 and will expect some discount. The discount should compensate any expected loss due to the default of the counterparty.

Therefore,

Risk value of product = risk-free value – CVA.

However, the calculation of CVA is not as simple as this. First of all, CVA is not calculated at the individual instrument level. Since the business involves multiple, and possibly two-way, trades with the counterparty, the CVA must be calculated at netting set level. There can be some type of correlation among the trades, but the correlation must be considered in calculating the CVA. Once the CVA is calculated at a higher level, it is allocated or distributed to individual trades based on certain calculations.

The other important fact is that the CVA has a time dimension. Since the EE varies based on time horizon, the CVA also varies based on time horizon. Therefore, the CVA calculated based on EE over next year cannot be used to assume that the expected loss in next two years would be same as that of one year. The other fact to consider while calculating CVA is wrong-way risk.

There is an approximate formula to calculate CVA that avoids the dimensional problem of CVA. Since the EPE provides the weighted average over time of EE, EPE can be assumed as constant EE over the period. So then instead of calculating PD × LGD, one can use the credit spread on the counterparty. The credit spread, approximately, represents the PD × LGD.

Therefore,

$$CVA = EPE \times \text{credit spread.}$$

This formula may be approximate for amortization-style transactions like swaps where the exposure is reset periodically, but it is not suitable for directional exposures, such as forwards.

In our previous formula, we used the probability of default. As discussed earlier, the PD can be calculated either from historical data or from current market conditions, which provides market implied probability. Now the question is, which one should be used in a CVA calculation? Since the CVAs are calculated to price the expected loss and are intended for a short-term purpose, it would be better to use risk-neutral PDs. For long-term strategic hedging and risk management, it would be better to use real world PDs. The regulators did not insist on which PD must be used and left it to financial institutions to choose based on their risk strategy.

If the institution is capable of actively managing its counterparty credit risk by means of a CVA desk and full hedging strategies through CDS and credit indices like the iTraxx or the CDX and measure risk at a short time horizon, the risk-neutral probabilities are good. It is very simple to explain that since the goal is to dynamically manage the positions, the main focus must be on market prices. On the other hand, for long-term strategies and a long-term real-world measure of risk or in regards to economic capital calculations, the real-world PDs are good.

Impact of Jump-to-Default on CVA

Jump-to-default is the risk that the spread of credit widens too quickly for a counterparty to make an adjustment in mark-to-market price. This risk is more pronounced in certain types of products, such as insurance-style products, and less sensitive in swap-style products. Jump-to-default risk creates a very strong asymmetry in the risk profile of insurance-style products. A way to explain the impact of jump-to-risk on CVA is that, in interest-rate swaps, since the initial price of the swap is zero, there is no impact of default of the counterparty on CVA. As time passes, the exposure may increase, and CVA may increase as the counterparty approaches default, but the maximum loss is bounded because of the approaching reset date.

Impact of Recovery on CVA

One of the parameters used in the calculation of CVA is loss given default, which is equal to 1 − recovery rate. The recovery-rate calculation is critical to CVA. Most recovery rates obtained from vendors are based on the outstanding amount as of default date. In reality, the higher value of exposure may have already been decreased because of the prior knowledge of default of the issuer. For example, consider a bond that is issued by Party A and priced at $98. The investor purchased CDS from Counterparty B. Because of the stressed market conditions, the bond may have decreased to $80. If the recovery rate is given as 50 percent, then the question is whether the rate is on $98 or $80. The CVA calculations must consider the recovery rate very carefully.

Incremental CVA

Incremental CVA refers to the CVA that is added with a new trade. This is different from the CVA that is calculated based on the characteristics of individual trades. This is because, when adding a trade to the portfolio, because of the impact of netting agreements and correlations, the risk that is brought by the individual trade may come down. The incremental risk is calculated as the difference between the portfolio CVA with and without the trade. The incremental CVA is not additive. In other words, the incremental CVA added by two new trades might be less than the sum of two incremental CVAs that are calculated individually.

Marginal CVA

After the global CVA is calculated, it is then decomposed as the sum of individual marginal CVAs, which gives the variation of the global CVA with respect to a given deal. It is used to find individual contributions of trade. This is different from incremental CVA. The marginal CVA is calculated after trading activity and is allocated to the trade. While the incremental CVA represents the contribution of individual trade, the marginal CVA represents the portion of CVA that was allocated to the individual trade based on certain criteria. The incremental and marginal CVAs may sometimes be the same depending on allocation criteria.

Impact of Margin Period of Risk on CVA

The margin period of risk refers to, with respect to a netting set subject to a collateral agreement, the period from the most recent exchange of collateral with a counterparty until the next required exchange of collateral, plus the period required to sell and realize the proceeds of the least liquid collateral that can be delivered under the terms of the collateral agreement and, where applicable, the period required to rehedge the resulting market risk upon the default of the counterparty.

The CVA increases as the margin period of risk increases. The CVA is typically zero at the zero value of the margin period of risk and is half of that of collateralized value at the margin period of risk of thirty calendar days and touches that of uncollateralized value as the margin period increases.

Standard Guidelines to Calculate CVA

CVA refers to adjustments to transaction valuation to reflect the counterparty's credit quality. CVA is the fair-value adjustment to reflect CCR in valuation of derivatives. As such, CVA is the market value of CCR and provides a market-based framework for understanding and valuing the CCR embedded in derivative contracts. CVA may include only the adjustment to reflect the counterparty's credit quality (a one-sided CVA or just CVA), or it may include an adjustment to reflect the banking organization's own credit quality. The latter is a two-sided CVA, or CVA plus a debt valuation adjustment (DVA).

For the evaluation of the credit risk due to the probability of default of counterparties, one-sided CVA is typically used. For the evaluation of the value of derivatives transactions with a counterparty or the market risk of derivative transactions, a two-sided CVA should be used.

Although CVA is not a new concept, its importance has grown over the last few years, partly because of a change in accounting rules that requires banking organizations to recognize the earnings impact of changes in CVA. During the 2007–2009 financial crisis, a large portion of CCR losses were attributable to CVA losses rather than actual counterparty defaults. As such, CVA has become more important in risk management as a mechanism to value, manage, and make appropriate hedging decisions, and to mitigate banking organizations' exposure to the MTM impact of CCR.

CVA calculations should include all products and counterparties, including margined counterparties. The method for incorporating counterparty credit quality into CVA should be reasonable and subject to ongoing evaluation. CVA should reflect the fair value of the CCR for OTC derivatives, and inputs should be based on current market prices when possible.

Credit spreads should be reflected in the calculation where available, and banking organizations should not overly rely on non-market-based probability of default estimates when calculating CVA. Banking organizations should attempt to map credit quality to name-specific spreads rather than spreads associated with broad credit categories. Any proxy spreads should reasonably capture the idiosyncratic nature of the counterparty and the liquidity profile. The term structure of credit spreads should be reflected in the CVA calculation

The CVA calculation should incorporate counterparty-specific master netting agreements and margin terms; for example, it should reflect margin thresholds or minimum transfer amounts stated in legal documents. Banking organizations should identify the correlation between the counterparty's creditworthiness and its exposure to the counterparty and seek to incorporate the correlation into their respective CVA calculation. CVA management should be consistent with sound risk management practices for other material MTM risks. Business units engaged in trades related to CVA management should have independent risk management functions overseeing their activities.

Systems that produce CVA risk metrics should be subject to the same controls as are used for other MTM risks, including independent validation or review of all risk models and alternative methodologies. Upon transaction execution, CVA costs should be allocated to the business unit that originated the transaction.

As a sound practice, the risk of CVA should be incorporated into the risk-adjusted return calculation of a given business. CVA cost allocation provides incentive for certain parties to make prudent risk-taking decisions and motivates risk-takers to support risk mitigation, such as by requiring strong collateral terms. Banking organizations should measure sensitivities to changes in credit and market risk factors to determine the material drivers of MTM changes. On a regular basis, but no less frequently than quarterly, banking organizations should ensure that CVA MTM changes are sufficiently explained by these risk factors (for example, through profit and loss attribution for sensitivities, and back testing for VaR).

Banking organizations hedging CVA MTM should gauge the effectiveness of hedges through measurements of basis risk or other types of mismatches. In this regard, it is particularly important to capture nonlinearity, such as the correlation between market and credit risk, and other residual risks that may not be fully offset by hedging.

5.2.3   Debt Value Adjustment

For simplicity, let's assume that transactions are taking place between a counterparty and financial institution (FI) and the CVA calculation is based on the probability of default by the counterparty. Therefore, the FI charges the CVA to the counterparty as a measure of hedging default risk. This concept assumes that the FI is risk-free, as the accountancy concept of "going concern" requires financial statements to be based on the assumption that the business will remain in existence for an indefinite period.

In reality, the FI may also default. This was not a concern until the financial crisis occurred in 2008. The perception has been changed since the last crisis. No FI is assumed default-remote. Therefore, the FI also needs to calculate something similar to CVA to the counterparty for exposure to the counterparty, such as collaterals or any other transactions. This is nothing but saying the CVA charges must be bilateral.

The value adjustment made to the FI is called *debt value adjustment*. In other words, appropriately, the CVA of one party will become DVA to the other party. While CVA considers only positive exposure, the DVA considers only negative exposure. The net charge is calculated using the sum of CVA and DVA (actually, DVA is negative). In other words,

$$\text{Net CVA} = \text{CVA} - |\text{DVA}|.$$

The net CVA is also called *bilateral CVA* or simply *BVCA*. However, the way we calculate CVA and DVA for the purpose of BCVA slightly differs from that of the unilateral version of CVA. The CVA component of BVCA is calculated as

$$(\text{PV of EPE to counterparty}) \times \text{LGD} \times$$
$$\text{PD of counterparty} \times (1 - \text{PD of institution}).$$

The last parameter is needed because we calculate CVA only if the institution survives. The value (1 − PD of institution) gives survival probability.

Similarly, the DVA component of BVCA is calculated as

$$[\text{PV of EPE (or ENE to CP) to Institution}] \times \text{LGD} \times$$
$$\text{PD of institution} \times (1 - \text{PD of counterparty}).$$

The last parameter is needed because we calculate DVA only of the counterparty survives. The value (1 − PD of Counterparty) gives survival probability.

Just as we have used EPE to calculate the CVA, we can use the ENE to calculate the DVA. ENE gives the weighted average over time of expected exposure but only negative exposure. Rewriting BCVA in terms of EPE and ENE,

$$\text{BCVA} = \text{credit spread of counterparty} \times \text{EPE} +$$
$$\text{credit spread of institution} \times \text{ENE}.$$

5.2.4   Funding Value Adjustment

In all trading transactions, the funds are either supplied by internal groups or borrowed. Even if they are supplied by internal groups, there is an implicit interest component that must be considered. For example, if funds are deposited in highly rated Treasuries, they receive some interest called an *opportunity cost*. If the amount is applied in trading activities and the counterparty defaults, it assumed that collateral and CVA charges cover the losses. However, who covers the interest that should be paid to the borrowed funds (in case of internal funds, it is opportunity cost)? It is necessary to calculate the funding value adjustments in addition to CVA and DVA in order to better estimate and hedge the credit risk.

Overnight index swap (OIS) discounting, which is very similar to LIBOR, is used to calculate funding costs. OIS is an interest-rate swap where a floating leg is linked to an overnight rate. OIS discounting is now the market standard for pricing collateralized deals and is being mandated by clearinghouses.

As with the BCVA calculation, the FVA calculation also involves two components—positive (EPE) and negative (ENE) exposure components. However, the use of PDs differ because it is assumed that both the institutions should survive to calculate the funding costs. Therefore,

$$FVA =$$

$$\text{(PV of EE to counterparty)} \times \text{LGD} \times$$
$$(1 - \text{PD of counterparty}) \times (1 - \text{PD of institution})$$

$$+$$

$$\text{(PV of EE to institution)} \times \text{LGD} \times$$
$$(1 - \text{PD of institution}) \times (1 - \text{PD of counterparty}).$$

Just as we used EPE and ENE to calculate the BCVA, we can calculate FVA using the spreads as follows:

$$FVA = \text{funding spread of borrowed funds} \times$$
$$EPE + \text{funding spread of lending funds} \times ENE.$$

As discussed earlier, OIS is the most suitable risk-free rate to use as a funding spread.

5.2.5   Cross Gamma

While the gamma gives the rate of change of delta with respect to the underlying asset price, the cross gamma give the rate of change of delta of one asset with respect to changes in the price of another asset in the basket. In essence, it captures the correlation effect.

5.3 Managing Counterparty Credit Risk

Like any other risk, the CCR cannot be eliminated completely. Hedging out the counterparty risk completely does not fulfill the needs of underlying transactions. However, counterparty risk can be reduced or transformed to other manageable risks. Use of collateral, nettings, ISDA master agreements, and central-clearing parties are a few of several ways of reducing the exposure.

5.3.1   *ISDA Master Agreement*

The International Swaps and Derivatives Association (ISDA) was founded in 1985 to make OTC derivatives markets safe and efficient. ISDA has over eight hundred member institutions from sixty countries. These members include corporations, investment managers, government and supranational entities, insurance companies, energy and commodities firms, international and regional banks, exchanges, clearinghouses, and repositories, as well as law firms, accounting firms, and other service providers. The three key areas of ISDA's work are reducing CCR, increasing transparency, and improving the industry's operational infrastructure. ISDA provides support for the G20's initiatives to reduce systemic risk and work with policymakers to adopt a prudent, effective regulatory framework.

The ISDA developed an industry standard framework called the *master agreement*. According to this agreement, the participants can trade any number of OTC derivative products under a single agreement. It contains terms and conditions to govern transactions between parties. The key mechanisms provided in a master agreement are netting of payments, closeout netting upon default, and seamless addition of various trades to existing portfolios.

The first step in the ISDA life cycle is confirmation. Let's first discuss ISDA confirmation, and then we'll examine various other components of the ISDA master agreement.

Once the terms of each trade subject to an ISDA master agreement are agreed upon, the trade is live. The parties must then confirm their agreement to these terms with a paper or electronic form of confirmation. The forms vary from product to product, and ISDA publishes these forms in the definitional booklets for various products. These confirmations concentrate on the economic terms of the trades, such as price, the notional amount, the underlying asset, and payment dates.

There remain many noneconomic terms that must or may be applied to the confirmation that cause trade confirmations to be long and cumbersome to negotiate. Historically, there used to be a huge delay in trade confirmations. Delays in confirming trades can cause operational risk as the trades become subject to an incomplete set of terms. To simplify and standardize the negotiation of trade confirmations, ISDA has been developing a number of forms of master confirmation agreements (MCAs) for various jurisdictions.

5.3.2   Single Agreement

By entering into ISDA master, the two parties are implicitly entered into a single agreement. The benefits of the single agreement are as follows:

- netting of payments
- closeout netting
- ability to collateralize portfolio as unit

5.3.3   Netting of Payments

In financial markets, transactions are two-way, meaning one party will have to make payments on certain transactions while the opposite party also needs to make payments to the first party on some other transactions. If the currency is the same for both payments and they both are due on the same date, the payments can be netted. This reduces operational risk. Netting is not possible if the payments involve two currencies, even if they are due on the same day.

5.3.4   Cross-Product Netting

Financial institutions engage in several types of product categories, such as OTC derivatives, repo-style transactions, eligible margin loans, and deposits. Each product category will have various instrument types—for example, interest-rate derivatives, FX derivatives, and equity derivatives are all OTC derivative categories.

All product types under one product category can be combined in single netting so that the net exposure amount can be reduced. Such a concept is called *cross-product netting*. Netting across different product categories is not possible.

5.3.5   Close-Out Netting

In the event of a default or another termination event with respect to the defaulting party, the surviving party is entitled to terminate all the outstanding transactions, value them, and net out the exposures owed by the defaulting party from any exposures that may be owed by the surviving party.

According to the document "Interagency Supervisory Guidance on Counterparty Credit Risk Management" from the Office of the Comptroller of the Currency (http://www.fdic.gov/news/news/press/2011/pr11113a.pdf), sound practices for managing a closeout should include the following:

- "requirements for hypothetical close-out simulations at least once every two years for one of the banking organization's most complex counterparties"
- "standards for the speed (typically four hours) and accuracy with which the banking organization can compile comprehensive counterparty exposure data and net cash outflows"
- "the sequence of critical tasks, and decision-making responsibilities, needed to execute a close-out"
- "closeout methodologies that are practical to implement, particularly with large and potentially illiquid portfolios"
- a consideration by dealers of "using the 'close-out amount' approach for early termination upon default in inter-dealer relationships"

5.3.6   Terminations

Derivative contracts cover both the short term and long term. The current exposure may increase over time for both short- and long-term derivatives. The exposed party may think that it may not be safe to have a bigger exposure to one single party. If it is short-term, then it may not be an issue. In the case of long-dated transactions, there should be a provision where the party can reset or wind down the transactions.

Reset agreements are most useful in swap-style transactions. When one leg is in the money and continuously increasing, the party can ask the counterparty to pay down on a certain date and then reenter the agreement. It is very similar to closing the transaction and replacing it with a new transaction.

Not all derivative transactions are swap-style. As discussed above, the exposure may be increased significantly over time for long-dated transactions, such as ten-year maturity contracts. The credit quality of the counterparty may be very good at the time of inception but deteriorate over time.

ISDA provides break clauses called "additional termination events" that provide for an institution to terminate a trade before the counterparty's credit quality deteriorates. The terms are set in such a way that termination may be possible only after passing certain prespecified times and dates thereafter.

There are three types of termination events: mandatory, optional, and trigger-based. In mandatory events, reset or termination occurs on the specified date. In optional termination events, one party or both the parties have the option to terminate at specified dates. The trigger-based options give the right to terminate when an event occurs, such as a rating downgrade.

5.3.7   *Walkaway Features*

Walkaway features are different from closeout netting. In walkaways, the party that is obligated to pay a certain amount to the counterparty can cease the payments in case the counterparty defaults.

5.3.8   *Multilateral Netting*

In the case of bilateral netting, the exposure is reduced if there are two-way payments between the parties. In some cases, one party may have a debt to the other while the other party does not have any exposure. Such parties may engage with a third party to gain the benefit of netting if there are compatible exposures. Such a concept is called *multilateral netting.*

5.3.9   *Deliverables*

Under the ISDA schedule, corporations, partnerships, and other conventional entities typically deliver annual and quarterly financial statements, whereas hedge funds and other investment vehicles typically deliver annual and monthly financial statements. These periodic financial statements provide parties with a snapshot of the financial health of their counterparties.

Publicly traded entities should ensure that the timing of the delivery of their financials under the ISDA is similar to (or more lenient than) the timing mandated by their regulator. Private entities delivering financial statements should ensure that they can meet the agreed-upon delivery timing and should have a system in place that guarantees timely delivery. Hedge funds, for instance, typically obtain their monthly statements from their administrators and should check with the administrator to determine how much time is needed after the end of each month to prepare and deliver the statements.

5.3.10   Collateral Management

Collateral is another way of reducing the exposure to a counterparty by receiving liquid assets as a guarantee of repayment. Such a mechanism is called *collateralization* or *margining*. Collateralization is used in conjunction with netting or as a standalone. There may be situations where the exposure is still positive even after netting. To mitigate the counterparty risk from the residual exposure, collateral agreements are kept in place. Collateral agreements are negotiated before the transactions take place, or prior to increasing the exposure, or after finding the net-positive exposure.

The collateral receiver is not an economic owner until the collateral giver defaults. Collateral agreements can be two-way, meaning both parties agree to post collateral depending on who has negative exposure. On a periodic basis, the positions are MTM, and if negative exposure is found, collateral agreements are checked for the conditions and then collateral is requested if conditions are met. As requesting, receiving, and posting collateral involves certain operational costs, the collateral reposting usually occurs at certain intervals.

While collateral management is mainly intended to reduce net exposure, it is also required in order to be eligible to receive certain ratings. On the negative side, collateral management introduces market risk, liquidity risk, and operational risk, which must be managed as part of counterparty risk.

Significant stress events have highlighted the importance of sound margining practices, adequate margin, and collateral haircut guidelines for all products with counterparty credit risk. According to "Interagency Supervisory Guidance on Counterparty Credit Risk Management," sound practices for managing a collateral should include the following:

- "Periodically review minimum haircuts."
- "Evaluate the volatility and liquidity of the underlying collateral."
- "Ensure that haircuts on collateral do not decline during periods of low volatility."
- "Set guidelines for cross-product margining [including] limiting the set of eligible transactions to liquid exposures, and having procedures to resolve margin disputes."

- Control and monitor "the extent to which collateral agreements expose a banking organization to collateral risks, such as the volatility and liquidity of the securities held as collateral."
- Control and monitor the "concentrations of less liquid or less marketable collateral asset classes."
- Control and monitor "the risks of re-hypothecation or other reinvestment of collateral ... received from counterparties, including the potential liquidity shortfalls resulting from the re-use of such collateral."
- Monitor "margin agreements involving third-party custodians" and "identify the location of the account to which collateral is posted, or from which it is received."
- "Obtain periodic account statements or other assurances that confirm the custodian is holding the collateral in conformance with the agreement."
- "Understand the characteristics of the account where the collateral is held ... and the legal rights of the counterparty or any third-party custodian regarding this collateral."

5.3.11   Credit Support Annex

The ISDA master agreement includes a standard form collateral agreement called the credit support annex. The CSA enables parties to an ISDA master agreement to receive and provide collateral so as to reduce counterparty credit risk. CSA governs the issues of collateral, including the following:

- valuation methods and timings
- valuation of collateral
- collateral transfer methods and timings
- collateral eligibility
- collateral substitutions
- collateral dispute resolutions
- rehypothecation of collateral
- events that may change the collateral condition

5.3.12   Margin Calls

The margin call is the mechanism through which adequate collateral is posted during the life of the transaction. All trades and collateral are marked-to-market periodically—usually daily, weekly, or monthly—and the net exposure is calculated internally by each party. The net exposure is then compared to a predefined acceptable exposure level that is set in collateral agreements. A margin call is made to the counterparty if the exposure limit is exceeded. Both the parties come to an agreement on how much needs to be posted.

If both the parties agree about the additional collateral requirement, then it is posted by the losing counterparty to the winning counterparty. If either of the parties dispute the additional requirement, the disputed portion may be negotiated. The parties may agree for longer margin-call frequencies in order to reduce operational costs. However, daily margining is becoming standard for OTC derivatives because of the perceived higher volatilities.

5.3.13   Collateral Threshold

A *threshold amount* is the unsecured credit exposure that the secured party is willing to allocate to the pledger. That means the pledger is not required to post additional collateral unless and until the secured party's exposure equals or exceeds the threshold amount. The level threshold amount is subject to the creditworthiness of the counterparty and negotiations. While the threshold amounts were commonly negotiated in favor of broker-dealers in the past, they have become rare in the post-Lehman market.

Another tool is the *minimum transfer amount* (MTA). Since the collateral calls for amounts smaller than MTAs are not permitted under the CSA, having an MTA prevents the call of smaller amounts and allows the parties to avoid unnecessary costs involved in small transfers.

5.3.14   Collateral Disputes

After marking the trading and collateral positions to the market, the party that has negative net exposure will get a margin call for additional collateral posting. If the party does not accept the evaluating criteria, then a dispute occurs that is subject to negotiation. The most frequently occurring collateral disputes include the following:

- *Ineligible collateral* is related to the incidence where the losing counterparty attempts to post securities having less quality than required, or the quality of the collateral has dropped below the required threshold. For example, an investment-grade bond has been downgraded to B and is no longer eligible collateral.

- *Valuation disagreements* occur when curves or prices are captured at different times, from different data sources, using different price samples, or the theoretical valuation is done using different valuation models or settings.
- *Portfolio mismatches* occur because of missing trades in the portfolio, which creates net exposure calculation differences. This may be for operational issues, such as the front office failing to properly enter trades at one of the counterparties.

Once a dispute is raised, both parties check the rules and reference data to resolve the issues. The resolving procedures include, but are not limited to, checking the collateral value using market-data-like FX rates, interest rates, and bond prices; verifying the CSA; checking the net collateral requirement and thresholds; and walk-through with counterparty regarding revaluation criteria.

If the counterparties are still in disagreement with collateral requirements, formal dispute-resolution procedures governed by the appropriate CSA are followed. These include getting additional external quotes from third-party dealers, banks, and valuation consultants, and getting one or more appraisals done.

5.3.15   Credit Limits

While the CVA focuses on evaluating counterparty risk at trade exposure and counterparty level, credit limits act at the portfolio level by limiting exposure concentrations. The idea of diversification is to avoid having all exposures with a single party and so reducing the weighted average default probability. Credit limits can also be imposed at instrument type, geography, and market sector, among other things. Meaningful limits on exposures must be incorporated into an exposure-monitoring system independent of relevant business lines. It should perform ongoing monitoring of exposures against such limits, to ascertain conformance with these limits and adequate risk controls that require action to mitigate limit exceptions.

A sound limit system, as described in "Interagency Supervisory Guidance on Counterparty Credit Risk Management," includes the following:

- "Establishment and regular review of counterparty limits and ... a process to escalate limit approvals to higher levels of authority, depending on the size of counterparty exposures, credit quality, and tenor."

- "Establishment of potential future exposure limits, as well as limits based on other metrics."
- "[Limits to] the market risk arising through CVA, with a limit on CVA or CVA VaR. However, such limits do not eliminate the need to limit counterparty credit exposure with a measure of potential future exposure."
- "Individual CCR limits ... based on peak exposures rather than expected exposures. Peak exposures are appropriate for individual counterparty limit monitoring purposes because they represent the risk tolerance for exposure to a single counterparty."
- "Expected exposure [as] an appropriate measure for aggregating exposures across counterparties in a portfolio credit model, or for use within CVA."
- "Consideration of risk factors such as the credit quality of the counterparty, tenor of the transactions, and the liquidity of the positions or hedges. "
- "Sufficiently automated monitoring processes to provide updated exposure measures at least daily."
- "Monitoring of intra-day trading activity for conformance with exposure limits and exception policies. Such controls and procedures can include intra-day limit monitoring, trade procedures and systems that assess a trade's impact on limit utilization prior to execution, limit warning triggers at specific utilization levels, and restrictions by credit risk management on allocation of full limits to the business lines."

5.3.16   Concentrations

Since the CCR is exposed to both market values and the credit quality of the counterparties, it can contribute to unexpected large losses in the event of counterparty default. This makes it necessary for firms to have an enterprise-wide process in place to effectively identify, measure, monitor, and control concentrated exposures on both a legal entity and enterprise-wide basis.

Concentration refers to a situation where an exposure or group of exposures meet the following conditions:

- Exposures exceed risk tolerance levels established to ensure appropriate diversification.

- Deterioration of the exposure could result in material loss.
- Exposures are concentrated in a specific category—such as loans, OTC derivatives, names in bespoke, index CDO credit tranches, security settlements, and money market transactions.
- Individual counterparties have large potential exposures, with a single market factor or transaction type driving those exposures.
- Exposures are concentrated with individual legal entities, or across affiliated legal entities at the parent entity level, or in the aggregate for all related entities.
- Exposures are concentrated within industries or other obligor groupings.
- Exposures are concentrated within geographic regions or country-specific groupings sensitive to similar macroeconomic shocks.
- Exposures are concentrated across counterparties when the same drives potential exposure or similar risk factors.
- Crowded trades exist where closeout risk may be heightened under stressed market conditions.
- There are collateral concentrations, including both risk concentrations with a single counterparty and risks associated with portfolios of counterparties.
- There is a concentration of noncash collateral for all product lines covered by collateral agreements, including collateral that covers a single counterparty exposure and portfolios of counterparties.
- Collateral concentrations involve special-purpose entities (SPEs), since the collateral typically represents an SPE's paying capacity.
- Concentrations involve on- and off-balance-sheet activities, contractual and noncontractual risks, contingent and noncontingent risks, as well as underwriting and pipeline risks.

5.3.17   Stress Testing

The stress-testing framework, which is an integral part of enterprise risk management, must be designed to monitor factors including the following:

- day-to-day exposure and concentrations
- extreme market conditions that could excessively strain the financial resources of the organization
- day-to-day portfolio and hedging needs
- the strength of assumptions made about the legal enforceability of netting and the ability to collect and liquidate collateral.

A sound stress-testing framework is tightly coupled with concentration management, discussed in 5.3.16. In addition, it should include the following:

- measurement of the largest counterparty-level impacts across portfolios
- measurement of material concentrations within segments of a portfolio, such as industries or regions
- measurement of relevant portfolio-specific and counterparty-specific trends.
- capturing of aggregated exposures across all forms of trading at the counterparty-specific level, including transactions that fall outside of the main credit system
- a stress test on all principal market risk factors, such as interest rates, foreign exchange, equities, credit spreads, and commodity prices for all material counterparties
- identification of the counterparties that are not material on an individual basis but are material on a consolidated basis
- assessment of nondirectional risks, such as yield-curve exposures and basis risks
- assessment of the joint movement of exposures and related counterparty creditworthiness
- stress testing of CVA to assess performance under adverse scenarios, incorporating any hedging mismatches
- concurrent stress testing of exposure and noncash collateral for assessing wrong-way risk
- identification and assessment of exposure levels for certain counterparties, such as sovereigns and municipalities, above which the banking organization may be concerned about willingness to pay
- integration of CCR stress tests into firm-wide stress tests.

5.3.18   Central Counterparties

Prior to the 2007 financial crisis, counterparties were undercapitalized, meaning they were not holding enough capital to fulfill the claims made by clients. The sudden increase in the number of claims made a number of counterparties file for bankruptcy. The failure of counterparties in turn increased the severity of the financial crisis. In other words, though the counterparties did not trigger the crisis, they were not immune to the failure, and the failure in turn helped to fuel the crisis.

For example, American International Group (AIG) London was offering credit protection through a product called *credit default swap (CDS)*. The notional credit risk exposure reached close to half a trillion by the end of June 2008. However, there were not enough financial resources to cover potential claims. The widespread bond defaults during the crisis imposed substantial losses on AIG and similar counterparties.

The policymakers identified the need for centralized clearing to strengthen the financial system and included it in a framework that was proposed for regulation and oversight of the OTC derivatives market. The goal of the central counterparties (CCPs) was to increase the transparency in OTC transactions and reduce the exposure. EU and other regulators also identified the need for centralized clearing. Basel III provides incentives for the transactions going through CCPs by reducing the capital requirements for such OTC derivatives.

Structure of CCPs

A CCP is an independent legal entity that acts as an intermediary between the buyer and the seller of a derivative transaction. Like a non-CCP transaction, the single contract between two initial counterparties is still executed. It is replaced by two new contracts, between the CCP and each of the two contracting parties. At that point, the buyer and seller are no longer counterparties to each other; instead, each acquires the CCP as its counterparty.

In the beginning, the CCP provides valuation of the OTC derivatives and associated settlement functions. During the life of the transaction, the CCPs evaluate the contract on a daily basis through a concept called *variation margin*. At the end of the day, margin calls are made to the parties to post the additional collateral. CCPs have the authority to make intraday margin calls also if large price movements shorten the margin funds.

In the event of default, the CCP auctions the positions of the defaulted member, transfers the client positions to surviving clearing members, and allocates any excess losses to surviving clearing members.

Benefits of Central Clearing

There are many benefits to CCPs based on the structure we just discussed. For example, CCPs increase transparency. In a non-CCP market, the party does not know how many other parties are exposed to the counterparty, what are the types of that exposure, and what is the exposure amount. It is common that factors pertaining to one type of transaction may increase the exposure amount drastically. If several parties purchased put options and if the underlying company fails, then there will be a pressure on the counterparty. Using the CCPs, the details of all the parties are known to the CCP, and the CCP can monitor each product by its capacity and plan the trading by client accordingly. The transparency is also useful to the regulators to measure systemic risk from time to time.

All the derivative transactions going through the CCP will need to go through daily valuation and margining, making the transactions similar to future contracts. This mechanism makes the transactions more liquid. The CCP acts as a counterparty to each party and provides not only bilateral netting but also multilateral netting. In simple bilateral netting, only transactions that are eligible for netting can be netted. If the bilateral transactions are more heterogeneous, then the benefit of netting cannot be used. In multilateral netting, the CCP identifies the eligible parties for netting and will reduce the exposure.

The panic of default will further decrease the recovery value and increase the replacement cost. Structured management of CCP will make the auction process centralized, and so the panic can be reduced, yielding more recovery value to the parties.

From earlier discussions, we learned that the counterparties were undercapitalized during the crisis and losses exceeded financial commitments. In a CCP structure, the CCP can evenly distribute the default losses to all the participants and reduce the default probability. This concept is called *loss mutualization*.

The introduction of CCPs alone is not likely to be sufficient to ensure that OTC derivatives markets operate efficiently and withstand large shocks. CCPs will need to be complemented by improvements in trading and settlement infrastructure. This includes the greater use of automated trading, maintaining all trades in central-data depositories and enhancing risk management and disclosure requirements for market participants themselves.

5.3.19   CVA Desk

Modern risk management practices have been separating CCR management out of trading desks and sourcing it to dedicated CVA desks. This will make it easier for the traders to work in the risk-free world as if the credit risk has been removed from the instruments.

The CVA desk reduces the traders' workload and responsibilities, accessing the whole portfolio that may have legs booked in different systems and handling the whole set of market data required to compute CVA. The CVA desk dedicates staff to concentrate on developing adapted simulation models and pricing algorithms, validating proxies, hedging CVA, and so on.

CVA desk responsibilities include but are not limited to:

- delivering on-demand pre-deal or incremental CVA expressed as a fee or spread to the trading desks
- integrating real-time executed trades with the global CVA process
- analyzing CVA and calculating marginal CVA per trade
- hedging the risks, such as credit and wrong-way risk

5.3.20   CVA VaR

CVA VaR models, which are based on CVA to measure potential losses, are currently in the early stages of development. These models will serve as effective tools for risk management purposes. CVA VaR models capture the variability of CCR exposure, the variability of the counterparty's credit spread, and the dependency between them. They are considered effective tools when compared with traditional CCR metrics.

Developing VaR models for CVA is significantly more complicated than developing VaR models for market risk positions. The percentile and time horizon for the VaR model must match those appropriate for the management of this risk and include all significant risks associated with changes in the CVA.

It may be possible to use the same percentile for CVA VaR as that of market risk VaR—for example, the 95th or 99th percentile. However, the time horizon for CVA VaR may need to be longer than for market risk because of the potentially illiquid nature of CVA. The following are important considerations in developing a CVA VaR model:

- All material counterparties covered by CVA valuation should be included in the VaR model.

- A CVA VaR calculation that keeps the exposure or the counterparty probability of default static is not adequate. It will not only omit the dependence between the two variables, but also the risk arising from the uncertainty of the fixed variable.
- CVA VaR should incorporate all forms of CVA hedging.

5.3.21   Significant Changes Under Basel III

An institution that comes under Basel regulation is allowed to recognize the credit risk mitigation benefits of financial collateral for repo-style transactions, eligible margin loans, and OTC derivative contracts. Subject to eligibility and approval, there are three approaches to measure the CCR and collateral benefit: the collateral haircut approach, simple VaR methodology, and the internal model methodology (IMM).

The definition of financial collateral has been modified as follows:

- The resecuritizations no longer qualify as financial collateral. This is because during the crisis, it was observed that resecuritizations have shown more market value volatility than other types of financial collateral.
- The conforming residential mortgages are not allowed to show as financial collateral.
- All noninvestment-grade debt securities were removed from the definition of financial collateral.

The definition of *investment grade* was also modified. Investment grade means that the entity to which the institution is exposed has adequate capacity to meet financial commitments for the projected life of the asset or exposure.

The advanced-approaches rule was amended so that the capital requirement for IMM exposures is equal to the larger of the capital requirement for those exposures calculated using data from the most recent three-year period and data from a three-year period that contains a period of stress reflected in the credit default spreads of the banking organization's counterparties.

Large financial institutions are interconnected through an array of complex transactions. In recognition of this interconnectedness, and to mitigate the risk of contagion from the banking sector to the broader financial system and the general economy, Basel III includes enhanced requirements for the recognition and treatment of wrong-way risk in the IMM. The advanced-approaches rule requires banking organizations' risk management procedures to identify, monitor, and control wrong-way risk throughout the life of an exposure. These risk management procedures should include the use of stress testing and scenario analysis.

If the banking organization identifies an IMM exposure with specific wrong-way risk, the organization is required to treat that transaction as its own netting set. The proposed rule defined *specific wrong-way risk* as a type of wrong-way risk that arises when either the counterparty or issuer of the collateral supporting the transaction, or the counterparty and the reference asset of the transaction, are affiliates or the same entity.

If the banking organization identified an OTC derivative transaction, repo-style transaction, or eligible margin loan with specific wrong-way risk for which the banking organization otherwise applies the IMM, the banking organization would set the PD of the counterparty and an LGD equal to 100 percent.

6 Liquidity Risk Management

6.1 Understanding Liquidity Risk

Prior to the 2007 financial crisis, financial institutions did not recognize the liquidity issue as a mainstream agenda and did not make liquidity management a prudent program. The rapid availability of funding suddenly took the reverse direction and quickly evaporated for an extended period. The events triggered the central banks to step in to ensure the proper function of financial markets.

Traditional asset-pricing models like CAPM (capital asset pricing model) assume that all assets are infinitely divisible as to the amount that may be held or transacted and can be transacted at no cost. Traditional value-at-risk models assume that portfolio positions are fixed over-the-horizon. The above models do not consider the fact that a portfolio cannot be liquidated without a significant impact on market prices. *Liquidity risk* is the degree to which a portfolio manager cannot trade a position without excess cost. Liquidity risk takes two forms: funding liquidity risk and market liquidity risk.

Liquidity is a financial institution's capacity to meet its cash and collateral obligations at a reasonable cost. Maintaining an adequate level of liquidity depends on the institution's ability to efficiently meet both expected and unexpected cash flows and collateral needs without adversely affecting either daily operations or the financial condition of the institution. Liquidity risk is the risk that an institution's financial condition or overall safety and soundness is adversely affected by an inability (or perceived inability) to meet its obligations.

An institution's obligations, and the funding sources used to meet them, depend significantly on its business mix, balance-sheet structure, and the cash-flow profiles of its on- and off-balance-sheet obligations. In managing their cash flows, institutions confront various situations that can give rise to increased liquidity risk. These include funding mismatches, market constraints on the ability to convert assets into cash or in accessing sources of funds (market liquidity), and contingent liquidity events. Changes in economic conditions or exposure to credit, market, operation, legal, and reputation risks also can affect an institution's liquidity risk profile and should be considered in the assessment of liquidity and asset/liability management.

Funding liquidity risk arises from either the demand for payment from investors or margin calls from the lender—which may lead to involuntary liquidation of the portfolio at unfavorable prices—and from liabilities, assets, or both when there are mismatches in timing of payments from one side to the other. It is also called *liquidity-at-risk* or *cash-flow-at-risk*. Market liquidity risk arises when a trade cannot be executed at prevailing market prices because of the size of the position relative to normal market lots. Over-the-counter (OTC) derivatives usually have relatively high liquidity risk.

Alternative investments engage either in leveraged portfolios or use futures to hedge portfolio positions. In either case, there will be a margin call from prime brokers when the mark-to-market value of collateral falls. If the fund manager does not have enough funds to meet the margin demands, some of the positions will be forced to liquidate at unfavorable prices.

Fund managers reduce downside risk by hedging the market position using futures, thus reducing VaR (value at risk). However, because of possible margin calls, there is the possibility of cash outflow, which increases cash-flow-at-risk or liquidity-at-risk (LAR). Therefore, even though the hedged positions have small VaR, they will be subject to larger LAR. On the other hand, European options, which do not demand margin calls, have zero LAR but potentially large VaR prior to maturity.

The asset side of funding liquidity risk arises where there is a demand from investors for redemptions. Since most hedge funds invest in illiquid assets, such as distressed debt or structured products, hedge-fund managers should impose a longer lockup period and longer notice periods.

A mismatch in timing of payments also causes liquidity risk. One such example is that most commercial banks fund long-term loans using short deposits. Mismatch occurs when there is a demand for withdrawal from depositors or when customers use an unused portion of their line of credit, thus forcing the bank into liquidity risk. Another example is when the coupon-payment dates in a collateralized debt obligations (CDO) special purpose vehicle (SPV) do not match with the interest receiving date.

One can ask whether liquidity risk is a standalone risk or falls under market risk, credit risk, or operational risk. What are the major sources of liquidity risk? What are the corresponding risk factors to measure and hedge the liquidity risk? In fact, there is no single source of liquidity risk, and there is no risk factor that can be mapped to liquidity risk.

Liquidity risk is not a standalone risk. Liquidity risk is a complex risk and can arise from unexpected tail risks, operational failures, internal imbalances, funding issues, counterparty failures, market crises, systemic risks, or from the combined effects of all those shocks. Internal imbalances arise when market conditions alter the value of assets and collateral, or when external factors disrupt the funding sources.

The economic cycle is also one of the sources of liquidity risk. In a rising economy, more banks lend money. When the economy starts falling, the value of collateral will also fall, and banks will demand more margins or ask to sell some of the assets. In order to meet margin requirements, clients will sell the assets. However, there may not be interested buyers to buy the assets that the client wants to sell. Instead, buyers will ask for the assets they are interested in. This situation will make even liquid assets illiquid.

Liquidity risk cannot be hedged with a single processor model. The risk management culture must be tuned to aim to routinize unexpected events. The liquidity risk management process should have governing rules and should deeply root within the corporate culture as an immune system. Assessing liquidity risk should involve both quantitative and qualitative approaches. Hedging liquidity risk is very expensive and cannot be priced accurately because of its complexity. It may not be advantageous to remove illiquid positions completely from a portfolio; instead, proper liquidity risk management should be in place in order to sustain the portfolio from unfavorable and extreme market movements.

6.2 Characteristics of Liquidity Risk

- *It cannot be measured accurately.* While there are certain models developed and certain measures available, it cannot be measured accurately as bid-ask prices cannot be predicted accurately.

- *It is heterogeneous.* Liquidity risk is applicable to all departments, such as lending, capital markets, and business planning. It is also classified as day-to-day, weekly, monthly, short-term, long-term, tactical, and strategic.
- *It cannot be hedged.* Liquidity risk cannot be hedged or avoided, as it is an integral part of business. Avoiding liquidity risk means avoiding a business. The only way to minimize liquidity risk is through prudential risk-taking, having effective liquidity risk management practice in place, and establishing proactive relationships with financing intermediaries.
- *It is tightly coupled with other risks.* It is true that all risk is interrelated. For example, market risk can influence credit risk and vice versa, and operational risk can lead to internal credit risk. However, the influence of liquidity risk on other risks is very high.
- *It is more sensitive.* Liquidity risk can arise with no prior notice, as it is tightly coupled to consumer fear and run on the bank. A sudden risk aversion in the market to any major event can make the assets more illiquid.
- *It can arise from a variety of sources.* Because of the heterogeneity of liquidity risk, it can arise from any source. For example, a downgrade or another loss of market confidence will impact the security firms' ability to refinance current unsecured debt obligations. For insurers, a downgrade-triggering event would typically cause many policyholders to consider surrendering their policies. For banks, a downgrade can result in reduced market access to unsecured borrowing from institutional investors, a reduction or cancellation of interbank credit lines, or a reduction of deposits. Funding liquidity risk also arises from systemic events, such as the near collapse of Long-Term Capital Management (LPCM), or external events and catastrophes resulting in large claims on insurers.
- *It cannot be detected easily.* Because of the nature of liquidity risk, it cannot be detected early, though certain early warning indicators can be designed.
- *VaR is not appropriate for liquidity risk.* Liquidity risk arises mostly from tail events—such as mass downgrades, run on banks, and contagion risk—and the VaR is not a good tool to capture tail risk.
- *It is more global than any other risk.* Liquidity risk is very closely correlated to the dynamics of global events. Liquidity risk in one place may lead to contagion risk, or contagion risk of other forms of risk may cause illiquidity everywhere. In particular, the squeeze of liquidity in 2008, which implied a drying-up of liquidity among financial institutions,

forced many banks and investors to repatriate capital to finance investment and meet redemption calls, thus triggering a flight-to-quality phenomenon.

- *It can lead to catastrophic losses.* Liquidity risk can cause catastrophic losses even to successful business.

6.3   Historical Scenarios of Liquidity Risk

6.3.1   LTCM and Liquidity Risk

Long-Term Capital Management (LTCM) was a hedge fund founded in 1994 by former employees of Solomon Brothers. It was a multistrategy fund that involved relative value and equity volatility with positions in fixed income, equity, and derivatives. It engaged in both balance-sheet leverage and soft leverage using derivatives.

The relative-value strategy was built on the assumption that although the yield differences between risky and risk-free fixed-income securities varied over time, the risk premium or credit spread would tend to revert to average historical levels. Similarly, the equity volatility strategy was built on the assumption that implied volatility on options would tend to revert to long-term average levels.

LTCM shorted the volatility when the volatility implied by equity options was abnormally high. The fund performed very well until 1998. In 1998, the unexpected default of Russia on its debt caused the soaring of Russian interest rates and the devaluation of the ruble. This economic shock caused an increase in yields and a flight to quality government bonds of developed countries. As a result, credit spreads increased opposite the assumption of decreased credit spread. In addition, Brazil devalued its currency, further increasing interest rates and credit spreads. The overall panic also caused an increase in volatility, which generated losses in equity volatility strategies.

The severe impact in mark-to-market values of positions resulted in margin calls and cash-flow problems. Although relative value strategies sometimes diverge temporarily and converge ultimately, LTCM could not wait until convergence returned, as it had to force the liquidation of some of its positions in order to meet funding requirements for margin calls. As an added disadvantage, many other hedge funds, which had mimicked the LTCM strategy, flooded the forced liquidation of positions into market. The unfavorable price movements ultimately caused the US government to bail out LTCM and close the fund.

Even though LTCM implemented various risk management strategies—such as implementing longer redemption periods for investors and conducting stress tests in historical returns—it failed to adjust VaR measures with stress scenarios of the possibility that a larger portion of the fund might be liquidated, and other fund managers might be holding similar positions that might also require liquidation at the same time in the event of extreme market movements.

6.3.2   MGM and Liquidity Risk

Metallgesellschaft Corporation (MG) is the subsidiary of Metallgesellschaft A.G., a German conglomerate. MG Refining and Marketing (MGRM) is MG's trading division. In 1993, MGRM entered into a huge number of energy derivatives (futures and swaps) to hedge its price exposure on its forward supply contracts to deliver gasoline, diesel fuel, and heating oil to its customers over a period of ten years at fixed prices. The counterparties to forward contracts were retail gasoline suppliers, large manufacturing firms, and some government entities.

MGRM offered the following different levels of programs:

- *firm-fixed*, offering a fixed monthly delivery of oil products at a set price
- *firm-flexible*, offering extensive rights to customers to set the delivery schedule for up to 20 percent of its needs in any year, besides the fixed price commitments
- *guaranteed margin* contracts under which it agreed to make deliveries at a price that would assure the independent operator a fixed margin relative to the retail price offered by its geographical competitors

At the discretion of MGRM, the contracts could be extended annually for a defined period. The first two programs involved 154 million barrels of obligations for periods up to ten years. The obligations to the MGRM meant it was short in oil.

Contracts were negotiated during the summer of 1993, when energy prices were low. The contracts came with a cash-out option if the energy price was to rise above the contractually fixed prices. Under the cash-out provision, the buyer could choose to sell the remainder of its forward obligations back to MGRM for a cash payment of one-half the difference.

This strategy exposed MGRM to the risk of rising energy prices. Therefore, MGRM hedged this price risk with OTC swaps and with energy futures contracts of between one to three months to maturity at the New York Mercantile Exchange (NYMEX). MGRM would gain substantially from its derivative positions if energy prices rose. During the latter part of 1993, however, energy prices fell, resulting in unrealized losses and margin calls on derivative positions in excess of $900 million. To complicate the matter, the futures market went into a contango price relationship for almost entire year, increasing cost each time it rolled its derivatives.

Since there were not many firms in the market selling long-dated contracts, and since MGRM's credit rating was low, it could not buy hedged contracts for the same maturity. If energy prices had risen rather than fallen, MGRM would not have had a problem. It would have had unrealized gains on its derivatives positions. Although it would have had unrealized losses on its forward contracts, this would not have mattered, as they would have been offset by unrealized gains on its derivative positions.

MGRM's hedging strategy included short-dated energy futures contracts and OTC swaps—known as a *stack and roll*. Under this strategy, MGRM opened a long position in futures staked in the near-month contract. Each month, MGRM would roll the stack over into the next near-month contract, gradually decreasing the size of the position. But when markets are in contango—that is, when futures prices are higher than spot prices—this strategy will result in losses.

MG's supervisory board responded to the situation of mounting margin calls by liquidating MGRM's derivative positions and forward supply contracts, ending MG's involvement in the oil market. The company suffered derivative-related losses of $1.3 billion by the end of 1993.

Based on the analysis, we can observe that MGRM's strategy was exposed to the following three risks:

1. Rollover risk
2. Funding risk
3. Credit risk

Proper funding would have saved the firm from not liquidating the long-dated forwards, which would have offset the losses in short-dated futures and swaps. Since there was demand for margins, there was a need for funding, and therefore the company had to forgo the expected profits from the forward contracts.

6.3.3   Year 2007 and Liquidity Risk

The economic crisis that began in 2007 has been of broad scope, severely affecting many markets and diverse institutions. The crisis started with declines in US housing prices and the associated rise in delinquencies on subprime mortgages. Since the expansion of subprime mortgages was only part of a much larger credit boom, other forms of credit were soon affected. Because of the complex nature of the credit instruments and the opacity of their markets, investors became increasingly uncertain about the magnitude and location of the risks underlying these instruments. They reacted by becoming more risk averse and either stopped trading or asked for substantially higher compensation to take on risk.

A broad range of asset markets, such as those for securitized products, became impaired. Financial institutions dependent on these markets suffered losses on their investments and cut back on their lending. The crisis became more acute in September of 2008 when the failure or near-failure of major financial firms resulted in financial markets freezing up.

6.4   How Hedge Funds Manage Liquidity Risk

Most alternative assets have much lower liquidity than stocks or bonds, and lower liquidity is one of the reasons alternative-investment investors expect a higher return on investment as a premium for illiquidity. When investors choose to invest in illiquid investments—such as venture capital, real estate, and hedge funds—they need to ensure that the range of allocations that may occur over time is acceptable. Since alternative investments are long-term investments, investors must also have a long enough time horizon to ensure that they are able to benefit from the expected higher returns of the illiquid investments.

Attempting to withdraw the investments, either partially or fully, will impact the performance of the fund, which in turn impacts the profits of other investors. Since a run on redemption hurts the performance of the fund and eventually the profit of other investors, the fund manager should impose restrictions on redemptions. However, overimposing the restrictions will not attract the investor, as there are always certain investors who want to redeem earlier than committed. As a trade-off between redemption restrictions and performance compromise, the fund manager should adopt additional liquidity management principles, including the following:

- *Enforce lockup periods.* A lockup period is an interval during which the investor is not allowed to withdraw from a particular fund. After the specified lockup period, investors are free to withdraw funds as defined in the disclosure document of each hedge fund. Almost all hedge funds have a lockup period ranging from as little as three months to longer than two years. The more established the fund, the longer the lockup period.

  Lockup periods are established to give enough opportunity to the fund manager to draw the strategy and deploy the money. While managers prefer to establish lockup periods, investors often view them as an inconvenience. Managed futures, on the other hand, do not have lockup periods. There are a few that have lockups, ranging anywhere from three months to a year, but this is not a stringent requirement in the futures-fund industry.

- *Enforce longer redemption notice periods.* Longer redemption notice periods provide the fund manager time to assess the pros and cons of selling assets and decide which assets to sell that will have the least impact on the fund.

- *Enforce redemption gates.* Redemption gates protect the fund manager from the flooding of deinvestments by investors. When few investors demand withdrawals, the manager may have to sell a portion of the assets, and since most funds invest at aggregated level rather than individual level, it may often require the sale of the investments of other investors as well. This will negatively impact the other investors. Withdrawing the funds may also result in negative tax consequences. Redemptions gates allow managers to restrict the amount of withdrawals to a ceiling of between certain percentages of quarterly assets..

- *Utilize side pockets.* Side pockets hold special investments. A special investment is typically an illiquid asset or any asset that the fund manager determines is difficult to establish a market value for or should be held until the conclusion of a special event. However, managers do not label every asset in the fund as special. Each investor participating in illiquid investments will redeem a pro rata portion of their illiquid investments.

  Side pockets enable managers to invest and manage funds efficiently, because side pockets provide protection from unforeseen redemption pressures. Side-pocketing allows fund managers to participate in private and less liquid investments in a way that is intended to be beneficial as well as fair and equitable to all investors. Side pockets are quite common in private equity funds.

- *Have capital reserves.* Reasonable cash reserves allow fund managers to fulfill redemption requests that they are obligated to meet as per the law.
- *Make payment in kind.* Payment in kind is more common in private equity investments. This provision allows fund managers to substitute cash redemptions with additional shares in the fund.

6.5 Modeling Liquidity Risk

Modeling liquidity risk is nothing but measuring the cost of liquidity. Liquidity cost is an additional cost at which the firm will be able to liquidate the assets in a desired time. Liquidity cost depends on a variety of factors, such as instrument, market scope, business cycle, and geography. While the measurement of liquidity cost requires both subjective and quantitative tools, there are typically three standard approaches: the constant spread approach, the exogenous spread approach, and the endogenous price approach.

The three methods look at different aspects of liquidity, and the researcher should select the appropriate method based on the nature of liquidity, sophistication, and ease of implementation. Consider the following factors:

- The *constant spread approach* is the simplest. It assumes that the bid-ask spread is constant. The liquidity cost (LC) is equal to the product of half the spread and the size of the position to be liquidated. Half the spread has been used here as the liquidity risk incorporating selling the asset, which is a one-way trip as opposed to a round-trip.
- The *exogenous spread approach* assumes that the bid–ask spread is not constant, but the trades of a single trader do not impact the spread. This assumes that the spread is stochastic, which follows normal distribution.
- The *endogenous price approach* assumes that there exists a downward pressure on prices in response to trading. The downward pressure can simply be included in the cost using elasticity and the size of the trade relative to the entire market.

6.6 Sources of Liquidity Risk

Liquidity risk arises from many sources, including firm-specific sources, customer business tactics, and systemic events.

6.6.1   Firm-Specific Sources

Firm-specific sources come from unfavorable movements in transactions. They include derivative-style transactions, collateral calls, products with embedded options, misalignment between loans, and funding sources.

The payments in derivative-style transactions are two-way and impact both outflows and inflows of cash. Certain derivatives—such as options and credit default swaps—receive the initial premium but can lead to huge payouts in unanticipated market movements of prices or events like bankruptcy, default, or ratings downgrade. The premium received may not be sufficient to cover payment obligations. Similarly, the delay or failure to receive the payments because of counterparty default will impact the cash inflows; or, in a securities borrowing transaction, sharp and unanticipated market movements or events— such as an unanticipated bankruptcy, default, or rating downgrade—could cause demand for additional collateral from counterparties.

Similar pressures on a firm's liquidity positions can arise from the following:

- collateral calls from exchanges in connection with foreign exchange and securities transactions
- margin and collateral agreements in the OTC derivative market or repo market
- liability mismatches arising from settlement systems requiring effective hedging or increased collateralization
- short positions in financial options with cash delivery

Off-balance-sheet exposures also contribute to liquidity risk at banking firms during times of stress. Key off-balance sheet products that can give rise to sudden material demands for liquidity at banking firms include committed lending facilities to customers, committed backstop facilities to commercial paper conduits, and committed backup lines to special purpose vehicles.

Insurance contracts offering policyholders the right, at regular intervals, to surrender a contract on guaranteed terms gives rise to liquidity risk. Another commonly mentioned product is linked funds, where investors are entitled to demand redemptions; funds holding illiquid assets, such as real estate, are especially problematic. Other products mentioned by a few firms include swaps, futures, and put options sold by the firm that might need collateralization, and reinsurance or other contracts containing rating triggers.

The bonds with embedded options, such as callable and puttable bonds, also impact the liquidity. The sudden recall of bonds by issuers or surrender from investors will lead to imbalances in the portfolio.

Liquidity risk also arises when long-term loans are issued using the proceeds from short-term instruments, such as commercial paper. When the CPs mature, typically in one to five years, there will be a need for the cash to return to the CP investors, whereas those funds are used to issue long-term loans with maturities greater than five years.

6.6.2   *Customer-Driven Transactions*

Customer deposits or transactions are a typical and more volatile tactic. Deposits are withdrawn when there are other attractive investments. The opposite transactions show a similar impact. For example, if customers borrowed money and prepay it earlier than the anticipated due date, there may be a reinvestment risk.

6.6.3   *Systemic Risk*

Ratings downgrades or other negative news leading to a loss of market confidence in a firm were cited as the most significant firm-specific sources of liquidity risk across the sectors, due the following concerns:

- *For securities firms*, a downgrade or other loss of market confidence would impact the firms' ability to refinance current unsecured debt obligations, which are their primary sources of funding for activities that cannot be self-financed.
- *For insurers*, such a triggering event would typically cause policyholders to consider surrendering their policies provided that the contractual and economic conditions are fulfilled. In addition, many reinsurance contracts include a ratings-downgrade trigger under which collateral is required when the rating of the counterparty falls below investment grade.
- *For banking organizations*, a downgrade can result in reduced market access to unsecured borrowings (such as CP) from institutional investors, a reduction or cancellation of interbank credit lines, or a reduction of deposits. Downgrades or other material, negative, firm-specific news or rumors can also increase liquidity demands through margin calls, requirements to post additional collateral, the need to

provide credit enhancements or backup lines for securitizations, and the need to fund assets no longer capable of being sold or transferred via securitization.

Funding liquidity risk also arises from systemic events, such as LTCM's near-collapse following the 1998 Russian bond default, or external events and catastrophes resulting in large claims on insurers. Financial groups find that preparing for systemic events presents challenges because scenario analysis requires in-depth and detailed determinations of appropriate assumptions regarding different sources of systemic risk, the speed and timing of the event, its impact across the various firms within the group, and the behavior of counterparties—information that is not easily derived from historical data.

6.7   Effective Liquidity Risk Management for Banking

Measuring liquidity risk accurately is highly difficult, and so it cannot be priced. The liquidity risk cannot be hedged, as it is difficult to measure, and also the hedging will cause loss of profit from core business opportunities. To minimize the losses occurring from liquidity risk in both normal markets and stressed markets, it is imperative to set up an effective liquidity risk management team as part of the enterprise risk management team. This section looks at how such a practice can be set up and what the goals should be.

6.7.1   Corporate Governance

Since liquidity risk is more enterprise in nature than any other risk, it is the responsibility of the board of directors to ensure the following:

- The institution's liquidity risk tolerance is established.
- The approach to managing the trade-offs between liquidity risk and short-term profits is defined.
- The nature of the liquidity risks is understood.
- Management's duties to identify, measure, monitor, and control liquidity risk are enforced.
- The institution's cash-flow projections (CFPs) for handling potential adverse liquidity events are understood and periodically reviewed.
- The liquidity-risk profiles of significant subsidiaries and affiliates as appropriate are understood.

Institutions should have documented strategies for managing liquidity risk and clear policies and procedures for limiting and controlling risk exposures that appropriately reflect the institution's risk tolerances. Strategies should identify primary sources of funding for meeting daily operating cash outflows, as well as seasonal and cyclical cash-flow fluctuations including but not limited to the following:

- cash-flow projections that include discrete and cumulative cash flow mismatches
- target reserves of unencumbered liquid assets
- measures used to identify unstable liabilities and liquid asset coverage ratios
- asset concentrations that could increase liquidity risk through a limited ability to convert to cash
- funding concentrations that address diversification of funding sources
- funding concentrations that address the nature of the assets they fund
- contingent liability exposures, such as unfunded loan commitments, lines of credit supporting asset sales or securitizations, and collateral requirements for derivatives transactions and various types of secured lending
- exposures of material activities, such as securitization, trading, and international activities.

6.7.2   Cash-Flow Projections

Firms should have a robust liquidity risk management framework providing prospective dynamic cash-flow forecasts that include assumptions on the likely behavioral responses of key counterparties to changes in conditions. Firms should make realistic assumptions about future liquidity needs for both the short and long term that reflect the complexities of their underlying businesses, products, and markets. In estimating the cash flows arising from liabilities, a firm should assess the stability of its funding sources to ensure its sources will not dry up quickly under stress.

6.7.3   Maturity Gap Analysis

The firm should obtain a maturity distribution for the sources and uses of funds by managing the timing of incoming flows in relation to known outgoing sources.

6.7.4   Monitoring the Quality of Products

The firm should analyze the quality of assets that could be used as collateral in order to assess their potential for providing secured funding in stressed conditions.

6.7.5   Monitoring Collateral and Margins

A firm should incorporate cash flows related to the repricing, exercise, or maturity of financial derivatives contracts in its liquidity risk analysis, including the potential for counterparties to demand additional collateral in the event of a decline in the product credit rating, for example, or a decline in the price of the underlying asset. Timely confirmation of OTC derivatives transactions is fundamental to such analyses, because unconfirmed trades call into question the accuracy of a firm's measures of potential exposure.

Collateral levels must be monitored by the legal entity jurisdiction and currency exposure. The shifts between intraday and overnight must be monitored.The institutions must have the ability to assess the potential demand on collateral arising from various types of contractual contingencies during periods of both market-wide and institution-specific stress.

6.7.6   Monitoring Wrong-Way Risk

Wrong-way risk refers to the phenomenon that counterparty credit quality deteriorates at the same time that firms need to claim it against their credit-quality deterioration. A firm should consider the liquidity needs it would encounter if it had wrong-way risk with a counterparty that provides guarantees on its assets. For example, a firm that holds assets whose creditworthiness is dependent on the guarantees of a third party or has raised funds against such assets could face significant demands on its funding liquidity if the third party's credit standing deteriorates. In such cases, the firm could be required to write down the value of assets backed by a third party—or repurchase, or post additional margin against, such assets.

6.7.7   Liquidity Across Currencies, Legal Entities, and Business Lines

Liquidity risk exposures and funding needs must be monitored within and across currencies, legal entities, and business lines, regardless of the organizational structure. It should be noted that there are some operational limitations in the transferability of liquidity. The institution must maintain sufficient liquidity to ensure compliance with applicable legal and regulatory restrictions on the transfer of liquidity among regulated entities.

6.7.8   *Intraday Liquidity Position Management*

Intraday liquidity monitoring is an important component of the liquidity risk management process and must include, but is not limited to, the following:

- monitoring and measuring expected daily gross liquidity inflows and outflows
- managing and mobilizing collateral when necessary to obtain intraday credit
- identifying and prioritizing time-specific and other critical obligations in order to meet them when expected
- settling other less-critical obligations as soon as possible
- controlling credit to customers when necessary
- ensuring that liquidity planners understand the amounts of collateral and liquidity needed to perform payment-system obligations when assessing the organization's overall liquidity needs

6.7.9   *Imposing Limits*

A firm should set limits to control its liquidity risk exposure and vulnerabilities and should regularly review such limits and corresponding risk-escalation procedures. Limits should be relevant to the business in terms of its location, complexity of strategy, nature of products, currencies, and markets served. Limits should be used for managing day-to-day liquidity within and across lines of business and legal entities under normal conditions.

6.7.10   *Liquidity Cushion*

A firm should maintain a cushion of unencumbered, high-quality liquid assets to be held as insurance against a range of liquidity stress scenarios, including those that involve the loss or impairment of unsecured and typically available secured funding sources. A critical element of a firm's resilience to liquidity stress is the continuous availability of an adequate cushion of unencumbered, high-quality liquid assets that can be sold or pledged to obtain funds in a range of stress scenarios. This requires explicitly relating the size of the cushion of unencumbered, high-quality liquid assets held as insurance against liquidity stress to the estimates of liquidity needs under stress.

Estimates of liquidity needs during periods of stress should incorporate both contractual and noncontractual cash flows, including the possibility of funds being withdrawn, and they should assume the inability to obtain unsecured funding as well as the loss or impairment of access to funds secured by assets other than the safest and most liquid. The size of the liquidity cushion should be aligned with established risk tolerance. Key considerations include assumptions of the duration and severity of stress and the liquidation or borrowing value of assets in stress situations.

6.7.11   Early-Warning Indicator System

A firm should design a set of indicators to identify the emergence of increased risk or vulnerabilities in its liquidity-risk position or potential funding needs. Such early-warning indicators should identify any negative trends and cause an assessment and potential response by management in order to mitigate the firm's exposure to the emerging risk. Early-warning indicators can be qualitative or quantitative in nature and may include but are not limited to the following:

- rapid asset growth, especially when funded with potentially volatile liabilities
- growing concentrations in assets or liabilities
- increases in currency mismatches
- a decrease of weighted average maturity of liabilities
- repeated incidents of positions approaching or breaching internal or regulatory limits
- negative trends or heightened risk associated with a particular product line, such as rising delinquencies
- significant deterioration in the firm's earnings, asset quality, and overall financial condition
- negative publicity
- a credit-rating downgrade
- stock-price declines or rising debt costs
- widening debt or credit-default-swap spreads
- rising wholesale or retail funding costs
- counterparties that begin to request additional collateral for credit exposures when the value of assets deteriorates
- correspondent firms that eliminate or decrease their credit lines

- difficulty accessing longer-term funding
- difficulty placing short-term liabilities

6.7.12   Funding-Source Diversification

A firm should diversify available funding sources in the short term, medium term, and long term. The desired diversification should include limits on counterparty-secured versus unsecured market funding, instrument type, securitization vehicle, currency, and geographic market. Diversification does not mean simply spreading across multiple funding sources; it is also related to proportionate mixing. The most common debt instruments banks include are client deposits, unsecured money market funds, straight bonds, MTN programs, secured lending like repos, covered bonds, and securitization.

If long-term loans are backed by short-term money market rollovers, the liquidity dries up during the crisis and the money market funds may not be able to roll over. While secured lending (borrowing) transactions somewhat guarantee the liquidity, it also depends on the quality of collateral being posted by the bank. If the quality deteriorates, the lenders leading to liquidity dry-up will withdraw the funds. The funding mix should consider every characteristic of every instrument of funding sources and will need to be optimized.

6.7.13   Contingency Funding Plan

A CFP sets out the strategies for addressing liquidity shortfalls in emergency situations. A CFP should delineate policies to manage a range of stress environments, establish clear lines of responsibility, and articulate clear implementation and escalation procedures. Contingent liquidity events are unexpected situations or business conditions that may increase liquidity risk. The events may be institution-specific or arise from external factors and may include the following:

- the institution's inability to fund asset growth
- the institution's inability to renew or replace maturing funding liabilities
- customers unexpectedly exercising options to withdraw deposits or exercise off-balance-sheet commitments
- changes in market value and price volatility of various asset types
- changes in economic conditions, market perception, or dislocations in the financial markets
- disturbances in payment and settlement due to operational or local disasters

A CFP provides a documented framework for managing unexpected liquidity situations. The objective of the CFP is to ensure that the institution's sources of liquidity are sufficient to fund normal operating requirements under contingent events.

Contingent liquidity events can range from high-probability and low-impact events to low-probability and high-impact events. Institutions should incorporate planning for high-probability and low-impact liquidity risks into the day-to-day management of sources and uses of funds. All financial-institution CFPs will typically focus on events that, while relatively infrequent, could significantly impact the institution's operations. A CFP should do the following:

- identify stress events
- assess levels of severity and timing
- assess funding sources and needs
- perform liquidity gap analysis
- perform stress tests
- identify potential funding sources
- establish liquidity-event management processes
- establish a monitoring framework for contingent events

6.7.14   Stress Test

A firm should conduct stress tests on a regular basis for a variety of institution-specific and market-wide stress scenarios to identify sources of potential liquidity strain and to ensure that current exposures remain in accordance with the firm's established liquidity risk tolerance. A firm should use stress-test outcomes to adjust its liquidity risk management strategies, policies, and positions and to develop effective contingency plans.

While a firm typically manages liquidity under normal circumstances, it should also be prepared to manage liquidity under stressed conditions. A firm should perform stress tests or scenario analyses on a regular basis in order to identify and quantify its exposure to possible future liquidity stresses, analyzing possible impacts on the institution's cash flows, liquidity position, profitability, and solvency. The results of these stress tests should form the basis for taking remedial or mitigating actions to limit exposure, build up liquidity buffers, and adjust its liquidity profile to fit its risk tolerance. The results of stress tests should also play a key role in shaping the firm's contingency planning and in determining the strategy and tactics to deal with events of liquidity stress. As a result, stress testing and contingency planning are closely intertwined.

6.8   Liquidity Risk Under Basel III

To promote awareness of the liquidity issue, the Basel Committee on Banking Supervision (BCBS) in 2008 published principles for "Sound Liquidity Risk Management and Supervision," providing detailed guidance on liquidity risk management. The committee has further strengthened its liquidity framework in Basel III by developing two minimum standards for funding liquidity: liquidity coverage ratio (LCR) to promote short-term resilience of a bank's liquidity risk profile by ensuring that it has sufficient high-quality liquid assets to survive a significant stress scenario lasting for one month; and net stable funding ratio (NSFR) to promote resilience over a longer time horizon (one year) by creating additional incentives for banks to fund their activities with more stable sources of funding on an ongoing basis.

Certain parameters pertaining to these standards contain elements of national discretion to reflect jurisdiction-specific conditions and thus require transparency in the regulations of each jurisdiction to provide clarity both within the jurisdiction and internationally. To further strengthen liquidity risk management, the committee has developed a set of monitoring tools to be used in the ongoing monitoring of the liquidity risk exposures of banks, and in communicating these exposures among home and host supervisors.

6.8.1   Liquidity Coverage Ratio

LCR is designed to ensure that the bank maintains an adequate level of unencumbered, high-quality liquid assets that can be converted into cash to meet its liquidity needs for a thirty-calendar-day time horizon under a significantly severe liquidity stress scenario, by which time it is assumed that appropriate corrective actions can be taken by management and, if needed, by supervisors if further needed to resolve the bank in an orderly way.

The LCR is the ratio of stock of high-quality liquid assets to total net cash outflows over the next thirty calendar days. As per the guidelines, this ratio must be greater than or equal to 100 percent.

Banks are expected to meet this requirement continuously and hold a stock of unencumbered, high-quality liquid assets as a defense against the potential onset of severe liquidity stress. As stated in the December 2010 BCBS document "Basel III: International Framework for Liquidity Risk Measurement, Standards and Monitoring" (http://www.bis.org/publ/bcbs188.pdf):

> Given the uncertain timing of outflows and inflows, banks and supervisors are also expected to be aware of any potential mismatches within the 30-day period and ensure that sufficient liquid assets are available to meet any cashflow gaps throughout the period.

> The scenario for this standard entails a combined idiosyncratic [firm-wide] and [systemic] market-wide shock that would result in:

>   • the run-off of a proportion of retail deposits;
>   • a partial loss of unsecured wholesale funding capacity;
>   • a partial loss of secured, short-term financing with certain collateral and counterparties;
>   • additional contractual outflows that would arise from a downgrade in the bank's public credit rating by up to and including three notches, including collateral posting requirements;
>   • increases in market volatilities that impact the quality of collateral or potential future exposure of derivative positions and thus require larger collateral haircuts or additional collateral, or lead to other liquidity needs;
>   • unscheduled draws on committed but unused credit and liquidity facilities that the bank has provided to its clients; and
>   • the potential need for the bank to buy back debt or honor noncontractual obligations in the interest of mitigating reputational risk.

LCR is equal to the stock of high-quality liquid assets divided by total net cash outflows over the next thirty calendar days

Stock of High-Quality Liquid Assets

Assets that can be easily and immediately converted into cash at little or no loss of value are considered to be high-quality liquid assets. The underlying stress scenario, the volume to be monetized, and the time frame all influence the liquidity. Assets that are less risky tend to have higher liquidity. High credit standing of the issuer and a low degree of subordination increases an asset's liquidity. Low duration, low volatility, low inflation risk and denomination in a convertible currency with low foreign exchange risk all enhance an asset's liquidity.

An asset's liquidity increases if market participants are more likely to agree on its valuation. According to "Basel III: International Framework for Liquidity Risk Measurement, Standards and Monitoring":

> The pricing formula of a high-quality liquid asset must be easy to calculate and not depend on strong assumptions. The inputs into the pricing formula must also be publicly available. In practice, this should rule out the inclusion of most structured or exotic products. ...

> The stock of high-quality liquid assets should not be subject to wrong-way (highly correlated) risk. For example, assets issued by financial institutions are more likely to be illiquid in times of liquidity stress in the banking sector. Listing on a developed and recognized exchange market increases ... an asset's transparency.

> The asset should have active outright sale or repo markets at all times(which means having a large number of market participants and a high trading volume). There should be historical evidence of market breadth and market depth (price impact per unit of liquidity) and market depth (units of the asset that can be traded for a given price impact). ...

> Quotes will most likely be available for buying and/or selling a high-quality liquid asset. ... A diverse group of buyers and sellers in an asset's market increases the reliability of its liquidity.

> Historically, the market has shown tendencies to move into these types of assets in a systemic crisis [exhibiting flight to quality].

In order to be considered for flight to quality, the liquidity generation through the sale or secured borrowing should remain intact even in periods of severe idiosyncratic and market stress. Lower-quality assets will exhibit the large fire-sale discount or haircut to compensate for high market risk under the conditions of severe market stress. This will "erode the market's confidence in the bank, but would also generate mark-to-market losses for banks holding similar instruments and add to the pressure on their liquidity position, thus encouraging further fire sales and declines in prices and market liquidity. In these circumstances, private market liquidity for such instruments is likely to disappear extremely quickly."

"Basel III: International Framework for Liquidity Risk Measurement, Standards and Monitoring" goes on to state:

> High-quality liquid assets should also ideally be eligible at central banks for intraday liquidity needs and overnight liquidity facilities. In the past, central banks have provided a further backstop to the supply of banking system liquidity under conditions of severe stress. Central bank eligibility should thus provide additional confidence that banks are holding assets that could be used in events of severe stress without damaging the broader financial system. That in turn would raise confidence in the safety and soundness of liquidity risk management in the banking system. It should be noted, however, that central bank eligibility does not by itself constitute the basis for the categorization of an asset as a "high-quality liquid asset."

Operational Requirements

Again quoting "Basel III: International Framework for Liquidity Risk Measurement, Standards and Monitoring":

> Assets must be available for the bank to convert into cash at any time to fill funding gaps between cash inflows and outflows during the stressed period. The assets must be unencumbered ... [meaning] not be pledged (either explicitly or implicitly) to secure, collateralize, or credit-enhance any transaction. [The collaterals received must not be rehypothecated.]

The stock of liquid assets should not be co-mingled with or used as hedges on trading positions, be designated as collateral or be designated as credit enhancements in structured transactions or be designated to cover operational costs … and should be managed with the clear and sole intent for use as a source of contingent funds. …

The stock should be under the control of the specific function or functions charged with managing the liquidity risk of the bank (typically the treasurer). A bank should periodically monetise a proportion of the assets in the stock through repo or outright sale to the market in order to test its access to the market, the effectiveness of its processes for monetization, and the usability of the assets, as well as to minimise the risk of negative signalling during a period of stress.

At the consolidated level, banks may also include in the stock qualifying liquid assets that are held to meet legal entity requirements … to the extent that the related risks (as measured by the legal entity's net cash outflows) are also reflected in the consolidated LCR. Any surplus of liquid assets held at the legal entity can only be included in the consolidated stock if those assets would be freely available to the consolidated (parent) entity in times of stress.

In addition, banks and regulators should be aware that the LCR stress does not cover expected or unexpected intraday liquidity needs that occur during the day and disappear by the end of the day.

While the LCR is expected to be met and reported in a single common currency, banks are expected to be able to meet their liquidity needs in each currency and maintain high-quality liquid assets consistent with the distribution of their liquidity needs by currency. The bank should be able to use the stock to generate liquidity in the currency and jurisdiction in which the net cash outflows arise. As such, the LCR by currency is expected to be monitored and reported to allow the bank and its supervisor to track any potential currency mismatch issues that could arise.…

In managing foreign exchange liquidity risk, the bank should take into account the risk that its ability to swap currencies and access the relevant foreignexchange markets may erode rapidly under stressed conditions, and that sudden, adverse exchange-rate movements could sharply widen existing mismatched positions and alter the effectiveness of any foreign exchange hedges. In order to mitigate cliff effects that could arise, if an eligible liquid asset became ineligible (eg due to rating downgrade) a bank would be allowed to keep the asset in its stock of liquid assets for an additional 30 calendar days. This would allow the bank additional time to adjust its stock as needed or replace the asset.

Categorization of Liquid Assets

There are two categories of assets, namely Level 1 assets, which do not have limit, and Level 2 assets, which can comprise up to 40 percent of the pool. According to "Basel III: International Framework for Liquidity Risk Measurement, Standards and Monitoring":

> National supervisors may wish to require haircuts for Level 1 securities based on, among other things, their duration, credit and liquidity risk, and typical repo haircuts. The following assets are considered Level 1 assets are limited to:
>
> - cash
> - central bank reserves, to the extent that these reserves can be drawn down in times of stress
> - marketable securities representing claims on or claims guaranteed by sovereigns, central banks, non-central government PSEs, the Bank for International Settlements, the International Monetary Fund, the European Commission, or multilateral development banks and satisfying all of the following conditions:
>   - assigned a 0% risk weight under the Basel II Standardized Approach;
>   - traded in large, deep and active repo or cash markets characterised by a low level of concentration;

           o   proven record as a reliable source of liquidity in the markets (repo or sale) even during stressed market conditions; and

           o   not an obligation of a financial institution or any of its affiliated entities.

- for non–0% risk-weighted sovereigns, sovereign, or central bank debt securities issued in domestic currencies by the sovereign or central bank in the country in which the liquidity risk is being taken or in the bank's home country; and,

- for non–0% risk-weighted sovereigns, domestic sovereign or central bank debt securities issued in foreign currencies, to the extent that holding of such debt matches the currency needs of the bank's operations in that jurisdiction.

Level 2 assets can be included in the stock of liquid assets, subject to the requirement that they comprise no more than 40% of the overall stock after haircuts have been applied. As mentioned above, the Level 2 cap also effectively includes cash or other Level 1 assets generated by secured funding transactions (or collateral swaps) maturing within 30 days. … The portfolio of Level 2 assets held by any institution should be well diversified in terms of type of assets, type of issuer (economic sector in which it participates, etc.) and specific counterparty or issuer.

A minimum 15% haircut is applied to the current market value of each Level 2 asset held in the stock. Level 2 assets are limited to the following:

- Marketable securities representing claims on or claims guaranteed by sovereigns, central banks, and non-central government PSEs or multilateral development banks that satisfy all of the following conditions:
  - o assigned a 20% risk weight under the Basel II Standardised Approach for credit risk;
  - o traded in large, deep, and active repo or cash markets characterized by a low level of concentration;

- o proven record as a reliable source of liquidity in the markets (repo or sale) even during stressed market conditions (ie maximum decline of price or increase in haircut over a 30-day period during a relevant period of significant liquidity stress not exceeding 10%); and
- o not an obligation of a financial institution or any of its affiliated entities.
- • Corporate bondsand covered bonds that satisfy all of the following conditions:
  - o not issued by a financial institution or any of its affiliated entities (in the case of corporate bonds);
  - o not issued by the bank itself or any of its affiliated entities (in the case of covered bonds);
  - o assets have a credit rating from a recognized external credit-assessment institution (ECAI) of at least AA− or do not have a credit assessment by a recognized ECAI and are internally rated as having a probability of default (PD) corresponding to a credit rating of at least AA−;
  - o traded in large, deep, and active repo or cash markets characterized by a low level of concentration; and
  - o proven as a reliable source of liquidity in the markets (repo or sale) even during stressed market conditions: ie, maximum decline of price or increase in haircut over a 30-day period during the relevant period of significant liquidity stress not exceeding 10%.

Both credit ratings and additional qualitative and quantitative criteria determine the eligibility of Level 2 assets. The additional criteria are not meant to exclude qualifying Level 2 assets, but to address assets that are not liquid, as well as to provide measures in addition to credit ratings with which to evaluate the liquidity characteristics of assets so as not to place undue reliance on external ratings alone. The Committee will test a number of qualitative and quantitative criteria during the observation period to determine the appropriate set and calibration of the criteria to use. These tested criteria will include volume, bid-ask spread, turnover, and other possible criteria to be further developed by the Committee.

As these criteria become more robust, there should be less emphasis placed on external ratings and more on the additional criteria.

Total Net Cash Outflows

"Basel III: International Framework for Liquidity Risk Measurement, Standards and Monitoring" specifies that:

> The term *total net cash outflow* is defined as the total expected cash outflows minus total expected cash inflows in the specified stress scenario for the subsequent 30 calendar days. Total expected cash outflows are calculated by multiplying the outstanding balances of various categories or types of liabilities and off-balance sheet commitments by the rates at which they are expected to run off or be drawn down. Total expected cash inflows are calculated by multiplying the outstanding balances of various categories of contractual receivables by the rates at which they are expected to flow in under the scenario up to an aggregate cap of 75% of total expected cash outflows:
>
> Total net cash outflows over the next 30 calendar days = outflows – Min {inflows; 75% of outflows}.
>
> While most roll-off rates, drawdown rates, and similar factors are harmonized across jurisdictions as outlined in this standard, a few parameters are to be determined by supervisory authorities at the national level. Where this is the case, the parameters should be transparent and made publicly available. ...

Banks will not be permitted to double-count items—ie if included as part of the "stock of high-quality liquid assets" (ie the numerator), the assets cannot also be counted as cash inflows. Where there is potential that an item could be counted in multiple outflow categories, (eg committed liquidity lines granted to cover debt maturing within the 30 calendar day period), a bank only has to assume up to the maximum contractual outflow for that product.

Retail Deposit Run-Off

According to "Basel III: International Framework for Liquidity Risk Measurement, Standards and Monitoring":

> Retail deposits are defined as deposits placed with a bank by a natural person. Deposits from legal entities, sole proprietorships or partnerships are captured in wholesale deposit categories. Retail deposits subject to the LCR include demand deposits and term deposits, unless otherwise excluded …
>
> These retail deposits are divided into "stable" and "less stable" portions of funds as described below, with minimum run-off rates listed for each category. The run-off rates for retail deposits are minimum floors, with higher run-off rates established by individual jurisdictions as appropriate to capture depositor behavior in a period of stress in each jurisdiction. …
>
> Stable deposits, which receive a minimum run-off factor of at least 5% in every jurisdiction, are those deposits that are fully covered by an effective deposit insurance scheme or by a public guarantee that provides equivalent protection and where:
>
> - the depositors have other established relationships with the bank that make deposit withdrawal highly unlikely; or,
> - the deposits are in transactional accounts (eg accounts where salaries are automatically deposited)

[For less-stable deposits,] supervisory authorities are expected to develop additional buckets with higher run-off rates as necessary to apply to buckets of potentially less stable retail deposits in their jurisdictions, with a minimum run-off rate of 10%. These jurisdiction-specific run-off rates should be clearly outlined and publicly transparent. Buckets of less stable deposits could include deposits that are not covered by an effective deposit insurance scheme or sovereign deposit guarantee, high-value deposits, deposits from sophisticated or high net worth individuals, deposits that can be withdrawn quickly (eg internet deposits) and foreign currency deposits, as determined by each jurisdiction.

An "effective deposit insurance scheme" refers to a scheme (i) that guarantees that it has the ability to make prompt payouts, (ii) for which the coverage is clearly defined and (iii) of which public awareness is high. The deposit insurer in an effective deposit-insurance scheme has formal legal powers to fulfill its mandate and is operationally independent, transparent, and accountable. A jurisdiction with an explicit and legally binding sovereign deposit guarantee that effectively functions as deposit insurance can be regarded as having an effective deposit insurance scheme.

The presence of deposit insurance alone is not sufficient to consider a deposit "stable." If a bank is not able to readily identify which retail deposits would qualify as "stable" according to the above definition (eg the bank cannot determine which deposits are covered by an effective deposit insurance scheme or a sovereign deposit guarantee) it should place the full amount in the "less stable" buckets as established by its supervisor.

Foreign currency deposits are deposits denominated in any other currency than the domestic currency in a jurisdiction in which the bank operates. Supervisors will determine the run-off factor that banks in their jurisdiction should use for foreign currency deposits. Foreign currency deposits will be considered as "less stable" if there is a reason to believe that such deposits are more volatile than domestic currency deposits. Factors affecting the volatility of foreign currency deposits include the type and sophistication of the depositors, and the nature of such deposits (for example, whether the deposits are linked to business needs in the same currency, or whether the deposits are placed in a search for yield).

The maturity of fixed or time deposits with a residual maturity or withdrawal notice period of greater than 30 days will be recognised (ie excluded from the LCR) if the depositor has no legal right to withdraw deposits within the 30-day horizon of the LCR, or if early withdrawal results in a significant penalty that is materially greater than the loss of interest.

If a bank allows a depositor to withdraw such deposits without applying the corresponding penalty, or despite a clause that says the depositor has no legal right to withdraw, the entire category of these funds would then have to be treated as demand deposits. ... Supervisors in each jurisdiction may choose to outline exceptional circumstances that would qualify as hardship, under which the depositor could withdraw the exceptional term deposit without changing the treatment of the entire pool of deposits.

Unsecured Wholesale Funding Run-Off

Unsecured wholesale funding is defined by "Basel III: International Framework for Liquidity Risk Measurement, Standards and Monitoring" as

> those liabilities and general obligations that are raised from non–natural persons (ie legal entities, sole proprietorships, and partnerships) and are *not* collateralised by legal rights to specifically designated assets owned by the borrowing institution in the case of bankruptcy, insolvency, liquidation, or resolution.

> The wholesale funding ... is defined as all funding that is callable within the LCR's horizon of 30 days or that has its earliest possible contractual maturity date situated within this horizon (such as maturing term deposits and unsecured debt securities) as well as funding with an undetermined

maturity.. … Wholesale funding that is [embedded with callable options] subject to a contractually defined and binding notice surpassing beyond the 30-day horizon are not included.

Unsecured wholesale funding is categorized "based on the assumed sensitivity of the funds providers to the rate offered and the credit quality and solvency of the borrowing bank." Each scenario is given a run-off rate, as follows:

- 5 percent, 10 percent, and higher for unsecured wholesale funding provided by small business customers
- 25 percent for operational deposits generated by clearing, custody. and cash management activities
- 25 percent or 100 percent for treatment of deposits in institutional networks of cooperative banks
- 20 percent or 40 percent for unsecured wholesale funding provided by nonfinancial corporates and sovereigns, central banks, multilateral development banks, and PSEs
- 100 percent for unsecured wholesale funding provided by other legal entity customers

Secured Funding Run-Off

"Basel III: International Framework for Liquidity Risk Measurement, Standards and Monitoring" defines *secured funding* as "those liabilities and general obligations that are collateralized by legal rights to specifically designated assets owned by the borrowing institution in the case of bankruptcy, insolvency, liquidation, or resolution.… All outstanding secured funding transactions with maturities within the 30 calendar day stress horizon," including customer short positions that do not have a specified contractual maturity, are categorized and are given the percentage of amount to be added to outflows, as follows:

- 0 percent for outflows backed by Level 1 assets or central banks
- 15 percent for outflows backed by Level 2A assets
- 25 percent for secured funding transactions with domestic sovereign, PSEs, or multilateral development banks that are not backed by Level 1 or 2A assets (PSEs that receive this treatment are limited to those that have a risk weight of 20 percent or lower, backed by RMBS and eligible for inclusion in Level 2B)
- 50 percent for outflows backed by other Level 2B assets
- 100 percent for all others

Derivatives Cash Outflows

The sum of net-cash outflows will receive a 100 percent factor. Banks should use their existing valuation methodologies to calculate cash flows. If a master netting agreement exists, then the cash flows may be calculated on a net basis by a counterparty. According to "Basel III: International Framework for Liquidity Risk Measurement, Standards and Monitoring":

> Often, contracts governing derivatives and other transactions have clauses that require the posting of additional collateral, drawdown of contingent facilities, or early repayment of existing liabilities upon the bank's downgrade by a recognized credit rating organization. The scenario therefore requires that for each contract in which "downgrade triggers" exist, the bank assumes that 100% of this additional collateral or cash outflow will have to be posted for any downgrade up to and including a 3-notch downgrade of the bank's long-term credit rating. ...

> Observation of market practices indicates that most counterparties to derivatives transactions typically are required to secure the mark-to-market valuation of their positions and that this is predominantly done using cash or sovereign, central bank, multilateral development banks, or PSE debt securities with a 0% risk weight under the Basel II standardised approach. When these Level 1 liquid asset securities are posted as collateral, the framework will not require that an additional stock of liquid assets be maintained for potential valuation changes. If however, counterparties are securing mark-to-market exposures with other forms of collateral, to cover the potential loss of market value on those securities, 20% of the value of all such posted collateral will be required to be added to the stock of liquid asssets by the bank posting such collateral.

This collateral includes the following:

- 100 percent of the nonsegregated collateral that could contractually be recalled by the counterparty because the collateral is in excess of the counterparty's current collateral requirements.

- 100 percent of the collateral that is contractually due but where the counterparty has not yet demanded the posting of such collateral.
- 100 percent of the amount of HQLA collateral that can be substituted for non-HQLA assets without the bank's consent that have been received to secure transactions that have not been segregated.

"Basel III: International Framework for Liquidity Risk Measurement, Standards and Monitoring" explains, "As market practice requires full collateralisation of mark-to-market exposures on derivative and other transactions, banks face potentially substantial liquidity risk exposures to these valuation changes. Inflows and outflows of transactions executed under the same master netting agreement can be treated on a net basis."

Any outflow generated by increased needs related to market valuation changes should be included in the LCR calculated by identifying the largest absolute net thirty-day collateral flow realized during the preceding twenty-four months. The absolute net collateral flow is based on both realized outflows and inflows. Supervisors may adjust the treatment flexibly according to circumstances.

The scenario for loss of funding on asset-backed securities, covered bonds, and other structured financing instruments assumes the outflow of 100 percent of the funding transaction maturing within the thirty-day period, when these instruments are issued by the bank itself. Loss of funding on asset-backed commercial paper, conduits, securities investment vehicles and other such financing facilities, involved 100 percent of maturing amount and 100 percent of returnable assets.

Cash Inflows

The cash inflows include contractual inflows including interest payments from outstanding exposures that are fully performing. Such exposures must not be expected to default within the thirty-day time horizon. Contingent inflows are not included in total net-cash inflows. The inflows are categorized into four sections.

There is a special relationship that must be balanced among the stock of HQLA, inflows, and flows. The amount of inflows that can offset outflows is capped at 75 percent of total expected cash outflows as calculated in the standard. This will in turn make a bank maintain a minimum amount of stock of HQLA equal to 25 percent of the total cash outflows. For example, if outflow is OF, the inflow is capped at 0.75OF.

$$LCR = \text{stock of HQLA}/(OF - 0.75 \, OF) = \text{stock of HQLA}/0.25OF.$$

This will make stock of HQLA to be maintained at 0.25OF in order to achieve LCR of 100 percent.

Secured Lending, Including Reverse Repos and Securities Borrowing

Since maturing repos or securities borrowing agreements secured by Level 1 assets are assumed to be rolled over, their inflows are given 0 percent weight.

- maturing repos or securities lending agreements secured by Level 2 HQLA will lead to cash inflows equivalent to the relevant haircut for the specific assets.
- Since the maturing repos or securities borrowing agreements secured by non-HQLA assets are assumed not to be rolled over, their inflows are given 100 percent weight.
- Collateralized loans or margin loans extended to customers for the purpose of taking leveraged trading positions are considered a form of secured lending. If such margin loans are backed by non-HQLA collateral, inflows are given 50 percent weight.

If the collateral obtained is rehypothecated to cover short positions that could be extended beyond thirty days, a bank should assume that such reverse repo-style arrangements will be rolled-over and will not give rise to any cash inflows (0 percent).

Committed Facilities

No credit facilities, liquidity facilities, or other contingent funding facilities that the bank holds at other institutions for its own purposes are assumed to be able to be drawn. Such facilities receive a 0 percent inflow rate, meaning that this scenario does not consider inflows from committed credit or liquidity facilities. This is to reduce the contagion risk of liquidity shortages at one bank causing shortages at other banks and to reflect the risk that other banks may not be in a position to honor credit facilities, or may decide to incur the legal and reputational risk involved in not honoring the commitment, in order to conserve their own liquidity or reduce their exposure to that bank.

Other Inflows by Counterparty

According to "Basel III: International Framework for Liquidity Risk Measurement, Standards and Monitoring":

> For all other types of transactions, either secured or unsecured, the inflow rate will be determined by counterparty. In order to reflect the need for a bank to conduct ongoing loan origination/roll-over with different types of counterparties, even during a time of stress, a set of limits on contractual inflows by counterparty type are applied.

Other Cash Inflows

The sum of all net-cash inflows should receive a 100 percent inflow factor. The amount of derivatives cash inflows and outflows should be calculated. Where derivatives are collateralized by HQLA, cash inflows should be calculated net of any corresponding cash or contractual collateral outflows that would result, all other things being equal, from contractual obligations for cash or collateral to be posted by the bank, given these contractual obligations would reduce the stock of HQLA. This is in accordance with the principle that banks should not double-count liquidity inflows or outflows.

"Basel III: International Framework for Liquidity Risk Measurement, Standards and Monitoring" adds that "Other contractual cash inflows should be captured here, with explanation given to what comprises this bucket. Inflow percentages should be determined as appropriate for each type of inflow by supervisors in each jurisdiction. Cash inflows related to non-financial revenues are not taken into account in the calculation of the net cash outflows for the purposes of this standard."

6.8.2   Net Stable Funding Ratio

The net stable funding ratio (NSFR) is the ratio of the available amount of stable funding and required amount of stable funding. The guidelines ensure that the ratio must be greater than 100 percent. The goal of NSFR is to ensure that long-term assets are funded with at least a minimum amount of stable liabilities in relation to their liquidity risk profiles. This limits overreliance on short-term wholesale funding during times of buoyant market liquidity and encourages better assessment of liquidity risk across all on- and off-balance-sheet items.

"Basel III: International Framework for Liquidity Risk Measurement, Standards and Monitoring" defines stable funding as:

> the portion of those types and amounts of equity and liability financing expected to be reliable sources of funds over a one-year time horizon under conditions of extended stress. ... Available stable funding (ASF) is defined as the total amount of a bank's:
>
> - capital;
> - preferred stock with maturity of equal to or greater than one year;
> - liabilities with effective maturities of one year or greater;
> - that portion of non-maturity deposits and/or term deposits with maturities of less than one year that would be expected to stay with the institution for an extended period in an idiosyncratic stress event; and
> - that portion of wholesale funding with maturities of less than a year that is expected to stay with the institution for an extended period in an idiosyncratic stress event.
>
> The objective of the standard is to ensure stable funding[and to raise awareness among investors and customers about]:
>
> - A significant decline in profitability or solvency arising from heightened credit risk, market risk or operational risk and/or other risk exposures;
> - A potential downgrade in a debt, counterparty credit, or deposit rating by any nationally recognized credit rating organization; and/or
> - A material event that calls into question the reputation or credit quality of the institution. ...
>
> Extended borrowing from central bank lending facilities outside regular open-market operations are not considered in this ratio, in order not to create a reliance on the central bank as a source of funding.

The ASF is calculated by first assigning the carrying value of an institution's equity and liabilities to one of the following five categories, quoted from Table 1, "Components of Available Stable Funding and Associated ASF Factors," in the BCBS document "Basel III: International Framework for Liquidity Risk Measurement, Standards and Monitoring":

1. *100% ASF factor*—the total amount of capital, including both Tier 1 and Tier 2 as defined in existing global capital standards issued by the Committee; the total amount of any preferred stock not included in Tier 2 that has an effective remaining maturity of one year or greater taking into account any explicit or embedded options that would reduce the expected maturity to less than one year; the total amount of secured and unsecured borrowings and liabilities (including term deposits) with effective remaining maturities of one year or greater excluding any instruments with explicit or embedded options that would reduce the expected maturity to less than one year; options include those exercisable at the investor's discretion within the one-year horizon

2. *90% ASF factor*—"stable" non-maturity (demand) deposits and/or term deposits with residual maturities of less than one year provided by retail customers and small business customers

3. *80% ASF factor*—"less stable" non-maturity (demand) deposits and/or term deposits with residual maturities of less than one year provided by retail and small business customers

4. *50% ASF factor*—unsecured wholesale funding, nonmaturity deposits and/or term deposits with a residual maturity of less than one year, provided by non-financial corporates, sovereigns, central banks, multilateral development banks and PSEs

5. *0% ASF factor*—all other liabilities and equity categories not included in the above categories

Secondly, the amount assigned to each category should be multiplied by an ASF factor. The total ASF is the sum of the weighted amounts.

Required Stable Funding

According to "Basel III: International Framework for Liquidity Risk Measurement, Standards and Monitoring," required stable funding is measured

using supervisory assumptions on the broad characteristics of the liquidity risk profiles of an institution's assets, off-balance sheet exposures and other selected activities. [It] is calculated as the sum of the value of the assets held and funded by the institution, multiplied by a specific required stable funding (RSF) factor assigned to each particular asset type, added to the amount of OBS activity (or potential liquidity exposure) multiplied by its associated RSF factor. The RSF factor applied to the reported values of each asset or OBS exposure is the amount of that item that supervisors believe should be supported with stable funding. Assets that are more liquid and more readily available to act as a source of extended liquidity in the stressed environment identified above receive lower RSF factors (and require less stable funding) than assets considered less liquid in such circumstances and, therefore, require more stable funding.

Table 2 in the BCBS document "Basel III: International Framework for Liquidity Risk Measurement, Standards and Monitoring," titled "Detailed Composition of Asset Categories and Associated RSF Factors," outlines the following components for seven factor levels:

1. *0% RSF factor*—cash immediately available to meet obligations, not currently encumbered as collateral and not held for planned use (as contingent collateral, salary payments, or for other reasons); unencumbered short-term unsecured instruments and transactions with outstanding maturities of less than one year; unencumbered securities with stated remaining maturities of less than one year with no embedded options that would increase the expected maturity to more than one year; unencumbered securities held where the institution has an offsetting reverse repurchase transaction when the security on each transaction has the same unique identifier (example, ISIN number or CUSIP); unencumbered loans to financial entities with effective remaining maturities of less than one year that are not renewable and for which the lender has an irrevocable right to call

2. *5% RSF factor*—unencumbered marketable securities with residual maturities of one year or greater representing claims on or claims guaranteed by sovereigns, central banks, BIS, IMF, EC, non-central government PSEs) or multilateral development banks that are assigned a 0 percent risk weight under the Basel II standardized approach, provided that active repo or sale-markets exist for these securities

3. 20% RSF *factor*—unencumbered corporate bonds or covered bonds rated AA– or higher with residual maturities of one year or greater satisfying all of the conditions for Level 2 assets in the LCR; unencumbered marketable securities with residual maturities of one year or greater representing claims on or claims guaranteed by sovereigns, central banks, non-central government PSEs that are assigned a 20% risk-weight under the Basel II standardized approach, provided that they meet all of the conditions for Level 2 assets in the LCR.

4. 50% RSF factor—unencumbered gold; unencumbered equity securities, not issued by financial institutions or their affiliates, listed on a recognized exchange and included in a large cap market index; unencumbered corporate bonds and covered bonds that have central bank eligibility for intraday liquidity needs and overnight liquidity shortages in relevant jurisdictions, aren't issued by financial institutions or their affiliates (except in the case of covered bonds), aren't issued by the respective firm itself or its affiliates, have a credit assessment by a recognized ECAI of A+ to A- or do not have a credit assessment by a recognized ECAI and are internally rated as having a PD corresponding to a credit assessment of A+ to A-, and are traded in large, deep and active markets characterized by a low level of concentration; unencumberd loans to non-financial corporate clients, sovereigns, central banks, and PSEs having a remaining maturity of less than one year

5. *65% RSF factor*—unencumbered residential mortgages of any maturity that would qualify for the 35 percent or lower risk weight under Basel II Standardized Approach for credit risk; other unencumbered loans, excluding loans to financial institutions, with a remaining maturity of one year or greater, that would qualify for the 35 percent or lower risk weight under Basel II Standardized Approach for credit risk

6. *85% RSF factor*—unencumbered loans to retail customers (natural persons) and small business customers (as defined in the LCR) having a remaining maturity of less than one year (other than those that qualify for the 65 percent RSF above)

7. *100% RSF factor*—all other assets not included in the above categories

Off-Balance-Sheet Exposures

Off-balance-sheet exposures require little initial funding but can lead to significant liquidity drains in times of market or idiosyncratic stress. As a result, the application of an RSF factor to various OBS activities require the institution to establish a reserve of stable funding. This requirement could be viewed as promoting the stable funding of the stock of liquid assets that could be used to meet liquidity requirements arising from OBS contingencies in times of stress.

An RSF Factor of 5 percent of the currently undrawn portion to the conditionally revocable and irrevocable credit and liquidity facilities to any client national supervisors can specify the RSF factors based on their national circumstances for the following, quoted from Table 3, "Composition of Off-balance Sheet Categories and Associated RSF Factors," in the BCBS document "Basel III: International Framework for Liquidity Risk Measurement, Standards and Monitoring,":

- Unconditionally revocable "uncommitted" credit and liquidity facilities;
- Guarantees;
- Letters of credit;
- Other trade finance instruments; and
- noncontractual obligations, such as:
    - Potential requests for debt repurchases of the bank's own debt or that of related conduits, securities investment vehicles and other such financing facilities;
    - Structured products where customers anticipate ready marketability, such as adjustable rate notes and variable rate demand notes (VRDNs); and
    - Managed funds that are marketed with the objective of maintaining a stable value, such as money market mutual funds or other types of stable value collective investment funds

6.8.3   Monitoring Tools and Metrics

The Basel Committee has recommended five monitoring metrics to help capture elements of liquidity risk specific to their jurisdictions, as outlined in "Basel III: International Framework for Liquidity Risk Measurement, Standards and Monitoring":

Contractual maturity mismatch

The contractual maturity mismatch profile identifies the gaps between the contractual inflows and outflows of liquidity for defined time bands. These maturity gaps indicate how much liquidity a bank would potentially need to raise in each of these time bands if all outflows occurred at the earliest possible date. This metric provides insight into the extent to which the bank relies on maturity transformation under its current contracts. ... Contractual cash and security inflows and outflows from all on- and off-balance sheet items [are] mapped to defined time bands based on their respective maturities.

Concentration of funding

This metric is meant to identify those sources of wholesale funding that are of such significance that withdrawal of this funding could trigger liquidity problems. The metric thus encourages the diversification of funding sources recommended in the Committee's *Sound Principles*. [Funding liabilities are sourced from each significant counterparty as a percentage of total liabilities, and from each significant product/instrument as a percentage of total liabilities.]

Available unencumbered assets

This metrics provides supervisors with data on the quantity and key characteristics, including currency denomination and location, of banks' available unencumbered assets. These assets have the potential to be used as collateral to raise additional secured funding in secondary markets and/or are eligible at central banks and as such may potentially be additional sources of liquidity for the bank. Definition and practical application of the metrick: Available unencumbered assets that are marketable as collateral in secondary markets and/or eligible for central banks' standing facilities.

LCR by significant currency

While the standards are required to be met in one single currency, in order to better capture potential currency mismatches, banks and supervisors should also monitor the LCR in significant currencies. This will allow the bank and the supervisor to track potential currency mismatch issues that could arise. Foreign currency LCR = Stock of high-quality liquid assets [HQLA] in each significant currency/Total net cash outflows over a 30-day time period in each significant currency. Note: Amount of total net foreign exchange cash outflows should be net of foreign exchange hedges).

Market-related monitoring tools

Supervisors can monitor information both on the absolute level and direction of major markets and consider their potential impact on the financial sector and the specific bank. Market-wide information is also crucial when evaluating assumptions behind a bank's funding plan. Valuable market information to monitor includes, but is not limited to, equity prices (ie overall stock markets and sub-indices in various jurisdictions relevant to the activities of the supervised banks), debt markets (money markets, medium-term notes, long term debt, derivatives, government bond markets, credit default spread indices, etc.); foreign exchange markets, commodities markets, and indices related to specific products, such as for certain securitized products (eg the ABX).

7 Risk Data Aggregation and Reporting

7.1 BCBS Principles for Effective Risk Data Aggregation

In the analysis of the global financial crisis of 2007, it was observed that one of the several significant factors fueling the crisis was the lack of adequate information technology (IT) and data architecture to view the broader financial risks. As a result, there was no clear picture for senior management of the aggregated risk exposures to identify concentrations at the bank group level, across business lines and between legal entities. These weaknesses affected the banks and the stability of the overall financial system.

The Basel Committee on Banking Supervision (BCBS) emphasized that a sound risk management system should have appropriate management information systems at the business and bank level and provided the principles to enhance banks' ability to identify and manage bank-wide risks. The principles cover four closely related topics:

1. Overarching governance and infrastructure
2. Risk data aggregation capabilities
3. Risk reporting practices
4. Supervisory review, tools, and cooperation

The Basel Committee believes that aggregate risk data management will improve their resolvability. The following are the highlights of a list of ways that, according to BCBS, data aggregation helps banks:

- anticipating the problems ahead
- finding a suitable merger partner in case of severe stress
- improving the decision-making process

- comprehensive assessment of risk exposures at the global consolidated level
- reducing the probability and severity of losses
- improving the speed at which information is available
- tracking the risks relative to the bank's risk tolerance/appetite
- providing early warning indicators of any potential breaches of risk limits
- conducting a flexible and effective stress testing

For convenience, the list of principles from the Basel Committee's January 2013 document "Principles for Effective Risk Data Aggregation and Risk Reporting" (January 2013; http://www.bis.org/publ/bcbs239.pdf) have been reproduced in boxes below. I've then elaborated on specific principles at the micro level based on my opinions.

7.2 Analysis of BCBS Principle on Data Governance

Principle 1

Governance—A bank's risk data aggregation capabilities and risk reporting practices should be subject to strong governance arrangements consistent with other principles and guidance established by the Basel Committee.

A bank's board and senior management should promote the identification, assessment and management of data quality risks as part of its overall risk management framework. The framework should include agreed service level standards for both outsourced and in-house risk data-related processes, and a firm's policies on data confidentiality, integrity and availability, as well as risk management policies.

A bank's board and senior management should review and approve the bank's group risk data aggregation and risk reporting framework and ensure that adequate resources are deployed.

A bank's risk data aggregation capabilities and risk reporting practices should be:

- Fully documented and subject to high standards of validation. This validation should be independent and review the bank's compliance with the Principles in this document. The primary purpose of the independent validation is to ensure that a bank's risk data aggregation and reporting processes are functioning

---

as intended and are appropriate for the bank's risk profile. Independent validation activities should be aligned and integrated with the other independent review activities within the bank's risk management program,and encompass all components of the bank's risk data aggregation and reporting processes. Common practices suggest that the independent validation of risk data aggregation and risk reporting practices should be conducted using staff with specific IT, data and reporting expertise.

- Considered as part of any new initiatives, including acquisitions and/or divestitures, new product development, as well as broader process and IT change initiatives. When considering a material acquisition, a bank's due diligence process should assess the risk data aggregation capabilities and risk reporting practices of the acquired entity, as well as the impact on its own risk data aggregation capabilities and risk reporting practices. The impact on risk data aggregation should be considered explicitly by the board and inform the decision to proceed. The bank should establish a timeframe to integrate and align the acquired risk data aggregation capabilities and risk reporting practices within its own framework.

- Unaffected by the bank's group structure. The group structure should not hinder risk data aggregation capabilities at a consolidated level or at any relevant level within the organization (e.g. sub-consolidated level, jurisdiction of operation level). In particular, risk data aggregation capabilities should be independent from the choices a bank makes regarding its legal organization and geographical presence.

A bank's senior management should be fully aware of and understand the limitations that prevent full risk data aggregation, in terms of coverage (e.g. risks not captured or subsidiaries not included), in technical terms (e.g. model performance indicators or degree of reliance on manual processes) or in legal terms (legal impediments to data sharing across jurisdictions). Senior management should ensure that the bank's IT strategy includes ways to improve risk data aggregation capabilities and risk reporting practices and to remedy any shortcomings against the Principles set forth in this document taking into account the evolving needs of the business. Senior management should also identify data critical to risk data aggregation and IT infrastructure initiatives through its strategic IT planning process, and support these initiatives through the allocation of appropriate levels of financial and human resources.

The bank's board is responsible for determining its own risk reporting requirements and should be aware of limitations that prevent full risk data aggregation in the reports it receives. The board should also be aware of the bank's implementation of, and ongoing compliance with the Principles set out in this document.

From "Principles for Effective Risk Data Aggregation and Risk Reporting," Basel Committee on Banking Supervision, January 2013, http://www.bis.org/ publ/bcbs239.pdf.

Based on the above guidelines, there are eight critical micro level requirements that a bank must address.

1. Promoting Data-Driven Culture

Decision making was rapidly switched to data-driven decision making from management-style decision making. Competitive advantage is driven by the effective use of quality data. Quality data does not come from a single group. It is the responsibility of all the groups who participate in data collection and processing. While the dedicated data quality group can ensure the accuracy of data to some extent, it does have limitations because of the nature of banking and capital-markets data. Senior management must ensure that everybody in the path of the data flow feels ownership. The measures taken by senior management should include, but not be limited to, understanding of the following:

- the data and the truth behind the data.
- how the data is captured
- how and when the data gets changed
- where the data is used
- the impact of having incorrect data
- relationships among various data elements
- products
- trading systems
- risk calculations
- various regulations.
- the full path of the data from source to destination

2. Service Level Agreements

In a data-driven world, data changes hands many times on the way to its destination. There is a possibility for conflicts to arise, especially from the point of view of what is expected, what is provided, and how is it being monitored. To make the data life cycle easy, it is necessary to establish service-level agreements (SLAs). An SLA is a negotiated agreement designed to establish a common minimum understanding about expected services, priorities, and responsibilities.

The SLA acts as a communication tool, conflict-prevention tool, and living document. A living document is something that is continuously referred to, in contrast to an archived document. The SLA contains service and management elements that describe how the agreed-upon services will be monitored. When applying these concepts to a data-driven world, the SLA specifies the following:

- the nature of data provided in the files
- the type of the file
- the intervals
- the transfer mode
- the monitoring mechanism
- the escalation procedure
- procedures to request changes
- dependencies
- required manual efforts, if any
- resources responsible
- system information

The SLAs plays a key role in data aggregation and smooths the service and management tasks.

3. Resource Allocation

Risk data aggregation is a time-consuming process and is not specific to a particular skill set or group. It is mainly driven by work culture while requiring skills speeded across technology, business, and information. The resources and funds must be allocated accordingly.

4. Full Documentation

Risk data management is not a product that can be validated against business requirements. While the initiative is strategic, the nature of management is more of the tactic. The standards cannot be self-validated by the governance program. The internal compliance and audit group must ensure that the governance program is designed and functioning in line with the bank's strategy and is capable of performing all the required jobs of risk data aggregation and reporting.

5. Compatibility with Future Initiatives

Banks' business is assumed to be continuously evolving. New products are added frequently. New businesses are acquired from time to time. Stressed banks merge with healthy banks. In a changed regulator environment, it is essential to evaluate new additions from the risk and regulatory point of view. Knowing the risk profiles of two entities simply does not provide enough information to make a decision about whether the addition of new business will fit into an organization's risk profile.

Determining the aftereffect risk profile requires the same mechanisms that are used to determine the current risk profile. This requires seamless data integration and data aggregation capabilities. Banks will need to incorporate such forward-looking necessaries in the information and risk architectures.

6. Insulation from Bank Structure

Risk data aggregation is not an isolated job. The group is also not an independent group, even though some part of risk data aggregation can exist on its own. It is a system within a system. It is heavily dependent on the matrix structure. In other words, it is a virtual group. The organization structure, either from a business point of view or a structuring point of view, should not limit risk data aggregation capabilities.

7. Managing the Limitations

There are certain limitations that prevent full data aggregation. The limitations spread across technical difficulties, entity separations, and jurisdiction restrictions. Such restrictions will severely impact the overall risk calculations. Senior management should intervene and ensure that the operations are smooth in such a restricted environment and plan a workaround in order to ensure full risk data aggregation.

8. Data Sharing Agreements

This requirement is tightly related to the above requirement. The purpose of these agreements is to define how sensitive data will be provided to cross jurisdictions and methods used by the organization for the secure and legal management, accessing, and processing of that data.

7.3   Analysis of BCBS Principle on Data Architectures

Principle 2

Data architecture and IT infrastructure—A bank should design, build and maintain data architecture and IT infrastructure which fully supports its risk data aggregation capabilities and risk reporting practices not only in normal times but also during times of stress or crisis, while still meeting the other Principles.

Risk data aggregation capabilities and risk reporting practices should be given direct consideration as part of a bank's business continuity planning processes and be subject to a business impact analysis.

A bank should establish integrated data taxonomies and architecture across the banking group, which includes information on the characteristics of the data (metadata), as well as use of single identifiers and/or unified naming conventions for data including legal entities, counterparties, customers and accounts.

Roles and responsibilities should be established as they relate to the ownership and quality of risk data and information for both the business and IT functions. The owners (business and IT functions), in partnership with risk managers, should ensure there are adequate controls throughout the lifecycle of the data and for all aspects of the technology infrastructure. The role of the business owner includes ensuring data is correctly entered by the relevant front office unit, kept current and aligned with the data definitions, and also ensuring that risk data aggregation capabilities and risk reporting practices are consistent with firms' policies.

From "Principles for Effective Risk Data Aggregation and Risk Reporting," Basel Committee on Banking Supervision, January 2013, http://www.bis.org/ publ/bcbs239.pdf.

Integrating with a Business Continuity Plan

As businesses move toward data-driven decision making, storage technology becomes a critical asset on which business continuity relies. Financial organizations have sufficient internally generated data, yet there is a tendency to rely on sample data. In addition, the regulatory reporting needs more structured data. And as data collections become more structured and sophisticated, the need for continuous availability of data also increases. Data availability and business continuity offer a vital competitive edge.

In addition to storage technologies, firms must adopt proven recovery management strategies to successfully address operational risk, availability, and security challenges. The architectures must support real-time data integration to provide the ability to respond and adapt to many external and internal demands. The architectural concepts that help organizations continue business operations without any significant impact include the following:

- storage technology
- high availability
- recovery management
- real-time data integration

Integrated Taxonomies and Architectures

Even in the abstract, data under such conditions are likely to be incompatible. Typically, each system uses a different data model—that is, it stores and works with data in different ways. Even where data models are similar, they are not always aligned. With each system marching to a different drummer, the structure of the data, the applicable taxonomy, and the methods with which data are used and processed differ from application to application. This puts enormous strain on the links between applications. Links are commonly custom-made for each connection, with developers writing extensive code to make the data from the source application compatible with the application that draws from it. In some cases, especially where legacy systems are involved, some functionality is coded into the interface, so that data are processed and not merely transferred.

This muddies the distinction between applications (which manipulate and calculate data) and interfaces (that transfer it). Firms then have to spend time and resources to analyze systematically the different data models used by applications and interfaces, because they can't be sure the data definitions used by the source application are equal to the data definitions of the receiving application. In some cases, weak or missing documentation means that firms must spend even more time reverse-engineering data to understand how it is being used and transformed.

All this makes reconciliations quite challenging, and does so as well for the upgrade or replacement of applications. Flaws in the data layer make it harder to convert data into insightful information, and contribute to delays in the creation of risk reports. Point-to-point interfaces are a hindrance to risk aggregation. Capabilities that are becoming more important for many firms are new risk indicators, especially for liquidity management, and simulation support for scenario analysis, stress testing in all its forms, and pre-deal analysis.

On the last point, risk IT/ops should integrate a new generation of front-office simulation tools. These can simulate the effect of a new product or a new deal on funding, liquidity, profitability, or limit utilization. They can also simulate the effect of the exogenous change in, say, the yield curve or credit spreads, on business P&Ls, products, and individual deals.

Because these new tools are designed to, among other tasks, measure and manage certain risks, their methodology, data model, taxonomy, and so on should be aligned with risk standards, and they should be integrated with the risk IT architecture. If not, firms are in danger of worsening any inconsistency in data models and methodologies from which they already suffer.

Single identifiers and Unified Naming Conventions

The Financial Stability Board recommends the development and implementation of the global legal entity identifier (LEI) system to facilitate counterparty risk aggregation. The adoption of the LEI is a great initiative in establishing standards for data aggregation, as this BCBS principle mandates standards and identifiers. In addition to identifiers, it is essential to establish unified naming conventions for all these entities.

Ownership of Risk Data

Firms should define clear ownership of end-to-end risk-related processes and indicators to help owners manage the process and assess their performance, and establish ownership for the task of continually reviewing, redesigning, and implementing improvements in processes that will enhance end-to-end consistency and efficiency. Clear process ownership, accountability for continual end-to-end improvement, and new workflow-management tools are necessary, complementary techniques firms should use to improve processes and information flows.

Firms can analyze steps in processes and data flows, grouping similar activities, to determine genuine process ownership. They should then formalize this by charging owners with their redesign (where needed) and management, documenting the new processes, drafting performance management principles, and so on. In many instances, conducting this analysis and assigning ownership can mean a radical redesign of the whole process layout.

Quality of Risk Data

Data quality can be improved by making quality assurance a bigger component of more roles. Incentives can also have a powerful beneficial effect. Even as firms pursue these initiatives to strengthen their data, many will continue to find that in certain well-defined circumstances, risk reports will be better served by speedy approximations than by slower, if more precise calculations.

Roles and Responsibilities

Roles and responsibilities should be established as they relate to the ownership and quality of risk data and information for both business and IT functions. This requirement will be discussed in more detail in Chapter 8.

7.4   Analysis of BCBS Risk Data Aggregation Principles

BCBS has provided a timeline of January 2016 to all the global systematically important banks (G-SIBs) to meet risk data aggregation and reporting principles. By meeting these guidelines, banks will help strengthen the financial industry.

Principle 3

Accuracy and Integrity—A bank should be able to generate accurate and reliable risk data to meet normal and stress/crisis reporting accuracy requirements. Data should be aggregated on a largely automated basis so as to minimise the probability of errors.

A bank should aggregate risk data in a way that is accurate and reliable.

- Controls surrounding risk data should be as robust as those applicable to accounting data.
- Where a bank relies on manual processes and desktop applications (eg spreadsheets, databases) and has specific risk units that use these applications for software development, it should have effective mitigants in place (eg end-user computing policies and procedures) and other effective controls that are consistently applied across the bank's processes.
- Risk data should be reconciled with bank's sources, including accounting data where appropriate, to ensure that the risk data is accurate.
- A bank should strive towards a single authoritative source for risk data per each type of risk.
- A bank's risk personnel should have sufficient access to risk data to ensure they can appropriately aggregate, validate and reconcile the data to risk reports.

As a precondition, a bank should have a "dictionary" of the concepts used, such that data is defined consistently across an organisation.

There should be an appropriate balance between automated and manual systems. Where professional judgements are required, human intervention may be appropriate. For many other processes, a higher degree of automation is desirable to reduce the risk of errors.

Supervisors expect banks to document and explain all of their risk data aggregation processes whether automated or manual (judgement based or otherwise). Documentation should include an explanation of the appropriateness of any manual workarounds, a description of their criticality to the accuracy of risk data aggregation and proposed actions to reduce the impact.

Supervisors expect banks to measure and monitor the accuracy of data and to develop appropriate escalation channels and action plans to be in place to rectify poor data quality.

From "Principles for Effective Risk Data Aggregation and Risk Reporting," Basel Committee on Banking Supervision, January 2013, http://www.bis.org/ publ/bcbs239.pdf.

Principle 4

Completeness—A bank should be able to capture and aggregate all material risk data across the banking group. Data should be available by business line, legal entity, asset type, industry, region and other groupings, as relevant for the risk in question, that permit identifying and reporting risk exposures, concentrations and emerging risks.

A bank's risk data aggregation capabilities should include all material risk exposures, including those that are off-balance sheet.

A banking organisation is not required to express all forms of risk in a common metric or basis, but risk data aggregation capabilities should be the same regardless of the choice of risk aggregation systems implemented. However, each system should make clear the specific approach used to aggregate exposures for any given risk measure, in order to allow the board and senior management to assess the results properly.

Supervisors expect banks to produce aggregated risk data that is complete and to measure and monitor the completeness of their risk data. Where risk data is not entirely complete, the impact should not be critical to the bank's ability to manage its risks effectively. Supervisors expect banks' data to be materially complete, with any exceptions identified and explained.

From "Principles for Effective Risk Data Aggregation and Risk Reporting," Basel Committee on Banking Supervision, January 2013, http://www.bis.org/ publ/bcbs239.pdf.

Principle 5

Timeliness—A bank should be able to generate aggregate and up-to-date risk data in a timely manner while also meeting the principles relating to accuracy and integrity, completeness and adaptability. The precise timing will depend upon the nature and potential volatility of the risk being measured as well as its criticality to the overall risk profile of the bank. The precise timing will also depend on the bank-specific frequency requirements for risk management reporting, under both normal and stress/crisis situations, set based on the characteristics and overall risk profile of the bank.

A bank's risk data aggregation capabilities should ensure that it is able to produce aggregate risk information on a timely basis to meet all risk management reporting requirements.

The Basel Committee acknowledges that different types of data will be required at different speeds, depending on the type of risk, and that certain risk data may be needed faster in a stress/crisis situation. Banks need to build their risk systems to be capable of producing aggregated risk data rapidly during times of stress/crisis for all critical risks.

Critical risks include but are not limited to:

- The aggregated credit exposure to a large corporate borrower. By comparison, groups of retail exposures may not change as critically in a short period of time but may still include significant concentrations;
- Counterparty credit risk exposures, including, for example, derivatives;
- Trading exposures, positions, operating limits, and market concentrations by sector and region data;
- Liquidity risk indicators such as cash flows/settlements and funding; and
- Operational risk indicators that are time-critical (eg systems availability, unauthorised access).

Supervisors will review that the bank specific frequency requirements, for both normal and stress/crisis situations, generate aggregate and up-to-date risk data in a timely manner.

From "Principles for Effective Risk Data Aggregation and Risk Reporting," Basel Committee on Banking Supervision, January 2013, http://www.bis.org/ publ/bcbs239.pdf.

Principle 6

Adaptability—A bank should be able to generate aggregate risk data to meet a broad range of on-demand, ad hoc risk management reporting requests, including requests during stress/crisis situations, requests due to changing internal needs and requests to meet supervisory queries.

A bank's risk data aggregation capabilities should be flexible and adaptable to meet ad hoc data requests, as needed, and to assess emerging risks. Adaptability will enable banks to conduct better risk management, including forecasting information, as well as to support stress testing and scenario analyses.

Adaptability includes:

- Data aggregation processes that are flexible and enable risk data to be aggregated for assessment and quick decision-making;
- Capabilities for data customisation to users' needs (eg dashboards, key takeaways, anomalies), to drill down as needed, and to produce quick summary reports;
- Capabilities to incorporate new developments on the organisation of the business and/or external factors that influence the bank's risk profile; and
- Capabilities to incorporate changes in the regulatory framework.

Supervisors expect banks to be able to generate subsets of data based on requested scenarios or resulting from economic events. For example, a bank should be able to aggregate risk data quickly on country credit exposures as of a specified date based on a list of countries, as well as industry credit exposures as of a specified date based on a list of industry types across all business lines and geographic areas.

From "Principles for effective risk data aggregation and risk reporting," Basel Committee on Banking Supervision, January 2013, http://www.bis.org/ publ/bcbs239.pdf.

There are several questions that must be addressed before even starting the big program:

- How do we interpret the principles?
- Do these principles need to be met on an individual basis?
- Are these principles meaningful on an individual basis?
- Where does the responsibility fall?
- Is the given time frame enough to implement the principles?
- What is the metric that says that the bank is in compliance with the principles?

The answer to the first question above is a prerequisite for answering all the rest. There are four principles that pertain to RDA, and they are accuracy and integrity; completeness; timeliness; and adaptability. That number may seem small, but the list of requirements tied to those four principles is much longer:

1. Accuracy
2. Reliability
3. Robust controls
4. Effective mitigants for manual processes
5. Reconciliation of sources and accounting
6. A single authoritative source per each type of risk
7. Sufficient access
8. A dictionary of the concepts
9. A high degree of automation
10. A balance between automated and manual systems
11. Documentation pertaining to manual workarounds
12. Measurement and monitoring of data accuracy
13. Escalation channels
14. Inclusion of all material risk exposures
15. Identification and explanation of exceptions
16. Timeliness
17. Speed based on risk type
18. Operating limits
19. Liquidity risk indicators
20. Operational risk indicators
21. Adaptability
22. Flexibility
23. Data customizations
24. Reaction to changes in the regulatory framework
25. Subsets of data

My opinions about each of these micro-level requirements are shared below.

1. Accuracy

This requirement is very simple. Data should be accurate, otherwise it will lead to poor decision making. At the same time, it is complex because of the dimensions of data elements and measurement techniques involved in certain data elements. For example, exposure of a security has two dimensions: amount and currency. The trading system may have both values, but it is useless if we are unable to capture the currency element.

It should be noted here that exposure is different from initial purchase price. Since the price varies on a daily basis because of market conditions, the current price mark-to-market as of the date must be captured. Trading sources may get the data from market data providers, but in some cases—depending on product type and internal needs—the firm may use its own mark-to-market value application. In such cases, the accuracy is tied to using the right source and ensuring that the entire transaction record is consistent. Here the accuracy also points to how accurate the system calculates the mark-to-market value. Depending on the product type, if the other system calculates the mark-to-market value in a currency other than that of the trading system, there will be inconsistency.

Accuracy doesn't simply reflect the propagation of the data through channels all the way to a centralized store; it also depends on the dimension of the data element and the way it is captured. The complexity varies based on the nature of the data element.

2. Reliability

While the above examples deal with the way the data element is defined, reliability deals with the confidence level on the data that is collected into a centralized source. Reliability depends on several factors, such as how old the data is and whether the process of collecting the data is consistent every day. This in turn is tied to both the data quality procedures and automation of the collection process. Collecting data manually on spreadsheets and loading the data store, for example, may lead to human errors and reduce confidence in the reliability of the data.

3. Robust Controls

Controls are a wider subject, related to both technical point and functional point. From a technical perspective, controls include ensuring that the files are processed in time with no issues, and from a functional perspective, whether all the required files were processed.

As in our mark-to-market value case, if the file from a trading system is applied while the other is missed, this will lead to inaccuracy and inconsistency in the data. There should be some controls that determine any unexpected jumps in the values. For example, if the mark-to-market value is not in an appropriate range for a given trade when compared with the previous value, that could raise suspicion that there is something wrong in the calculation process. In such a case, if there are some controls implemented in the calculation system itself to compare the reasonableness of the value, that will solve some problems.

4. Effective Mitigants for Manual Processes

While the principles of accuracy and integrity are tightly coupled with the process of automating the data flows, there could be unavoidable situations where a manual process is needed—perhaps because of sudden additions to the list of products traded, addition of new systems, or migrating to a new system. Alternatively, there could be situations where certain elements of the record in a centralized store need to be edited. Both types of manual processes (manual uploads and manual edits) should have sophisticated and easy mechanisms and must incorporate appropriate mitigants.

5. Reconciliation to Sources and Accounting

Excluding the intermediate systems through which data flows to the destination, the three sources where the data is viewed as reliable are the original source, the target (enterprise data source), and the GL accounting system. The data in all these sources must be reconciled. While the reconciliation process can be manual during the development of risk data aggregation systems, such a process must be automated to ensure the data is consistent in these places. Therefore, the reconciliation process itself will turn into a new system that needs to be maintained and monitored. Proper monitoring tools need to be developed that describe the results of the reconciliation.

6. A Single Authoritative Source for Each Type of Risk

This requirement does not seem to be clear. While the purpose of risk data aggregation is to establish an authoritative data source, using the word *per* each type of risk is somewhat confusing. There is no clarity about the risk type based on risk category—such as market risk, credit risk, liquidity risk—or based on risk factor—such as interest rate risk, currency risk. Either way, this requirement conflicts with enterprise risk management, as having a single source for multiple risk types and risk factors makes it easier to analyze the interconnectedness among the risks and risk factors. This requirement may be helpful from the point of view of generating reports, but risk management involves more than this.

7. Sufficient Access

While this is very much required during the development process, the challenge lies in having such access to the aggregated data source post-production because of jurisdiction restrictions. Therefore, it is very much desired to build sophisticated and meaningful access levels into the risk data aggregation system.

8. A Dictionary of the Concepts

Having such a dictionary in place will help bank personnel clearly understand the truth behind the data element, and will be helpful to ensure the consistency of the data across all destinations, such as source, GL accounting, and risk data aggregation system. Such a dictionary can be embedded in the metadata repository system.

9. A High Degree of Automation

While a high degree of automation prevents errors in data aggregation, it also reduces the flexibility to incorporate the changes needed because of changes in the business. Therefore, this requirement is tightly coupled with #4, "Effective Mitigants for Manual Processes."

10. A Balance Between Automated and Manual Systems

This requirement is not clear, as it is not known whether the allowed manual processes are due to any jurisdiction restrictions or if there is a limit on an allowed number of manual processes. However, if for some reason a manual process is found to be a good process, proper justification needs to be documented.

11. Documentation Pertaining to Manual Workarounds

While the above requirement is related to the manual system, this requirement is related to temporary workarounds while the automation is being changed. In such cases, there should exist a document that describes the need for such a workaround, what steps are being taken to retire it, how the workaround is used without introducing any errors, and so on.

12. Measure and Monitoring of Data Accuracy

This requirement deals with establishing scorecards and metrics that communicate the accuracy ratio of the data.

13. Escalation Channels

This is one of the most challenging and critical tasks in risk data management. Because of the large number of involved parties and systems, it is critical to identify the right person to escalate an issue during the post-development process. It is tightly coupled with the work culture. One of the issues that slows down the escalation process is people's behavior, especially from the point of view of not owning the responsibility. Proper channels need to be identified and documented, and they must ensure that the assigned person will hold the responsibility to get the things corrected in a timely and efficient manner.

14. Inclusion of All Material Risk Exposures

Material risk is the risk that impacts the value of the position. Examples of material risks include market risk, credit risk, liquidity risk, and operational risk. All positions and trades must be identified if they are exposed to any material risk and must be included in the risk data aggregation system.

15. Identification and Explanation of Exceptions

If a certain set of records is not included in the risk data aggregation or if they are moved to a different category than they usually belong to, there should be clear documentation explaining why those records have been excluded from the usual set.

16. Timeliness

Exposure amounts based on certain criteria will change on a daily basis or even during the day. Such information is critical in stressed periods. For example, senior management may want to restrict further exposure to a certain counterparty after hearing news about that counterparty. Alternatively, there may be a need for restrictions by market sector.

While certain exposure types change slowly, there are others that change rapidly. For example, issuing loans is a slower process, while transacting the derivatives is rapid and can occur several times during the day. There should be a mechanism to calculate the aggregated exposure by certain criteria routinely as well as on an on-demand basis.

17. Speed Based on Risk Type

As explained above, the speed at which the exposure reports are needed varies based on risk type. There should be some mechanism to configure the aggregating intervals as well as a configurable mechanism that can be used to adjust the intervals.

18. Operating Limits

The trading system may need to know if it can further extend the exposure to a certain party or if it is reaching the limits. In order for feedback on the limits to the trading system to take place, all the sublevel details must be captured in the record.

19. Liquidity Risk Indicators

Every transaction will have its own level of liquidity. The liquidity is associated with collaterals, derivatives, cash flows, funding availability, and so on. Liquidity indicators must be captured for each transaction.

20. Operational Risk Indicators

This requirement is related to the systems and access. It is required to ensure that all systems are available at all times. If a system is not available at the time it is critical to conduct certain transactions, then those incidents must be logged and stored. Similarly, if there are any attempts by unauthorized users trying to perform certain transactions, those violations must be captured.

21. Adaptability

Risk management is both a strategic and a tactical process. Adaptability in risk data aggregation will enable banks to conduct better risk management, including forecasting information, and support stress testing and scenario analyses.

22. Flexibility

Risk data aggregation must be flexible enough to modify the aggregation processes to incorporate the data based on the trends. For example, if there is a new type of macroeconomic data available, it needs to be made part of existing data so that it can be combined to make forecasts about counterparties or marker prices.

23. Data Customizations

The requirements are tightly related in the way the enterprise data store is logically built. If the data is structured effectively and logically, then it is easy to produce various reports, by using either business intelligence tools or ad hoc queries. There should be a mechanism to customize the logical model even after it is built and moved to production.

24. Reaction to Changes in the Regulatory Framework

Regulatory requirements change often. Rules may change, or the variety of data called for may be adjusted. The enterprise architectures and risk data aggregation must be capable of meeting such deadlines.

25. Subsets of Data

There should be sufficient attributes included in the records so that the reports can be filtered based on subcriteria—for example, exposure to a particular market sector or geography.

7.5   Analysis of BCBS Principles on Risk Reporting Practices

The Basel Committee provided five high-level principles on risk reporting practices dealing with accuracy, comprehensiveness, clarity, usefulness, frequency, and distribution.

> **Principle 7**
>
> **Accuracy—Risk management reports should accurately and precisely convey aggregated risk data and reflect risk in an exact manner. Reports should be reconciled and validated.**
>
> Risk management reports should be accurate and precise to ensure a bank's board and senior management can rely with confidence on the aggregated information to make critical decisions about risk.
>
> To ensure the accuracy of the reports, a bank should maintain, at a minimum, the following:

- Defined requirements and processes to reconcile reports to risk data;
- Automated and manual edit and reasonableness checks, including an inventory of the validation rules that are applied to quantitative information. The inventory should include explanations of the conventions used to describe any mathematical or logical relationships that should be verified through these validations or checks; and
- Integrated procedures for identifying, reporting and explaining data errors or weaknesses in data integrity via exceptions reports.

Approximations are an integral part of risk reporting and risk management. Results from models, scenario analyses, and stress testing are examples of approximations that provide critical information for managing risk. While the expectations for approximations may be different than for other types of risk reporting, banks should follow the reporting principles in this document and establish expectations for the reliability of approximations (accuracy, timeliness, etc) to ensure that management can rely with confidence on the information to make critical decisions about risk. This includes principles regarding data used to drive these approximations.

Supervisors expect that a bank's senior management should establish accuracy and precision requirements for both regular and stress/crisis reporting, including critical position and exposure information. These requirements should reflect the criticality of decisions that will be based on this information.

Supervisors expect banks to consider accuracy requirements analogous to accounting materiality. For example, if omission or misstatement could influence the risk decisions of users, this may be considered material. A bank should be able to support the rationale for accuracy requirements. Supervisors expect a bank to consider precision requirements based on validation, testing or reconciliation processes and results.

From "Principles for Effective Risk Data Aggregation and Risk Reporting,"
Basel Committee on Banking Supervision, January 2013, http://www.bis.org/
publ/bcbs239.pdf.

Accuracy and precision are twin measures in statistics. Before explaining how these two measures are important for risk reporting, let's discuss them from a statistics point of view and identify the common causes for inaccuracy and lack of precision. In statistics, accuracy is defined as the ratio of

$$\frac{number\ of\ true\ positives + number\ of\ true\ negatives}{number\ of\ true\ positives + false\ positives + true\ negatives + false\ negatives}$$

Precision is defined as the ratio of

$$\frac{true\ positives}{number\ of\ true\ positives + false\ positives}$$

These individual components are very statistically intensive and related to Type I and Type II errors. For the purposes of this chapter, let me explain them with real-life examples:

- *True positive* is an access system that lets in the authorized user. A system designed to identify positives is functioning correctly. In other words, it is a test result that detects the condition when the condition is present.
- *False positive* is an access system that allows an unauthorized user. A system designed to identify positives is functioning incorrectly. It is a test result that detects the condition when the condition is absent.
- *True negative* is an antivirus detecting the virus properly. Therefore, a system that is designed to identify negatives is functioning properly. In other words, it is a test result that detects the condition when the condition is absent.
- *False negative* is an antivirus *not* detecting the virus. Therefore, a system that is designed to identify negatives is not functioning properly. In other words, it is a result that does not identify the condition when the condition is present.

When it comes to risk management, accuracy and precision are related to justifying whether a decision made by the trading department or business is accurate and precise and analyzing the decision making. For that purpose, the report should be accurate and precise. Inaccuracy and lack of precision in reporting is often due to poor-quality data—both incorrect data and lack sufficient data to make decisions. Especially in the case of illiquid assets, there will not be sufficient data points because of lack of active trading in the market.

While database providers try to maintain as much accuracy as possible, they may sometimes be subject to the following biases, which overstate returns and understate risk and may sometimes make funds more attractive than is justifiable:

- *Survivorship bias* can be explained by taking fund performance as an example. Survivorship bias occurs when the hedge-fund database excludes funds that have gone out of business. The perception is that only poorly performing hedge funds would go out of business. If nonperforming funds are excluded, then the database may contain a majority of positively performing funds. It is quite likely that funds will exhibit high volatile returns before operations are ceased. Therefore, the survivorship bias will overstate the returns and understate the risk of the fund index. In an academic study conducted during 2006, Fung and Hsieh found that survivorship bias added 3 percent per year to the reported hedge-fund returns. However, as the hedge-fund industry matures, survivorship bias declines.

- *Self-selection bias* can be explained by taking fund performance as an example. Since hedge funds are little-regulated, they have a choice as to whether to report performance at any and all times. Some fund managers that want to market their fund may suddenly decide to report hedge-fund data providers, and they report only if they are performing well. On the other hand, the hedge fund may stop reporting if it is not performing well. This is *self-selection bias*. It can be compared to a forum where exam candidates discuss an exam. When the results are announced, candidates may post theirs. It is quite possible that only candidates who pass the exam will come back to the forum and post as passed. Out of a hundred posts during the exam day, we may find 70 percent "passed" posts, but that does not necessarily mean that 70 percent of the aspirants passed the exam. On the other hand, a successful candidate who was not a member of the forum until the day results were announced may register and post a message like "passed." The self-selection bias will lead to an upward bias in performance measurement.

- *Backfill or instant history bias* occurs when positively performing funds are added to the database and backfill all the historical data as well. Since hedge-fund managers have the option of when to report performance, it is rational that they'll report only when the numbers look attractive. A study by Princeton professor Burton Malkiel published in the *Financial Analysts Journal* found that backfill bias overstated hedge-fund returns by 5 percent per year.

- *Liquidation bias* is somewhat similar to survivorship bias but occurs before the fund goes out of business. Unsuccessful hedge funds, before they liquidate operations, will be busy with preparing internal reports and other formalities. During this time, they may stop reporting their performance to hedge-fund databases. While closing the fund may take months, the database will lose the tail part of the data stream. This may cause the index to overestimate returns and underestimate risk. Liquidation bias is also called *catastrophe bias*.

Quantifying bias issues is not an easy task, and investors should apply subjective analysis when comparing fund performance with a corresponding index. Investors should try to get custom data that includes any excluded funds and then make the necessary adjustments to calculate unsmoothed risk and returns.

In addition to the bias issue, another issue that investors should keep in mind after adding the fund to the portfolio is performance reports. There are three main things to make sure of related to reports:

1. The fund is publishing the report periodically.
2. The report does not contain lagged data. For example, some funds may publish the data the first day of every quarter but may include data only until the last day two quarters prior.
3. The report is easy to interpret and understand.

Requirements Defined

The system should be linked to the requirements document. There should be clear documentation and tracing of both automated and manual edits and reasonableness checks, including an inventory of the validation rules that are applied to quantitative information. The system should have integrated procedures for identifying, reporting and explaining data errors or weaknesses in data integrity via exception reports.

Reconciliation Reports

The aggregated-risk data system should have an internal component that reconciles source data with aggregated data.

Mathematical and Logical Relationships

Risk data contains a large number of quantitative measures. These measures are used to observe the behavior of price movements with respect to changes in the market. The same quantitative measure for the same type of instrument will have different interpretations. For example, if we take delta, which gives the rate of change of the option price with respect to the underlying stock, it may work in a different way for the call option on the same stock if the call option has some exotic features, such as barrier options or average options.

The duration that measures the rate of change of bond price with respect to yield may not work in all the ranges of yields if the bond has some embedded options, such as callable and puttable. The reporting system must have some sort of auxiliary components that describe the nature of mathematical measures and such factors as how they are applicable to the instruments listed in the report, how they behave at different regimes of underlying risk factors like interest rates, and how they behave in stressed conditions.

Exception Report

Most instruments are sensitive to multiple risk factors. Similarly, most instruments exhibit multiple sensitivities. For example, if we take a bond that is issued in a foreign market, it is exposed to both interest-rate risk and currency risk. If certain assumptions are made such that the currencies are automatically reflected in the interest rate changes, then the risk calculation is simple. While this assumption works sometimes, it may not necessarily be true in all periods. If any assumptions are made, then such assumptions and exceptions must be reflected in the auxiliary component of the reports.

While the instruments exhibit nonlinearity with respect to risk factors, the intensity of severity is high in a certain type of instrument. For example, a bond exhibits some kind of nonlinearity with respect to interest-rate changes, which can be captured using convexity. Convexity gives the second-order changes and measures the rate of change of duration with respect to interest rate. Similarly, the option on the bond (let's assume the seller guarantees the bond price) is classified nonlinear as the exposure to the option seller changes so drastically if the interest rates are rising.

Both the bond and bond option exhibit nonlinearity. For simplicity purposes, bonds may be classified as linear products while bond options are classified as nonlinear options. In such case, the exceptions must be explained in the auxiliary report so that risk managers and senior management can interpret them accordingly.

Depth and Scope of Reports

Traditional risk management reports have an eye toward selective attributes, such as exposure amount by group, instrument type, and region. These reports were generated from limited data sets or silos. New regulations and the evolution of enterprise risk management consider risk from a much broader scope and depth by looking the risk from the angles of strategic, operational, and interrelated portfolios. The scope of risk management responsibility has been expanded to include business-continuity planning that focuses on how to make informed decisions about uncertainties that impact the organization's future.

Risk-based strategic decisions across the organization are guided by risk appetite statements on both the enterprise and operational level. The depth and scope of the reports must be designed by thinking from an enterprise point of view to do the following:

- make better decisions about uncertainties that affects our future
- establish an overarching framework for managing the organization's most significant risks
- enhance the achievement of strategic objectives and board risk oversight
- identify key threats that the firm faces in achieving the business objectives and responding
- establish a process for proactively managing threats to the business
- treating risk as an expense item and managing it through hedging

---

Principle 8

Comprehensiveness—Risk management reports should cover all material risk areas within the organisation. The depth and scope of these reports should be consistent with the size and complexity of the bank's operations and risk profile, as well as the requirements of the recipients.

Risk management reports should include exposure and position information for all significant risk areas (eg credit risk, market risk, liquidity risk, operational risk) and all significant components of those risk areas (eg single name, country and industry sector for credit risk). Risk management reports should also cover risk-related measures (eg regulatory and economic capital).

Reports should identify emerging risk concentrations, provide information in the context of limits and risk appetite/tolerance and propose recommendations for action where appropriate. Risk reports should include the current status of measures agreed by the board or senior management to reduce risk or deal with specific risk situations. This includes providing the ability to monitor emerging trends through forward-looking forecasts and stress tests.

Supervisors expect banks to determine risk reporting requirements that best suit their own business models and risk profiles. Supervisors will need to be satisfied with the choices a bank makes in terms of risk coverage, analysis and interpretation, scalability and comparability across group institutions. For example, an aggregated risk report should include, but not be limited to, the following information: capital adequacy, regulatory capital, capital and liquidity ratio projections, credit risk, market risk, operational risk, liquidity risk, stress testing results, inter- and intra-risk concentrations, and funding positions and plans.

Supervisors expect that risk management reports to the board and senior management provide a forward-looking assessment of risk and should not just rely on current and past data. The reports should contain forecasts or scenarios for key market variables and the effects on the bank so as to inform the board and senior management of the likely trajectory of the bank's capital and risk profile in the future.

From "Principles for Effective Risk Data Aggregation and Risk Reporting," Basel Committee on Banking Supervision, January 2013, http://www.bis.org/ publ/bcbs239.pdf.

Sufficient data history for important risk factors and comprehensive data sets for such risks are important to risk management and meeting supervisory requirements. Rules for depth and comprehensiveness of data history should be defined conservatively, in consultation with the firm's supervisors. Where necessary and possible, missing internal data values should be filled in with high-quality proxies or external data sources agreed on between the firm and its supervisors.

Creation of a dedicated function to manage data quality, either as part of the firm's risk management function or as the foundation of a cross-business-unit risk team. A dedicated team manages routine data aggregation and also assures fulfillment of specific requests. Its tasks include ensuring the consistency of data from various risk systems on the same risk type (credit, for example);

delivering comprehensive aggregated exposure reports for all risk types for each counterparty; producing regular reports on limits and exposures by subcategory (such as industry and region); and performing monthly cross-checks with the firm's finance group on limit and exposure data, taking any necessary steps to achieve consistency. For certain firms, this unit will need to work closely with front-office quantitative teams to align on methodologies across businesses.

Significant Risk Areas and Components of Those Risk Areas

The risk reporting system must be able to identify the areas of the risk that products are exposed to. Instead of having a spate mechanism to generate credit risk, market risk, liquidity risk, and operational risk exposures, the system should generate the unified view of risks that products are exposed to. In other words, the reports must be based on the products, including all the areas of risk the products are exposed to. At the same time, the risk exposures must be broken down by single name, country, industry sector, and so on. In addition, the same must be capable of producing risk-related measures, such as regulatory and economic capital.

Emerging Risk Concentrations and the Ability to Monitor Emerging Trends

Risk management is not about avoiding risk, as the business is driven by the commitments to fulfill the needs of customers. The demand for certain products is seasonal and may be concentrated for a significant period of time. Avoiding risk means missing business opportunities. Instead of avoiding the risk, the risk must be managed and manageable. Therefore the risk reporting system must be capable of identifying emerging risk concentrations and monitoring emerging trends through forward-looking forecasts and stress tests. The reports must be able to provide information needed to react effectively to evolving risks.

Principle 9

Clarity and usefulness—Risk management reports should communicate information in a clear and concise manner. Reports should be easy to understand yet comprehensive enough to facilitate informed decision-making. Reports should include meaningful information tailored to the needs of the recipients.

A bank's risk reports should contribute to sound risk management and decision-making by their relevant recipients, including, in particular, the board and senior management. Risk reports should ensure that information is meaningful and tailored to the needs of the recipients.

Reports should include an appropriate balance between risk data, analysis and interpretation, and qualitative explanations. The balance of qualitative versus quantitative information will vary at different levels within the organisation and will also depend on the level of aggregation that is applied to the reports. Higher up in the organisation, more aggregation is expected and therefore a greater degree of qualitative interpretation will be necessary.

Reporting policies and procedures should recognize the differing information needs of the board, senior management, and the other levels of the organisation (for example risk committees).

As one of the key recipients of risk management reports, the bank's board is responsible for determining its own risk reporting requirements and complying with its obligations to shareholders and other relevant stakeholders. The board should ensure that it is asking for and receiving relevant information that will allow it to fulfill its governance mandate relating to the bank and the risks to which it is exposed. This will allow the board to ensure it is operating within its risk tolerance/appetite.

The board should alert senior management when risk reports do not meet its requirements and do not provide the right level and type of information to set and monitor adherence to the bank's risk tolerance/appetite. The board should indicate whether it is receiving the right balance of detail and quantitative versus qualitative information.

Senior management is also a key recipient of risk reports and it is responsible for determining its own risk reporting requirements. Senior management should ensure that it is receiving relevant information that will allow it to fulfil its management mandate relative to the bank and the risks to which it is exposed.

A bank should develop an inventory and classification of risk data items which includes a reference to the concepts used to elaborate the reports.

Supervisors expect that reports will be clear and useful. Reports should reflect an appropriate balance between detailed data, qualitative discussion, explanation and recommended conclusions. Interpretation and explanations of the data, including observed trends, should be clear.

> Supervisors expect a bank to confirm periodically with recipients that the information aggregated and reported is relevant and appropriate, in terms of both amount and quality, to the governance and decision-making process.
>
> *From "Principles for Effective Risk Data Aggregation and Risk Reporting," Basel Committee on Banking Supervision, January 2013, http://www.bis.org/ publ/bcbs239.pdf.*

Information in the Context of Limits

The process of fulfilling customer needs is subject to limits set based on the customer risk profile and the bank's risk appetite. It is crucial for banks to maintain a balance between customer needs and risk appetite. The risk reports should provide meaningful and easily interpretable information in the context of limits.

Risk Appetite/Tolerance

The risk reporting system must act as a liaison between portfolio managers and the limit-management system in order to effectively communicate the limits from a context of risk appetite and tolerance. The system must promote and enhance the understanding of the risk appetite and the limits to risk management so that the board will be prepared accordingly.

Aggregated Risk Reports

The liquidity coverage ratio involves three components:

1. Stock of high-quality liquid assets
2. Outflows
3. Inflows requiring some level of business optimization

In order to continuously monitor and optimize the ratio, the reports must take an aggregated view that includes, but is not be limited to, the following information:

- capital adequacy
- regulatory capital
- capital and liquidity ratio projections

- credit risk
- market risk
- operational risk
- liquidity risk
- stress-testing results
- inter- and intra-risk concentrations
- funding positions and plans

Governance Mandate

It is the bank board's responsibility to provide the reporting requirements that are useful to governance mandate and design the bank's risk appetite and tolerance policy.

Principle 10

Frequency—The board and senior management (or other recipients as appropriate) should set the frequency of risk management report production and distribution. Frequency requirements should reflect the needs of the recipients, the nature of the risk reported, and the speed, at which the risk can change, as well as the importance of reports in contributing to sound risk management and effective and efficient decision-making across the bank. The frequency of reports should be increased during times of stress/crisis.

The frequency of risk reports will vary according to the type of risk, purpose and recipients. A bank should assess periodically the purpose of each report and set requirements for how quickly the reports need to be produced in both normal and stress/crisis situations. A bank should routinely test its ability to produce accurate reports within established timeframes, particularly in stress/crisis situations.

Supervisors expect that in times of stress/crisis all relevant and critical credit, market and liquidity position/exposure reports are available within a very short period of time to react effectively to evolving risks. Some position/exposure information may be needed immediately (intraday) to allow for timely and effective reactions.

From "Principles for Effective Risk Data Aggregation and Risk Reporting," Basel Committee on Banking Supervision, January 2013, http://www.bis.org/ publ/bcbs239.pdf.

Qualitative Explanations

The meaning of quantitative measure varies based on the context, business group, product, or even season. The reports must contain clear qualitative explanations indicating how the numbers are relevant based on the context.

Ability to Generate Reports in a Stressed Environment

Decision making is driven by the business data. It may be more dynamic when the markets are under stress and when there are opportunities to acquire a troubled business. The demand for special types of data and reports is subject to the situation as of the day of decision making. The reporting must be capable of generating required reports in a stressed environment.

Intraday Reports

There may be situations where certain liquidity risk management decisions are taken based on intraday events. In such cases, there must be a capability to generate the reports by including the intraday data.

Principle 11

Distribution—Risk management reports should be distributed to the relevant parties while ensuring confidentiality is maintained.

Procedures should be in place to allow for rapid collection and analysis of risk data and timely dissemination of reports to all appropriate recipients. This should be balanced with the need to ensure confidentiality as appropriate.

Supervisors expect a bank to confirm periodically that the relevant recipients receive timely reports.

From "Principles for Effective Risk Data Aggregation and Risk Reporting," Basel Committee on Banking Supervision, January 2013, http://www.bis.org/publ/bcbs239.pdf.

Risk management reports should be distributed to the relevant parties while ensuring confidentiality is maintained. Procedures should be in place to allow for rapid collection and analysis of risk data and timely dissemination of reports to all appropriate recipients. This should be balanced with the need to ensure confidentiality as appropriate. Supervisors expect a bank to confirm periodically that the relevant recipients receive timely reports.

7.6 Analysis of BCBS Supervisory Review, Tools, and Cooperation

For convenience, the remaining BCBS principles that pertain to supervisory review, tools, and cooperation are reproduced in the boxes below.

Principle 12

Review—Supervisors should periodically review and evaluate a bank's compliance with the eleven Principles above.

Supervisors should review a bank's compliance with the Principles in the preceding sections. Reviews should be incorporated into the regular program of supervisory reviews and may be supplemented by thematic reviews covering multiple banks with respect to a single or selected issue. Supervisors may test a bank's compliance with the Principles through occasional requests for information to be provided on selected risk issues (for example, exposures to certain risk factors) within short deadlines, thereby testing the capacity of a bank to aggregate risk data rapidly and produce risk reports. Supervisors should have access to the appropriate reports to be able to perform this review.

Supervisors should draw on reviews conducted by the internal or external auditors to inform their assessments of compliance with the Principles. Supervisors may require work to be carried out by a bank's internal audit functions or by experts independent from the bank. Supervisors must have access to all appropriate documents such as internal validation and audit reports, and should be able to meet with and discuss risk data aggregation capabilities with the external auditors or independent experts from the bank, when appropriate.

Supervisors should test a bank's capabilities to aggregate data and produce reports in both stress/crisis and steady-state environments, including sudden sharp increases in business volumes.

From "Principles for Effective Risk Data Aggregation and Risk Reporting,"
Basel Committee on Banking Supervision, January 2013, http://www.bis.org/
publ/bcbs239.pdf.

Principle 13

Remedial actions and supervisory measures—Supervisors should have and use the appropriate tools and resources to require effective

and timely remedial action by a bank to address deficiencies in its risk data aggregation capabilities and risk reporting practices. Supervisors should have the ability to use a range of tools, including Pillar 2.

Supervisors should require effective and timely remedial action by a bank to address deficiencies in its risk data aggregation capabilities and risk reporting practices and internal controls.

Supervisors should have a range of tools at their disposal to address material deficiencies in a bank's risk data aggregation and reporting capabilities. Such tools may include, but are not limited to, requiring a bank to take remedial action; increasing the intensity of supervision; requiring an independent review by a third party, such as external auditors; and the possible use of capital add-ons as both a risk mitigant and incentive under Pillar 2.

Supervisors should be able to set limits on a bank's risks or the growth in their activities where deficiencies in risk data aggregation and reporting are assessed as causing significant weaknesses in risk management capabilities.

For new business initiatives, supervisors may require that banks' implementation plans ensure that robust risk data aggregation is possible before allowing a new business venture or acquisition to proceed.

When a supervisor requires a bank to take remedial action, the supervisor should set a timetable for completion of the action. Supervisors should have escalation procedures in place to require more stringent or accelerated remedial action in the event that a bank does not adequately address the deficiencies identified, or in the case that supervisors deem further action is warranted.

From "Principles for Effective Risk Data Aggregation and Risk Reporting," Basel Committee on Banking Supervision, January 2013, http://www.bis.org/ publ/bcbs239.pdf.

Principle 14

Home/host cooperation—Supervisors should cooperate with relevant supervisors in other jurisdictions regarding the supervision and review of the Principles, and the implementation of any remedial action if necessary.

Effective cooperation and appropriate information sharing between the home and host supervisory authorities should contribute to the robustness of a bank's risk management practices across a bank's operations in multiple jurisdictions. Wherever possible, supervisors should avoid performing redundant and uncoordinated reviews related to risk data aggregation and risk reporting.

Cooperation can take the form of sharing of information within the constraints of applicable laws, as well as discussion between supervisors on a bilateral or multilateral basis (eg through colleges of supervisors), including, but not limited to, regular meetings. Communication by conference call and email may be particularly useful in tracking required remedial actions. Cooperation through colleges should be in line with the Basel Committee's *Good practice principles on supervisory colleges.*

Supervisors should discuss their experiences regarding the quality of risk data aggregation capabilities and risk reporting practices in different parts of the group. This should include any impediments to risk data aggregation and risk reporting arising from cross-border issues and also whether risk data is distributed appropriately across the group. Such exchanges will enable supervisors to identify significant concerns at an early stage and to respond promptly and effectively.

From "Principles for Effective Risk Data Aggregation and Risk Reporting," Basel Committee on Banking Supervision, January 2013, http://www.bis.org/ publ/bcbs239.pdf.

8 Information and Risk Architectures

8.1 Governance Program

Two primary preconditions to ensure compliance with BCBS principles are to have a strong data governance framework and to have risk data architecture and information technology (IT) infrastructure in place. As such, risk data aggregation capabilities and risk reporting practices should be subject to effective data governance and data management. In addition, the bank should have sophisticated and manageable data architecture and IT infrastructure to fully support risk data aggregation capabilities and risk reporting methods not only in normal times but also during times of stress or crisis.

While the Basel Committee provides a high-level view of these principles, it is the bank's responsibility to frame the governance and build data architecture and IT infrastructure in line with Basel principles.

Traditionally, data has been seen as an integral part of technology both by technology teams and business teams. The high level of separation between technology and business teams was making it difficult to make optimal decisions about data management. Technology challenges were transforming into organizational challenges because of the decreased compatibility across the systems over time. Firms may have acquired other firms that followed different data architectures, or different business groups were using different vendor products.

Regulatory scrutiny is becoming more intrusive and forcing financial institutions to resolve data quality challenges. Traditionally, IT functions were concentrating more on infrastructure development, availability, performance, database management, and database design—paying less attention to data flow documentation, data quality, and metadata. As companies are realizing that data is a tangible asset in a changing economy, data management is gaining importance.

It should be noted that the fourteen Basel principles are not just intended to provide Basel III regulatory reports. They are applicable to the overall risk management of the bank. If the bank is building a data management infrastructure for the purpose of Basel III regulation, it may not want to have redundant infrastructures for internal and other risk management purposes. Therefore, banks should build more general data management infrastructures that fulfill the needs of overall risk management.

Risk management does not serve its purpose as long as various departments own different pieces of risk calculations. The implicit inconsistency among silo-based calculations raises concerns about the reliability of the outcome. Lots of reworking is needed while aggregating the risk data and metrics that were collected in the form of Excel spreadsheets. Performing risk calculations with aggregated data will give an accurate view of enterprise risk. Aggregating risk data needs sound enterprise data management.

The goal of enterprise data management is establishing a single authoritative source of data that everyone can trust and rely on. Such a source of data is not only used for risk management but also to feed back to valuation models of the securities or traded products. Building such an authoritative data store requires a lot of effort, tactics, strategies, and resources. The process building and maintaining such a store is collectively referred to as *enterprise data management*.

Enterprise data management will also play a key role in transforming the data into information. The difference between *data* and *information* is that data is provided in raw form while information provides context. Data is an asset. Though data does not appear in the balance sheet, it provides incredible value to the firm in informing effective decisions. As the assets have owners, the data should have owners, called *data stewards*. As the assets need management, the data also needs management, called *data management*. The data management program is the collaborative responsibility of several parties within the organization.

To perform various functions of enterprise data management, there must be an effective data governance program that involves all relevant technology teams and business teams. Data governance takes the responsibility of setting policy for IT and data groups to follow while establishing their architectures and implementation. Data governance creates a framework that sets the desirable behavior in the valuation, creation, movement, transforming, storage, use, archiving, and deletion of data. Data governance defines processes, roles, standards, and metrics that ensure the effective and efficient use of data.

Data governance is an imperative program for companies that want to implement enterprise risk management. Data governance programs are also required for firms going for big data. The traditional valuation methods and risk analytics are quantitative models. These models were built based on a sample set of data and then applied to the larger set of data to predict the future. As the markets are maturing and volatilities are increasing, such quantitative models require the use of heavy data. The combination of quantitative finance and huge data is called *data science*, and it's more about mining data and searching for patterns. Mining huge volume of data needs big-data technologies.

Data governance programs are not limited to enterprise data. They are equally important for silo-based databases to promote a unified process and standards. Various institutions define the data governance in different ways, but the ultimate interpretation leading to it is the same.

The MDM Institute defines data governance as "the formal orchestration of people, processes, and technology to enable an organization to leverage data as an enterprise asset." Forrester defines it as "the process by which an organization formalizes the fiduciary duty for the management of data assets critical to it success." The Data Governance Institute states that "data governance is a system of decision rights and accountabilities for information-related processes, executed according to agreed-upon models, which describe who can take what actions with what information, and when, under what circumstances, using what method." DAMA defines it as "the exercise of authority over the management of data assets and the performance of data management functions."

A data governance program does not directly involve technology operations. The program does not involve developing or marinating any technology systems. It does not involve business. Its core focus is to deal with policies and standards.

Building enterprise data storage requires interaction with a large number of teams. Each team has its own responsibilities. Work culture may be different for each team, even in the same organization. There is potential for conflicts when dealing with such teams. One of the uppermost goals of data governance programs is promoting the work culture and preventing any conflicts.

Data governance programs should promote unified standards, such as naming standards, data modeling standards, and other data architecture standards. This will, in turn, increase the team's efficiency, especially when working with cross-functional groups. Data governance programs should define the policies that explain the rules controlling the integrity, security, and use of data during its life cycle and state of change.

The ultimate goal of a data governance program is to increase the economic value of the data. The economic value comes from decreasing the risk of regulatory fines, reducing the capital reserve, detecting the risks, and helping the firm profit from such risk areas by properly managing the risk. Enterprise data management (EDM) helps the risk to be managed efficiently, thus reducing the required capital reserves. From an infrastructure point of view, EDM eliminates the redundancy of the data and data storage, reducing operational costs. EDM helps to lower development costs, as much of the required data is obtained from clearly defined, trusted sources. EDM serves as a single source of trusted data to mine for trading opportunities.

Banks must design, build, and maintain data architectures that fully support risk data aggregation and reporting—hedging methods not only in normal times, but also during times of stress. Such infrastructure should help the firm to predict and quickly react to changing market conditions.

To ensure the completeness of data by capturing and aggregating all material risk data across groups, data should be available by business line, legal entity, asset class, industry, and region. Banks should have the ability to generate and aggregate up-to-date risk data in a timely manner to meet all risk management practices and improve the adaptability to meet a broad range of on-demand, ad hoc risk management reporting requests in a dynamic environment. In certain cases, the retrieval of the ad hoc piece of data may take a day, whereas the data is useful for only a few seconds in a decision-making meeting. Having the data in place does not serve its purpose if it cannot be used quickly as and when needed. A data governance program should draw out accessibility procedures and make them available to users.

Data and model governance (DMG) is a relatively new program and requires a restructuring of the data-related groups with a mix of new and existing roles. Let's discuss the various roles needed in a data governance program. It may be that one person will fill many roles.

8.1.1   Chief Data Officer

As companies start building enterprise-wide interconnected architectures to integrate their applications and systems across the company, it is no longer efficient to have standards, policies, and procedures for each silo. Therefore, the new role of chief data officer (CDO) has emerged. The main responsibilities of the CDO include framing data strategies, standards, procedures, and accountability at the enterprise level. The CDO is also responsible for ensuring proper implementation of this framework. On the executive management team, the CDO is the voice of data, representing it as a strategic business asset. CDOs work proactively by exposing data as a driver of revenue.

The CDO develops a data strategy that will enable the most effective use of data assets while keeping costs within reasonable limits, and is responsible for every job of data management and governance that is highlighted in this chapter. The CDO must possess a balance of technical skill, business knowledge, and people skills to smoothly navigate the technical and political hurdles of shepherding valuable enterprise data. Of the three, the most challenging job is dealing with cultural responsibilities.

In every firm, there are staff members who are dealing with data; staff members who are not dealing with data; leaders who can make decisions in the absence of data; people who deal with analysis; people who deal with the application that generates the data; and so on. It will take more than hardware and software to establish regimes of data sharing, to educate employees, and to institutionalize data-driven decisions. The functions of the CDO will touch nearly every staff member within an organization.

Human resources are a significant asset to any firm, even though the value does not appear in the balance sheet. Firms make valuable decisions based on data, but data doesn't appear on the balance sheet either. Data is taking center stage in predicting the future and making decisions. Data governance programs should create data-driven culture and promote data as an asset to gain proper attention from everyone and demonstrate how critical data elements support business processes and what the risks to the business are if data is unavailable or incorrect.

8.1.2   Data Steward

The data steward is the central point of contact for all queries and issues related to data. Data stewardship must be a formal job role in any business where there is well-defined data management and governance. Data stewards must perform as business users with expert knowledge of business processes and architectures. They act as a liaison between the IT department and information users. They are the people who must know everything about how the data is created, flows, and is used within those processes. Data stewards must hold the responsibility for validating the accuracy, completeness, and comprehensiveness of data within a business context.

In any business, there can be a chief data steward responsible for overseeing and guiding multiple stewards. The general responsibilities of the data steward include, but are not limited to, the following:

- Manage an inventory of data sources.
- Ensure consistency in reference data and master data definitions.
- Create and manage business metadata.
- Manage the business logic and rules behind the data transformations.
- Create an overall data quality program.
- Coordinate with other data stewards for enterprise stewardship needs.
- Create new policies or standards for ensuring appropriate data entry, usage, and transformation in collaboration with the chief data steward and/or chief data officer.
- Define data validation and reconciliation processes.
- Set access requirements for the data and approve the provisioning requests for access to source data.
- Collaborate with data custodians to implement validations, controls, and data transformations, and to resolve any data issues.

8.1.3   Data Custodian

Data custodians are part of the IT function and own the repositories and technical infrastructure to manage the data. They oversee the safe transport and storage of data, focusing on the technical activities required to keep the data intact and available to users at all times. Responsibilities of data custodians include, but are not limited to, the following:

- Assist data stewards and other data custodians in researching data issues and inquiries.
- Collaborate with data stewards as described in the responsibilities of the data steward.
- Guide data stewards in establishing escalation processes.
- Implement data transformations, controls, validations, and documents through which the data flows.
- Perform the reconciliation processes following completion of data.
- Provide appropriate communication of issues with delivery or quality of source data.
- Partner with data repository teams to establish a process to request changes to data source feeds.
- Provide the source team with appropriate communication of issues with delivery or quality of source data.
- Define, capture, and maintain technical metadata.

8.1.4   Data Architect

While the role of data architect is not a new one in traditional data environments, the role must be fine-tuned from the DMG point of view. As the organization start generating, storing, and retrieving exponentially more data every month, the complexity in operating these tasks efficiently and effectively is also growing. That is why data architects are so important. Their duties include, but are not limited to, the following:

- Optimize the storage, access, movement, and organization of data by using processes, systems, technology, and human performance.
- Balance the potentially conflicting requirements of fast responding transaction systems, business intelligence involving large quantities of data, and a clear and concise view of reporting.
- Define enterprise-wide, non-redundant product standards to efficiently manage data architecture components.
- Draft an enterprise-wide asset-management strategy to enable resource sharing and reduce operational costs.
- Bridge the business and technology worlds from a data and information perspective.

- Provide valuable input and raise awareness of significant issues requiring data governance attention.
- Be involved in most data management decisions.
- Have a good understanding of the context, subject, and quality that the business needs.
- Determine and provide architectural approaches for data environments.

8.1.5   Metadata Manager

Metadata is data about data. It represents the details about where a data element is stored, its characteristics, its definition, where it is used, how it flows through different stores, what systems it is flowing through, how it is being transformed on the way, what are its different controls, what is the frequency of updates, who owns it, and more.

Metadata management is a governing function that gathers these details and manages them. Metadata management is an as-is documentation process and does not dictate how and what the actual data should be. Metadata provides business details to technical professionals, including but not limited to business definitions, business rules, algorithms and calculations, system of records, data stewards, group owners, business use, business impact, and business constraints.

Metadata improves the confidence level among business users about the data obtained from different databases, analytical applications, and application systems. The technical details provided to business users include, but are not limited to, mappings, transformations, database names, table names, column names, data types, job schedules, job dependencies, retention rules, purging rules, source systems, feed names, feed types, and audit controls.

Metadata provides the details of data stewardship—including, but not limited to, data owners, data stewards, business groups, data-sharing rules, data-sharing agreements, business goals, and subject areas. It helps the organization in identifying and reducing data redundancy. Metadata management makes the ad hoc report generation process less hectic. It increases the value of strategic information and improves the data management lifecycle.

Implementing effective metadata management involves several phases, including drafting a strategy, promoting the metadata culture, educating the team about business terminology and processes, gathering metadata, and choosing metadata management tools.

Metadata management—and, for that matter, all of data management—comes under IT department. However, the team should be fully aware of business definitions, where the data is used, and what the business impact will be. Team management should have sufficient documentation about the business and business processes. This information does not have to be part of the metadata. The team management should frequently arrange sessions with business teams.

Choosing the metadata management tool is the responsibility of the data management group. In the beginning, it may be possible to collect the metadata in the form of Excel sheets. However, for the purposes of the visibility and modification group, there should be a user-interface-based tool where users can retrieve, view, and make changes as and when needed. There are several metadata management tools on the market. Developing the tool from scratch may be expensive for any firm.

Metadata can be broken down into three types:

1. *Technical metadata*, such as the name of the source table, the source table column name, data type, feed names, and transportation mechanism
2. *Business metadata*, such as the business term's name, definition, stewards, and associated reference data
3. *Operational metadata*, such as the date last updated, number of times accessed, or date last accessed

There are a lot of metadata management strategies, but the firm needs to come up with a strategy based on its own needs in order to avoid overfitting or underfitting. Data lineage is the core part of metadata management. Data lineage is used to trace the path of any data element, controls, or transformations.

Business teams provide the list of data elements that are needed in a centralized database. The metadata manager should collect the definitions of each element and a short business description, priority, and business impact. Business teams also tell the originating source of these elements. If not then, it is required to identify the source application systems with the help of other business teams. For example, if the elements correspond to repo trading and if the enterprise risk management does not have a list of repo trading systems, it is helpful to approach the trading desk to get a list of source systems.

From there onward, it is the metadata team's responsibility to trace the flow of the elements—how the data is being transferred to the other system. It is flowing like a flat file or SQL (structured query language). Questions to ask include the following:

- What is the time and frequency of data flow?
- On which database and table does it get loaded?
- What is the data type?
- Is there a transformation of the element between two systems? (For example, one system may call it as liquidity flag while they may prefer to store it as illiquid flag, in which case the element gets flipped.)
- Who owns each system?
- Who is the subject-matter expert of each system?
- Who is the data steward?
- What are the controls and checks implemented at element level and flow level?

It is also necessary to collect the checks performed to ensure data integration. For example, how do you know if the data has been loaded on a particular day? If the data is not loaded, then who will contact whom? What is the mode of communication?

There is no doubt that metadata management is one of the most frustrating jobs in the organization. The team does not own any database or business. It needs a lot of attention from application owners and database-subject experts. The metadata management team is comprised of semi-technical people with domain knowledge. Since the team is responsible for documenting the processes owned by other teams, there might be potential for conflict. Technical teams may not care about business knowledge. While the teams are capable of explaining the systems technically, it may sometimes be difficult to describe them in terms of business. The metadata management team should first proactively identify the potential conflicts and promote the work culture accordingly.

The big challenge in data aggregation is dealing with different levels of people having different job profiles. Each silo team has its own responsibilities and priorities and may feel no incentive to work with the EDM team to provide a required level of service. At the same time, it may not be economical to dedicate resources at silos to work with the EDM team. The ideology should come by building a work culture across the firm. Silos should feel that they would indeed become direct or indirect owners of the enterprise data.

8.1.6   Data Quality Manager

The data quality framework deals with agreed-upon service-level standards and policies on data confidentiality, integrity, and availability. Data quality managers are responsible for ensuring that the data meets the specified characteristics. The quality program design phase must be appropriate for the business context and therefore must, at least initially, be designed and guided by the data stewards. The process must be capable of uncovering data anomalies, inconsistencies, and redundancies by analyzing content, structure, and relationships within the data.

The quality program must have a transformation phase consisting of running the correction mappings that are used to correct the source data. The quality program must have the data monitoring capability to examine the data over time and raise an alert when the data violates any business rules that are set.

The top desired qualities of data are as follows:

- accuracy
- accessibility
- adaptability
- comprehensiveness
- consistency
- timeliness
- granularity
- precision

8.1.7   Data Privacy Officer

Bringing the data to a centralized data management system does raise some privacy issues. Some privacy rules pertain to the proprietary nature of the silo data, while others pertain to jurisdictional laws. The data management team must have data-sharing and privacy agreements in place and stored in such a way that they are accessible to all relevant parties.

There are three stages involved in this effort: identifying the sensitivity of the data, preparing the agreements, and implementing an enterprise data management system. When collecting sensitive data, identifiers must de-identified in such a way that they can later be re-identified by the silos when using the enterprise data. The governance team must be able to convince the silos of the importance of moving to centralized system and must take all precautionary steps to protect data from misuse, unauthorized access, disclosure, and destruction. One of the required tasks of data management is transforming the data into a unique format in a way that will not lead to misinterpretation.

The individual trading teams must have reasonable access to the enterprise data but be kept from broader data. Privacy checks must be implemented in the enterprise data management system accordingly. There are several legal impediments to data-sharing across jurisdictions as well. The framework must maintain the balance and trade-offs among the vendor processes, in-house processes, data confidentiality, integrity, and availability.

8.1.8   Internal Data Auditor

EDM must include a component to perform logging and auditing of information usage, which helps in timely detection of, and response to, unauthorized information-processing activities. The governance framework must establish policies for logging, auditing, monitoring the information usage, event tracking, recording, and monitoring of the data as determined by the critical nature of the application. There are certain legal and regulatory requirements as wells as business needs, and storage and processing capacities that determines the retention periods for log data.

8.2 Information Architectures

According to the Basel Committee's Principle 2 on data architecture and IT infrastructure ("Principles for Effective Risk Data Aggregation and Risk Reporting," January 2013, http://www.bis.org/publ/bcbs239.pdf), "A bank should design, build and maintain data architecture and IT infrastructure which fully supports its risk data aggregation capabilities and risk reporting practices not only in normal times, but also during times of stress or crisis, while still meeting the other Principles."

8.2.1   *Enterprise Data Architecture*

Financial institutions collect and maintain data from various source systems. The list includes trading systems, customer databases, and market-data systems. The same data is called different things in different systems. For example, the principal amount in one system is called *face value*, whereas in another system it is called *par value*. A centralized metadata system with a unique data element ID with different aliases should be integrated with the systems.

The customer for certain transactions in one system may be a parent customer for a different set of transactions in another system. In this case, it is required to know both the legal identifier as well as parent identifier. For such purposes, a customer hierarchy system must be Integrated with the source systems.

Data architecture and IT infrastructure teams should have a clear understanding of the nature of data, where and how it is used, and how is it related to other data elements in order to build aggregated data system. The purpose of data varies from time to time. It depends on how risk managers treat the data. In normal markets, a certain portion of data may be sufficient to make certain decisions, whereas a stressed market demands an additional set of parameters to be included in the data. The architecture should be able to support enhancing or shrinking the sets with minimal manual intervention.

For example, there is a report with list of positions espoused to a certain counterparty. In a stressed market, the risk manager may need to know the exposures of all counterparties within the legal hierarchy of that counterparty. For such purposes, the entire customer database should be up to date. It may be possible that a different person than the one aggregated owns that customer hierarchy database, while the owner of a customer hierarchy database did not find a need for updating his database. In such cases, there must be clarity in the roles and responsibilities of ownership and who should do what and when.

In a different example, if a new customer arrives and positions are entered into the trading system and customer database, the data travels to the aggregated system through intermediate systems. If the two intermediate systems that store position data and customer data are not synced for the first time to capture the customer data, there will be missing customer data in the aggregated data for certain transactions. There should be periodic checks and controls to ensure that the transaction data set is complete.

Enterprise data architecture is more than simply building a data warehouse, bringing the data from multiple sources, and storing it to create a centralized data store where a set of regulatory reports can be generated. If that's all it was, there would be no point in investing millions of dollars on risk data aggregation. When building enterprise data architecture, it is necessary to consider the fundamental rules of Basel regulation, other regulations, and all the principles of risk data aggregation and reporting. That will provide a baseline for not only centralized data storage but also the upstream data transfer mechanisms used to collect data from silos, downstream mechanisms for analytics, data quality architectures, and more.

For example, Basel III requires daily calculation of CVA (credit value adjustment) VaR (value-at-risk), even though there is no such need of reporting the same to regulators. The effective management of CVA risk and liquidity risk does need intraday real-time calculations. The real-time risk calculations are not just limited to CVA but also to several other metrics.

On the other hand, trading speed is increasing multifold. Trading desks are moving to a new era of embedding risk data in the front office and implementing trading strategies that optimize regulatory risk, portfolio risk, and traders' performance in real time. This may require pre-trading risk analysis. By this time, we understand what kind of enterprise data system and transfer mechanisms we need in order to be in compliance with RDA principles. The enterprise data management system needs to support much faster risk data aggregation to provide real-time updates.

Firms preferred to have silo databases, but not because they were not aware of enterprise data system. It was because silo owners wanted to have control over agility. Agility refers to the ability to make changes to the system effectively and efficiently in order to meet the dynamics of the business. However, higher management loses control over the risk data they want.

Moving to enterprise data management can help firms get control over risk data by integrating data into a single trusted form. At the same time, front-office teams will lose the ability to make their risk function customizable to meet their specific needs. Lack of agility in an enterprise data management system can lead to trading and risk-function-technology systems being separated. This will hamper collaboration.

Collaboration among different silos is needed to allow firms to get a clear view of risk across the enterprise and to increase accountability, responsibility, and transparency. Hence, enterprise data architecture must focus on maintaining balance between control and agility. In order to compensate the silo owner for the loss of control, enterprise data management must support enterprise risk management by providing real-time data to perform real-time calculations based on a variety of data types and using a higher volume of data than ever before while meeting the specific needs of silos.

Some risk calculations are very specific to a silo, even though data from multiple silos is required. Enterprise risk management and data management systems must be able to handle specific risk calculations. The challenge comes from the use of vendor systems for trading, as vendor systems are not usually flexible enough to receive custom feeds and fine-tune trading decisions.

While following traditional procedures to collect and manage master data, organizations should utilize the unstructured data available from different sources to capture the advantages of big data. The following examples describe how unstructured and text data can add value to the traditional master data:

- Attaching the insights from social media to the counterparty's record will improve monitoring of the counterparty.
- Unstructured financial information from 10-K and 10-Q reports can dynamically update changes in ownership structures.
- Unstructured data about macroeconomics in the counterparty's region can help to predict the counterparty's future state.

The data management team needs to adopt, but not be limited to, the following best practices to align with master data management (MDM):

- Assess the master data to support the risk reports and analytics.
- Leverage the big data to increase the strategic value of master data.
- Improve the consistency of key reference data to support the big datamanagement program.
- Extract meaning from unstructured text to enrich master data.
- Continuously monitor the relationships among various reference data elements to support the dynamics of big analytics.
- Eliminate the duplicity to reduce the manual interventions.

8.2.2   *Effective ETL with Big Data Technologies*

Traditionally, extract-transform-load (ETL) has been used to extract data from multiple sources, transform it to fit business needs, and load it into a data warehouse. If the data sets from the sources are very large and require a good amount of data transformation, traditional ETL can become challenging because it is too complex and takes too long to execute. The nature of risk data, as explained in previous sections, requires an infrastructure to process ETL cost-effectively and at a much faster speed. But the historical hardware and software were not enough to cost-effectively store, transform, and load the data into a centralized data store.

With the emergence of big data technologies, using the Hadoop-based big data hub in enterprise data architecture, we now have a cost-effective, scalable, extreme-performance environment in which to extract, transform, and analyze the data without traditional ETL. *Big data* refers to the large amounts of heterogeneous data that flows continuously through the organization. While the Hadoop has become a synonym for big data, the maturity in big-data technologies will enable several traditional technologies to meet the characteristics of big data.

Because of the nature of the structured data in capital markets, the use of big data must be managed in a very carefully designed manner. Big data is not meant just for unstructured data. Proper design can make the best use of big data for a mix of structured and unstructured data. Let me mention few of the big-data technologies and their primary use in the data driven world.

The first product to be mentioned in big data is Hadoop. It's a database that relies on the core principle of "no schema-on-write." That means there is no need to predefine the data schema before loading data into it. This is true for both structured data, such as transaction data, and unstructured data, such as content tagging and web logs. The data can rapidly load as-is into Hadoop, where it is available for downstream analytic processes. The raw data can be offloaded and transformed by parallel processing at scale. There is also a provision to perform the traditional ETL tasks of cleansing, normalizing, aligning, and aggregating data for the enterprise data warehouse (EDW) by employing the massive scalability of MapReduce.

Hadoop is a core part of data-driven computing infrastructures. It's designed to execute queries and other batch operations against massive data sets that can be petabytes in size. It runs on a large cluster of low-cost machines or cloud-computing services. It is designed to gracefully handle frequent hardware malfunctions. It allows users to quickly write efficient parallel code and to scale linearly to handle massive data by adding more nodes to the cluster.

Why do we need Hadoop to process the data while there exists several relational databases that use SQL? A relational database management system (RDBMS) runs on high-end propriety machines and storage systems. If we want to increase the data size, we will either need a powerful machine or additional servers. There is no single server available with the capabilities of processing so much data in a timely manner. Since Hadoop architecture runs on a cluster of low-cost commodity servers, adding hundreds or thousands of computers to the cluster is not so expensive.

While RDBMS is meant for processing structured data, Hadoop can be used to process structured, semi-structured, or unstructured data. Modern applications deal with data types that won't fit into the RDBMS model. Text documents, images, audio files, video files, and XML files are a few examples of data types. Since Hadoop uses key/value pairs, and since unstructured data can easily be transformed into key/value pairs, it is more flexible for working with unstructured data.

How does Hadoop work? Hadoop is an ecosystem of software packages, including MapReduce, Hadoop Distributed File System (HDFS), and a lot of other libraries. The ecosystem is designed to detect and handle failures at the application layer, thus providing high-available service. Software packages are used to load or append the data to HDFS. Hadoop then scans through the data to produce results that are output into other files. Hadoop's processing system, MapReduce, helps the data to be processed in a more general fashion.

Hadoop uses MapReduce to split up a problem and send it to different servers. Each sub-problem is solved by a different server in parallel. The individual solutions are then merged together and written into files that may in turn be used as inputs into additional MapReduce steps. Hadoop adds the ability to store and access data that might be needed but may never be loaded into the data warehouse. It allows organizations to store the data cost-effectively in Hadoop and retrieve it as needed—using Hive or other analytic tools native to the platform—without affecting the EDW environment.

The next useful thing is NoSQL (not only SQL). It is a high-performance, highly available, rich query language that is easily scalable. NoSQL is not a relational database and does not adhere to the traditional RDBMS structure. It is not built on tables and does not employ SQL to manipulate data. It may not provide full ACID (atomicity, consistency, isolation, durability) guarantees. However it has a distributed and fault-tolerant architecture.

While the common goal for Hadoop and NoSQL is massive scalability and support for massive data, they both have their own places where they perform better. NoSQL is good for storing information of a certain type, with great retrieval speed based on key write performance. Hadoop is good for inexpensive storage of lots of data, structured and semi-structured.

There are several NoSQL databases on the market. Some of the more prominent are Apache Cassandra, MongoDB, Voldemort, Apache HBase, SimpleDB, and BigTable. The Apache Cassandra database is the right choice for scalability and high availability without compromising performance. HBase is an open-source, no relational, column-oriented database. It runs directly on Hadoop. It is not a MapReduce implementation. A principal differentiator of HBase from MapReduce implementations, such as Pig and Hive, is the ability to provide real-time read-and-write random access to very large data sets. MongoDB is a document database that provides high performance, high availability, and easy scalability.

MapReduce is a powerful and flexible tool used to parse unstructured or semi-structured data. But this tool is useful only when there is massive data. Financial organizations have plenty of data scattered across multiple systems. If all that data can be brought to HDFS, it can be used more efficiently. But actually doing so is a cumbersome task.

Consider an example where counterparty events information is obtained from blogs and websites. Actually matching these events against their profiles or their previously recorded history requires that we look up information in a database. Running several MapReduce programs would possibly cause performance issues. The solution is to periodically dump the contents of the events database and the history database to HDFS and let the MapReduce programs join against the data stored there.

Going one step further, we could take the in-HDFS copy of the counterparty database and import it into a system similar to a data warehouse. This will allow us to perform ad hoc SQL queries against the entire database without working on the production database.

Hive is like a data warehouse system. It is used for data summarization, ad hoc queries, and analysis of large data sets stored in Hadoop distributed-file systems. Hive provides a mechanism to query the data using an SQL-like language called HiveQL. Statements are broken down by the Hive service into MapReduce jobs and executed across a Hadoop cluster.

Sqoop is another tool in the big data family. It stands for SQL-to-Hadoop. It is a straightforward command-line tool. Sqoop allows easy import and export of data from structured data stores, such as relational databases, enterprise data warehouses, and NoSQL systems. The data set being transferred is sliced up into different partitions, and a map-only job is launched with individual mappers responsible for transferring a slice of this data set. It provides the ability to import from SQL databases or HDFC straight into the Hive data warehouse.

Next comes Pig. Financial firms produce large numbers of larger log files. These contain a great deal of useful information—for example, who initiated the transaction, whether it was discarded before fulfilling, and whether the same transaction was processed later. The files need to be cleansed, precompiled, and loaded to retrieve any insights. Pig is useful for such ETL operations. It provides an engine for executing data flows in parallel on Hadoop. It comes with Pig Latin, a language used to express data flows. It also provides traditional data operations, such as join, sort, and filter.

Pig is used in conjunction with MapReduce. Pig Latin scripts are first written into a series of one or more MapReduce jobs. Pig then compiles and executes them. Why do we need use Pig instead of directly using MapReduce? Because Pig Latin provides all of the standard data processing operations, such as join, filter, and group by, order by, and union. Pig can analyze Pig Latin scripts, understand the data flows, and provide early error checking. Pig does a similar job to what Hive does, but Pig has a scripting language where as Hive is query-based system.

Other useful tools include the following:

- *ZooKeeper*, a centralized service for maintaining configuration information, naming, providing distributed synchronization, and providing group services

- *Cascading*, a Java application framework that enables typical developers to quickly and easily develop rich data analytics and data management applications that can be deployed and managed across a variety of computing environments
- *Oozie*, a workflow engine used to run Hadoop jobs, such as MapReduce, Pig, Hive, and Sqoop
- *Mahout*, an open-source, highly scalable, machine-learning library from Apache
- *Apache Flume*, a distributed system used to collect, aggregate, and move large amounts of data from multiple sources into HDFS or another central data store

8.3 In-Memory Analytics and Real-Time Risk Calculations

Traditional risk management systems relied on overnight batch risk calculations, predefined queries, or Excel-based spreadsheet calculations. As the dynamics of trading and markets change every minute, more real-time or on-the-fly risk calculations are needed, and need to be integrated with pricing engines.

While the historical data is readily available in structured databases, they don't reflect the intraday data. There needs to be a mechanism where the intraday data is cached and readily available to use in conjunction with historical data. The intraday data-flows involve heavy computations, such as streaming market data, analyzing dependencies, and making calculations. Simple caching solutions cannot provide the scalability of the intraday data under such write-intensive flows and therefore require in-memory analytics. The architecture requires intraday data to reside in memory and historical data in relational database or Hadoop/NoSQL, and depends on a holistic view of the multi-tier architecture.

8.4 Market Risk Analytics

When we talk about market risk, the first thing that comes to mind is value-at-risk (VaR)—with market risk management just a matter of calculating VaR on a daily basis and providing those numbers to risk managers. However, the financial crisis challenged this misconception. Sophisticated market risk management starts at the technology division, with multidimensional changes to traditional market risk strategies. The following changes must be made to implement a sophisticated market risk management system:

1. Don't rely on traditional VaR measurement procedures; implement high-performance VaR calculation systems.
2. Do not simply use traditional VaR numbers; consider alternative VaR measures as well.
3. Monitor and measure short volatility risk.
4. Implement sophisticated sensitivity analysis.
5. Conduct scenario analysis and stress testing using static and dynamic simulations.
6. Integrate real-time and event-driven analysis with market risk measurement.
7. Implement sophisticated interaction systems with risk managers.

In Chapter 4, I discussed three techniques of VaR measurement: parametric, historical simulation, and Monte Carlo simulation. The parametric approach can be developed using the variance-covariance matrix or delta-normal method. However, there is some limitation in using variance-covariance matrix methods because of limitations in the traditional hardware and software.

For example, portfolio risk is derived from the historical data of profit and loss of individual positions. Some of the instruments may not have historical data for longer periods. An illiquid security may have a very short record, and other OTC instruments may not have any history at all. In such cases, it may be possible to identify comparable instruments for which we do not have sufficient data.

After collecting historical data from each instrument, we calculate the volatility of each. We also need to obtain correlations between the instruments. If there are n instruments in the portfolio, there will be n (n-1)/2 correlations. The total of n volatilities and n (n-1)/2 correlations account to n (n+1)/2 data points.

As n increases, the number of data points grows exponentially. If there are 1,000 instruments in portfolio, then there will be 500,500 calculations needed. With the traditional hardware and software, it is very difficult to collect and process the data involved.

To overcome this problem, the traditional practice is to map the asset against a market risk factor. For example, all stocks in the portfolio are mapped to single stock-market factors represented by the stock-market index; bonds are mapped to interest-rate risk factor. The computing time to perform risk simulations is thereby greatly reduced. The individual assets in the portfolio can be classified into a limited number of categories, such as interest-rate products, currency products, and equity positions. Each of these categories has its own risk factor—for example, beta for equities, duration for bonds.

The VaR is then calculated assuming the returns follow normal distribution. For example, VaR using beta is calculated as follows:

> Assume that n is the number of stocks in portfolio. An amount, Si, is invested in the stocks of firm i. After using capital asset pricing model (CAPM) and applying risk calculation, the VaR on investment i is calculated as

$$Var = -Z \times \sigma i \times \beta i \times Si$$

> The total VaR on all investments is calculated as

$$VaR = -Z \times \sigma m \text{ (sum of all } \beta i \times Si)$$

> The VaR of other asset classifications is calculated similarly. This process reduces the number of computations from $n(n+1)/2$ to n.

The problem with such a simplified mechanism is that the underlying correlations are not captured efficiently, and the correlation between individual instruments and market risk factors is only appropriate and not accurate. Moreover, the VaR calculations assume that the returns follow normal distribution. Yet the financial markets are not always normal.

The evolution of big data brings several strong capabilities to address the issues, surrounded by computational time and collection of required historical data. Performing $n(n+1)/2$ computations can be done in minutes.

VaR is used to measure the potential loss in a portfolio over a defined period at a given confidence interval. For example, if the VaR of a portfolio is calculated as $100 million at 95 percent confidence level for a period of ten days, there is a only a 5 percent chance that the value of the asset will drop more than $100 million over any given ten days.

First of all, the VaR does not tell what the loss is that can occur beyond the 95 percent confidence level. In other words, the 5 percent chance of loss can be huge and cannot be determined by this model. The calculation of VaR assumes the returns of the portfolio are normally distributed. The normal distribution means the returns drawn as a graph are bell-shaped. Or in simple terms, the model assumes normal market conditions and also assumes that the conditions will remain the same in the future.

But in competitive markets, the returns exhibit non-normal pattern. For example, the value of a stock of a particular company may rise by a lot because of certain events, such as successful invention of new product, and may become stable over that period. Or a liquidity crisis, which is a low-probability catastrophic event, can create a loss that wipes out the capital and creates a client exodus.

All VaR models use historical data to some degree or another, and therefore the VaR model is a function of the time period over which the historical data is collected. If that time period is a relatively stable one, the computed VaR will be a low number and will understate the risk looking forward. Conversely, if the time period examined was volatile, VaR will be set too high. Therefore, there is a potential for the model to give an underestimated or overestimated VaR.

The VaR provides only an estimate under normal market conditions. It cannot be used as an authoritative measure. It also depends on the methodologies used to calculate it. We do not have to eliminate the VaR completely. Instead, there are several ways to address the drawback by using the data efficiently and using the high-powered IT infrastructure.

Even alternative VaR measures are not enough to forecast the risk profile, as all these models depend on historical data that does not include current and possible events that can occur. Nonlinear products, such as derivatives or even some investment strategies, involve exposure to short volatility risk. The market risk measurement system should be capable of monitoring and measuring short volatility risk.

Some strategies calculate net exposure based on value, while other strategies are built based on net beta exposure. When there is change in beta of either long or short positions, the manager readjusts the long or short positions to achieve the desired net beta exposure. The beta expansion risk is the risk that beta of long and short positions will change disproportionately.

Beta expansion risk is more common in small-capacity strategies, such as convertible arbitrage strategies. In a convertible arbitrage strategy, managers purchase convertible bonds or preferred stocks and then short the same company's or a similar company's stock. As more and more managers implement the same strategy on the same company's convertible bonds or preferred stocks, there will be more shorting of the stock. This will add downward pressure on the stock, and the beta of the stock will expand.

When many managers short-sell the stock at the same time, there will be an added downward pressure on that stock that will make the stock price more volatile. The increased standard deviation in turn increases the covariance with the stock market. This will cause the beta to be expanded more than the manager anticipates. The increased beta of a short position will require more positions to be added on the long side in order to achieve the previously desired net beta exposure. The other source of beta expansion is increased demand for hedging when the markets start declining. In order to protect from downside risk, managers who have not yet hedged the portfolio will start selling the stock short, which will result in downward pressure. This will reduce their anticipated profits. In other words, risk management will become expensive during market declines.

Short volatility risk is also quite common in insurance strategies where the returns are consistent in terms of premium. However, the sale of insurance contracts is a short volatility investment strategy that can result in occasional large losses. Short volatility risk appears in any traditional or nontraditional strategies that closely resemble insurance strategies.

For example, an option seller receives an upfront premium when he writes either a put option or a call option. If the option expires, then the profit will be the premium that was received upfront. However, if the market moves in an unfavorable direction, then the losses can be large. If the price of the underlying asset on which the put (call) option was sold goes down (up), then the option seller has to bear the losses. Since the exposure is synthetic and off-balance-sheet, the transparency of the position is not apparent. The strategy makes the manager attractive in nonvolatile markets but can bring huge losses. In other words, the received premium shows short-term profits but the volatility increases the chances of option execution demanding the option writer to purchase the underlying securities at unfavorable prices and deliver to the option buyer.

Unfortunately, short volatility strategies are exposed to negative events only; they are not exposed to positive events. Therefore, the upside potential is either limited or zero. Short volatility risk is quite common in fixed-income investments as well. The returns are consistent with limited or no upside potential. If the issuer defaults, then the investor loses an amount that is equivalent to par value minus recovery value. Experts describe relative-value hedge-fund strategies and event-driven hedge-fund strategies as selling economic disaster insurance.

Short volatility risk has been practically demonstrated using the merger arbitrage strategy. Consider the merger announcement that Company ABC will merge with Company XYZ in a one-for-one stock swap. After the announcement, Company ABC's stock price is $10, and Company XYZ's stock price is $8. The merger spread is $2. This is the premium that the hedge-fund manager expects to earn. The hedge-fund manager will short Company ABC's stock at $10 and buy Company XYZ's stock at $8.

At the closing of the deal, the stock prices of the two companies must converge. Convergence occurs either from the drop of Company ABC's stock, making money on its short position, or the rise of Company XYZ's stock, making money on its long position. Alternatively, the merged company may end up with a stock price between $8 and $10, and the hedge-fund manager will make money on both the short position and the long position. However, the maximum profit the merger arbitrage manager can earn is the merger spread of $2.

Merger arbitrage managers take a bet that the merger will be completed. They analyze antitrust regulations, consider whether the bid by the acquiring company is hostile or friendly, and check on potential shareholder opposition to the merger. If the merger is completed, the merger arbitrage manager will earn the spread that it previously locked in through its long and short stock positions. However, if the merger falls through, the merger arbitrage manager may incur a considerable loss that cannot be known in advance. From this perspective, merger arbitrage hedge funds can be viewed as merger insurance agents. They insure against the risk of loss should the merger deal collapse.

By buying the stock of the target company and selling the stock of the acquiring company from investors who do not have as much confidence in the merger deal, merger arbitrage hedge funds accept and insure against the risk of the deal collapsing. If the merger is successfully completed, the merger arbitrage manager will collect a known premium. However, if the merger fails to be completed, the merger arbitrage manager is on the hook for the loss, instead of the shareholders from whom he purchased shares or to whom he sold shares. In essence, shareholders of the two companies can "put" their losses back to the merger arbitrage manager if the deal falls through.

Similarly, the risk of senior tranches in a collateralized debt obligation (CDO) can be compared with short volatility risk. The returns are consistent in the form of the coupon and have no upside potential. However, if the correlations among the pool assets increase and the losses exceed the junior tranches, then the investor in senior tranches faces large losses. Therefore, the buying of a senior tranche resembles an insurance contract in systemic economic risk.

Many hedge funds use a short volatility strategy to enhance their returns. However, as explained earlier, the key issue is that short volatility strategies are often synthetic, off-balance-sheet, and not apparent from position transparency. This will result in a reasonable return as long as the insurance premiums continue to be collected. However, when a volatility event occurs, the results can be disastrous. Investors, in effect, "put" their losses to the hedge-fund manager, resulting in large declines in value.

This exposure can be hedged by buying put options on the VIX (market volatility) index equivalent to the short volatility exposure embedded in strategies. This is an active strategy that requires the rolling of put options to maintain a continuous hedge against the strategies. In addition, the amount of put options to purchase will change as the delta of the short put option changes. This requires a form of dynamic hedging known as *portfolio insurance*. Chasing deltas as the market declines rapidly can lead to a downward spiral of stock prices from which it is difficult to recover. Therefore, the alternative hedge against short volatility risk is to diversify the portfolio by including funds that tend to be long volatility. Prior empirical studies have indicated that managed futures, or commodity trading advisors, have investment strategies that tend to be long volatility.

8.5   Managing Counterparty Risk with Big Data

The demand for real-time risk calculations and regulatory capital optimization enables the traditional risk management functions to be integrated into the front office to involve them in the decision-making process. Traditional counterparty credit risk management relies heavily on individual traders, risk managers, middle office, and back office. The risk calculations were being done by overnight batch processes. This brings certain challenges when monitoring significant intraday counterparty and liquidity events and may not be noticed until the overnight risk calculations are performed. These challenges not only make it time-consuming but also lead to costly damages to profits. Building near-real-time environments with unparalleled scalability can solve the problem to some extent. This will enable globally visible real-time risk mitigation across all products, units, and geographies.

While traditional risk management examines measures like current exposure and concentration, the effectiveness of risk management comes from the comprehensive analysis of overall credit risk in the trading book. Comprehensive measures include potential future exposure (PFE), credit valuation adjustments (CVA), debit valuation adjustments (DVA), funding value adjustments(FVA), and several other advanced metrics.

8.5.1   The CVA Desk

In order to allocate CVA in near real time and as trades are executed, it is necessary to continuously monitor risk sensitivities and trading events of counterparties and counterparty exposures. Therefore, the initiative to improve the effectiveness of counterparty risk management starts with building a centralized CVA desk. The idea behind creating the CVA desk is to enable traders to think as if they are dealing with risk-free trades. In other words, all the risk-taking will be outsourced to the dedicated CVA desk. This disconnects the trades from the responsibilities of, for example, evaluating a whole portfolio and dealing with market data required to compute CVA.

The dedicated CVA desk is responsible for delivering on-demand incremental CVA expressed as a fee or a spread for a predeal to the trading desks, thus integrating real-time executed trades in the global CVA process; analyzing CVA and allocating marginal CVA per trade; hedging the risks, such as credit and wrong-way risk; and satisfying the capital deployment.

While aggregating the overall trading data and maintaining quality of data— one key for successful counterparty risk—the key behind the CVA desk is architecting the infrastructure and database. There are several components involved, including portfolios, market data, reference data, collateral data, agreements, and risk engines. In addition, there are engines to generate scenarios, calculate the price, and calculate the aggregated CVA. In addition, primary trades will have companion protection trades.

The market data needed for the CVA desk includes the regular market data that is needed at the trading desk; credit-related market data, such as CDS spread and recovery curves; and correlation matrices between the underlying and credit-market data in order to handle the wrong-way risk. The internal data includes the collateral data, margin calculations, and netting agreements.

CVA desks need timely and accurate risk-factor sensitivities—such as deltas, gammas, cross gammas, and scenario analysis—to make informed hedging decisions. The effectiveness of risk management relies not only on measuring the volatility in time but also on understanding the dynamics that are driving the volatility. These things are required on an intraday basis. Because of the limitations of traditional hardware, software, and data management procedures, the required computations are not refreshed on an intraday basis. This will limit the ability to use a large number of scenarios. Therefore, in addition to computational intensity and time, the way the batches are linked and monitored is highly critical. If one batch process fails while another continues, then overall numbers can go into doom.

The trading book is dynamic in multiple dimensions. While the book keeps changing throughout the day, the dynamics at counterparty also keep changing, and so do market factors. Therefore, the real-time monitoring process must be scalable and automated. Triggers and events must be continually monitored throughout the trading day. Events include, but are not limited to, additional termination events (ATEs) like rating downgrades, large movement in volatilities, interest rates, foreign-exchange rates, limit breaches, and other credit-related events. Detection of such triggers and events should in turn trigger an automated intraday call to update sensitivities or an alert to alter a hedge.

The scenario engine uses various techniques, such as Monte Carlo simulations and analytical models. For the purpose of this discussion, the engine details are not needed. The scenario engine requires interaction with the portfolio data. The pricing engines interact with the generated simulation data, market data, collateral data, and margin requirements. So finally, the aggregated CVA calculation requires interaction with netting agreements.

The effective CVA desk must also integrate intraday liquidity risk management with the collateral management and identify monitor, and control wrong-way risk, which arises from the correlation between the counterparty's default probability and exposure. Basel III requires CVA calculations to include wrong-way risk. The CVA desk must monitor general wrong-way risk by product, region, industry, or other relevant data. This is needed so the senior management and the board can step in to understand and redefine the risk-tolerance profile.

Basel III requires banks to calculate effective expected positive exposure (EEPE), which in turn must use the greater of the portfolio-level capital using current market data and the portfolio-level capital charge based on stress calibration. In addition, since either the firm or the counterparty can default, the CVA should be treated as bilateral, requiring calculation of the DVA—CVA from the point of view of the counterparty—and then subtract DVA from CVA.

8.5.2   How Does the CVA Desk Work?

The CVA desk can be either centralized or decentralized. While decentralized CVA desks can put more focus on specific trading activities, the centralized desk can significantly reduce operational cost, improve efficiency, and add economic benefit by using netting at a broader level. The netting benefit is higher especially if the individual desks are trading cross-asset classes. The other advantage is the loss distribution across the desks. For example, if a desk is doing business on a particular asset class and the market is under stress on that asset class, the losses can be absorbed indirectly by other desks through a centralized CVA desk.

At the inception of the trade, the CVA desk calculates the CVA premium and charges for the trading desk. The trader then incorporates the price in his transaction with the counterparty. Upon the default of the counterparty, the CVA desk pays the replacement cost amount to the trader. In other words, the CVA desk acts as an internal insurer.

8.5.3   Counterparty Credit Risk Management

Proper management of counterparty credit risk requires the following sequential steps:

1. Gather data about positions, markets, and counterparties. The challenges are too much data, too dynamic, and too much variety.
2. Estimate potential exposures, such as PFE, EPE (expected positive exposure) , ENE (estimated negative exposure), and EEPE. The challenge is very fast, and very large Monte Carlo simulations are needed.Requirements include fast analysis of terms and conditions of all trades, market data across all asset classes, historical market data, fast interpretation of netting and CSA (credit support annex), and counterparty hierarchies.

3. Compare aggregated exposures against limits. The challenge is inconsistent and incompatible data coming from multiple trading desks.
4. Monitor wrong-way risk. The challenge lies in fast analysis of structured and unstructured data.
5. Perform stress testing and scenario analysis. The challenge lies in identifying appropriate and multiple scenarios and avoiding ad hoc analysis.
6. Calculate predeal CVA measures to identify risk-reducing trades and provide traders with a competitive pricing advantage. Pre-deal CVA facilitates proactive pricing of counterparty credit risk on a trade-by-trade basis, in the context of the portfolio exposure, to a given counterparty.
7. Calculate intraday CVA to continuously monitor hedging needs.
8. Determine capital and provisions. The challenge lies in increasing profitability and reducing capital requirements.
9. Integrate market risk management and intraday liquidity risk management with CCR (counterparty credit risk). The challenge lies in different ownerships and different goals.
10. Legal risk mitigation requires fast analysis and organized management of counterparty and collateral documents.
11. Limit the damage. The key challenge is maintaining quality of credit data.
12. Inform senior management and stakeholders. Require well-advanced interactive dashboards.
13. Tune the counterparty risk management to react to market dynamics.

8.6   Liquidity Risk Analytics with Big Data

From the very first chapter, we learned that one of the causes for the severe financial crisis was the lack of proper liquidity risk management. In subsequent chapters, we discussed how liquidity issues fueled the crisis at Long-Term Capital Management (LTCM) and Metallgesellschaft Corporation (MGRM), firms that clearly understood the need for liquidity risk managed to limit the damages. However, even those firms that were managing the liquidity risk were following traditional spreadsheet-based calculations. As we have been discussing in other chapters, managing liquidity risk on spreadsheets cannot address real-time liquidity issues and can only provide approximate information.

Liquidity risk is not standalone; it is tightly linked to market risk, credit risk, and other risks. Therefore, even a single unfavorable event can lead to catastrophic funding problems or trading problems for the firm. The liquidity issue may not necessarily arise from internal sources but can be spilled over from other organizations and impact the overall portfolio and firm. Therefore, firms must use both in-house real-time data on daily positions and the market data of different asset classes to continuously monitor liquidity conditions and unfavorable market conditions. Upon detecting any events, the firm must react to the changes in order to remain credible in the market.

Traditionally, liquidity management heavily relied on experience and individual expertise, going to central bank user interface and payment systems and talking to traders. This is no longer an effective option, and therefore operational liquidity management has to be improved.

Various regulatory authorities across the globe have provided strict and complex guidelines, rules, and regulations focusing on liquidity risk governance, measurement, monitoring, and disclosure. Because of the limitations in current hardware and software, the current systems are not equipped to handle these changes, and financial institutions worldwide are facing challenges to react to these regulatory measures in an appropriate and timely manner.

Effective liquidity risk management requires the following five major tasks:

1. enterprise data management
2. intraday view on liquidity positions
3. interaction between collateral management and liquidity risk
4. predictive analytics
5. sophisticated infrastructure

8.6.1   Enterprise Data Management

In silo-based data management environments, it becomes impossible to collate enterprise-wide liquidity positions. The data needs to be obtained at the transactional, product, business-line, legal-entity, and firm-wide levels. Tactical liquidity risk management requires transaction-level data in an aggregated format.Therefore, transaction- or operation-level data serves as foundational data for liquidity risk management.

Aggregating data across a transaction's life cycle requires information feed from numerous front-, middle-, and back-office systems, as well as data received from multiple counterparties, branches, and settlement systems through various channels. While gathering firm-wide liquidity data is an important task of sound liquidity risk management, it is equally important to create a link between enterprise data and the transaction level system to run the scenarios on a daily basis when necessary. Therefore, the enterprise data system and transaction system must be connected and bidirectional—one is to gather the aggregated data and the reverse is to run the scenarios in the transaction system. While the first can be asynchronous, the second must be synchronous or near real-time.

As the Basel III is being implemented globally, local regulators require significant amounts of liquidity to be held in their jurisdictions. This would require the implementation of the liquidity optimization system and efficient data management.

As the capital markets rely heavily on trading, and since timing is the most critical factor for trading, real-time visibility of liquidity requires timely collection of confirmations received from customers, counterparties, and clearing and settlement systems. Enterprise data management must focus on frequency, timeliness, and consistency of data. It should capture the overall picture of major markets and their linkage to the financial sector and the bank, as the market-wide information is crucial when evaluating assumptions behind a bank's funding plan.

The market information includes, but is not limited to:

- equity prices, such as stock-market indices and sub-indices in various jurisdictions relevant to the activities of the bank
- debt markets, such as money markets, medium-term notes, long-term debt, derivatives, government bond markets, and credit default spread indices
- foreign exchange markets
- commodities markets
- indices related to certain securitized products

Such information is used to monitor whether the market is losing confidence in a particular institution or has identified risks at an institution. Since some of the underlying processes use structured data, and since liquidity monitoring requires the use of unstructured data, there is a lack of data interoperability. Enterprise data management should, in a timely way, achieve interoperability among all the data formats.

Most of the trades in capital markets rely on credit spreads and interest rates. The real-time monitoring of credit spreads of different assets and the average credit spreads of various asset classes in various markets are needed to help traders make the decisions. Credit spread is one of the good indicators of liquidity risk. The liquidity risk management system should be capable of the calculating and monitoring of concentration of liquidity exposures and calculation of average daily peak of liquidity usage. In addition, intraday liquidity risk management must continuously monitor future views of liquidity flows, collaterals, and liquidity gaps across buckets, contingency fund planning, net interest income analysis, fund transfer pricing, and capital allocation. Upon detection of threshold breaches, alerts must be generated and escalated immediately to the relevant parties.

Intraday liquidity management is an integral part of improved liquidity risk management. The management and control of liquidity must be multidimensional and include the management of cross-currency risk, intragroup liquidity flows between legal entities, and the processes and controls around the intraday management of liquidity.

In addition to its multidimensional nature, the liquidity risk is multidirectional, meaning it must be managed in multiple ways. Cash management forecasts how much cash to lend or borrow to flatten its books; funding management to know which businesses require this cash, how they will get the funds, and at what cost; and liquidity management to ensure that payments and receipt flows are smoothed through the day within limits.

Effective intraday liquidity risk management is not only meant for regulatory compliance and risk mitigation but also results in savings for the bank. Financial costs can be substantial as a result of overcollateralization, intraday credit-line costs, higher funding costs, overdraft charges, and higher liquidity buffers. Improved management and monitoring of intraday positions across accounts and currencies should reduce the need for intraday credit lines. Derived detailed analytics and a review of market-wide stress-test scenarios will reduce liquidity buffers required to cover intraday liquidity shortfalls.

Intraday liquidity risk management increases productivity among trades as it avoids the waiting until toward the end of the trading day to flatten the bank's position and be at the mercy of wider spreads and tightening market liquidity. For this purpose, the front-, middle-, and back-office systems must be integrated to improve monitoring of all commitments made across business lines.

The contractual maturity mismatch and the gaps between the inflows and outflows of liquidity for defined time bands indicate how much liquidity a bank would potentially need to raise if all outflows occurred earlier than anticipated. This metric is used to draw insight into maturity transformation under its current contracts. This metric enables supervisors to build a market-wide view and identify market outliers and liquidity. It helps upper management plan and bridge any identified gaps in its internally generated maturity mismatches.

The metric, at a minimum, should use all the data on the categories, including derivatives, outlined in the liquidity coverage ratio. For liabilities, it should be assumed that there would not be any rollovers—meaning the liabilities are due at the end of maturity. For assets, it should be assumed that there would not be any new contracts. Contingent liability exposures, which are based on certain triggers like downgrades, need to be detailed. The customer collateral received that is permitted to be rehypothecated as well as the amount of collateral that is already rehypothecated needs to be included in the metric, as this would generate mismatches in the borrowing and lending of customer collateral.

A concentration of funding metric is used to identify those sources of wholesale funding that are of such significance that withdrawal of this funding could trigger liquidity problems. The concentration of a funding source can be identified using the ratios, such as

$$\frac{funding\ liabilities\ sourced\ from\ each\ significant\ counterparty}{the\ bank's\ balance-sheet\ total}$$

or

$$\frac{funding\ liabilities\ sourced\ from\ each\ significant\ product/instrument}{the\ bank's\ balance-sheet\ total}$$

It can also be identified based on asset and liability amounts by significant currency.

A *significant counterparty* can be a single counterparty or group of connected counterparties accounting in aggregate for more than 1 percent of the bank's total balance sheet. A *significant product/instrument* is defined as a single product/instrument or group of similar products/instruments that in the aggregate amount to more than 1 percent of the bank's total balance sheet. A currency is considered significant if the aggregate liabilities denominated in that currency amount to 5 percent or more of the bank's total liabilities.

8.6.2   Interaction Between Collateral Management and Liquidity Risk

The financial institution must be able to meet both expected and unexpected current and future collateral needs arising from different activities. Collateral is required to cover the margining requirements of a financial institution arising from its activities in different markets. Firms that are managing margining activity manually through e-mail, fax, and phone prevent the firm from monitoring and reporting on an intraday basis the impact of their margining activity on their present and predictive collateral positions.

Many firms have started implementing effective collateral management systems. If they have not already, they will eventually have to implement them because of changing regulatory needs. However, there should be an efficient linkage between collateral management systems and liquidity risk management systems, making collateral position management an integral part of a firm's liquidity risk program.

Such integration will be helpful in drawing an intraday view of metrics on the unencumbered collateral positions that could be mobilized in a timely manner. These metrics provide information about the quantity and key characteristics, including currency denomination and location of banks' available unencumbered assets.

Institutions should also assess the eligibility of each major asset class they hold for central-bank collateralization and the acceptability of their assets to major counterparties and providers of funds in secured funding markets. Many firms experience difficulties in monitoring the impact of the terms of funding or trading arrangements on their ability to mobilize collateral on an intraday basis. Depending on the business line and market practices, collateralization and margining could represent a large volume of agreements, which could in turn tie up significant amounts of cash.

This metric should be categorized by significant currency. A currency is considered significant if the aggregate stock of available unencumbered collateral denominated in that currency amounts to 5 percent or more of the associated total amount of available unencumbered collateral. The report should also include the estimated haircut that the secondary market would require for each asset. In addition to haircuts, the report should include expected monetized value of the collateral, rather than the notional amount, and where the assets are actually held, in terms of the location of the assets and what business lines have access to them.

It should be noted that the metric does not capture potential changes in counterparties' haircuts, and lending policies that could occur under either a systemic or idiosyncratic event could provide false comfort that the estimated monetized value of available unencumbered collateral is greater than it would be when most needed. To gain more meaningful insights, this report should be used in conjunction with the maturity mismatch metric and other balance-sheet data.

The measures mentioned above provide a better picture about real-time assessment of liquidity. None of them provides the ability to predict the future state of liquidity. Predictive liquidity management requires advanced analytics and risk intelligence. Monitoring predictive positions will involve the development of real-time information exchange capability between liquidity management systems, trading or payments applications, and reference data platforms.

8.7 Sovereign and Country Risk

Sovereign risk is a risk that a foreign government will default on its loan or fail to honor other business commitments because of a change in national policy. A country asserting its prerogatives as an independent nation might prevent the repatriation of a company or a country's funds through limits on the flow of capital, tax impediments, or the nationalization of property. The difference between sovereign risk and credit risk can be explained as follows: When a domestic party borrows money, he would either pay the entire promised principal or interest as per the agreement if the financial situation is good, or would seek to work out the loan with the lender by rescheduling part or all of the balance, or would likely proceed with bankruptcy filing and eventually liquidate the firm's assets.

Suppose that a high-grade corporation in a foreign country borrows funds from, for example, a US financial institution. If the dollar-reserve position of the foreign country's government runs into bad shape after lending, then the foreign government will refuse to allow any further repayment to be made in dollars to outside creditors. This will put the foreign borrower automatically into default, even though the corporation maintains good credit. Therefore, the sovereign credit rating acts as a ceiling for the ratings of that country's borrowers regardless of the health of the borrower and makes the lending decision to a foreign-country corporation a two-step process.

Lenders must assess the credit risk of the borrower and make necessary adjustments to credit spreads and credit limits, and then again readjust them by assessing the sovereign risk of the country in which the borrower resides. Sovereign-risk events may take one of the following two forms:

- *debt repudiation*, an outright cancellation of all of the borrower's current and future foreign debt and equity obligations
- *debt rescheduling*, in which a foreign country or a group of creditors in that country declare a moratorium or delay on its current and future debt obligations and then seek to alter contractual terms, such as interest rates and debt maturity

Though country risk and sovereign risk are related, they are two distinct phenomena. Country risk is associated with doing business in a particular country, while sovereign risk focuses only on the ability or willingness of debt repayment by government. In other words, country risk is the broadest measure, and it includes sovereign risk, political risk, and transfer risk—the risk that a transaction cannot take place because a government or central bank will not allow currency to leave a country.

Though there is a positive relationship between sovereign and country risk, the sovereign credit profile can improve without necessarily expecting improvement in the business environment. Similarly, deterioration in a country's risk condition does not necessarily imply a worsening in sovereign creditworthiness, though often that will be the case.

Sovereign risk can basically be evaluated using internal models, external models, and implied risk models. While these are basic models, credit-rating agencies will follow a rigorous evaluation process by applying a number of variables that will be discussed in the following sections. Because of the lack of historical data and because of the relatively small size of the statistical sample set, sovereign risk cannot be assessed as precisely as for corporations.

8.7.1   Internal Evaluation Models

Internal evaluation models evaluate various macroeconomic and microeconomic variables and ratios that forecast the country's probability of rescheduling. Internal evaluation models are statistical models that calculate credit score, similar to the z-score rating of probability of corporate bankruptcy. Some of the important variables that can forecast rescheduling probabilities are debt service ratio, import ratio, investment ratio, variance of export revenue, and domestic money supply growth.

Debt Service Ratio

A country's primary source of dollar inflow depends on the export of goods and services, and part or all of the inflow will be used to pay down any interest and amortization on debt. The larger the debt repayments in dollars proportionate to export revenue, the greater the probability of debt rescheduling.

$$Debt\ Service\ Ration(DSR) = \frac{interest + amortization\ of\ debt}{exports})$$

A higher value of DSR indicates a higher likelihood of debt rescheduling.

Import Ratio

Countries that depend heavily on imports for infrastructure development or consumer needs import goods from other countries and pay the required dollar amount from foreign exchange reserves. The greater the need for imports, the faster the depletion of its foreign exchange and the more likely to result in debt rescheduling.

$$Import\ Ratio(IR) = \frac{total\ imports}{total\ foreign\ exchange\ reserves}$$

A higher value of IR indicates a higher likelihood of debt rescheduling.

Investment Ratio

A country that invests heavily in infrastructure development and factory construction would likely see more production in the future.The investment ratio measures the ratio of real investment and the gross national product (GNP). The higher the investment ratio, the lower the probability of rescheduling.

$$Investment\ Ratio(INVR) = \frac{real\ investment}{GNP}$$

A higher value of INVR indicates less probability of debt rescheduling.

Variance of Export Revenue

Variance of export revenue reflects the fact that export revenue may be highly volatile because of quantity risk and price risk. While quantity risk is the risk that the production of raw commodities that a country can sell in other countries depends on surplus and shortage, price risk is the risk that the export of commodities is subject to supply and demand in international markets. A higher value of variance of export revenue indicates a higher likelihood of debt rescheduling.

Domestic Money Supply Growth

A country's inflation depends on the domestic growth rate of that country's money supply, and a higher growth rate will increase the inflation rate. Higher inflation will likely weaken the currency value. When a country's currency loses credibility as a medium of exchange, then the country must increasingly depend on hard currency for both domestic and international payments.

$$Domestic\ Growth(MG) = \frac{\Delta M}{M}$$

where ΔM is the change in money supply and M is the initial level of the money supply. A higher value of MG indicates a higher likelihood of debt rescheduling.

Disadvantages of Statistical Models

- The delay in collecting the economic variables makes the model stale.
- Statistical models estimate rescheduling probability on both interest and principal amortization, but in reality, some countries may reschedule only one component and pay the other as scheduled.

- Statistical models ignore political risk events, such as strikes, elections, corruption, and revolutions.
- Statistical models are not always stable because of the fact that rescheduling that occurred in the past due to inefficient ratios is not necessarily indicative of the future.

8.7.2   External Evaluation Models

Various external agencies provide country risk analysis, either in the form of detailed reports or ratings or a combination of rating and report. The main criteria used by the majority of country risk analysis firms are as follows. This list gives a general picture of country risk assessment and does not include every factor, and some of these factors may not be applicable in certain situations.

Internal political risk factors:

- fractionalization of the political spectrum
- fractionalization by language or region
- willingness to compromise
- potential social disturbances
- political effectiveness
- political instability
- corruption

External political risk factors:

- influences of regional political forces
- external conflicts
- foreign influence

Economic risk factors:

- gross domestic product (GDP) per head
- real GDP growth
- budget balance as percentage of GDP
- inflation rate
- level of economic development
- fiscal and monetary policy
- soundness of the banking system

External debt indicators:

- debt service ratio
- debt consumption
- history of default and rescheduling

Balance of payment:

- current account as percentage of GDP
- terms of trade
- export growth rate
- import ratio
- access to capital markets

The Economist Intelligence Unit (EIU) rates countries by combining economic policy risk, political risk, economic structure risk, and liquidity risk. It provides detailed reports on country analysis, as well as democracy indices for major countries. The EIU belongs to the Economist Group and was founded in 1949. It is known as the world's leading provider of country intelligence and covers more than a hundred countries. The EIU rates a company on a hundred-point scale. The higher the score, the riskier the country. It then divides the score into five bands from A to E, with A indicating low risk and E indicates high risk.

The US-based *Institutional Investor* magazine publishes institutional investors' credit ratings twice a year and covers about 150 countries. *Institutional Investor* specifically concentrates on the issue of a country's creditworthiness. *Institutional Investor* asks about a hundred global bankers to rate countries based on their perception of creditworthiness. All selected bankers are surveyed during the same window of two months that ends forty-five days before the publication date. Bankers are not allowed to rate their home country.

The *Institutional Investor* ratings models employ both advanced quantitative techniques and subjective appraisals. The magazine finally provides scores on the scale of zero to one hundred, with zero being the highest risk of default.

Rating agencies, such as Fitch, Moody's, and S&P, have developed rigorous models that employ both quantitative and subjective analysis to calculate sovereign risk. They cover more than a hundred sovereigns and provide ratings. For example, Fitch's scale starts from AAA (lowest default risk) through C (high default risk) and to DDD, DD, and D (default). Fitch is primarily concerned with a country's external debt, government policy, standard financial and macroeconomic indicators, long-term factors, and internal and external political risk factors. The team of analysts runs stress tests to assess the economy's ability to overcome international exogenous shocks.

8.7.3   Implied Sovereign Risk Model

Similar to the way implied credit risk can be calculated from market prices of bonds, implied sovereign risk can be estimated from the secondary market prices of sovereign debt. The factors that lead to a secondary market for sovereign debt are:

- Larger financial institutions want to reduce their exposure to sovereign debt.
- Financial institutions are willing to swap one country's debt for another's in order to rebalance the portfolio.
- Wealthy investors and hedge funds seek to engage in debt-for-equity swaps.

Sovereign debt is available in the secondary market in four ways: Brady bonds, sovereign bonds, performing bonds, and nonperforming bonds.

Brady Bonds

Brady bonds are bond-for-loan swaps where US and other financial institutions exchange their dollar loans for dollar bonds issued by sovereigns. These bonds typically have a longer maturity and lower coupon than was originally promised. However, the principal is usually collateralized through the issuing country's purchasing of US Treasuries. In the event that the sovereign defaults on its Brady bonds, the buyers of the bonds can access the dollar bonds held as collateral.

Sovereign Bonds

Sovereigns issue sovereign bonds to repurchase the country's US-dollar-denominated Brady bonds. Since Brady bonds are collateralized by US Treasuries, their value partly reflects the value of US Treasuries. In contrast, sovereign bonds are uncollateralized, and their price reflects the credit risk of the country.

Performing Bonds

Performing bonds are original or restructured outstanding sovereign loans on which the sovereign is making payments to lenders. Sovereigns that have a potential for rescheduling of payments may sell the bonds at a discount.

Nonperforming Bonds

Nonperforming bonds are original or restructured outstanding sovereign loans on which the sovereign is currently not making payments to lenders. These bonds are typically traded at deep discounts.

8.7.4   Implied Country Risk in Market Prices

Market prices on sovereign loans are available on a monthly basis. Managers construct a statistical country rating analysis (CRA) model to analyze which key economic or political events have led to changes in secondary market prices. The CRA model involves regressing periodic changes in secondary market prices on a set of key variables.

8.8   Operational Risk

Hedge funds are very heterogeneous in nature and are exposed to various risks, such as liquidity risk, market risk, counterparty risk, and so on, thus acting as market makers. Hedge funds implement various arbitrage and non-arbitrage trading strategies (such as fixed-income arbitrage) and distressed-security strategies that are potentially subject to large profits. These strategies require trading activities that can be considered less conventional than in the long-only universe and expose the manager to operational risk for which the manager does not receive a premium.

Recent studies reveal that operational risk greatly exceeds the risk related to the investment strategy, with at least half of hedge-fund collapses directly related to a failure of one or several operational processes. A weak operational environment will increase the impact of an external event, such as tough trading conditions or brutal changes in financing conditions. Indeed, few hedge funds failed purely because of operational issues.

While the main sources of observed hedge-fund operational issues are misrepresentation, misappropriation, and deliberate fraud, these could have been prevented to some extent by using practices like position pricing, procedures for calculating net asset value (NAV), client-reporting procedures, reconciliation capabilities, compliance controls, and risk management infrastructure. Not all hedge-fund frauds were necessarily intentional; some may have occurred because of loopholes in the systems and processes that could have been identified and prevented with a proper monitoring system.

Operational risk is as old as the industry, yet it has been neglected by firms. The banking industry has long recognized the importance of market risk and credit risk and developed various models to quantify them. Because of the broader nature of operational risk, there was no clear definition of it, and every risk that did not fall under market or credit risk used to be treated as operational risk. Basel II came up with a definition for operational risk, and based on this definition, the sources of operational risk can be detected, monitored, and controlled.

According to Basel, operational risk is defined as the risk of direct and indirect loss resulting from inadequate or failed internal processes, people, and systems, or from external events. Basel's definition includes legal risk but excludes business risk, strategic risk, and reputational risk where losses would be difficult to quantify. A few examples of operational risks are as follows:

- *inadequate processes*, such as systems with a lack of advanced features, missing functionalities, not enough automation, and redundancy
- *internal processes,* such as model error, availability of loss reserves, model complexity, transaction execution error, booking error, collateral confirmation, collateral netting error, erroneous disclosure, limit exceeds, volume risk, position reporting error, and profit-and-loss reporting error
- *people problems,* including incompetency, inadequate resources, key personnel, management, communication, internal politics, conflicts of interest, lack of cooperation, fraud, and organized labor activities
- *systems problems,* including system failures, network failures, system inadequacy, compatibility risk, supplier risk, data corruption, disaster recovery risk, system age, system support, hacking damage, and theft of information
- *external events,* such as politics, taxation, regulation, social tensions, competition, theft, forgery, check kiting, and natural disaster losses

Understanding of operational risk is more important in the modern era of investments because of the growing sophistication of financial technology and rapid deregulation and globalization of the financial industry. While it may not be feasible to eliminate operational-risk failures completely, a sound operational risk management framework must focus on minimizing the occurrence of events and potential losses. At a minimum, the following objectives should be considered by the operational risk management framework:

- Define and explain the operational risk in the context of the institution.
- Avoid potential catastrophic losses.
- Educate all employees at all levels and business units on enterprise-wide operational risk.
- Motivate all departments to anticipate all kinds of risks, thereby effectively preventing the failures from occurring.
- Make the firm less vulnerable to breakdowns.
- Identify potential problem areas in the firm.
- Prevent operational mishaps from happening.
- Establish clarity of roles, responsibilities, and accountability.
- Identify business units in the firm with high volume and high turnover.
- Identify business units with high complex support systems.
- Empower business units with the responsibility and accountability of the business risk they assume on a daily basis
- Monitor the danger signs of both income and expense volatilities.
- Ensure that there is compliance to all risk policies.
- Ensure that there is clear and concise measure of due diligence on all risk-taking and non-risk-taking activities of the firm.
- Regularly provide the executive committee with a concise report.

The Basel Committee on Banking Supervision, in its May 2001 document "Operational Risk Loss Data" (http://www.bis.org/bcbs/qisoprisknote.pdf), under Annex 1, breaks down loss events into seven general categories.

1. Internal Fraud

Internal fraud is defined as losses due to acts of a type intended to defraud, misappropriate property, or circumvent regulations, the law, or company policy, excluding diversity/discrimination events, which involve at least one internal party. Internal fraud is further classified as "unauthorized activity" and "theft and fraud." Examples of unauthorized activity include transactions not reported (intentional), transaction type unauthorized (with monetary loss), and mismarking of position (intentional). Examples of theft and fraud include fraud, credit fraud, worthless deposits, theft, extortion, embezzlement, robbery, misappropriation of assets, malicious destruction of assets, forgery, check kiting, smuggling, account takeover, impersonation, tax noncompliance, evasion (willful), bribes, kickbacks, and insider trading (not on firm's account).

2. External Fraud

External fraud is defined as losses due to acts of a type intended to defraud, misappropriate property, or circumvent the law by a third party. External fraud is further classified as "theft and fraud" and "systems security." Theft and fraud include theft, robbery, forgery, and check kiting. Systems security related include hacking damage and theft of information (with monetary loss).

3. Employment Practices and Workplace Safety

This category is defined as losses arising from acts inconsistent with employment, health or safety laws or agreements, payment of personal injury claims, or diversity/discrimination events. These events are further classified as "employee relation," including compensation, benefit, termination issues, and organized labor activities; "safe environment," including general liability (slips and falls, etc.), employee health and safety rules and events, and workers compensation; and "diversity and discrimination," encompassing all types of discrimination.

4. Clients, Products, and Business Practices

This category is described as "losses arising from an unintentional or negligent failure to meet a professional obligation to specific clients (including fiduciary and suitability requirements), or from the nature or design of a product." These events are further categorized into the following five types:

- *Suitability, disclosure, and fiduciary*, including fiduciary breaches, guideline violations, suitability, disclosure issues (KYC, etc.), retail consumer disclosure violations, breach of privacy, aggressive sales, account churning, misuse of confidential information, and lender liability
- *Improper business or market practices*, including antitrust, improper trade or market practices, market manipulation, insider trading (on firm's account), unlicensed activity, and money laundering
- *Product flaws*, including product defects and model errors
- *Selection, sponsorship, and exposure*, including failure to investigate client per guidelines and exceeding client exposure limits

- *Advisory activities,* including disputes over performance or advisory activities

5. Damage to Physical Assets

This category is described as "losses arising from loss or damage to physical assets from natural disaster or other events." Examples include natural disaster losses and human losses from external sources (such as terrorism and vandalism).

6. Business Disruption and Systems Failures

This category is described as "losses arising from disruption of business or system failures." Examples include events related to systems, such as hardware, software, telecommunications, and utilities

7. Execution, Delivery, and Process Management

This category is described as "losses from failed transaction processing or process management, and from relations with trade counterparties and vendors." These events are further classified as follows:

- *Transaction capture, execution, and maintenance,* including miscommunication; data entry, maintenance, or loading error; missed deadline or responsibility; model or system misoperation; accounting error or entity attribution error; other task misperformance; delivery failure; collateral-management failure; and reference data maintenance
- *Monitoring and reporting,* including failed mandatory reporting obligation or inaccurate external report (loss incurred)
- *Customer intake and documentation,* including client permissions/ disclaimers missed or legal documents missing or incomplete
- *Customer/client account management,* including unapproved access given to accounts, incorrect client records (loss incurred), or negligent loss or damage of client assets
- *Trade counterparties,* including nonclient counterparty misperformance or miscellaneous nonclient counterparty disputes
- *Vendors and suppliers,* including outsourcing vendor disputes

8.8.1   Measuring Operational Risk

Operational risk can be evaluated using top-down and bottom-up approaches. While the top-down approach is easy to implement, the bottom-up approach provides more accurate assessment, as it involves gathering the information from the micro level.

Top-Down Models

Top-down models use data that is readily available—such as firm-level financial performance or industry-level performance—to calculate the implied operational risk. These models are relatively simple and give a general picture of the company's operational risk. The most common top-down models available to measure operational risk are the implied capital model, income volatility model, income pricing model, and analogue model.

Bottom-Up Models

In contrast to top-down models, bottom-up models analyze risk factors at the source level and calculate the firm-level operational risk. The Basel II encourages banks to develop bottom-up models. Among the commonly used bottom-up models, the two most popular approaches are process approaches and the actuarial approach.

Loss Distribution Approach

The loss distribution approach (LDA) model, an actuarial type of bottom-up model, is one of the approaches used to model operational risk measurement. Under this approach, frequency of loss and severity of loss are modeled separately and then combined through a process called *convolution* to measure the operational loss. Unlike other models, the LDA uses both frequency of loss and severity of loss to measure the operational risk. Like market risk and credit risk measurement models, LDA also uses historical data to model the distribution. However, there is not adequate historical data available either internally or externally, as firms or data providers started recording operational risk data relatively recently. This poses some challenges in measuring operational risk.

It is standard practice that firms use internal data to estimate the frequency of losses and both internal and external data to estimate loss severity. External data providers include Operational Riskdata eXchange Association, Fitch Risk, and so on. External data may be biased because of the size and nature of the firm where the event occurred. A scale bias may be caused by the possibility that larger firms would have larger biases. A truncation bias may be caused when the firms do not capture loss data below a certain threshold level. The correlation between probability of loss and size also matters. Therefore, external data needs to be scaled when used in the loss-measurement models.

Loss Frequency Distribution

The probability-of-loss event, which has no time dimension, is translated into the loss frequency, which represents the number of loss events occurring during the risk horizon. *Risk horizon* refers to a fixed time period over which the events are to be observed and is usually set as one year for regulatory purposes. LDA models often use Poisson distribution, negative binomial distribution, or binomial distribution to model the frequency distribution.

In Poisson distribution, the mean and standard deviation are equal, and therefore only three parameters are required to measure the probability of losses. The three parameters are mean or standard deviation lambda, time horizon T, and number of losses.

Severity Distribution

While a little data may be sufficient to model the frequency distribution, modeling loss severity distribution requires a huge amount of data, and there is not adequate data available either internally or externally. This makes the modeling loss severity more challenging. Loss severity is usually modeled using lognormal distribution. High-frequency risks can have severity distributions that are relatively lognormal, but low-frequency risks can have distributions that are too skewed and leptokurtic to be well captured by lognormal density functions. Common density functions are gamma density, generalized hyperbolic, lognormal mixtures, and general mixture distributions.

Some external databases that are constructed from public, newsworthy events will have very few but extreme losses. There is an implicit high threshold for the losses included. In order to get values in the tail, analysts attempt to model the body and tail separately. Tails are typically modeled using generalized Pareto or other distributions in an EVT (extreme value theory) class of distributions.

Operational Loss Distribution

Loss frequency distribution and loss severity distribution will be combined into a single distribution called *operational loss distribution* through a convolution process. As with other types of risks, correlation among various components of operational risk may reduce the combined risk. Correlations observed in operational loss distribution modeling include the following:

- correlations among loss events within the cell
- correlations among severity samples within the cell
- correlation among loss events between cells
- correlation among severity samples between the cells
- correlation between frequency distribution and the severity distribution

For various practical reasons, only the dependencies of frequency distribution are taken into account and are often measured using Gaussian copulas.

9 Glossary

ABCP: See *asset-backed commercial paper*

ABS: See *asset-backed security*

Accreting swap: A swap in which the notional amount changes incrementally over a period until the contract matures. In regular swaps, one party pays a fixed interest rate and the opposite party pays a floating interest rate over a particular period. The notional amount stays the same throughout the contract. In an accreting swap, if the initial agreement is to exchange the fixed 4 percent and LIBOR plus 1 percent on a notional amount of $1 million, then at the end of every swap reset date the new notional will be $1 million plus n times 10 percent of $1 million, where n is the count of reset. In other words, at the end of first three months, the parties exchange the interest on $1 million; at the end of sixth month, the parties exchange the interest on $1.1 million, and at the end of ninth month the notional will be $1.2 million. Businesses prefers accrete swaps because as the business grows, its exposures that need to be protected from risk factors also change. In the above example, we have used interest rate, but in reality the accreting swap applies to many risk factors, including currency. Accreting swaps are also called *accumulating swaps*.

Accrued interest: The interest that is accumulated since the previous coupon date but not yet received by the bondholder. If the bondholder wants to sell the bond prior to receiving the interest or if the bondholder wants to calculate the exposure, then the accrued interest must be added to the bond price. Accrued interest is applicable to loans as well.

Accumulating swap: See *accreting swap*

Alpha: Alpha measures the excess return over the return predicted by the CAPM.

Amortizing swap: The opposite of accreting swap. In amortizing swaps, the notional on which the interest rates are exchanged decreases over time. This may be required if the underlying notional is tied to mortgage loans. For example, for a party owning mortgage loans, the notional decreases as the borrowers pay down part of the principal over time, and so the notional on which the protection is needed also decreases.

Arbitrage: A way of profiting from market inefficiencies or product preferences. For example, a bond that was issued recently sells at a higher price than one issued long ago, even though both have the same remaining maturity. There is an opportunity to profit from buying older bonds and short-selling the newly issued bond, and this is called *arbitrage*. This concept is not just limited to bonds; it applies to all financial products. It is a simultaneous purchase and involves selling the same or similar instrument in order to make a profit.

Arbitrage collateralized debt obligation (CDO): Bonds that are issued against a pool of actively managed underlying assets. A specialist investment-management company acquires the underlying assets in the market over a period known as the ramp-up phase and will actively manage them thereafter. An arranging bank provides support during the ramp-up to acquiring the assets. From then onward, the portfolio of assets will be large enough to generate sufficient interest receipts to warrant the issuance of CDO notes. The managers continually buy and sell the underlying assets in order to generate a profit to support the CDOs. In contrast to arbitrage CDOs, static CDOs contain the static underlying assets.

Asian option: Option in which the payoff amount is calculated by recording the underlying asset price at a sequence of intervals and then taking the average of those interval prices. Asian options are also called *average options*.

Asset-backed commercial paper (ABCP): Short-term notes ranging from 90 days to 180 days issued after a bank or conduit collects the expected cash flows of the receivables from the originators and issues. Originators sell the receivables to the bank or conduits to enhance liquidity.

Asset-backed security (ABS): A security similar to a mortgage-backed security, except that the underlying assets are non-mortgage-related assets, such as loans, leases, and credit-card debt. The difference between ABS and ABCP is that the ABCP is a corporate debt, backed by receivables, that is issued for a term of less than a year.

Asset swap: Swap in which a product that pays fixed interest is exchanged with a product that pays floating-rate interest for a specified period. In a regular swap, the fixed interest is exchanged with floating interest on a specified notional during the period of contract. In an asset swap, for example, a bond that pays fixed coupons is exchanged with an index that pays the floating interest rate.

At-the-money: A situation in which the underlying asset price meets the strike price of an option. Exercising the option at this point does not yield any profit to the option buyer and is said to be at loss, as the buyer paid some premium to purchase the contract.

Available-for-sale: Financial assets carried at fair value with the changes in fair value recorded in other comprehensive income. The fair value of a financial instrument on initial recognition is normally the transaction price. Subsequent to initial recognition, fair values for financial assets are determined by bid prices quoted in active markets. Securities that are classified as available-for-sale and do not have a readily available market value are recorded at cost. Available-for-sale securities are written down to fair value through income whenever securities, which are calculated on an average cost basis, are recognized in sundry income.

Average option: See *Asian option.*

Back-testing: When traders build an investment strategy, they need to test its ability. Testing with forward data may take several months. Back-testing assumes that if the strategy exists for a specified time in the past, the historical data can be used to generate the output of the strategy.

Bank run: A situation that occurs because of panic rather than a real problem at the bank, eventually leading to bank failure; also known as a run on the bank. This happens when a large number of customers become concerned about the bank's solvency and withdraw their deposits simultaneously. As more people withdraw their funds, the probability of default increases. And in turn, as the probability of default increases, the more people will withdraw their deposits. This will put the bank at default risk.

Balance-Sheet CDOs: In balance-sheet CDOs, the assets in the pool are typically loans. The originators of these loans are mostly banks. Banks use balance-sheet CDOs to reduce risky assets.

Barbell portfolio: A portfolio with a mix of high and low ends. For example, if a portfolio of bonds is filled half with short-term bonds and half with long-term bonds, it is called a *barbell portfolio*. The two groups have low duration and high duration respectively. Similarly, if portfolio stocks are half low-beta and half high-beta, such a portfolio is a barbell portfolio.

Barrier option: An option in which the payoff is linked to whether or not the underlying asset has hit the barrier. Here, barrier refers to a certain predetermined price. Knock-out and knock-in options are examples of barrier options. A knock-out option expires worthless if the underlying asset exceeds a certain price, limiting losses for the writer. In a knock-in style, there is no value to the option until the underlying asset reaches a set price.

Basel Accord: A set of regulatory agreements set by the Basel Committee on Banking Supervision (BCBS) in order to ensure the stability of financial institutions by requiring them to have the capital reserve to meet obligations and absorb unexpected losses.

Basel I: The first Basel Accord, issued in 1988, focused mainly on credit risk by creating a bank-asset classification system.

Basel II: The second Basel Accord created standards and regulations on how much capital a financial institution must set aside.

Basel III: Built on the Basel I and Basel II guidelines to improve the banking sector's ability to deal with systemic risk and economic stress, Basel III is intended to improve the risk management practice, strengthen the banks' transparency, and boost the liquidity of the firm.

Basis: A difference between two different products that represent the same underlying asset. For example, in commodities, it refers the variation between the spot price of a deliverable commodity and the price of the futures contract on the same contract that matures on the same day that the spot price is quoted for.

Basis point (BPS): One-hundredth of 1 percent, or 0.01 percent. Since interest rates move by a small fraction—for example, 0.01 percent, 0.02 percent, and so on—it is simple to use the basis point to refer the change.

Basis point value (BPV): A method used to quantify interest-rate risk for small changes in interest rates. It tells how much money the instrument or portfolio will gain or lose for one basis point or 0.01 percent parallel movement in the yield curve.

Basis risk: Risk that occurs when assets and hedged assets show a deviation in correlation. It is applicable to any hedged pair. For example, in the commodity market, the basis is the difference between the current cash price of a commodity and the futures price of the same or a similar commodity. Basis is usually computed in relation to the next futures contract to expire and may reflect different periods, product forms, grades, or locations. Basis risk exists when futures and spot prices do not change by the same amount over time. In other words, basis risk is the risk that remains after the hedging strategy has been implemented. For example, an airline company wants to hedge against a rise in jet-fuel prices and will purchase NYMEX heating-oil futures contracts. The contract may dictate various options for the grade of commodity, location, and chemical attributes. When spot and futures contracts are not perfectly correlated, basis risk will appear. The magnitude of basis risk depends on the degree of correlation between spot and futures prices.

Basis swap: A swap in which both parties exchange the floating rates on certain notionals, but the two floating rates refer to two different mechanisms. For example, LIBOR is exchanged with a Treasury-bill rate. This is useful in a situation where the bank lends in LIBOR and borrows at Treasury rates.

Basket option: A single option where the payoff is linked to two or more underlying assets; also called *rainbow option*. While the underlying assets can have different characteristics, such as the expiration date and strike price, they all must move in the intended direction in order for the option to be worthwhile.

BCBS: See *Basel Accord*

Bear spread: The writer of a bear spread believes that the stock price will not go up so that he earns premium, but on the safe side he buys a call option at a higher strike by paying a little premium just in case he has to sell the stock to the first buyer, thus minimizing the loss. This strategy involves the simultaneous purchase and sale of options (puts or calls, but only one type). An option with a higher strike price is purchased and simultaneously an option with a lower strike price on the same asset is sold. Both options will have the same expiration date.

Bermudan option: An option that can be exercised only on predetermined dates, typically every month. European-style options can be exercised only on the expiration date and American-style options can be exercised any time before the expiration date—and as Bermuda lies between Europe and America, so Bermudan options also lie in between.

Beta: A statistical measure of the volatility of a security with respect to market or any other standard index; also called *beta coefficient*. It is used to quantify the systematic risk of a security or a portfolio. Beta of the market, for example, S&P 500 or DJI, is one. A stock with a beta of 1.1 tells us that the swing in the stock price is 10 percent more than that of the market. Beta is used in the capital asset pricing model (CAPM) to calculate the expected return of an asset.

Binary option: An option that pays either a specified amount (if the option expires in the money) or nothing at all (if the option expires out of the money). For example, a binary option that is purchased at the strike of $40 with a specified payoff amount of $100 would pay $100 on the expiration date if the underlying stock price stays above the strike of

$40 on that day. If the underlying strike is below $40, the holder does not receive anything.

Binomial model: A model used to forecast option prices and interest rates. It is based on a special case in which the price of stock or interest rate can either go up or down by a certain percent.

Black-Scholes model: Financial model developed in 1973 by Fisher Black, Robert Merton, and Myron Scholes that is widely used to price options. The model has acted as a base model for several variants. This model assumes that the price of traded assets follows a geometric Brownian motion with constant drift and volatility. The option price is calculated by incorporating the volatility of the stock, the time value of money, the option's strike price, and the time to the option's expiration.

Black swan: A theory according to which hard-to-predict and rare events come as a surprise and have a major effect on the financial industry.

Bond: A fixed-income security that acts as a channel to the corporate or governmental entities to borrow the funds for a defined period at a specified interest rate. The purchasers of the bonds, who are called investors, act as lenders.

Bond Price: The present market value of the bond at which the seller is willing to sell the bond.

Book or trading indicator: An indicator that describes whether an asset is purchased for long-term holding or short-term trading. Typically the book is used for loans and trading is used for traded products.

Book value: The value of an asset that is carried on the balance sheet. It can be different from market value. By comparing the book value and market value, one can say that the traded asset is overpriced, underpriced, or fair.

Bootstrapping: A strategy used to determine the yields for Treasury zero-coupon securities with different maturities. A yield curve is drawn using Treasury bill rates of different maturities. However, the curve may not be complete, as T-bills offered by the government are not available for every period. The missing figures are calculated using interpolation in order to derive the yield curve.

BPS: See *basis point*

BPV: See *basis point value*

Brady bonds: Bonds that are issued by the governments of emerging nations are called *Brady bonds*. They are named after former US Treasury Secretary Nicholas Brady for the recognition of his sponsored effort to restructure emerging market-debt instruments.

Bull spread: The opposite of a bear spread. An option with a lower strike price is purchased, and simultaneously the higher strike price is sold. Both options have the same expiration date. Investors who are optimistic about the rise of the stock price purchase the call option, and if they are not too optimistic, they sell the call option at higher strike in order to compensate the premium paid. The strategy can be built with put also.

Bullet bond: A bond that repays the entire face value at once on the maturity date rather than a series of smaller repayment obligations spread over several dates.

Bullet portfolio: A portfolio designed using the bullet strategy has bonds with maturities that are highly concentrated at one point on the yield curve. In other words, the duration of all bonds is pretty much the same. The same concept can be applied to stocks but using the beta.

Butterfly spread: A combination of a bull spread and a bear spread. It involve four positions—two long and two short. The strike price for the middle positions is the same. In a bull spread, long call A and short call B are involved, and in bear spread, short call B and long call C are involved. Where A < B, butterfly is conservative strategy, meaning it has a limited profit and limited risk.

CVaR: See *conditional value at risk*

Call option: An agreement that gives an investor the right, but not the obligation, to buy an underlying asset at a specified price within a specified time period.

Callable bond: The call option in a callable bond gives the issuer the flexibility of withdrawing the bond prior to maturity and is usually less expensive, as the issuer pay the premium to the bond holder indirectly, either when the bond is called or by paying higher interest rate. The three most common callable features are:

- *American*—callable on any date, usually with thirty days notice;
- *European*—callable only at one specific future date; and
- *Bermudan*—callable only on interest-payment dates.

Callable swap: See *cancelable swap*

Cancelable swap: A swap where one party has the right but not the obligation to terminate the swap on one or more predetermined dates during the life of the swap. There are two types of cancelable swaps: a callable swap where the fixed-rate payer has the right to terminate the swap on a number of specified dates and a puttable swap where the fixed-rate receiver has the right to terminate the swap on a number of dates.

Capital asset pricing model (CAPM): A model used to calculate expected rate of return on investment. According to the CAPM, the expected return of a security or a portfolio equals the risk-free rate plus a risk premium. The risk premium equals the product of risk measure (beta), and the difference between the market return and risk free rate—β (rm–rf).

Caplet: Interval at which a cap payment is paid and reset if a borrower purchases caps on loans.

Caps: Limit placed to create a ceiling on floating-rate interest costs. When interest rates move above the cap rate, the cap seller pays the purchaser the difference. Borrowers who pay the variable interest on the loan typically purchase caps to get protected from rising interest rates.

Cash flow at risk (CFAR): An integrated corporate risk measure that explains how actual cash flows are deviated from the planned value in the budget because of changes in the underlying risk factors.

Catastrophic (CAT) bond: A high-yield debt instrument that is usually linked to protection from catastrophic events, such as hurricanes. These bonds are used to hedge against catastrophic risk.

CBO: See *collateralized bond obligation*

CBOE: See *Chicago Board Options Exchange*

CCP: See *central clearing party*

CDO: See *collateralized debt obligations*

CDO: *Chief Data Officer*

CDS: See *credit default swap*

CDS index: See *credit default swap index*

CDS spread: See *credit default swap spread*

CDX: One of two main families of CDS indices. CDX, which is administered by CDS Index Company and marketed by Markit, contains North American and emerging-market companies. The other family, iTraxx, contains companies from the rest of the world.

CEM: See *current exposure method*

Central clearing party (CCP): An independent legal entity that acts as an intermediary between the buyer and the seller of a derivative transaction; also called *central counterparty*. The single contract between two initial counterparties is still executed like a non-CCP transaction, but is then replaced by two new contracts, between the CCP and each of the two contracting parties. At that point, the buyer and seller are no longer counterparties to each other; instead, each acquires the CCP as its counterparty.

In the beginning, the CCP provides the valuation of OTC derivatives and associated settlement functions. During the life of the transaction, the CCPs evaluate the contract on a daily basis through a concept called *variation margin*. At the end of the day, margin calls are made to the parties to post the additional collateral. CCP has the authority to make intraday margin calls also if large price movements shorten the margin funds.

In the event of default, the CCP auctions the positions of the defaulted member, transfers the client positions to surviving clearing members, and allocates any excess losses to surviving clearing members.

CFAR: See *cash flow at risk*

CFTC: See *Commodity Futures Trading Commission*

Cheapest-to-deliver: A futures contract specifies what kind of relevant securities can be delivered upon maturity. The cheapest security that can be delivered to the long position satisfying the contract specifications is determined according to the specs. For example, in Treasury-bond futures contracts, the contract specifies that any Treasury bond can be delivered as long as it is within a certain maturity range and has a certain coupon rate.

Chicago Board Options Exchange (CBOE): According to its website (http://www.cboe.com/AboutCBOE/Corporate.aspx), "Chicago Board Options Exchange (CBOE), the largest US options exchange and creator of listed options, continues to set the bar for options trading through product innovation, trading technology, and investor education. CBOE offers equity, index, and ETF options, including proprietary products, such as S&P 500 options (SPX), the most active US index option, and options on the CBOE Volatility Index (VIX), the world's barometer for market volatility. CBOE is home to the world-renowned Options Institute and CBOE.com, named 'Best of the Web' for options information and education."

Chooser Options: A chooser option gives the holder of the option the right to choose whether the option is a call or put at a specific time during the life of the option.

Counterparty credit risk (CCR): Counterparty credit risk is the risk that the opposite party of the contract will not meet its contractual obligations plus the expected credit loss because of credit-quality deterioration.

Clawback clause: Clause that allows investors to take back the previously paid performance fee if the fund does not produce the hurdle rate over the agreed-upon period.

Clean price: The price of a coupon-paying bond not including any accrued interest. On each coupon payment date, the clean price will equal the dirty price, as there is no further interest accrued. Dirty price = clean price + accrued interest.

Clearing margin: Margin that clearing members are contractually required to deposit with the clearinghouse to cover their own and their customers' open positions. These margins are supposed to be high enough to protect against market risk and to safeguard the marketplace.

Cliff risk: The point at which a small shift in a bond's value can have a big impact on its price.

CLN: See *credit linked note*

CLO: See *collateralized loan obligation*

Closed-end fund: Fund created when publicly traded investment companies raise a fixed amount of capital through an initial public offering (IPO) and then structure, list, and trade as a stock.

CMBS: See *commercial mortgage-backed securities*

CMO: See *collateralized mortgage obligation*

Collar: An effective way to hedge rate risk at low cost. A collar is created by purchasing a cap and selling the floor or by purchasing a floor and selling the cap. The premium due for the cap (floor) is partially offset by the premium received for the floor (cap).

Collateral: Something that is provided as guarantee for a debt. If the borrower is not able to repay the debt, then the lender has the right to sell the collateral in the market and use the proceeds toward the debt. For example, if the mortgage loan is taken and if it is not paid, then the bank has the right to sell the house and use the proceeds toward the loan payment.

Collateral dispute: See *dispute*

Collateralized bond obligation (CBO): An investment-grade bond backed by a pool of several types of credit-quality bonds.

Collateralized debt obligation (CDO): Obligation similar to asset-backed securities or mortgage-backed securities in that a special purpose vehicle assembles all of these categories. However, with CDOs, an entire pool is structured based on credit risk exposures—with segments that divide exposure into different tranches with unique risk, return, and maturity profiles—and then issues CDO securities, transferring the risk to investors.

Collateralized loan obligation (CLO): Special CDO where payments from business loans are pooled together and passed on to different classes of owners in various tranches.

Collateralized mortgage obligation (CMO): Obligation that repackages the cash flow generated by the mortgage pool into different tranches, each tranche having a different mixture of prepayment risk/reward. A CMO is fundamentally similar to a CDO in that the risk of a portfolio of bonds has been redistributed such that some investors are exposed to more risk and some are exposed to less, but the main difference is that the CMO is designed to redistribute prepayment risk, whereas the CDO is designed to redistribute default risk.

Commercial mortgage-backed securities (CMBS): Securities issued by a real-estate mortgage investment conduit (REMIC) where the pool is backed by commercial mortgages. They are structured as multiple tranches and are different from mortgage pass-throughs.

Commercial paper: An unsecured, short-term debt instrument issued by a corporation to meet short-term liabilities. These are simple versions of asset-backed commercial paper.

Committee on Uniform Securities Identification Procesures (CUSIP): According to the US Securities and Exchange Commission, "A CUSIP number identifies most securities, including stocks of all registered U.S. and Canadian companies, and U.S. government and municipal bonds." ("CUSIP Number," http://www.sec.gov/answers/cusip.htm.)

Commodity: A marketable item produced to satisfy needs. Commodities are physical assets, such as precious metals; base metals; energy products, such as natural gas or crude oil; and food, such as wheat and corn.

Commodity Futures Trading Commission (CFTC): An independent US federal agency that regulates the commodity futures and options markets, promotes competitive and efficient futures markets, and protects investors against manipulation, abusive trade practices, and fraud.

Commodity swaps: Swaps used by producers and consumers to hedge against commodity price variations. The commodity swap can be settled in either cash or by physical delivery. Consumers whose businesses prefer fixed-rate payments for commodities hold the floating leg to receive the variance while the producers who agree to pay a floating rate hold the fixed leg. There are two main types of commodity swaps: fixed-floating commodity swaps, where both the legs are commodity based, and commodity for interest swaps, where a total return on the commodity is exchanged for some money market rate plus or minus a spread.

Component value-at-risk (VaR): The amount of risk an asset contributes to a portfolio of assets. Because of the diversification effect, it is less than the individual VaR of that asset. In other words, even though the asset is considered as risky, when added to a portfolio it may be seen as less risky because of the divarication benefit an asset brings to the portfolio.

Compound option: An option on an option—that is, the exercise payoff involves the value of another option. A compound option thus has two expiration dates and two strike prices. There are typically four types of compound options, including chooser options and barrier options. A compound option is a two-dimensional, second-order derivative.

Compounding swap: Variations on plain vanilla swaps where interest keeps on compounding forward until the end of the life of the swap instead of being received or paid on reset dates.

Conditional probability distribution (PD): An outcome that depends on the occurrence of a previous event or outcome. It is calculated by multiplying the probability of the preceding event by the probability of the succeeding event. Similarly, the conditional probability of default is conditional on the business cycle. This not only allows one to measure changes in risk as macroeconomic conditions change, but it also improves such measurement from an econometric and economic perspective, thus improving the measurement of loans' credit risk through time.

Conditional value at risk (CVaR): A weighted average between the value at risk and losses exceeding the value at risk. CVaR is also known as expected shortfall or tail VaR. This is different from credit VaR or CVA VaR.

Conduit: A government or private agency that pools mortgages and other loans to issue securities in its own name. Conduits are backed by mortgages, credit-card receivables, and other loans.

Constant maturity swap (CMS): A derivative with a payoff that is based on a swap rate of a specific maturity. The CMS note may pay semiannual coupons based on semiannual fixings of the ten-year semiannual swap rate.

Contango market: A market in which the futures price is above the expected future spot price is called *normal contango*. When hedgers are net long in futures, the futures price will be higher than the expected spot price to compensate speculators for the risk of selling short. For example, Kellogg's, a cereal company, wants to protect itself from pricing fluctuations of grain and buys long futures in grains. Speculators, on the other hand, bear the risk of pricing fluctuations and expect a risk premium. To compensate the speculators for bearing the risk, Kellogg's will pay more than the spot price for future deliveries. This will put upward pressure on prices. Speculators expect that the spot price at the time of delivery will be less than the price they receive for futures and cash in the profit. Normal contango occurs if hedgers are net long in futures and speculators are net short in futures.

There is a difference between normal contango and contango. Normal contango refers to a price pattern where the futures price is above the expected future spot price, while contango refers to a situation where the futures price is greater than the spot price. There are many factors that make the market contango. One such factor is storage cost. Holding a commodity requires storage costs, which may make the opportunity cost higher than the risk-free rate. So the parties may pay a higher premium for futures, which will result in a price higher than the spot price. Similarly, backwardation refers to a price pattern where futures prices are below spot prices. For example, a stock that pays a dividend falls, by an amount equivalent to the dividend, in price when the dividend is announced. So the futures buyer prefers to pay a lesser amount than the spot price. In the case of commodities, the lease rate replaces the role of dividend.

Convenience yield: The benefit that the holder of a commodity receives. The benefit can be in a form other than a lease. For example, a manufacturer may need raw materials on a continuous basis. If the manufacturer runs out of stock of the materials, then the production process may slow down or even shut down temporarily. As a result, the manufacturer may lose part of his business income. Having the material purchased ahead of need and keeping it ready for manufacturing purposes increases the benefit. This benefit is called the *convenience yield*. Convenience yield has the same effect as lease rate and represents the benefit the holder of a futures contract loses or the benefit the holder of a commodity receives.

Convergence: A movement in the price of the contract toward the price of the underlying asset. Alternatively, it is a situation where two prices moving in opposite directions change and move in the same direction.

Conversion factor: Factors calculated as the present value of the bond minus accrued interest divided by face value. In order to prevent market manipulation in the futures market, the exchanges set a rule that any government bond with more than fifteen years to maturity on the first day of the delivery month is deliverable on that contract. Since deliverable bonds have different market prices, the CBOT created a conversion factor.

Convertible bond: A bond that gives the investor the right to convert it into common stock in the future. The right to convert the bond into common stock can be interpreted as the issuer implicitly selling the call option to the investor to purchase the issuer's stock. This call option reduces the coupon payment on the convertible bond. The option also acts as a long put on the bond, as an investor can put the bond back to the issuer with an exchange of stock. In this case, the stock price acts as the exercise price. So convertible bonds comprise two components: a bond and equity option.

Convexity: The rate of change of duration with respect to yield. Duration is a first-order derivative. Convexity is a second-order derivative.

Copula: A tool that, unlike the correlation coefficient, works well for skewed distributions like option pricing and tail loss analysis. While the correlation coefficient explains the dependency between the returns of two or more assets, it works well only with normal distributions. The return distributions in financial markets are mostly skewed.

Correlation coefficient: Tool that explains the relative movement of one factor with another factor. It is a statistical measure that quantifies the correlation, and ranges between –1 and +1. A correlation coefficient of +1 indicates the perfect positive correlation, implying that as one security moves up or down, the other security will move in the same direction. A correlation coefficient of –1 indicates the perfect negative correlation, implying that as one security moves up or down, the other security will move in the opposite direction. The correlation coefficient of 0 implies that the securities are said to have no correlation. Correlation coefficient is used to build hedging strategies.

Corridor floating-rate note (FRN): A special type of FRN in which a higher coupon is paid if a particular reference rate is within a specific range (corridor) composed of a lower and an upper boundary. The coupon payments are calculated based on the number of days during the preceding coupon period in which a reference rate was stuck to a preset corridor.

Cost of carry: Costs incurred as a result of an investment position are called *cost of carry*. The cost of carry includes storage costs, borrowing costs, margin costs, and economic costs and is mainly influenced by interest rates. Fluctuations in interest rates will make margins and cost of carry fluctuate, which in turn will result in basis risk.

Cost of funds: The interest rate paid by financial institutions for the funds that they invest. Even if internal departments source the funds, there is some kind of cost of funds.

Counterbalancing capacity: The liquidity that a firm is expecting to be able to access over a given time frame to fund the gap between the sum of all cash inflow and the sum of all cash outflow over a certain time period.

Counterparty: The opposite party participating in a financial transaction. Every transaction must have a counterparty in order for the transaction to be executed.

Counterparty credit risk: The risk that a counterparty in a financial contract may default on obligations during the term of the contract. It is an unified view of market risk and credit risk.

Country risk: Risk is associated with doing business in a particular country. Though country risk and sovereign risk are related, they are two distinct phenomena, as sovereign risk focuses only on the ability or willingness of debt repayment by the government. In other words, country risk is the broadest measure, and it includes sovereign risk, political risk, and transfer risk. Though there is a positive relation between sovereign and country risk, the sovereign credit profile can improve without necessarily expecting improvement in the business environment. Similarly, deterioration in country risk conditions does not necessarily imply a worsening in sovereign creditworthiness, though often that will be the case.

Coupon: The interest rate that is stated on a bond issuance; also called *coupon rate*. The coupon is typically paid semiannually.

Coupon frequency: The frequency that the bond issuer pays the coupon on the bond.

Covariance: A statistical measure that explains the degree to which returns on two assets move in tandem. A positive covariance indicates that the asset returns move in the same direction. A negative covariance indicates that the returns move inversely. Covariance is used to calculate the correlation coefficient.

Covered call: Selling call option to the stock we own. Covered calls are good in downside markets, as we receive some premium, and not favorable in upside markets, as we have to forgo opportunities.

Covered position: A long position that comes with covered call.

Credit contagion: The credit deterioration of an entity that spills over to other entities and impacts their credit quality.

Credit correlation: Tool that describes how the credit risk among the products in a portfolio or basket is related. For example, the pricing of nth-to-default swaps depends on individual risks as well as on the way in which credit events on one name (instrument) relate to credit events on another. In other words, the credit correlations among individual names determine the price of the nth-to-default swap.

Credit default swap (CDS): A bilateral contract between two parties, where one party pays a periodic premium to buy protection against the risk of default or downgrade of an asset issued by a specified entity. In other words, he is purchasing the insurance to protect his assets. Upon a credit event (such as default or downgrade), the buyer of protection receives a payment intended to compensate against the loss on the investment.

Credit default swap (CDS) index: A standardized credit security used to hedge a portfolio of credit default swaps or bonds instead of buying many single names CDSs. These indices are considered to be highly liquid. Credit-default-swap indexes are used as benchmarks for protection of bonds against default, and so represent the changes in credit quality. CDX and iTraxx are the two main families of CDS indices.

Credit default swap (CDS) spread: The premium payed to the seller by the buyer of a CDS, who is the buyer of the protection. This is typically quoted in basis points per year of the contract's notional amount, and the payment is made periodically, usually on a quarterly basis. When we say the CDS spreads are widened, that means, buyers pay more as sellers see more risk and demand more compensation.

Credit derivative: Bilateral contact agreements mainly used to protect against credit deteriorations of assets. They are purchased over the counter and do not involve exchanges, and therefore they are called *OTC derivatives*. Examples of credit derivatives include asset swaps, credit default swaps, total return swaps, and credit linked notes.

Credit enhancement: Internal or external supports provided either at transaction level or program-wide or a combination of both. Credit enhancements protect the credit program against losses on the underlying asset portfolios.

Credit event: An event like a downgrade or default on a credit product. Examples of credit events are credit migration, bankruptcy (not applicable to sovereigns), failure to pay, obligation acceleration/default, repudiation/moratorium, and restructuring.

Credit indices: See *credit default swap index.*

Credit limit: The maximum amount a financial institution can extend to its customer. Credit limits are usually determined based on the borrowing entity's credit rating and the lending financial institution's existing exposure to that customer.

Credit linked note (CLN): A structured note where the principal repayment is linked to the creditworthiness of the CLN issuer as well as to reference entity. Here the reference entity is nothing but the issuer of the bond for which the CLN issuer is providing the protection. By purchasing the CLN, the investor is indirectly providing the protection on a bond issued by the reference entity.

Credit migration: The movement of credit quality of a debt security from one rating to another rating over a period. Also known as credit rating migration, it can be either an upgrade or downgrade from an existing rating.

Credit risk: The risk of loss of part or whole of principal or interest stemming from a borrower's failure to meet a contractual obligation.

Credit spread option: A financial derivative contract on a credit spread that transfers credit risk from one party to another. Buyers pay the premium, and the seller pays the compensation if a given credit spread changes from its current level.

Credit support annex (CSA): A standard-form collateral agreement included in the ISDA master agreement. The CSA enables parties to an ISDA master agreement to receive and provide collateral so as to reduce counterparty credit risk. CSA governs the issues of collateral, such as:

- valuation methods and timings
- valuation of collateral
- collateral transfer methods and timings
- collateral eligibility
- collateral substitutions
- collateral dispute resolutions
- rehypothecation of collaterals
- events that may change the collateral condition

Credit trigger: See *credit event*

Credit value adjustment (CVA): The difference between the risk-free value of the portfolio and its true value, accounting for the possible default of the counterparty. It is calculated at counterparty level and allocated to individual trades. It is calculated as the product of expected exposure, probability of default, and loss given default.

Credit value adjustment (CVA) desk: Primary responsibilities of the CVA Desk are pretrade pricing of CVA, Managing P&L of the CVA, and managing risk in the bank's portfolio.

Credit value adjustment VaR (CVA VaR): Basel III includes an explicit capital requirement for CVA risk and requires an institution to calculate risk-weighted assets for CVA risk. The rule reflects in risk-weighted assets a potential increase of the firm-wide CVA due to changes in counterparties' credit spreads, assuming fixed expected exposure (EE) profiles.There are two approaches for calculating the CVA capital requirement: the simple CVA approach and the advanced CVA approach.

Credit value at risk (CVaR): The difference between unexpected loss and expected loss.

Cross-currency swap: A swap used to manage the currency risk in foreign investment portfolios. A currency swap involves the exchange of payments denominated in one foreign currency for payments denominated in another.

Cross default: A provision in which the default of the borrower automatically triggers default on another debt held by the same lender. Such provisions are included in contracts.

Cross gamma: While gamma gives the rate of change of delta with respect to its underlying asset, the cross gamma gives the rate of change of delta with respect to another underlying asset. This is useful especially when the underlying assets in the portfolio are correlated.

Cross hedging: The concept of hedging a position in a portfolio by taking short position in an asset that shows similar behavior in price movements. For example, stock in a metal company can be hedged by taking short position in metal industry ETF.

Cross-product netting: Financial institutions engage in several types of product categories, such as OTC derivatives, repo-style transactions, eligible margin loans, and deposits. Each product category will have various instrument types—for example, interest-rate derivatives, FX derivatives, and equity derivatives are all OTC derivative categories. In cross-product netting, all product types under one product category are combined in a single netting so that the net exposure amount can be reduced. Netting across different product categories is not possible.

CSA: See *credit support annex*

Cum-dividend: See *dividend, ex- or cum-*

Current exposure method (CEM): One of the approaches used to measure counterparty credit risk, along with the standardized method (SM) and internal model method (IMM). As described by the Basel Committee on Banking Supervision, "Under the CEM, the EAD is calculated as the sum of the current market value of the instrument and a potential future exposure (PFE) add-on component that reflects the potential change in the instrument's market value between the computation date and a future date on which the contract is replaced or closed out in the case of a counterparty default." ("The Non-Internal Model Method for Capitalising Counterparty Credit Risk Exposures," September 2013, http://www.bis.org/publ/bcbs254.pdf.)

Current par value: Typically applicable to MBS where the prepayments are common. The sinking of pool is quantified as pool factor, which in turn is used to calculate the current face value of the mortgage-backed security.

Curvature: The way the linearity in the products varies at various points of the factor.For example, in bonds, the convexity describes how bond prices vary with respect to rates at different points of rates. Similarly, in options, the gamma describes how the option varies at different points of underlying stock prices.

CUSIP: See *Committee on Uniform Securities Identification Procedures*

CVA: See *credit value adjustment*

CVA desk: See *credit value adjustment desk*

CVA VaR: See *credit value adjustment VaR*

Debt value adjustment (DVA): The value adjustment made to the bank. In other words, CVA of one party will become DVA to the other party. While CVA considers only positive exposures the DVA considers only negative exposures.

Default probability: The probability that the counterparty can default.

Default risk: The risk that the borrower or counterparty can fail to meet the contractual obligations.

Delivery versus payment (DVP): A securities or commodities transaction in which the buyer is obligated to make payment only if the seller has made delivery of the securities or commodities, and the seller is obligated to deliver the securities or commodities only if the buyer has made payment.

Delta: The expected move in the price of an option for $1 change in the underlying asset.

Delta hedging: The process by which a fund manager adjusts the stock position from time to time—in response to delta changes and hedge-ratio changes—so that it remains delta-neutral; also called *delta-neutral hedging*. Delta is approximately 1 for deep in-the-money options, 0.5 for at-the-money options, and 0 for out-of-money options.

Derivative: A financial contract whose value is derived from the performance of underlying market factors, such as interest rates, currency exchange rates, and commodity, credit, and equity prices. While most derivative transactions do not involve the exchange of underlying assets, certain derivative contracts dealing with currencies do involve the exchange. Derivative transactions include options, forwards, futures, swaps, caps, floors, collars, and various combinations thereof.

Differential swap: A swap in which one party's interest payments are denominated in one currency while the notional principal is stated in another currency.

Dirty price: The price of a coupon-paying bond after including any accrued interest. On each coupon payment date, the clean price will equal the dirty price, as there is no further interest accrued.

Discount bond: A bond, also called a *zero-coupon bond* or *zero bond*, that does not pay regular interest payments. Instead, the investor buys the bond at a steep discount price—that is, at a price lower than face value. At the time of maturity, bondholders will receive the face value of the bond.

Discount rate: Also called *internal rate of return*, it is used to calculate net present value. The risk-free rate r represents the discount rate or opportunity cost.

Discount window: A window that allows eligible institutions to borrow money from the central bank on a short-term basis to meet liquidity shortages caused by internal or external disruptions.

Dispute: Disputes that occur when one or both parties disagree on the collateral valuation or margin deposits; also called *collateral disputes*. There are several types of collateral disputes: ineligible collateral, which occurs when the quality of the collateral has dropped below the required threshold whereas the posting party does disagree, or alternatively when the party attempts to post securities having less quality than required; valuation disagreements, which occur when there is no coherence between the parties about the use of curves, timings, data sources, and price samples used in valuation models; and portfolio mismatches, which occur when missing trades are not included in the portfolio, which causes differences in net exposure calculation.

Distressed securities: Securities issued by companies with poor performance, excessive level of debt financing, accounting problems, or rating downgrades from major credit rating agencies, which are called *distressed companies*. Traditional institutional investors, such as pension funds and endowments, who have floors on the credit quality of securities, may be forced to sell distressed securities in order to be in compliance. These securities are often sold at discount because of a fire sale.

Diversification: The process of spreading the investments across verities of instruments, sectors, regions, countries, and so on. Greater diversification also means low correlations among the assets in the portfolio. Greater diversification is achieved by employing nondirectional, market-neutral trading strategies. Diversification minimizes the risk, but there is a potential for poor performance.

Dividend: Funds distributed to shareholders when a corporation earns a profit. Alternatively, the corporation may choose to reinvest the profit in the business.

Dividend ex- or cum-: If a declared dividend belongs to the seller, then the stock will be given the ex-dividend status. Otherwise, it is called *cum-dividend*. This occurs based on the timing of the dividend announcement and dividend payment date.

Dodd-Frank Act: The Dodd-Frank Wall Street Reform and Consumer Protection Act, is established to lower risk in various parts of the U.S. financial system.

Drawdown: A decline in net asset value of a fund for a given day. In traditional investments, the drawdown is quite observable, as it is correlated with market declines. However, since the fund manager's goal is to protect the fund against market declines, the funds should, in theory, not exhibit drawdown.

Duration: The percentage change in a bond's price for a 1 percent change in its interest rate. Bond prices change when interest rates change. The new value of a bond can be calculated by revaluing the present coupon value and par value using the new or forecasted interest rate as the discount rate. However, this process is time-consuming. Duration is a simple and less-intensive measure.

DV01: The percentage change in a bond's price for a 1 basis point change in its interest rate.

DVA: See *debt value adjustment*

DVP: See *delivery versus payment*

Early amortization: A special type of credit enhancement for an ABS that is triggered when there is a sudden increase in delinquencies in the underlying loans or when excess spread falls below an acceptable level.

Early termination event: If at any time an event of default with respect to a party (the "defaulting party") has occurred and is then continuing, the other party (the "non-defaulting party") may, by not more than twenty days notice to the defaulting party specifying the relevant event of default, designate a day not earlier than the day such notice is effective as an early termination date in respect of all outstanding transactions.

ECL: See *expected credit loss*

Economic capital: Measurement of risk using economic realities rather than accounting and regulatory rules. Economic capital is the unexpected losses measured at a 99.9 percent confidence level over a one-year horizon.

EE: See *expected exposure*

Effective expected positive exposure (EEPE): A statistic calculated by replacing a short-dated transaction with a new transaction after maturity date. The calculation of EPE does not take maturity date into consideration. For example, assume that the basket has twenty transactions and ten of them of short-dated transactions. The effective exposure decreases after maturity of each transaction, and those short-dated transactions may be rolled over into new transactions, which are not considered by the EPE calculation.

Efficient frontier: An optimized portfolio that offers the highest expected return for a defined level of risk or the lowest risk for a given level of expected return.

Eligible collateral: A standard acceptable collateral. Certain securities are not accepted as collaterals or not recognized as collateral as per Basel rules.

Embedded option: A special provision attached to a bond that gives the holder or the issuer the right to perform a specified action at some point in the future. For example, a callable bond gives the issuer the right to withdraw the bond from the market and pay the principal, while a puttable bond gives an option to the holder to put the bond back to the issuer and demand the principal.

ENE: See *expected negative exposure*

EPE: See *expected positive exposure*

Equity swap: Some investors have restrictions on owning certain stocks. For example, some countries restrict which stocks can be owned by foreigners. But foreign investors may see opportunities in the stock market of that country. For example, let's say Party A, who is a foreign investor to Country B, wants to invest in the stocks of that country. Since he has restrictions on owning those stocks, he approaches Party B in Country B.

Party B borrows the funds from elsewhere and buys the stocks on behalf of Party A. The interest on the borrowed funds is either fixed or variable. Let's say the interest is LIBOR. At the end of reset period, typically three or six months, the party pays the interest on borrowed funds and Party B pays the returns on the stocks. In other words, if the stock prices go up then Party B pays the profit to Party A, and if the stock prices go down, then the party pays the loss amount to Party B.

In this case, Party B continuously earns some constant spread from the interest component. For example, if Party B is borrowing the funds at the LIBOR and if the Party A is paying the interest as LIBOR + 100bp, then 100bp is the commission for Party A.

Equity tranche: The tranche, also called *first-loss tranche*, that absorbs losses up to a predefined percentage of the sum of the notional on a portfolio of reference names. Once the equity tranche is exhausted, the mezzanine tranche starts to absorb the additional losses. The senior tranche is considered to be least risky and typically gets an AAA rating. The senior tranche performs well until both the equity and mezzanine tranches are exhausted, and then it too will experience losses.

ESL: See *expected shortfall*

ETF: See *exchange-traded funds*

ETL: See *expected tail loss*

ETL: Extract-Transform-Load.

ETO: See *exchange-traded option*

Eurobond: A bond issued in a currency other than the currency of the country or market in which it was issued.

Eurocurrency: Bank deposits of currency outside the country that issued the currency.

Eurodollar: US dollar deposits outside of the US.

EVT: See *extreme value theory*

Ex-ante analysis: An ex-ante analysis that considers future or potential events to give an idea of future movements in price or the future impact of a newly implemented policy. VaR uses only historical data and so is not considered as ex-ante analysis.

Ex-dividend: See *dividend ex- or cum-*

Ex-dividend date: The date on which the person who owns the security will be awarded the dividend, regardless of who currently holds the stock.

Excess spread: The difference between receipts from the underlying assets and all payables (including the expenses) in the securitization pool, such as ABS. Excess spreads act as a cushion against shortage of payments in difficult periods.

Exchange-traded funds (ETF): ETFs are essentially index funds that track the performance of a specific stock or bond market index or other benchmark. There are quite a few different real-estate funds available on the market. Investors can get exposure to global real estate, country-specific real estate, or REITs. Inverse ETFs are also available. There are even ETFs related to real estate, such as home-builder ETFs and mortgage-backed funds. They are highly liquid and tax efficient. Investors can take long or short positions.

Exchange-traded option (ETO): An option traded on a regulated exchange with a standardized contract specifying underlying asset, quantity, expiration date, and strike price, all known in advance.

Exercise price: The price specified in option contracts at which the underlying security can be purchased or sold.

Exotic option: Complex options built using simple options. The complexity gives more flexibility to investors and can be used to customize hedging needs or to build arbitrage strategies. The customization lies in exercise mechanism, strike prices, pay off amount, and so on.

Expected credit loss (ECL): An average cost of defaults expected over a period of time, calculated by using the exposure amount (EAD), probability of default (PD), and loss given default (LGD): $ECL = EAD \times PD \times LGD$.

Expected negative exposure (ENE): A weighted average over time of the negative exposures, where the weights are the proportion that an individual expected exposure represents of the entire time interval.

Expected positive exposure (EPE): A weighted average over time of the positive exposures, where the weights are the proportion that an individual expected exposure represents of the entire time interval.

Expected shortfall (ESL): ETL in which the VaR is measured relative to the benchmark. Expected shortfall is the same as ETL except that it measures the average of relative VaR beyond the confidence level. Both ETL and ESL are called conditional VaR.

Expected tail loss (ETL): The average of losses larger than VaR. Since the traditional VaR measurement does not consider kurtosis and skewness, the actual VaR is underestimated. This VaR acts as a benchmark for ETL, also called *expected shortfall*. ETL is not a substitute for VaR; it only supplements VaR. ETL is attractive because it reveals the loss hidden in tails, gives the losses beyond the VaR, and is subadditive, risk averse, and very useful for scenario-based portfolio optimization.

Expiration date: The date after which the contact has no value.

Extreme value theory (EVT): A special branch of statistics that attempts to make the best possible use of little information about the extremes of distribution and draw meaningful conclusions. EVT applies only to the tails and is inaccurate for the center of the distribution.

Face value: The amount paid to a bondholder at the maturity date, given the issuer doesn't default. Also called *par value*.

Fat tail: A term that refers to skew, a very important statistical measure in the analysis of return distribution, as it tells us how the returns deviate from the normal distribution. The normal distribution is a symmetrical distribution with equal frequency of loss and gains. Since alternative investments employ complex option-like strategies, the return distribution is not always symmetrical. The skewness refers to the extent to which the distribution is not symmetrical. The distribution may be either positively or negatively skewed.

Flight to quality: The action of investors moving their capital away from riskier investments to safe investments. This is usually caused by uncertainty in financial markets.

Floating-rate notes (FRNs): Floating-rate notes (FRNs) protect investors from fluctuations in interest rates. The coupon is linked to a specific index, such as the London Interbank Offered Rate (LIBOR).

Floor: Technique used by lenders to get protection from downward movement of interest rates. When a floor is created on floating-rate interest costs and interest rates move below the floor rate, the seller pays the purchaser the difference.

Floorlet: Any interval of a floor contract that is multi-period and involves periodical resets.

Forward: An agreement to buy or sell an asset on a specified date for a specified price. In a forward contract, the seller is obligated to sell the asset and the buyer is obligated to buy it as per the agreement, whereas in an option contract, the holder of the option has the option to buy or sell but is not obligated to do so.

Forward rate agreement (FRA): An agreement between two parties that one party will pay a certain interest rate on a certain principal amount at a specified future time. FRAs are traded over the counter and not on an exchange. Forward rate agreements are very flexible in nature and can be structured to mature on any date. They are off-balance-sheet instruments and do not require a notional amount to be exchanged; instead, only the interest differentials are exchanged.

Forward Start Options: Forward start options are options whose strike price will be determined at some later date. A forward start option is paid for in the present, but the strike price is not fully defined until an intermediate date before expiration.

Front running: The unethical practice of a broker using the information for trading before the research department even distributes it to the clients.

Futures: Contracts similar to forward contracts, with the difference being that forward contracts are bilateral, meaning buyer and seller can design the contract terms. Future contracts are executed on future exchanges, and both the buyer and seller need to obey the terms and conditions set by the exchange. Value to the buyer or seller is calculated on a daily basis, and the difference must be deposited with the exchange.

Gamma: Gamma gives the rate of change of delta with respect to stock price. Therefore, it is a second-order derivative of an option with respect to underlying asset price.

G-SIBs: See *global systemically important banks*

Geometric Brownian motion: A continuous-time stochastic process in which the logarithm of the randomly varying quantity follows a Brownian motion, also called a *Wiener process*, with a drift. The stochastic process, also called a random process, is a theory that explains that the process may take many unknown directions before evolving into some system over time.

Global systemically important banks (G-SIBs): Banks identified based on four main criteria: size, cross-jurisdiction activity, complexity, and substitutability.

Haircut: The European Repo Market defines the haircut as an "adjustment to the quoted market value of a collateral security to take account of the unexpected loss that the repo buyer in a repo may face because of the difficulty of selling a collateral security in response to a default by the repo seller." ("Haircuts and Initial Margins in the Repo Market," http://www.icmagroup.org/assets/documents/Maket-Practice/Regulatory-Policy/Repo-Markets/Haircuts%20and%20initial%20margins%20in%20the%20repo%20market_8%20Feb%202012.pdf). The fair amount that can be lent against the collateral is calculated as (1 − haircut) × market value of collateral.

Held-for-trading: Financial assets and financial liabilities that are purchased and incurred with the intention of generating profits in the near term. These instruments are accounted for at fair value with the change in the fair value recognized in indirect and administrative expenses.

Held-to-maturity: Securities that have a fixed maturity date, where the corporation intends and has the ability to hold to maturity. They are accounted for at amortized cost using the effective interest-rate method.

Historical simulation: A simulation that assumes near-future returns will likely follow the pattern of most-recent returns. The methodology uses historical performance data, both profit and loss, with the expectation that the past is a good indicator of the near future. It gets the profit/ loss for a longer historical period if available.

Hurdle rate: What the investor can earn on his own paying a management and performance fee to the fund manager. For example, if the return of the fund is 5 percent and the average S&P return is 5 percent, then the investor could invest in a passive index and pay a lower fee instead of a 2/20 fee structure. Hurdle rate is similar to opportunity cost.

Hybrid security: Securities that combine characteristics of both equity and debt. They can pay a fixed or floating rate of return, which can be in the form of interest or dividends. Convertible bonds are an example of hybrid securities.

Identifier: Unique IDs given to securities. ISIN, CUSIP, and SEDOL are examples of security identifiers.

Idiosyncratic risk: The risk that is specific to the firm. It is also called *firm-wide risk*. It has little or no correlation with market risk and is usually reduced by means of diversification. However, the 2007 financial crisis taught that a risk in a bigger firm will lead to systemic risk.

IDN: See *interest differential note*

IFRN: See *inverse floating rate note*

Illiquidity: How fast an asset can be sold without reducing the price substantially. The more time it takes, the more the illiquidity.

In-the-money: An option for which the underlying price is worth enough to exercise it, assuming that there is no premium paid. A call option is in-the-money when the underlying asset price crosses above the strike price, and a put option is in-the-money when the underlying asset price crosses below the strike price.

Incremental value at risk (VaR): The difference between the portfolio VaR after adding/deleting the position and the VaR before adding/deleting the position. While marginal VaR gives the impact of changing an existing position on the portfolio VaR, incremental VaR gives the change in VaR from the addition or deletion of an entire position in the portfolio.

Index amortizing swap: A variation of interest-rate swap based on a notional principal amount that may decrease over time in accordance with the path of future interest rates. This is the opposite of an accreting swap.

Index swap: A variation of interest-rate swap that involves the overnight rate being exchanged for a fixed interest rate. An overnight rate index can be any standard index, such as federal funding or commodity index.

Indexed amortizing notes: Notes on which the principal pay-down is amortized based on certain index.

Index-Linked Bonds: Bonds whose payment is linked to indexes, including GDP (gross domestic product), consumer price index (CPI), earning measures, and foreign exchange rates are called Index-Linked Bonds.

Inflation-indexed bonds: Bonds that protect the investor from inflation. Treasury inflation-protected securities (TIPS) protect investors from inflation risk.

Interest-differential note (IDN): Note designed to pay the difference between interest rates in two countries or currencies. Investors use these bonds to take advantage of higher rates in other countries without actually investing in that country, thus avoiding the exchange-rate risk.

Interest-only bond (IO): Bond on which the cash flow starts out big and gets smaller as time passes. In contrast to principal-only bonds, IO prices move in the same direction as interest rates. That is the reason certain hedge-fund managers prefer IOs during times of rising interest. If interest rates are falling, then the underlying pool will be paid off faster than expected, and IO investors will be left with no-interest cash flows.

Interest-rate (IR) derivative: Derivative used to manage the risk in the fluctuations of interest rates and to build arbitrage strategies to fulfill the specific needs of investors and borrowers. The most common derivative types used for interest rates are options, forwards, futures, swaps, or a combination.

Interest-rate (IR) swap: Swap used to exchange a fixed interest rate with a floating interest rate. In IR swaps, only interest payments are exchanged, not the principal.

Internal rate of return: See *discount rate.*

International Securities Identification Number (ISIN): A twelve-character alphanumerical code used to uniquely identify a security.

International Swaps and Derivatives Association (ISDA): Association founded in 1985 to make OTC derivatives markets safe and efficient. ISDA has over 800 member institutions from 60 countries. These members include corporations, investment managers, government and supranational entities, insurance companies, energy and commodities firms, international and regional banks, exchanges, clearinghouses and repositories, as well as law firms, accounting firms and other service providers. The three key area of ISDA's work are reducing counterparty credit risk, increasing transparency, and improving the industry's operational infrastructure. ISDA provides support for the G20's initiatives to reduce systemic risk and work with policymakers to adopt a prudent, effective regulatory framework. (ISDA, "About ISDA," http://www2.isda.org/about-isda/)

Intrinsic value: For call options, the difference between the underlying stock's price and the strike price; for put options, the difference between the strike price and the underlying stock's price. If the difference value is negative, the intrinsic value is given as zero.

Inverse floating rate note (IFRN): A note that pays the coupon that increases as prevailed market rates decline. IFRNs are the opposite of FRNs: while FRNs are good when interest rates are trending upward, they are not favorable in declining periods. Inverse floaters can be linked to any reference index.

IO: See *interest-only bond*

IR derivative: See *interest-rate derivative*

IR swap: See *interest-rate swap*

ISDA: See *International Swaps and Derivatives Association*

ISIN: See *International Securities Identification Number*

Issue: A term used to refer to a security.

Issue country code: The country to which the security is intended to sell.

Issuer: The borrowing party that issues the securities.

Issuer country code: The physical location of the issuer.

iTraxx: One of two main families of CDS indices. The other family, CDX, contains North American and emerging-market companies. iTraxx, which is managed by the International Index Company (IIC) and owned by Markit, contains companies from the rest of the world.

Jump-diffusion processes: Processes used in modern finance to capture discontinuous behavior in prices of assets, such as stocks, bonds, and interest rates.

KMV: Model that measures default in terms of distance to default. In contrast to the Merton model, Moody's KMV models assume that the firm contains two forms of debt—one long-term and the other short-term.

Knock-out option: An out-barrier option that pays off only if the stock finishes in the money and if the barrier is never crossed before expiration. A knock-out option expires worthless if the underlying asset exceeds a certain price, limiting losses for the writer.

Kurtosis: An important statistical measure for alternative investments, measuring the peakedness of the distribution. Distribution that is more peaked than a normal distribution is referred to as leptokurtic, whereas distribution that is less peaked than normal distribution is referred to as platykurtic. Kurtosis for a normal distribution is 3. The difference between nonnormal kurtosis and 3 is called excess kurtosis.

Excess kurtosis is negative for platykurtic distribution and positive for leptokurtic distribution. Leptokurtic distribution will have more returns either around the mean or far from the mean, whereas platykurtic distribution will have fewer returns around and far from the mean.

Ladder Options: Ladder options are special types of lookback options for which the highest asset price is set to the floor in the series for call options, and the lowest is set to the ceiling in the series for put options.

LDA: See *loss distribution approach*

LEAPS: See *long-term equity anticipation securities*

Legal entity identifier (LEI): A unique ID associated with a single corporate entity. The regulatory initiatives are driving the creation of a universal LEI standard for financial markets.

Leptokurtic distribution: See *kurtosis*

Leverage: The use of borrowed funds, such as margin, to increase the potential return of investment.

Leverage ratio: The ratio of borrowed funds to own funds.

LGD: See *loss given default*

LIBID: See *London Interbank Bid Rate*

LIBOR: See *London Interbank Offered Rate*

LIFFE: See *London International Financial Futures and Options Exchange*

Liquid asset: An asset that can be sold in the market quickly, without compromising on the price.

Liquidity: See *illiquidity*.

Liquidity coverage ratio: This standard is designed "to ensure that the bank maintains an adequate level of unencumbered, high-quality liquid assets that can be converted into cash to meet its liquidity needs for a 30 calendar day time horizon under a significantly severe liquidity stress scenario … by which time it is assumed that appropriate corrective actions can be taken by management and/or supervisors, and/or the bank can be resolved in an orderly way," according to the Basel Committee on Banking Supervision. The ratio of stock of high-quality liquid assets to total net cash outflows over the next thirty calendar days must be greater than or equal to 100 percent. ("Basel III: International framework for liquidity risk measurement, standards and monitoring," December 2010, http://www.bis.org/publ/bcbs188.pdf)

Liquidity preference theory: A term-structure theory that states that long-term investments pose a higher interest-rate risk than short-term investments, and therefore long-term bonds are less marketable and less liquid in nature. So investors either prefer short-term bonds or expect sufficient compensation for bearing interest-rate risk and liquidity risk in long-term bonds. As a result, yield premium increases with maturity.

Liquidity risk: The risk stemming from the lack of marketability of an investment that cannot be bought or sold quickly without wider bid–ask spreads or large price movements.

Lockout: The period beginning with an investment over which the investor cannot redeem any part of the investment; also called *lockup*.

Lognormal distribution: A lognormal distribution has a longer right tail compared with a normal, or bell-shaped, distribution. The model is based on a normal distribution of underlying asset returns, which is the same thing as saying that the underlying asset prices themselves are lognormally distributed. The lognormal distribution allows for a stock price distribution of between zero and infinity (i.e. no negative prices) and has an upward bias (representing the fact that the stock price can only drop 100 percent but can rise by more than 100 percent).

London Interbank Bid Rate (LIBID): The bid rate that banks are willing to pay for Eurocurrency deposits in the London interbank market.

London Interbank Offered Rate (LIBOR): The interest rate at which banks borrow money from other banks in the London interbank market. It is used as a reference for short-term investment interest rates. It is calculated by the British Bankers' Association as the average of the world's top rated banks' interbank deposit rates for larger loans with maturities between overnight and one full year.

London International Financial Futures and Options Exchange (LIFFE): A London-based futures exchange, now part of Euronext.

Long position: Refers to an asset that is bought and added to the portfolio.

Long-term equity anticipation securities (LEAPS): Options contracts with expiration dates that are longer than one year.

Longevity bonds or longevity derivatives: Bonds that allow insurers and pension plans to hedge aggregate longevity risk. The bonds' coupon would rise if a cohort lived longer than expected, offsetting higher annuity costs. Longevity bonds would lower capital requirements for insurers and reduce the risk for pension plan sponsors. Governments could take the lead in issuing such bonds and gradually shift most of the responsibility to the capital markets. These are a class of securities designed to offer a hedge against longevity risk.

Lookback option: An option that provides investors flexibility (if in the money) to buy at the ex-post low and sell at the ex-post high. The payoffs of lookback options depend on the maximum or minimum underlying asset price attained during the option's life. Therefore, lookback options are strongly path-dependent options.

Loss distribution approach (LDA): An actuarial type of a bottom-up model that is one of the approaches used to model operational risk measurement. Under this approach, frequency of loss and severity of the loss are modeled separately and then combined through a process called convolution to measure the operational loss.

Loss frequency distribution: The probability of the loss event, which has no time dimension, is translated into the loss frequency, which represents the number of loss events occurring during the risk horizon. Risk horizon refers to a fixed period over which the events are to be observed and is usually set as one year for regulatory purposes.

Loss given default (LGD): The estimated remaining portion after the recovery of exposure from the counterparty. Mathematically, LGD is expressed as 1–RR.

Macaulay's duration: Concept developed Frederick Macaulay equating the duration to the average time to maturity or the time required to receive half of the present value of the bond's cash flows. The relationship between modified duration and Macaulay duration can be expressed as follows:

$$D_m = \frac{D_{Mac}}{1 + \frac{y}{k}}$$

Where D_m = modified duration and D_{Mac} = Macaulay duration. As the number of payments per year increases, y/k will become smaller, and the value of modified duration will approach Macaulay duration. In other words, for continuous interest rate, k is equal to infinity and y/k will be zero, in which case modified duration and Macaulay duration will become equal.

Maintenance margin: The minimum amount of equity that must be maintained in a margin account.

Margin: Borrowed money that is used to purchase securities.

Margin account: A brokerage account in which the broker lends the customer cash to purchase securities.

Margin call: When the account balance falls below the minimum maintenance margin, the investor gets a call from the broker to deposit additional money or securities so that the margin account is brought up to the minimum maintenance margin.

Marginal cost of funds: Incremental cost or differential cost of each additional dollar borrowed.

Marginal value at risk (VaR): The per-unit change in a portfolio VaR with respect to an additional investment in a portfolio. That is, the marginal

VaR is the partial derivative of the portfolio VaR with respect to the position.

Mark-to-market (MTM): "Process of daily revaluation of a security to reflect its current market value instead of its acquisition price or book value. Also called marked to market or marking to market." (Business Dictionary, "Mark to Market," http://www.businessdictionary.com/definition/mark-to-market.html)

Mark-to-model: A practice of determining the value of an asset or portfolio using internal assumptions and financial models. This is in contrary to mark-to-market practice, where market quotes are used to calculate values of an asset or portfolio.

Market segmentation theory: A term-structure theory that states that the bond market is segmented by maturities and thus supply and demand are determined by bond maturities. Market inefficiencies also exist, as certain market participants are restricted from investing in noninvestment-grade securities. Some investors prefer high-liquid assets, while others want to take advantage of illiquidity. Alternative investment managers take advantage of market segmentation and earn excess returns. High-yield bonds and CDOs are examples of segmented markets.Maturity date: The date on which the last principal is paid back.

MBS: See *mortgage-backed securities*.

Mean reversion: A theory that states that prices and/or returns of an asset tend to the long-term average from the peak or bottom.

Measurement period: A period for which the performance of an asset is being valuated.

Mezzanine tranche: See *equity tranche*.

Minimum transfer amount (MTA): An amount below which collateral calls are not permitted under the CSA. Having an MTA prevents the call of nuisance amounts and allows the parties to avoid unnecessary costs involved in small transfers. The practical implications of the MTA are that the secured party is unsecured for any exposure that is less than the MTA.

Model risk: A risk that arises from using an inappropriate model or using a model with incorrect inputs. Any model is only as good as the input. A model does not generate all the required input on its own. For example, the Black-Scholes options valuation model asks a user for an estimate of future volatility and then translates that estimate into a fair option value. If the estimated volatility is not correct, the estimated option value may not be fair in reality. In other words, the model may be correct, but data like rates, volatilities, correlations, and spreads may be badly estimated. An insufficient number of factors make the model imperfect. For example, a one-factor model of interest rate may be reasonable for valuing Treasury bonds, but much less reasonable for valuing options on the slope of the yield curve. Similarly, a model that was developed to determine one type of variable will not work for other variables.

Modified duration: See *Macaulay duration*

Money market fund: An investment fund that has as its primary goal to earn interest for shareholders while maintaining a net asset value (NAV) of $1 per share.

Monotonicity: A concept that assumes that a portfolio with higher potential returns will likely have less risk.

Monte Carlo simulation: A technique depending on simulation run by computers that is flexible, powerful, and capable of taking into account all nonlinearity of the portfolio value with respect to its underlying risk factors.

Moral hazard: The risk that one party misleads the other party by providing misleading information about its assets, liabilities, or credit capacity.

Mortgage-backed security (MBS): Securitized assets backed by a pool of residential or commercial mortgages. The loans from banks, mortgage companies, and other originators are assembled into pools and then securities are issued representing claims on the principal and interest payments made by borrowers on the loans in the pool.

MTA: See *minimum transfer amount*

MTM: See *mark-to-market*

NAICS: See *North American Industry Classification System.*

Net asset value (NAV): Value calculated on a daily basis using the closing market prices of the securities in the fund's portfolio.

Net gross ratio (NGR): The ratio, used in Basel calculations, of the net current credit exposure to the gross current credit exposure. In calculating the NGR, the gross current credit exposure equals the sum of the positive current credit exposures of all individual OTC derivative contracts subject to a qualifying master netting agreement.

Net interest income: The difference between the revenue that is generated from a bank's assets and the expenses associated with paying out its liabilities.

Net present value: The difference between the present value of cash inflow and the present value of cash outflow.

Net replacement cost: The cost to replace an asset in the portfolio. For example, if an asset in the portfolio costs $100 and the counterparty defaults, then the same may cost $110 to replace with the same kind of asset.

Netting: In financial markets, transactions occur as two-way, meaning one party will have to make payments on a certain transaction while the opposite party also needs to make payments to the first party on some other transactions. If the currency is same for both the payments and they both are due on the same date, then the payments can be netted. This reduces operational risk. Netting is not possible if the payments involve two currencies, even if they are due on the same day.

Netting indicator: An indicator in a database that states if the asset is subject to netting.

Netting set: A set of assets under certain netting agreement.

NGR: See *net gross ratio.*

Normal backwardation: Phenomenon that occurs if hedgers are net short in futures and speculators are net long in futures. A market in which the futures price is below the expected future spot price is called a normal backwardation market. In the agriculture market, for example, farmers want to protect themselves from fluctuations that may be caused by weather. For this purpose, they sell the futures ahead of the harvest. Speculators, on the other hand, bear the risk and expect a risk premium. The risk aversion of farmers puts downward pressure on the futures prices, which fall below spot prices.

Normal distribution: A two-tailed distribution with a bell shape. Its skew value is 0, kurtosis is 3, and mean=mode=median.

North American Industry Classification System (NAICS): The standard used to classify business establishments.

Notional principal: In a swap, the agreed amount on which the two different types of payments are exchanged. In the transaction, the notional principal is not exchanged and so is called notional or theoretical.

Novation: The mechanism of replacing one party in a contract with another party.

Nth-to-Default Baskets: Nth-to-default swaps offer protection on a specified occurrence of default in a list of reference entities. For example, in a basket of ten reference entities, the basket-holder may want to purchase the protection only on the first default.

OCC: See *Office of the Comptroller of the Currency*

OECD: See *Organization for Economic Co-operation and Development*

Off-the-run bonds: Bonds that were issued in the past, as opposed to on-the-run bonds, which are recently issued and are more liquid. Off-the-run issues require liquidity premium and therefore are cheaper than on-the-run issues with the same remaining expiration time. Both prices converge to their par value at maturity.

Office of the Comptroller of the Currency (OCC): Organization whose primary mission is "to charter, regulate, and supervise all national banks and federal savings associations. … Headquartered in Washington, DC, the OCC has four district offices plus an office in London to supervise the international activities of national banks." ("About the OCC," http://www.occ.gov/about/what-we-do/mission/index-about.html)

On-the-run bonds: Bonds that are recently issued, as opposed to off-the-run bonds, which were issued in the past. On-the-run issues are more liquid than off-the-run issues, so off-the-run issues require liquidity premium and therefore are cheaper than on-the-run issues with the same remaining expiration time. Both prices converge to their par value at maturity.

Open-end fund: A mutual fund that does not have restrictions on the number of shares that can be issued.

Opportunity cost: See *discount rate*.

Option: A financial derivative that represents a contract sold by one party to another party. The contract offers the buyer the right, but not the obligation, to buy or sell an asset at an agreed-upon price called the strike price during a certain period of time or on a specific date called an exercise date.

Option-adjusted spread: Price that includes the adjustments to the option. MBS prices are more volatile because of the prepayment option that is embedded in mortgage loans. In the United States, mortgage borrowers can prepay the home loan at any time without penalty—that is, borrowers can avail themselves of the prepayment option at no explicit cost. However, mortgage loans include this option price implicitly. Since mortgage loans can be paid at any time, pricing MBS securities is a complex process, and therefore investors require a large premium for bearing prepayment risk.

Organization for Economic Cooperation and Development (OECD): Organization whose mission is to promote policies that will improve the economic and social well-being of people around the world.

OTC derivative: See *over-the-counter derivative*

Over-the-counter (OTC) derivative: A derivative that is traded in an informally organized market, the OTC, with little or no regulatory oversight. The contracts are bilateral and can be customized to fulfill the needs of buyers and sellers.

Overcollateralization: An internal credit enhancement to ensure that cash inflow is always greater than cash outflow. This is done using a loan to value ratio.

PAC: See *planned amortization class*

Par value: See *face value*

Parallel shift: "A shift in economic conditions in which the change in the interest rate on all maturities is the same number of basis points. In other words, if the three month T-bill increases 100 basis points (one percent), then the six-month, one-year, five-year, ten-year, twenty-year, and thirty-year rates all increase by 100 basis points, as well." (NASDAQ, "Parallel shift in the yield curve," http://www.nasdaq.com/investing/glossary/p/parallel-shift-in-the-yield-curve)

Pari passu: A Latin phrase meaning "equal footing" that is used to describe assets with the same characteristics. For example, securities in the top-rated tranche of CDO of a particular SPV will have the same characteristics and so are called *pari passu securities*.

Path-dependency analysis: Analysis that reveals whether any one period's action in a particular variable has any impact on the following period's movement. In other words, it reveals whether the frequency of upward movement in any period is conditional on prior upward movement, and likewise, whether the frequency of downward movement in any given period is conditional on prior downward movement. For example, refinancing activity in the mortgage market because of downward movement of interest rates depends on how many mortgages were referenced during the last downward movement of interest rates. If mortgage loans were already refinanced during the last decrease, then the refinancing activity may be less during the subsequent decrease in rates.

Pay-in-kind bond: A periodic form of payment in which the interest payment is not paid in cash but rather by accruing it to the principal amount of the security in the amount of the interest.

Payment frequency: The frequency with which bonds pay a coupon. While most bonds pay coupon semiannually, some bonds pay the coupon quarterly or yearly.

PFE: See *potential future exposure*

Plain vanilla bond: A regular bond that does not have any embedded options or conditions.

Planned amortization class (PAC): A class of CMOs that is amortized based on the sinking fund schedule that is established within a range of prepayment speeds, meaning that within a certain range of prepayment rates the payments to the PAC remain stable. A PAC security is structured with a companion tranche called the support tranche, which provides prepayment protection for the PAC security. If the prepayment rate is higher than the upper prepayment rate, then the support tranche absorbs the excess payment, while the PAC receives payments as originally scheduled. If the prepayment rate is less than the lower prepayment rate, then payments to the support tranche are deferred and paid to the PAC. Therefore, the stability of the PAC security cash flow comes at the expense of increased risk to the support tranche. If the excess continues until the support tranche is paid off, then the PAC tranche will start receiving the excess payments. Similarly, if the payments are less than supported by the support tranche, then the PAC will receive lesser payments. At this stage, the PAC is said to be broken or busted.

Platykurtic distribution: See *kurtosis*

PO: See *principal-only bond*

Portfolio: A set of financial assets, such as stocks and bonds managed by investors or investment managers.

Position: Indicates a security or loan that is held for the long term rather than trading purposes.

Potential future exposure (PFE): Represents possible future value of an exposure. The PFE for a single OTC derivative contract, including an OTC derivative contract with a negative mark-to-fair value, is calculated by multiplying the effective notional principal amount of the OTC derivative contract by the appropriate conversion factor.

Prepayment risk: The risk that is faced by investors or lenders because of earlier repayment of principal by the borrower due to lower market rates. Since the loan or bond, which was paying higher rates, is paid back, the investor or lender will have to relend or reinvest at lower rates because of lower market rates. In other words, prepayment risk causes reinvestment risk.

Price value of basis point (PVBP): A measure that describes how a basis point change in yield affects the price of a bond.

Principal-only bond (PO): Securities whose cash flow starts out small and substantially increase with the passage of time. The faster the prepayments occur, the faster PO securities receive their principal back and the higher the yield on the investment. PO tranches benefit from lower interest rates, where prepayments are much faster. This is because the borrowers, who borrowed at higher interest rate, would like to take advantage of current low interest rates and so will prepay the loans through refinancing. That means the yield on PO price is inversely related to interest rates and exhibits negative convexity at lower levels of interest rates.

Probability of default: See *default probability*

Protective Put: The protective put is an insurance-style strategy, meaning we buy insurance on the stock we own. In simple math, protective put = long stock + long put.

Pure expectation theory: A term-structure theory that states that the yield received in long-term investments is equivalent to the effective yield received by periodically reinvesting using short-term bonds. According to this theory, the rising term structure reflects that the market expects the short-term rates to rise in the future; the declining term structure reflects that the market expects the short-term rates to decrease in the future; and the flat-term structure reflects that the market expects the short-term rates to remain unchanged in the future. For example, if a one-year bond returns yield higher than that of a six-month bond, then investors anticipate that the yield six months from now should be higher than the six-month rate available now.

Put option: An option that gives the holder an option, but not the obligation, to sell an asset at a certain price on or before a certain date.

Puttable bond: Bonds on which holders pay the premium in terms of receiving a lower coupon rate or paying a certain amount at the time of putting it back. Just as the issuer of a callable bond has the flexibility of withdrawing the bond from market when interest rates go down, the bondholder may also want to put the bond back to the issuer when interest rates go up or when the issuer credit quality is trending down. Puttable bonds are known as *investor-friendly bonds*.

Puttable swap: See *cancelable swap*

PVBP: See *price value of basis point.*

Quanto: A swap that involves combinations of interest rate, currency, and equity-swap features. Payments are based on interest-rate movements in two different countries.

Rainbow option: See *basket option*

Rate reset frequency: Period over which the coupon is fixed in the interest-rate swap. At the end of the period, the floating rate is reset to reflect the benchmark rate of that time. It usually occurs quarterly but depends on contract terms.

Recovery rate: See *loss given default.*

Reference entity: The issuer of the bond for which the third party is providing protection. For example, by purchasing credit linked notes, which are issued by Party B, the purchaser of the bond is indirectly providing the protection on a bond issued by reference entity (Party A). Credit linked notes are structured such that the issuing institutions provide credit protection for the reference entity using a credit default swap (CDS) and receive regular fixed payment from the protection (CDS) buyer.

Regime shift: Rapid reorganization of systems from one relatively stable state to another. In financial markets, regimes may last for several years and shifts often appear to be associated with changes in economic conditions. With regime shift, relationships that existed among a set of variables will behave differently in the next regime.

Rehypothecation: When prime brokers provide margin, the customer or borrower will pledge the securities in their brokerage account to serve as collateral. The prime broker may, in turn, use this collateral as collateral against their loans through a process called *rehypothecation*.

Reinvestment risk: See *prepayment risk*.

Remaining maturity: The remaining portion of life of the bond from the current date.

Repo: The practice of short-term borrowing by dealers using securities. One party sells the securities to investors and buys them back after certain days (typically overnight but can be longer than a day in some cases) at an agreed-upon price. The difference in selling price and repurchase price is the interest paid to the investor. Repos are not derivatives as they involve the exchange of underlying assets. Security finance transactions are also considered to be repo-style transaction.

Repo rate: The difference between a security's sale price and repurchase price adjusted to per unit of days.

Repudiation: An outright cancellation of all of the borrower's current and future foreign debt and equity obligations.

Resecuritization: A mechanism of using the securities to create a pool of securitization. For example, if a CDO pool is backed by securities, such as MBS, then such CDO bonds are called *resecuritized securities*. Basel III has some restrictions on using resecuritized securities as collateral.

Reset date: See *rate reset frequency*

Reverse Repos: In a reverse repo, dealers buy at a lower price and then sell back the securities at a higher price at a later date, attributing the difference to the interest earned.

Rho: Rate of change of the option price with respect to interest rate.

Risk-free rate: A rate that can be earned by investing in risk-free assets, such as Treasuries.

Run on the bank: See *bank run*

Scenario analysis: An analysis that involves estimating the loss from extreme movements by applying historical scenarios.

Securitization: A process of pooling assets, dividing the proceeds into several parts, and selling the units as security.

Securitization pool: Pool of assets in the securitization, which are used as backing for the issued securities.

Shadow rating: The name given to a private bond rating given by a rating agency without any public announcement.

Short position or short-selling: Selling a security that is not owned. The seller borrows the security and sells it to the buyer. When the lender demands the security, the seller purchases it in the market and repays to the lender. Investors do this if they anticipate a decline in the price of securities.

Shout Options: In shout options, the special feature—the payoff upon shouting—is another derivative, with contractual specifications different from the original derivative.

Sinking fund: See *planned amortization class*

Skewness: Skewness refers to the extent to which the distribution is not symmetrical.

Source system: The original point of source of data gatherings, such as a trading system or order entry system.

Special purpose vehicle (SPV): A legal entity created by the sponsors or originators by transferring assets to the SPV. The SPV is intended to carry out some specific activity or a series of such activities. The SPV can be registered as a limited partnership, limited liability company, trust, or corporation. An SPV is a kind of virtual entity that has no employees, makes no substantive economic decisions, and has no physical location. SPVs cannot go bankrupt. Trustees perform the administrative functions, such as collection and distribution of cash.

Spot date: The day when a spot transaction is typically settled, meaning when the underlying assets like currency or the commodity involved in the transaction are transferred.

Spot market: A market in which assets—such as commodities, currency, or securities—are sold for cash and delivered immediately.

Spread option: A type of option where the value of an option is derived from the difference between the prices of two or more assets. Bull spreads, bear spreads, and butterfly spreads are examples of spread options.

SPV: See *special purpose vehicle.*

Standard deviation: See Volatility.

Start date: The date on which the transaction is initiated.

Step-down bonds: Bonds with coupon payments that decrease (step down) over the life of the security according to a predetermined schedule. In the case of one-step bonds, the coupon will reset once during the life of the bond; with multistep bonds, the coupon will reset multiple times. The initial coupon paid on a step-down is usually higher than comparable market rates, and the step-down may eventually decrease its future coupon payments and yield less than prevailing market rates.

Step-up bonds: Bonds that have coupon payments that increase (step up) over the life of the security according to a predetermined schedule. In the case of one-step bonds, the coupon will reset once during the life of the bond; with multistep bonds, the coupon will reset multiple times. The initial coupon paid on a step-up is usually lower than comparable market rates, and the step-up may eventually increase its future coupon payments and even yield higher than prevailing market rates. The step-up bondholder chooses to forgo some interest income in the near term in exchange for a potential of higher yield over the life of the investment.

Straddle: A strategy that involves purchasing the same number of call and put options at the same strike price with the same expiration date. If both the call and put positions are long, then the straddle is called a *long straddle*; if both the positions are short, then the straddle is called a *short straddle*. In other words, selling a long straddle is nothing but a short straddle. By employing a long straddle, a manager takes advantage of any sudden movement in the stock price regardless of the direction.

Straight bond: A bond that pays interest at regular intervals, and at maturity repays the principal that was originally invested.

Strangle: A strangle strategy is employed by taking a long position in a call option and a put option on the same underlying asset at the same maturity but different strike prices. These positions are cheaper to implement, as the options with strikes further from the current underlying price will have a lower theta. Managers typically take a call position with a higher strike than that of the put position. The profit is not realized for slow movement of the stock. Large movements are required to lock in profits. However, the cost of strategy establishment is low because of lower premiums.

Strike price: The price set in option contracts upon hitting the price at which the option will become exercisable.

Super senior tranche: The tranche in a CDO considered to be least risky and typically earning an AAA rating. The senior tranche performs well until both the equity and mezzanine tranches exhaust. At this time, a senior tranche will experience losses.

Swaps: Swaps involve returns on one type of product being exchanged with the returns on some other type of product.

Swaption: A swaption is nothing but swap + option. Interest-rate swaptions give the holder the right, but not the obligation, to enter into or cancel a swap agreement at a future date.

Synthetic collateralized debt obligation (CDO): A transaction that transfers the credit risk on a reference portfolio of assets made up of credit default swaps. Thus, a synthetic CDO is classified as a credit derivative.

TAC bonds: See *targeted amortization class bonds*

Tail loss: Losses in the tail part of a VaR model. Such models assume that the returns are normally distributed, whereas in reality they exhibit skewed distribution, meaning there can be concentrations of losses or profits on extreme. The skewed portions are called *tails*, and the tails sometimes can be fat. Expected tail loss, expected shortfalls, copulas, and extreme value theory are some of the useful tools to measure tail loss.

Targeted amortization class (TAC) bonds: According to a definition by Campbell R. Harvey, a professor of finance at Duke University, "Bonds offered as a tranche class of some CMOs, according to a sinking fund schedule. They differ from PAC bonds whose amortization is guaranteed as long as prepayments on the underlying mortgages do not exceed certain limits. A TAC's schedule is met at only one prepayment rate." (NASDAQ, "Targeted Amortization Class Bonds," http://www.nasdaq.com/investing/glossary/t/targeted-amortization-class-bonds)

TED Spread: TED stands for Treasuries over Eurodollars.

Term repo: Using term repo, a bank will agree to buy securities from a dealer and then resell them after few days or few months at a preset price. The difference between the purchase and sale prices represents the interest paid for the agreement. The difference between repo and term repo is that the repo is a means of overnight lending whereas term repos are meant for longer than a day.

Term structure theories: See *pure expectation theory, liquidity preference theory, and market segmentation theory.*

Theta: One of the option Greeks that give rate of change of option price with respect to time.

Threshold amount: The unsecured credit exposure that the secured party is willing to allocate to the pledger. After the party's exposure is determined, it may be qualified by certain credit terms in the CSA, and the parties may agree to a threshold amount. A secured party would likely only agree to a threshold amount when facing a financially stable and creditworthy counterparty. While at one point in time threshold amounts were commonly negotiated in favor of broker-dealers, threshold amounts have become rare in the post-Lehman market.

Tick: The minimum allowed upward or downward movement in the price of a security or commodity from trade to trade.

Total return swap (TRS): A bilateral agreement between two parties that exchanges the total return from an asset between them. This is designed to transfer the credit risk from one party to the other. In addition, total return swaps are used as synthetic repo instruments for funding purposes. The TRS is sometimes called a *total rate-of-return swap,* or TR swap.

Trading indicator: See *book or trading indicator*

TRS: See *total return swap*

Treasury inflation-protected securities (TIPS): Treasury inflation-protected securities (TIPS) protect investors from inflation risk. The US Treasury created these inflation-indexed notes just for this purpose. The value of the principal is adjusted to reflect the effects of inflation with the CPI as a guide, in addition to a fixed rate of interest. At maturity, if inflation has increased the value of the principal, the investor receives the higher, adjusted value back. If deflation has decreased the value, the investor nevertheless receives the original face amount of the security.

Treasury Securities: Treasury securities, or simply *Treasuries*, are backed by the "full faith and credit" of the US government, and thus by its ability to raise tax revenues and print currency.

Underlying exposure: The asset on which option contracts are written.

Undrawn amount: The remaining portion of allowed credit after drawing zero or a certain amount.

Unfunded credit derivatives: Certain credit derivatives where the seller makes no upfront payment to cover its potential future liabilities. The seller will make a payment in an unfunded credit derivative only if the conditions to settlement are met. Consequently, the buyer takes a credit risk on whether the seller will be able to pay any cash settlement amount or physical settlement amount. The most popular types of unfunded credit derivative products are single-name credit default swaps, index trades, basket products, credit spread options, swaptions, recovery swaps, constant maturity swaps, and CDS on ABS.

Unrealized gain: Gain that arises from holding onto an asset after it has increased in price but before it is sold to realize a gain.

Unrealized loss: A loss that arises from holding onto an asset after it has decreased in price but before it is sold to realize the loss.

Value-at-risk (VaR): The maximum loss that can occur over a defined period for a given confidence interval. If the VaR on a portfolio is calculated as $10 million at a one-week, 95 percent confidence level, then there is a 95 percent confidence that the loss of the portfolio will not exceed $10 million over any given week. In other words, there is a 5 percent chance that there will be a loss of at least $10 million over any given week.

Variance: A measure of how each sample in a set differs from the mean of the set. Variance is calculated by taking average of the squares of differences between each number in the set and the mean.

Variation margin: A margin payment made by clearing members to their respective clearinghouses when the future price decreases.

Vega: Rate of change of the option price with respect to volatility.

Vintage year: The year in which either investments are made or securities are issued.

Volatility: The fluctuations in value from its mean; also called *standard deviation*. See *variance*.

Volatility smile: A term structure of implied volatility can be plotted as differently implied volatilities extracted from options with different maturities. Volatility smiles present as different implied volatilities are extracted from options with different strikes. The combination of volatility term structure and volatility smiles, a three-dimensional plot, is called *volatility surface*.

When a volatility smile is detected, the manager buys the cheaper option in the volatility surface that is nearer the money and sells a more expensive option in the volatility surface that is further out of the money on the same underlying asset and at the same expiry. This type of spread trade can be constructed using either put or call options.

If the manager has a negative view of the underlying market, bear spread will be used; that is, long the put with a high strike and short the put with a low strike. Alternatively, writing a call option with a low strike and buying the long with a higher strike can also execute a bear spread. If the manager is positive on the market, bull spread will be implemented using call options, that is, long the call with a low strike and short the call with a higher strike. Alternatively, selling a put option with a high strike and buying the put with a low strike can execute a bull spread.

Volatility surface: See *volatility smile*.

Walkaway feature: A feature, different from closeout netting, that allows the party that is obligated to pay a certain amount to cease the payments in case the counterparty defaults.

Weakening of the basis: When the futures price increases faster than the spot price, basis decreases and weakening of basis is said to occur.

Yield: The return on investment. For example, if a bond of face value $100, which is paying a 5 percent annual coupon, is purchased for $100, then the yield is 5 percent. If the same bond is purchased for $98 in the market, then the yield is 5/98 percent, which is 5.1 percent. Therefore, the yield is different from the coupon.

Yield curve: A graph of interest rates taken from bonds of the same quality but with different maturities. Since the short-term rates are usually less than that of long-term bonds, the graph appear to slope upward. The yield curve compares the three-month, two-year, five-year and thirty-year Treasury bonds.

Yield to maturity (YTM): Amount calculated by taking into account the bond's current market price, par value, coupon interest rate, and time to maturity, and assuming that all coupon payments are reinvested at the same rate as the bond's current yield.

Zero-coupon bond: See *discount bond.*

Zero curve: Similar to yield curve but created by plotting the yields of zero-coupon Treasury bills and their corresponding maturities.